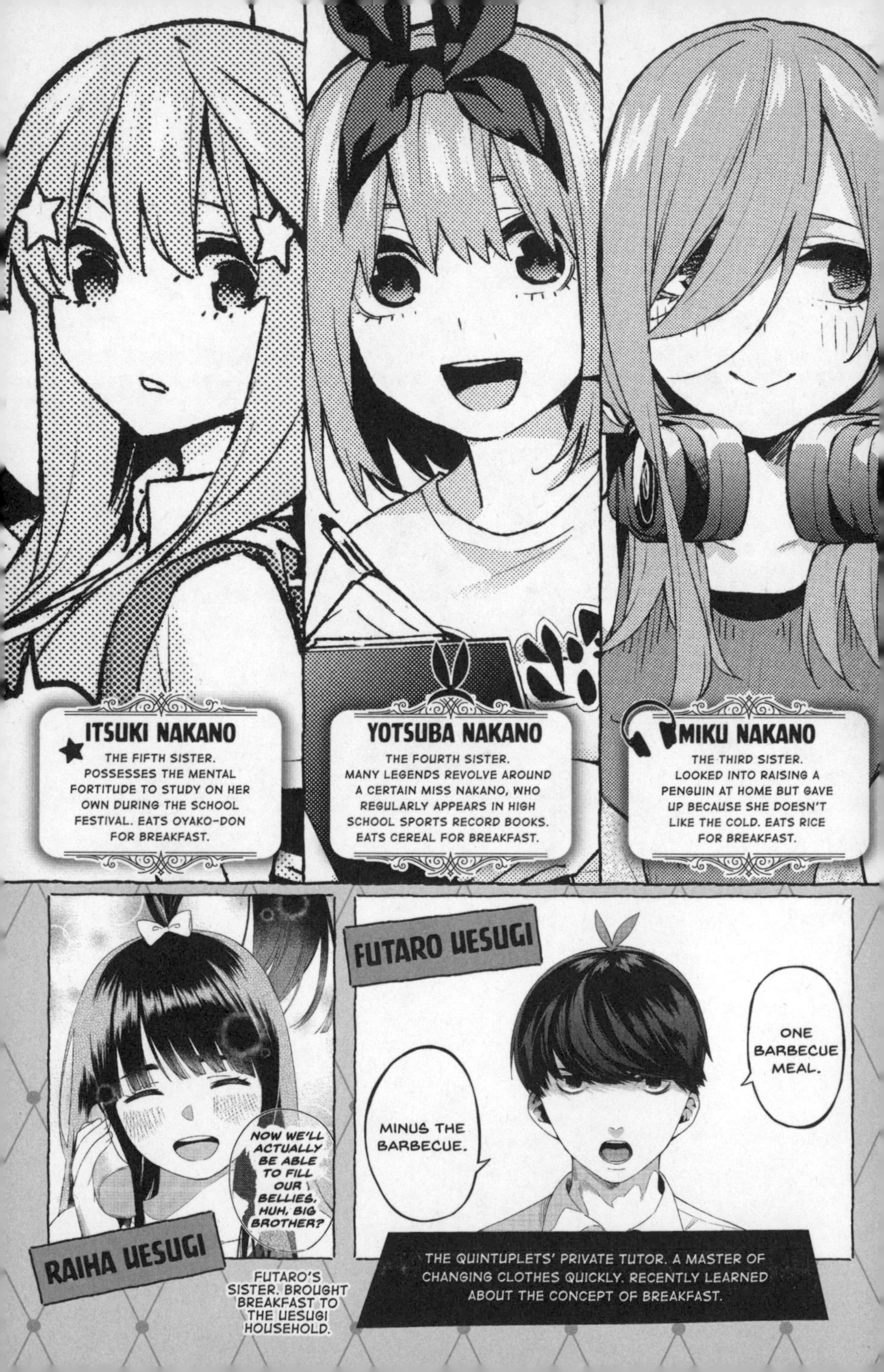

MIKU NAKANO
THE THIRD SISTER. LOOKED INTO RAISING A PENGUIN AT HOME BUT GAVE UP BECAUSE SHE DOESN'T LIKE THE COLD. EATS RICE FOR BREAKFAST.
YOTSUBA NAKANO
THE FOURTH SISTER. MANY LEGENDS REVOLVE AROUND A CERTAIN MISS NAKANO, WHO REGULARLY APPEARS IN HIGH SCHOOL SPORTS RECORD BOOKS. EATS CEREAL FOR BREAKFAST.
ITSUKI NAKANO
THE FIFTH SISTER. POSSESSES THE MENTAL FORTITUDE TO STUDY ON HER OWN DURING THE SCHOOL FESTIVAL. EATS OYAKO-DON FOR BREAKFAST.
FUTARO UESUGI
ONE BARBECUE MEAL.
MINUS THE BARBECUE.
THE QUINTUPLETS' PRIVATE TUTOR. A MASTER OF CHANGING CLOTHES QUICKLY. RECENTLY LEARNED ABOUT THE CONCEPT OF BREAKFAST.
NOW WE'LL ACTUALLY BE ABLE TO FILL OUR BELLIES, HUH, BIG BROTHER?
RAIHA UESUGI
FUTARO'S SISTER. BROUGHT BREAKFAST TO THE UESUGI HOUSEHOLD.

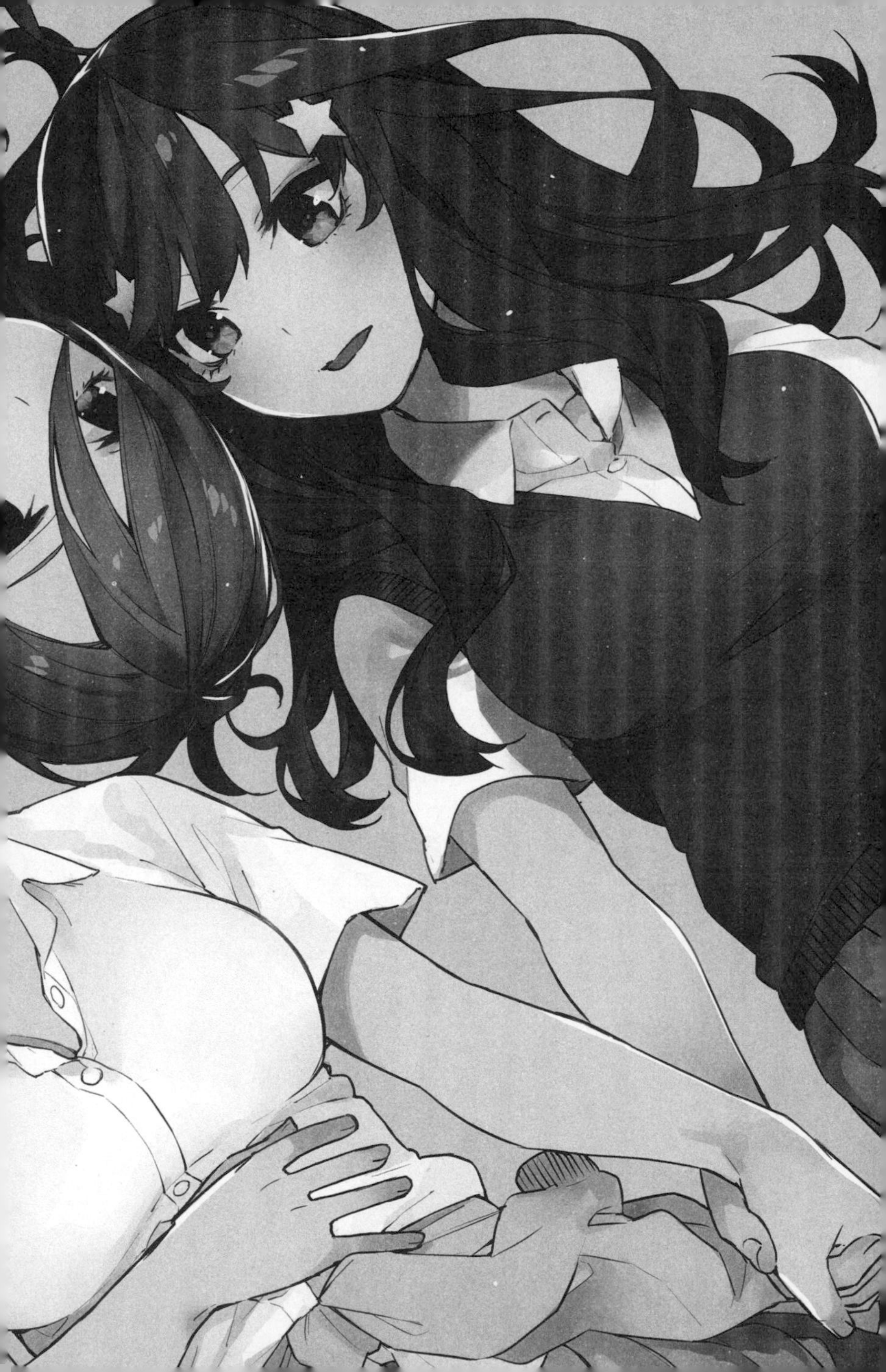

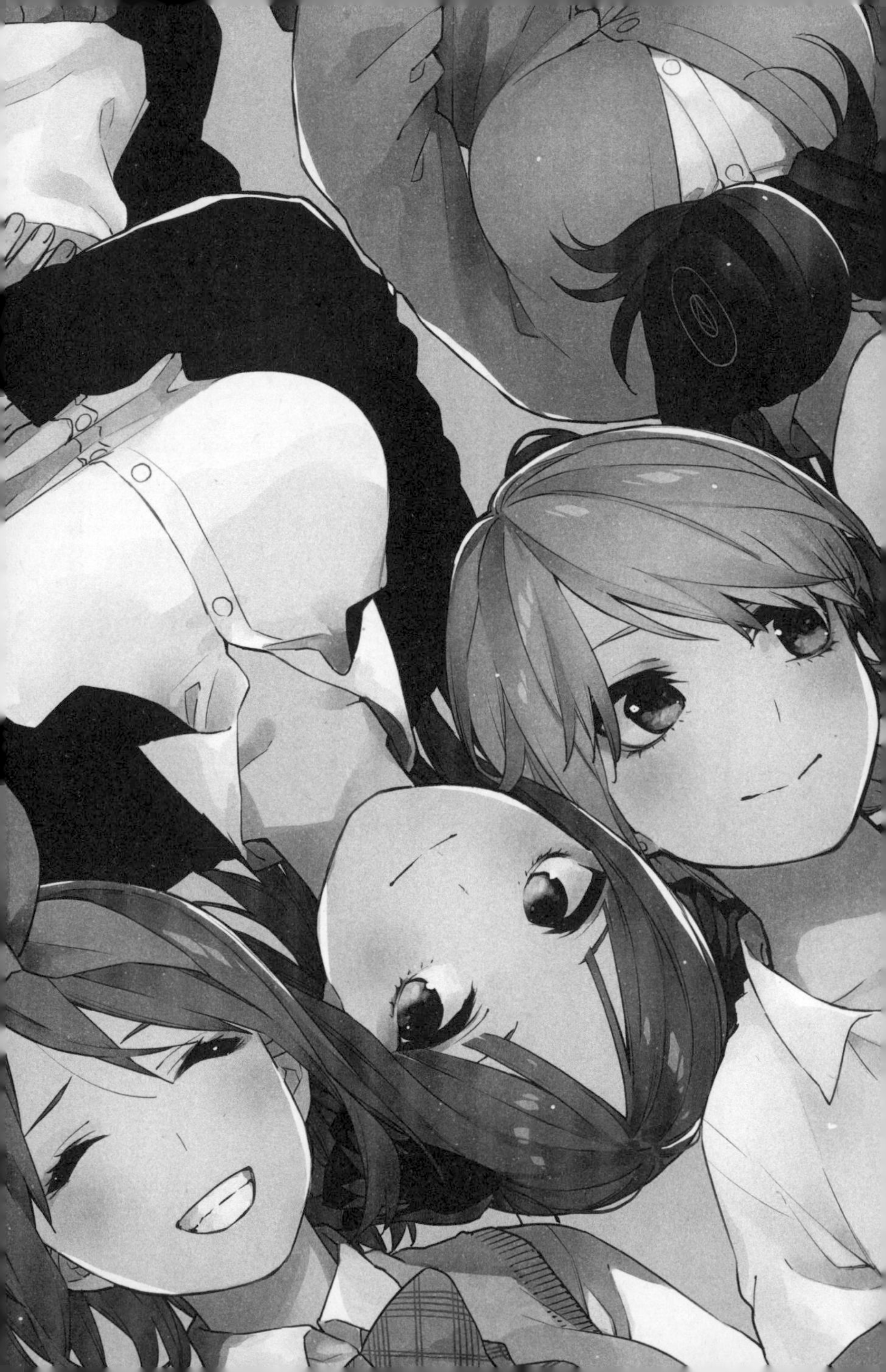

CONTENTS

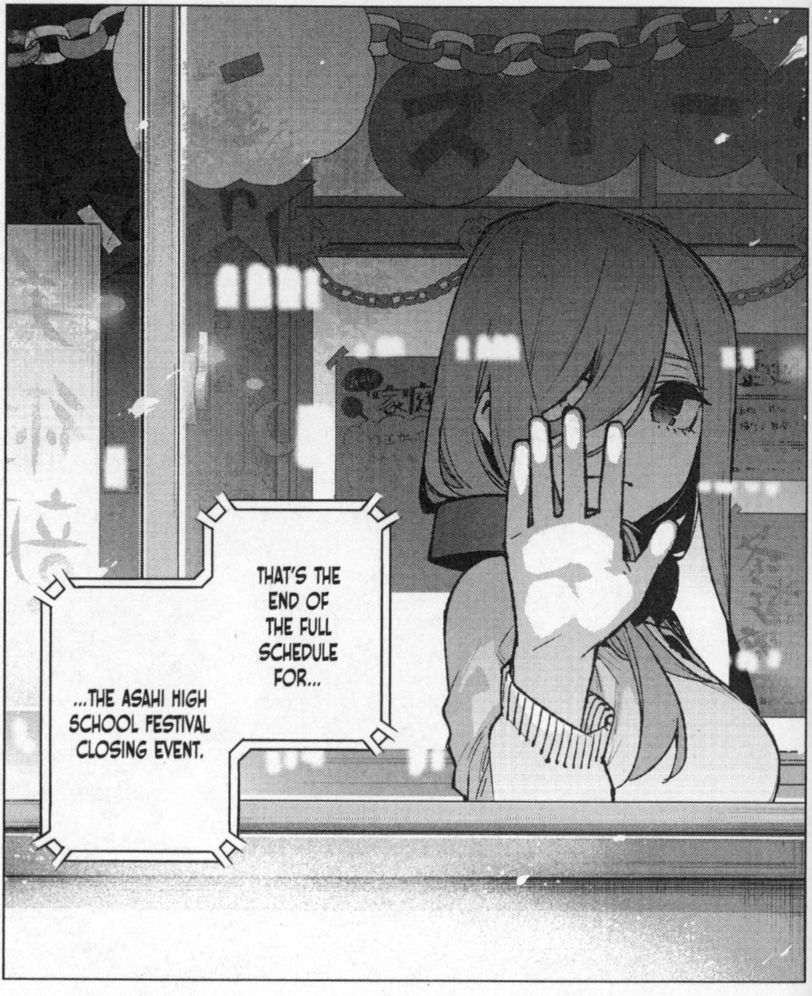
THAT'S THE END OF THE FULL SCHEDULE FOR...
...THE ASAHI HIGH SCHOOL FESTIVAL CLOSING EVENT.

CHAPTER 105 IF THE FINAL FESTIVAL WAS MIKU'S ①

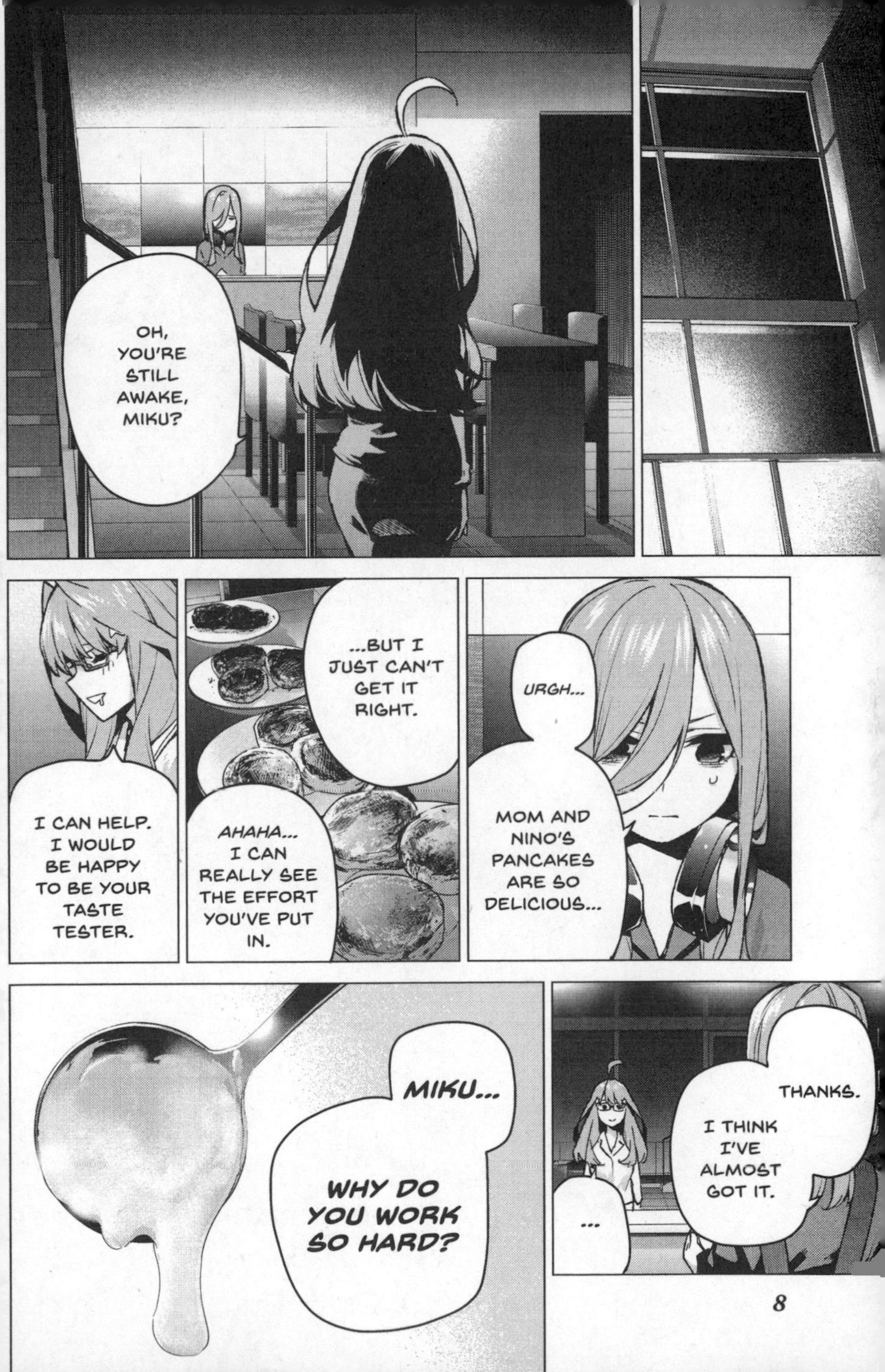
OH, YOU'RE STILL AWAKE, MIKU?
URGH...
MOM AND NINO'S PANCAKES ARE SO DELICIOUS...
...BUT I JUST CAN'T GET IT RIGHT.
AHAHA... I CAN REALLY SEE THE EFFORT YOU'VE PUT IN.
I CAN HELP. I WOULD BE HAPPY TO BE YOUR TASTE TESTER.
THANKS.
I THINK I'VE ALMOST GOT IT.
...
MIKU...
WHY DO YOU WORK SO HARD?

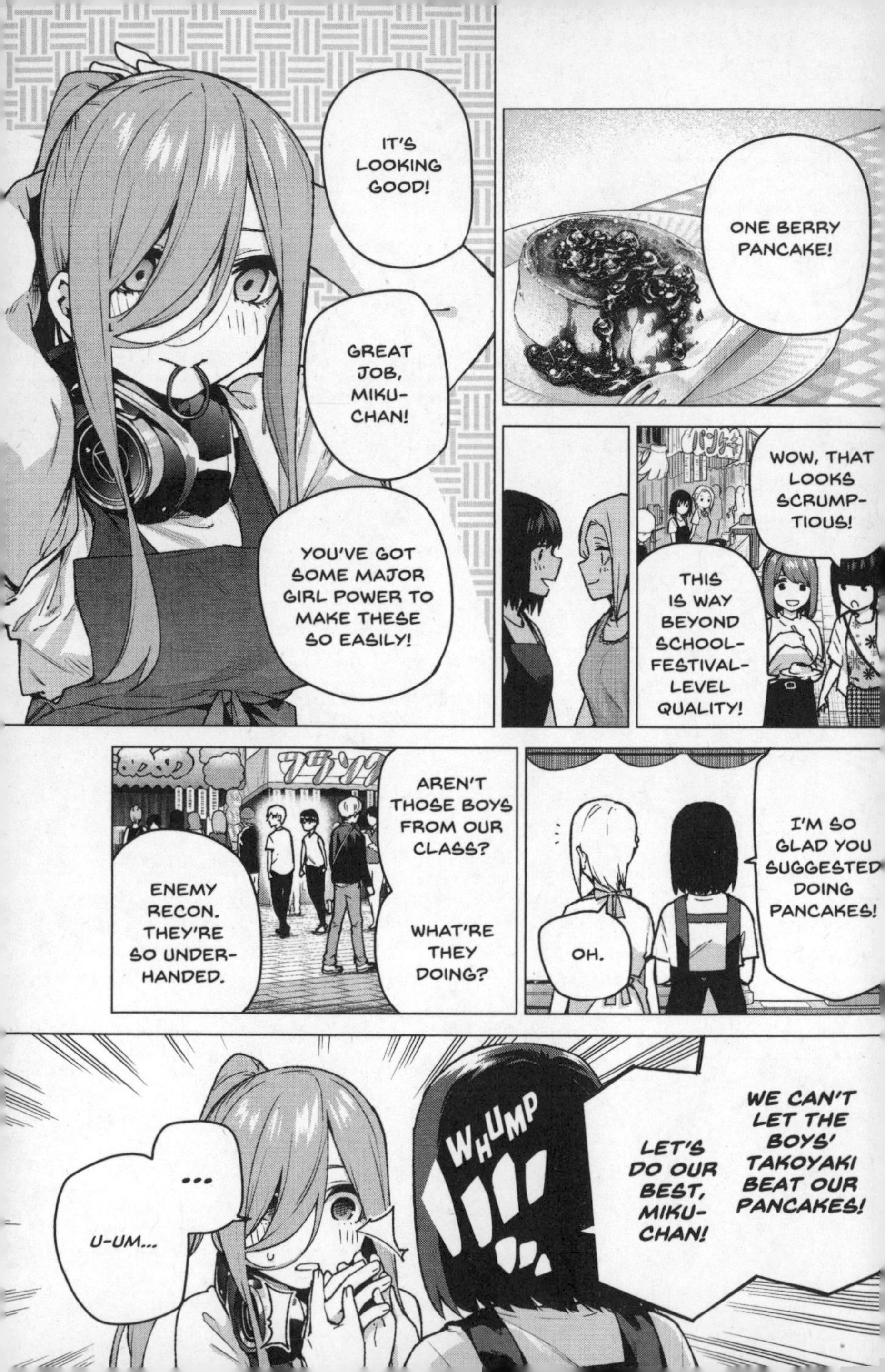
ONE BERRY PANCAKE!
WOW, THAT LOOKS SCRUMP-TIOUS!
THIS IS WAY BEYOND SCHOOL-FESTIVAL-LEVEL QUALITY!
IT'S LOOKING GOOD!
GREAT JOB, MIKU-CHAN!
YOU'VE GOT SOME MAJOR GIRL POWER TO MAKE THESE SO EASILY!
I'M SO GLAD YOU SUGGESTED DOING PANCAKES!
OH.
AREN'T THOSE BOYS FROM OUR CLASS?
WHAT'RE THEY DOING?
ENEMY RECON. THEY'RE SO UNDER-HANDED.
WE CAN'T LET THE BOYS' TAKOYAKI BEAT OUR PANCAKES!
LET'S DO OUR BEST, MIKU-CHAN!
WHUMP
...
U-UM...

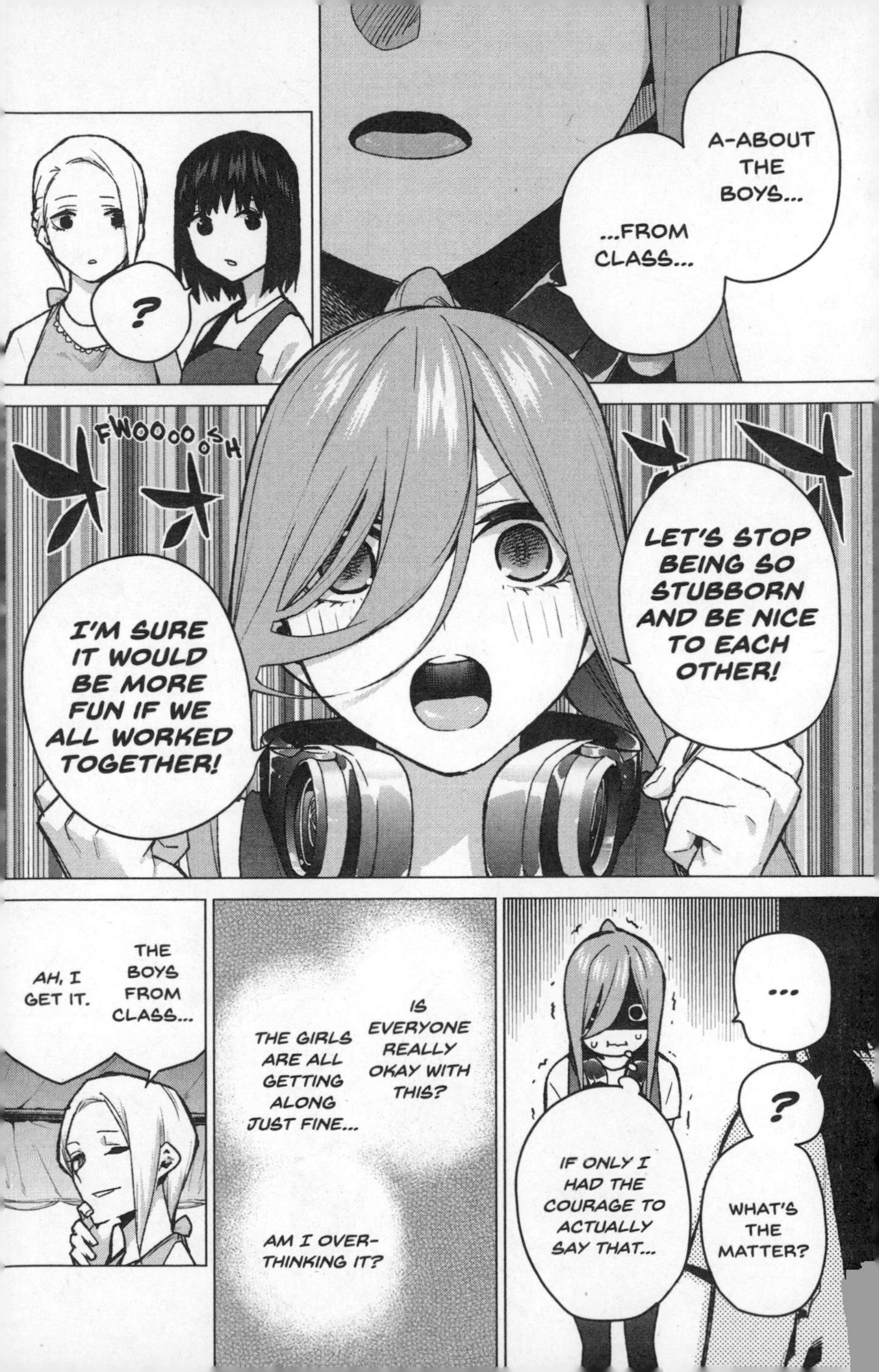
A-ABOUT THE BOYS...
...FROM CLASS...
?
LET'S STOP BEING SO STUBBORN AND BE NICE TO EACH OTHER!
I'M SURE IT WOULD BE MORE FUN IF WE ALL WORKED TOGETHER!
FWOOOOOSH
...
?
IF ONLY I HAD THE COURAGE TO ACTUALLY SAY THAT...
WHAT'S THE MATTER?
IS EVERYONE REALLY OKAY WITH THIS?
THE GIRLS ARE ALL GETTING ALONG JUST FINE...
AM I OVER-THINKING IT?
THE BOYS FROM CLASS...
AH, I GET IT.

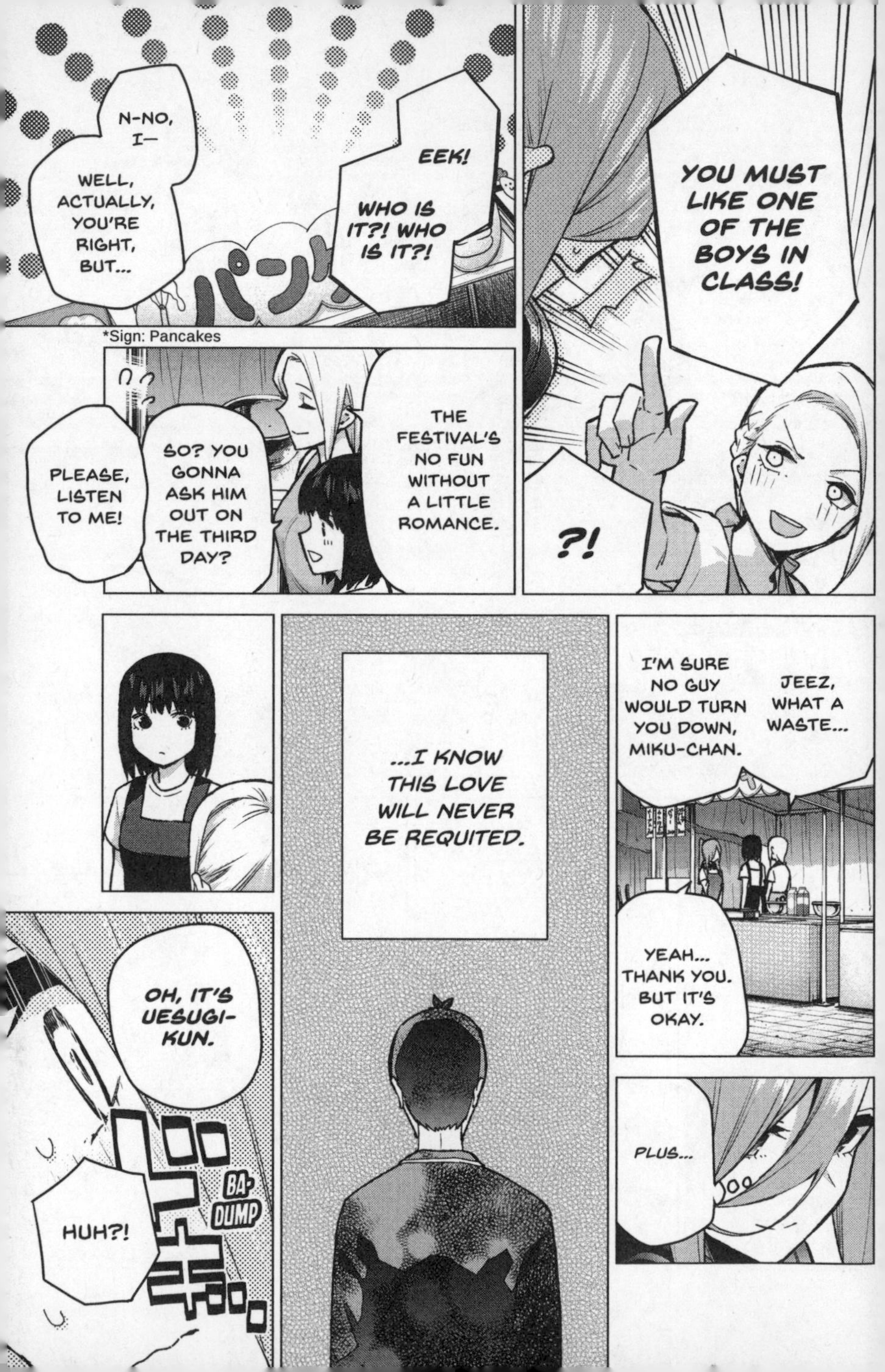
YOU MUST LIKE ONE OF THE BOYS IN CLASS!
?!
EEK!
WHO IS IT?! WHO IS IT?!
N-NO, I—
WELL, ACTUALLY, YOU'RE RIGHT, BUT...
*Sign: Pancakes
THE FESTIVAL'S NO FUN WITHOUT A LITTLE ROMANCE.
SO? YOU GONNA ASK HIM OUT ON THE THIRD DAY?
PLEASE, LISTEN TO ME!
JEEZ, WHAT A WASTE...
I'M SURE NO GUY WOULD TURN YOU DOWN, MIKU-CHAN.
YEAH... THANK YOU. BUT IT'S OKAY.
PLUS...
...I KNOW THIS LOVE WILL NEVER BE REQUITED.
OH, IT'S UESUGI-KUN.
BA-DUMP
HUH?!

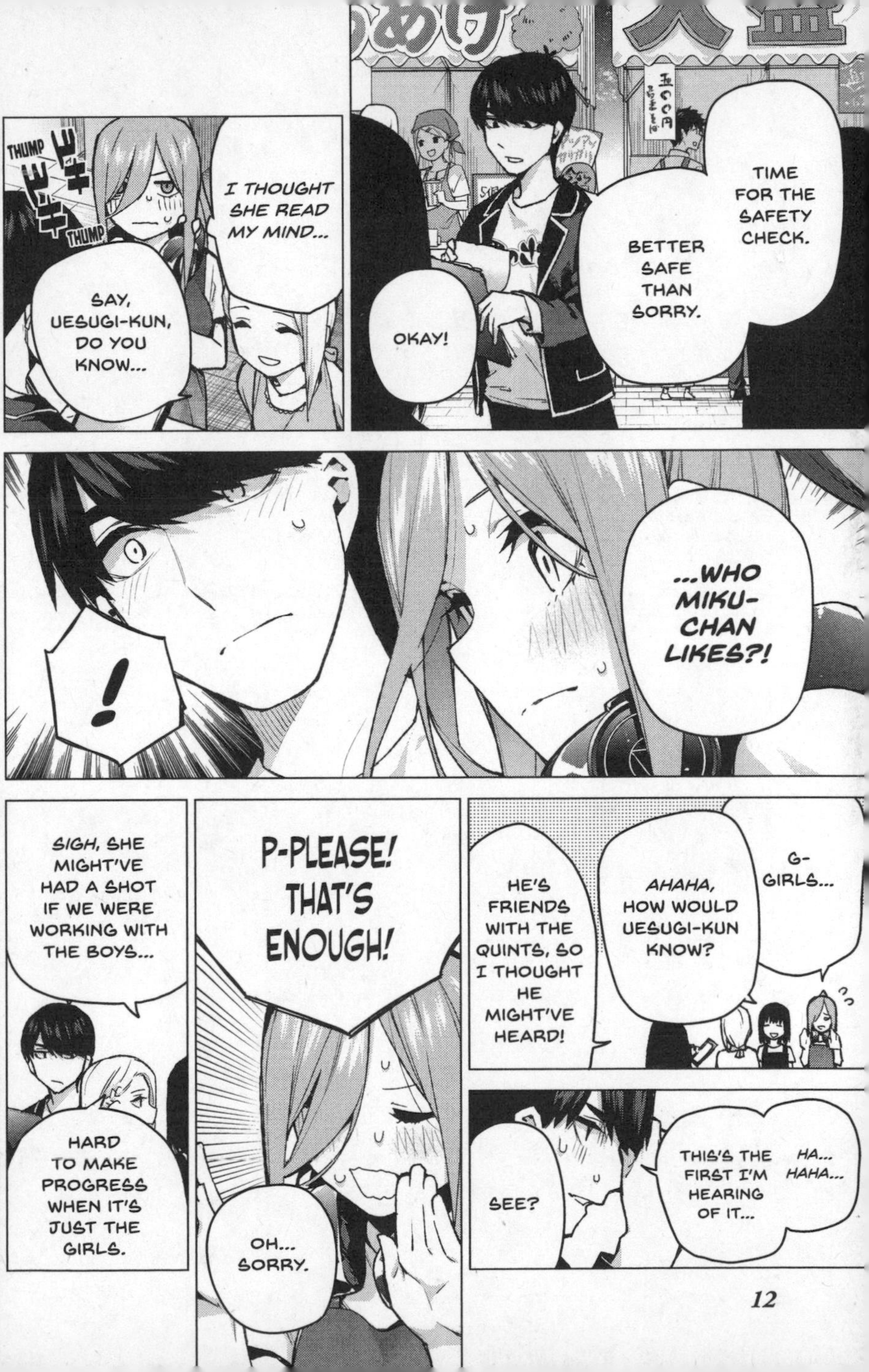
TIME FOR THE SAFETY CHECK.
BETTER SAFE THAN SORRY.
OKAY!
THUMP THUMP
I THOUGHT SHE READ MY MIND...
SAY, UESUGI-KUN, DO YOU KNOW...
...WHO MIKU-CHAN LIKES?!
!
G-GIRLS...
AHAHA, HOW WOULD UESUGI-KUN KNOW?
HE'S FRIENDS WITH THE QUINTS, SO I THOUGHT HE MIGHT'VE HEARD!
HA... HAHA...
THIS'S THE FIRST I'M HEARING OF IT...
SEE?
P-PLEASE! THAT'S ENOUGH!
OH... SORRY.
SIGH, SHE MIGHT'VE HAD A SHOT IF WE WERE WORKING WITH THE BOYS...
HARD TO MAKE PROGRESS WHEN IT'S JUST THE GIRLS.

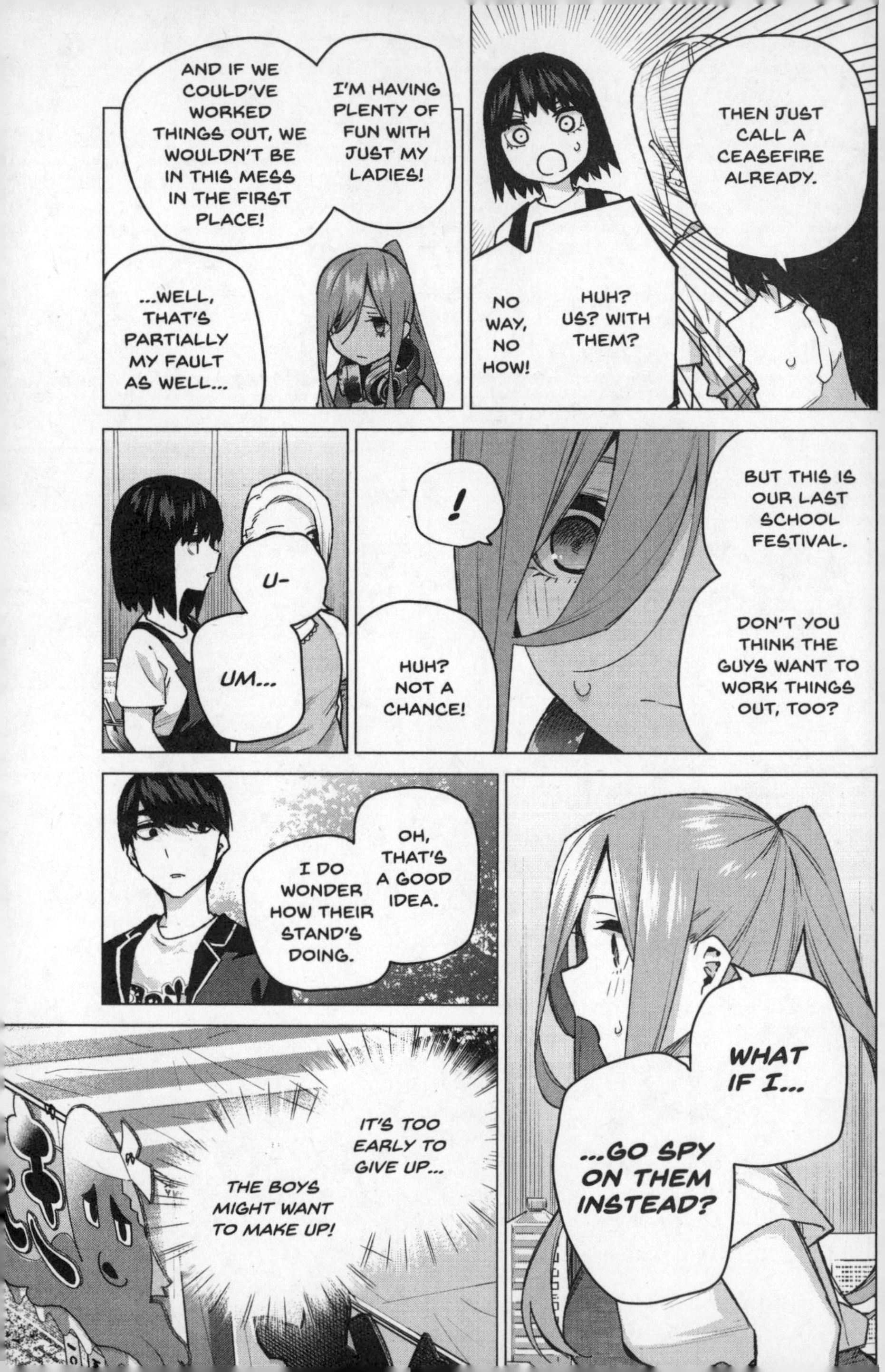
THEN JUST CALL A CEASEFIRE ALREADY.
HUH? US? WITH THEM?
NO WAY, NO HOW!
I'M HAVING PLENTY OF FUN WITH JUST MY LADIES!
AND IF WE COULD'VE WORKED THINGS OUT, WE WOULDN'T BE IN THIS MESS IN THE FIRST PLACE!
...WELL, THAT'S PARTIALLY MY FAULT AS WELL...
BUT THIS IS OUR LAST SCHOOL FESTIVAL.
!
DON'T YOU THINK THE GUYS WANT TO WORK THINGS OUT, TOO?
HUH? NOT A CHANCE!
U-
UM...
WHAT IF I...
...GO SPY ON THEM INSTEAD?
OH, THAT'S A GOOD IDEA.
I DO WONDER HOW THEIR STAND'S DOING.
IT'S TOO EARLY TO GIVE UP...
THE BOYS MIGHT WANT TO MAKE UP!

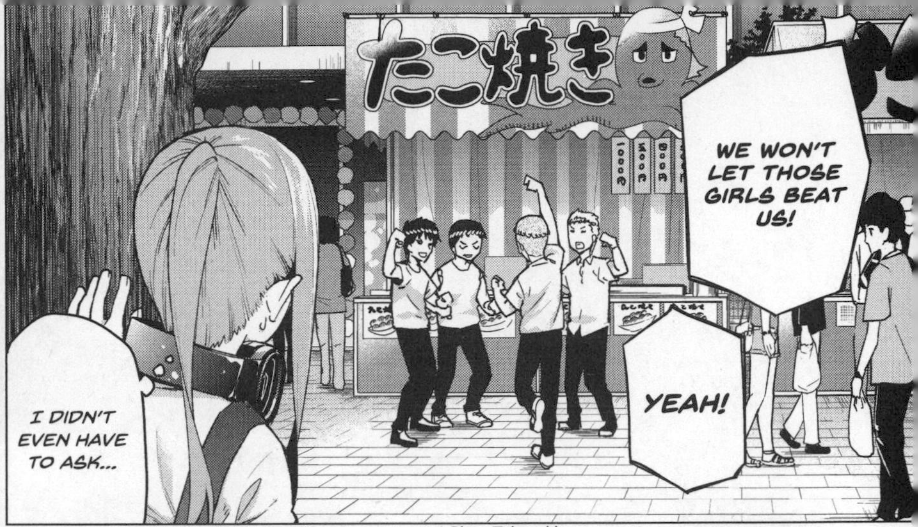
たこ焼き
WE WON'T LET THOSE GIRLS BEAT US!
YEAH!
I DIDN'T EVEN HAVE TO ASK...

* Sign: Takoyaki

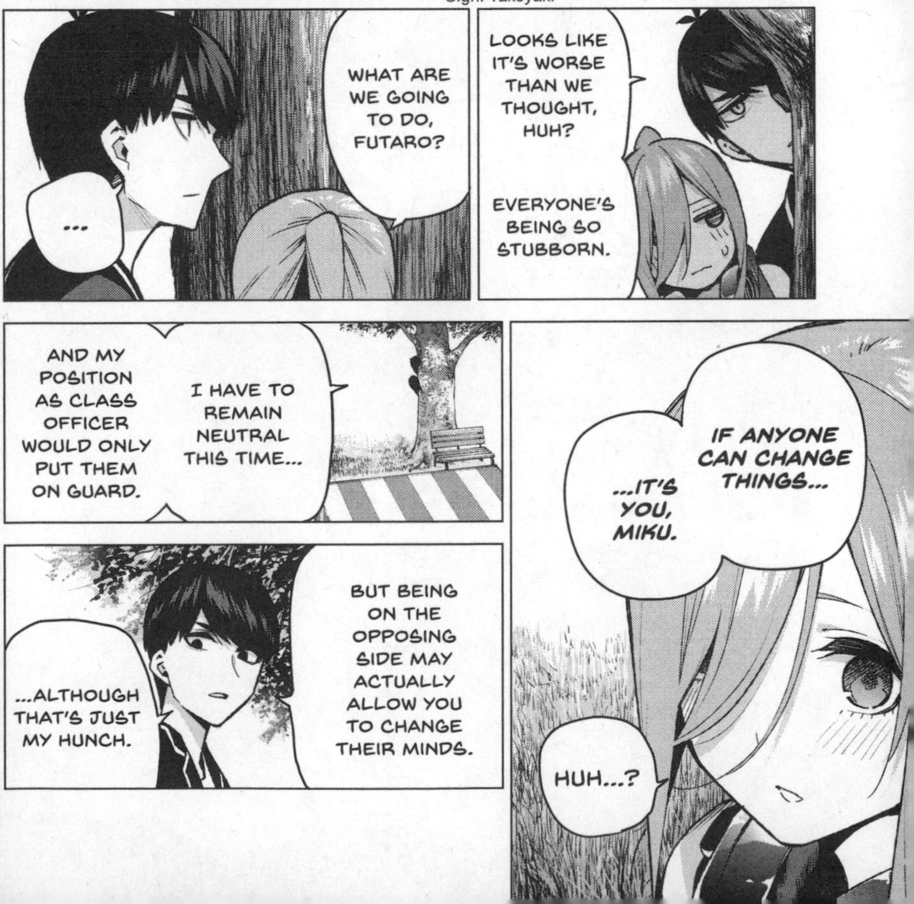
LOOKS LIKE IT'S WORSE THAN WE THOUGHT, HUH?
EVERYONE'S BEING SO STUBBORN.
WHAT ARE WE GOING TO DO, FUTARO?
...
IF ANYONE CAN CHANGE THINGS...
...IT'S YOU, MIKU.
HUH...?
I HAVE TO REMAIN NEUTRAL THIS TIME...
AND MY POSITION AS CLASS OFFICER WOULD ONLY PUT THEM ON GUARD.
BUT BEING ON THE OPPOSING SIDE MAY ACTUALLY ALLOW YOU TO CHANGE THEIR MINDS.
...ALTHOUGH THAT'S JUST MY HUNCH.

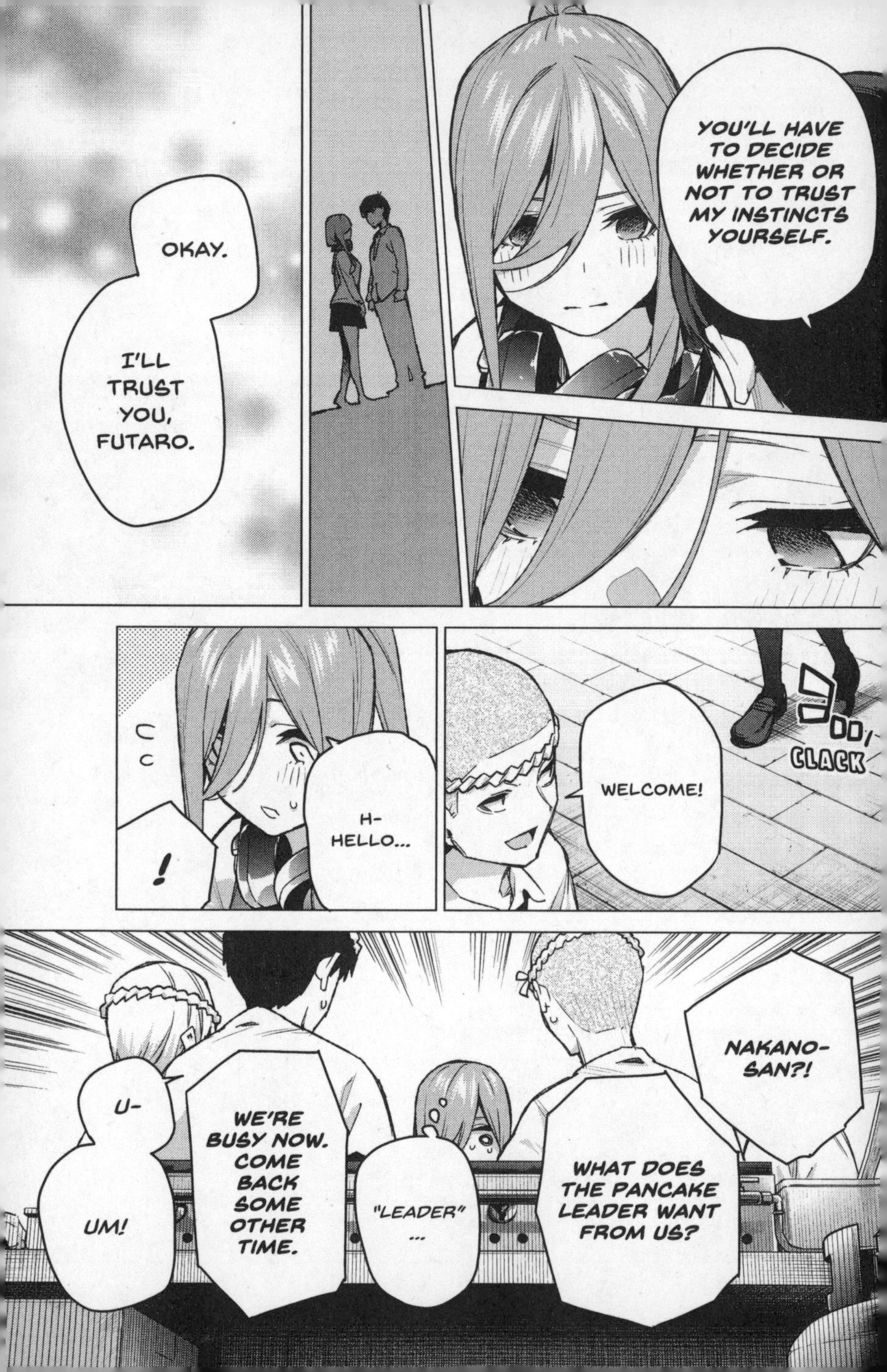
YOU'LL HAVE TO DECIDE WHETHER OR NOT TO TRUST MY INSTINCTS YOURSELF.
OKAY.
I'LL TRUST YOU, FUTARO.
CLACK
WELCOME!
H- HELLO...
!
NAKANO-SAN?!
WHAT DOES THE PANCAKE LEADER WANT FROM US?
"LEADER" ...
WE'RE BUSY NOW. COME BACK SOME OTHER TIME.
U- UM!

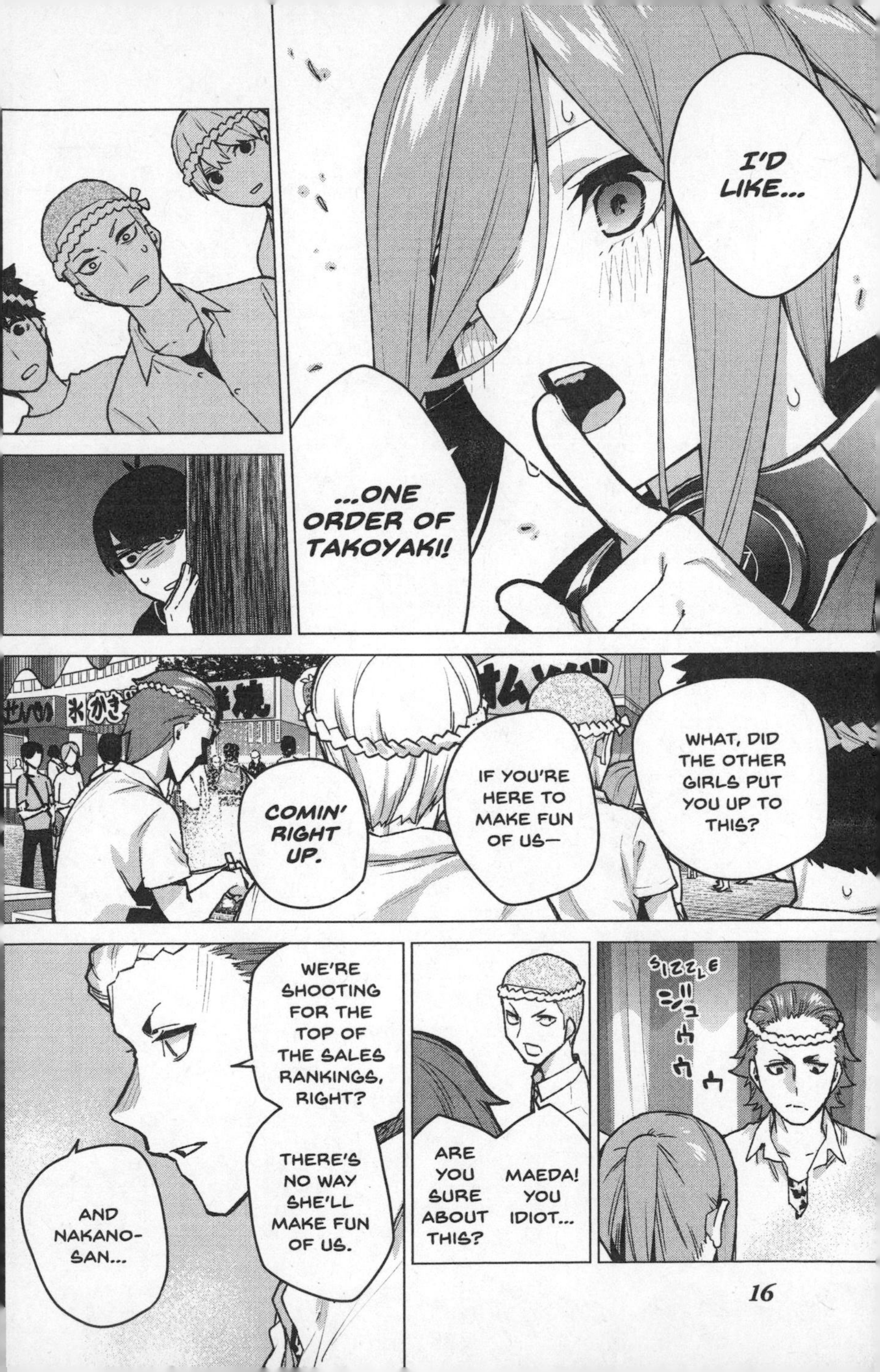
I'D LIKE...
...ONE ORDER OF TAKOYAKI!
WHAT, DID THE OTHER GIRLS PUT YOU UP TO THIS?
IF YOU'RE HERE TO MAKE FUN OF US—
COMIN' RIGHT UP.
SIZZLE
MAEDA! YOU IDIOT...
ARE YOU SURE ABOUT THIS?
WE'RE SHOOTING FOR THE TOP OF THE SALES RANKINGS, RIGHT?
THERE'S NO WAY SHE'LL MAKE FUN OF US.
AND NAKANO-SAN...

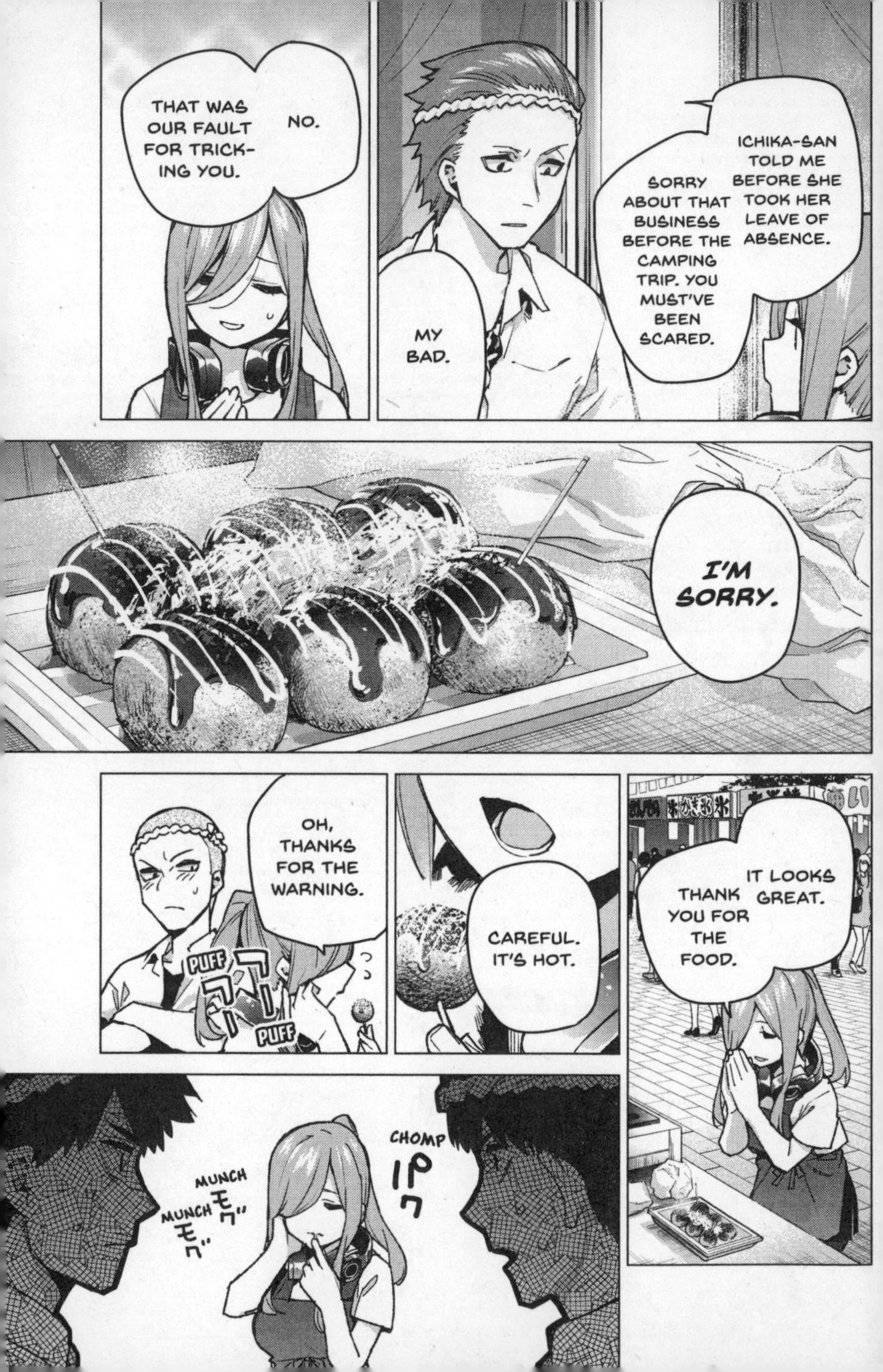
ICHIKA-SAN TOLD ME BEFORE SHE TOOK HER LEAVE OF ABSENCE.
SORRY ABOUT THAT BUSINESS BEFORE THE CAMPING TRIP. YOU MUST'VE BEEN SCARED.
MY BAD.
NO.
THAT WAS OUR FAULT FOR TRICKING YOU.
I'M SORRY.
IT LOOKS GREAT.
THANK YOU FOR THE FOOD.
CAREFUL. IT'S HOT.
OH, THANKS FOR THE WARNING.
PUFF
PUFF
CHOMP
MUNCH
MUNCH

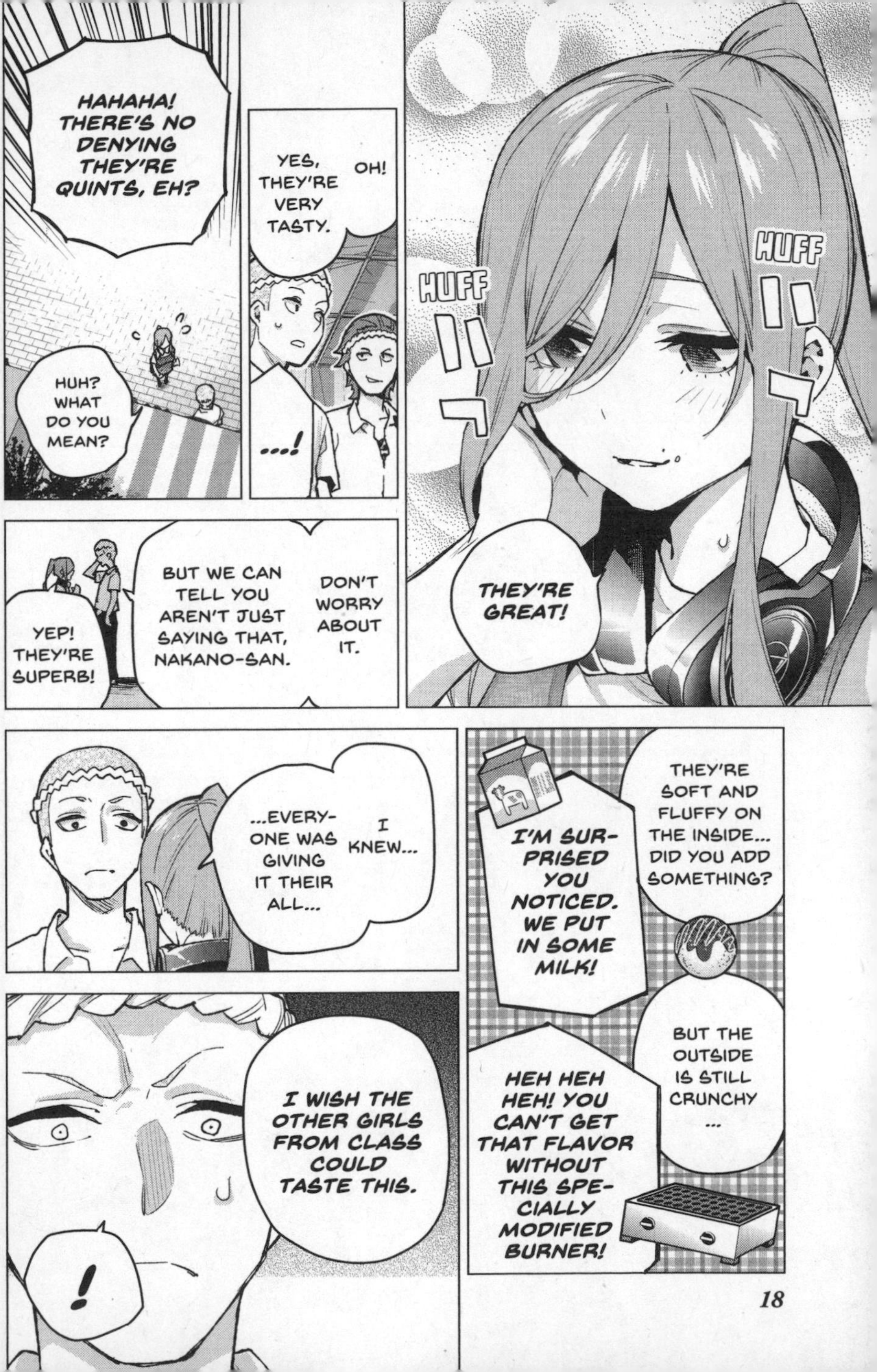
HUFF
HUFF
THEY'RE GREAT!
OH!
YES, THEY'RE VERY TASTY.
...!
HAHAHA! THERE'S NO DENYING THEY'RE QUINTS, EH?
HUH? WHAT DO YOU MEAN?
DON'T WORRY ABOUT IT.
BUT WE CAN TELL YOU AREN'T JUST SAYING THAT, NAKANO-SAN.
YEP! THEY'RE SUPERB!
THEY'RE SOFT AND FLUFFY ON THE INSIDE... DID YOU ADD SOMETHING?
I'M SURPRISED YOU NOTICED. WE PUT IN SOME MILK!
BUT THE OUTSIDE IS STILL CRUNCHY ...
HEH HEH HEH! YOU CAN'T GET THAT FLAVOR WITHOUT THIS SPECIALLY MODIFIED BURNER!
I KNEW...
...EVERYONE WAS GIVING IT THEIR ALL...
I WISH THE OTHER GIRLS FROM CLASS COULD TASTE THIS.
!

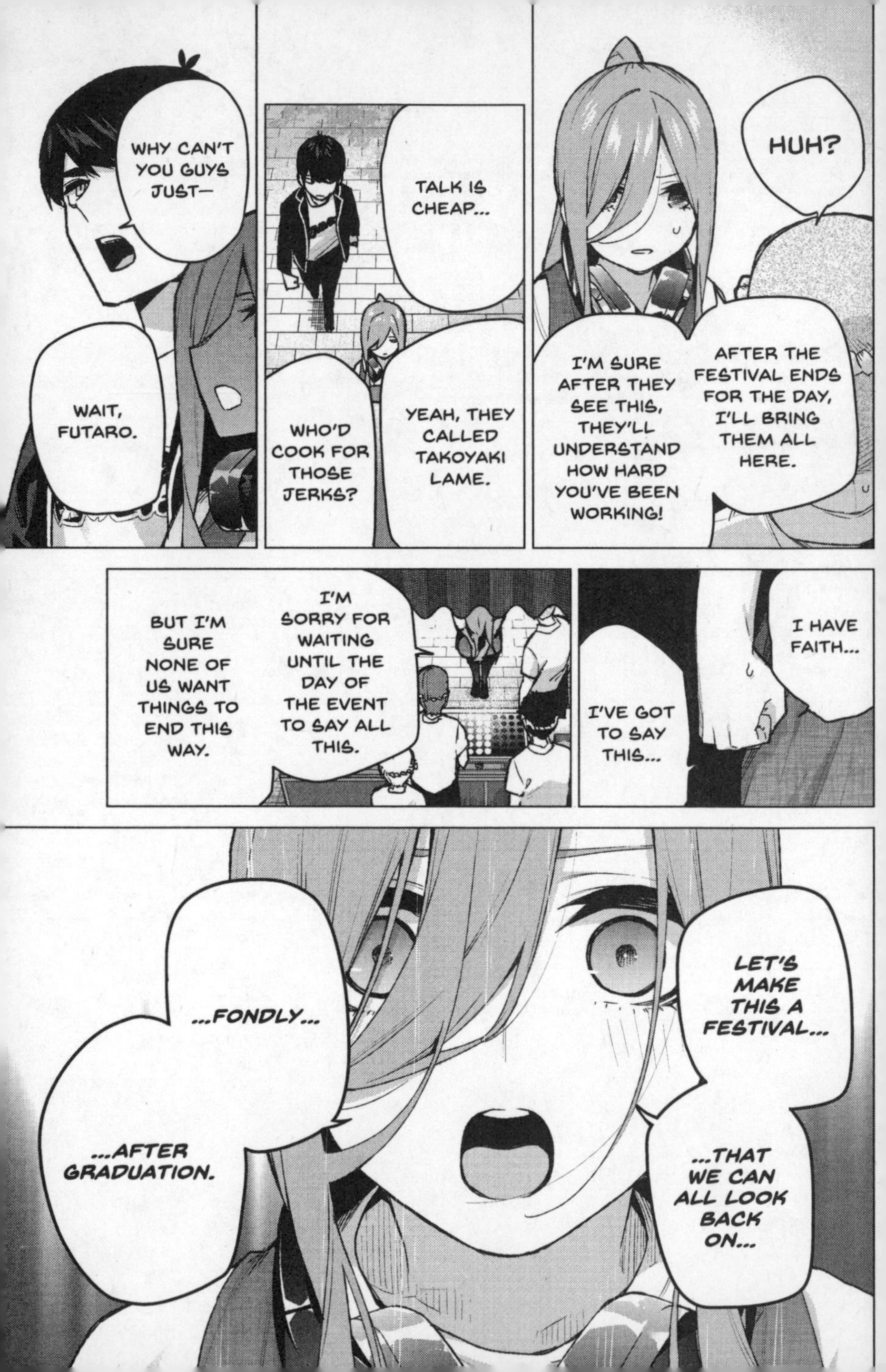
HUH?
AFTER THE FESTIVAL ENDS FOR THE DAY, I'LL BRING THEM ALL HERE.
I'M SURE AFTER THEY SEE THIS, THEY'LL UNDERSTAND HOW HARD YOU'VE BEEN WORKING!
TALK IS CHEAP...
YEAH, THEY CALLED TAKOYAKI LAME.
WHO'D COOK FOR THOSE JERKS?
WHY CAN'T YOU GUYS JUST—
WAIT, FUTARO.
I HAVE FAITH...
I'VE GOT TO SAY THIS...
I'M SORRY FOR WAITING UNTIL THE DAY OF THE EVENT TO SAY ALL THIS.
BUT I'M SURE NONE OF US WANT THINGS TO END THIS WAY.
LET'S MAKE THIS A FESTIVAL...
...THAT WE CAN ALL LOOK BACK ON...
...FONDLY...
...AFTER GRADUATION.

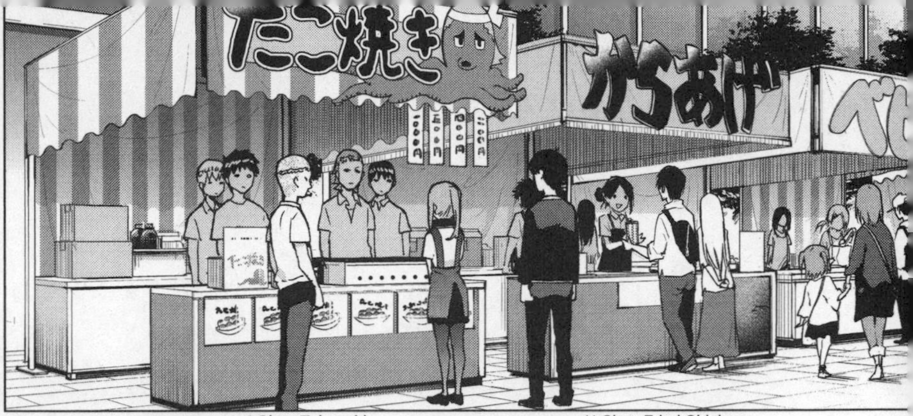
たこ焼き
からあげ
* Sign: Takoyaki ** Sign: Fried Chicken

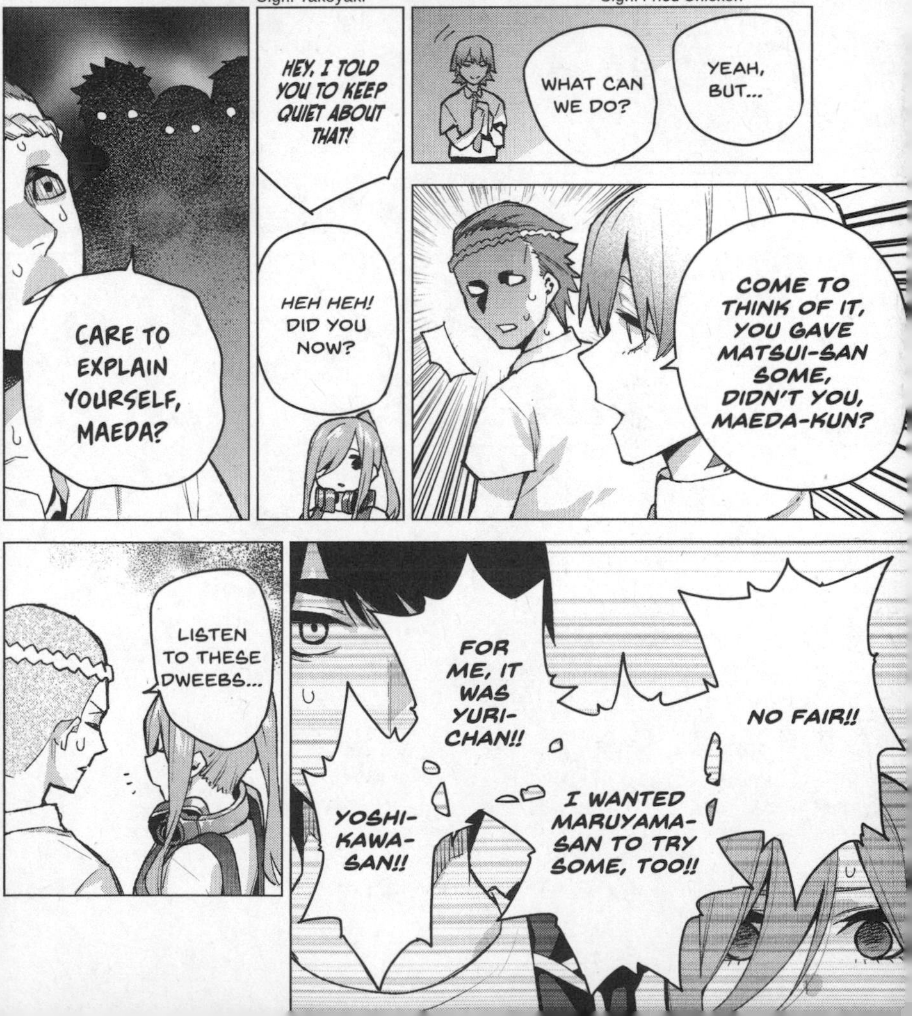
YEAH, BUT...
WHAT CAN WE DO?
COME TO THINK OF IT, YOU GAVE MATSUI-SAN SOME, DIDN'T YOU, MAEDA-KUN?
HEY, I TOLD YOU TO KEEP QUIET ABOUT THAT!
HEH HEH! DID YOU NOW?
CARE TO EXPLAIN YOURSELF, MAEDA?
NO FAIR!!
I WANTED MARUYAMA-SAN TO TRY SOME, TOO!!
FOR ME, IT WAS YURI-CHAN!!
YOSHI-KAWA-SAN!!
LISTEN TO THESE DWEEBS...

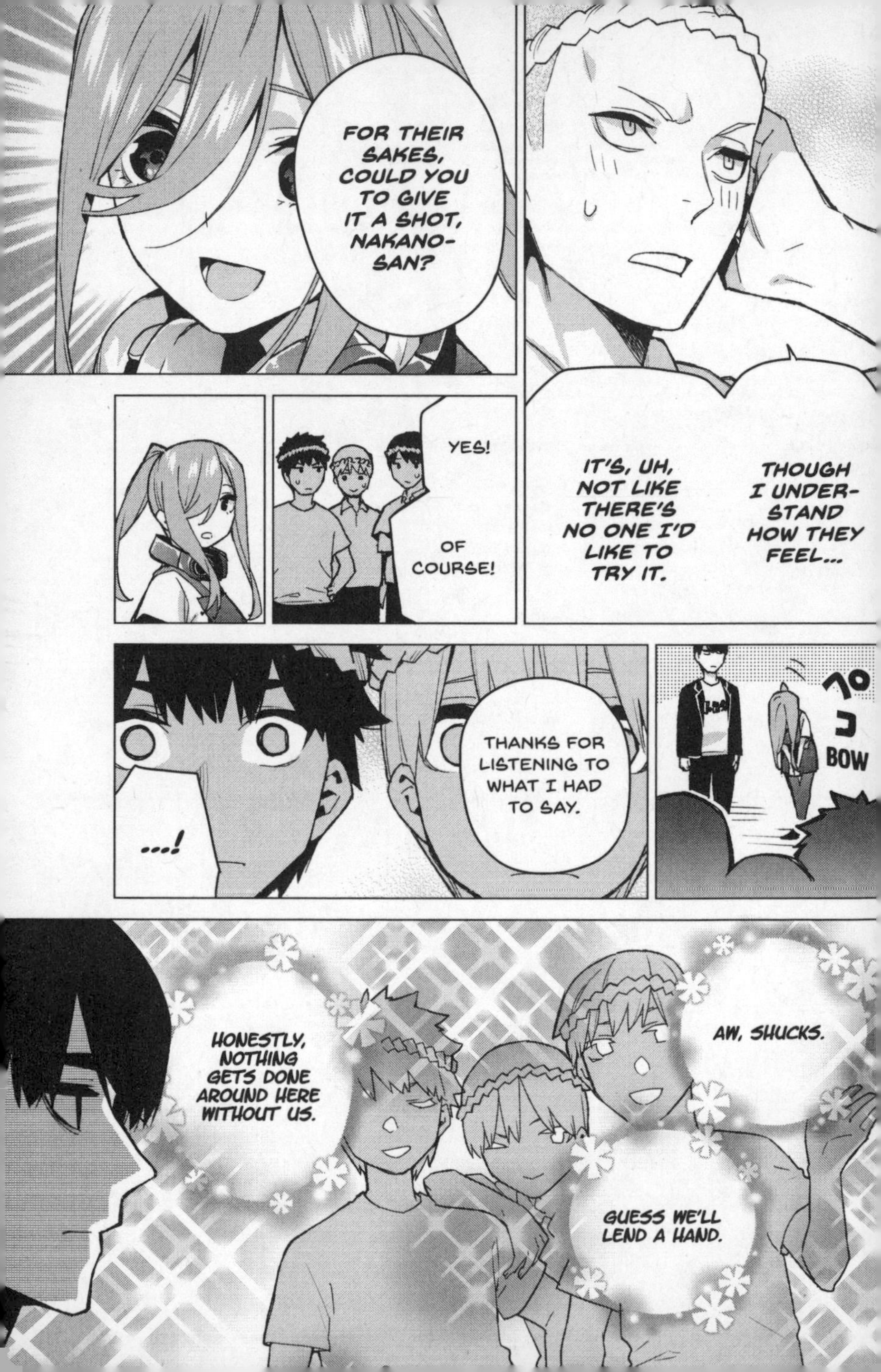
FOR THEIR SAKES, COULD YOU TO GIVE IT A SHOT, NAKANO-SAN?
THOUGH I UNDERSTAND HOW THEY FEEL...
IT'S, UH, NOT LIKE THERE'S NO ONE I'D LIKE TO TRY IT.
YES!
OF COURSE!
ヘコ
BOW
THANKS FOR LISTENING TO WHAT I HAD TO SAY.
...!
AW, SHUCKS.
GUESS WE'LL LEND A HAND.
HONESTLY, NOTHING GETS DONE AROUND HERE WITHOUT US.

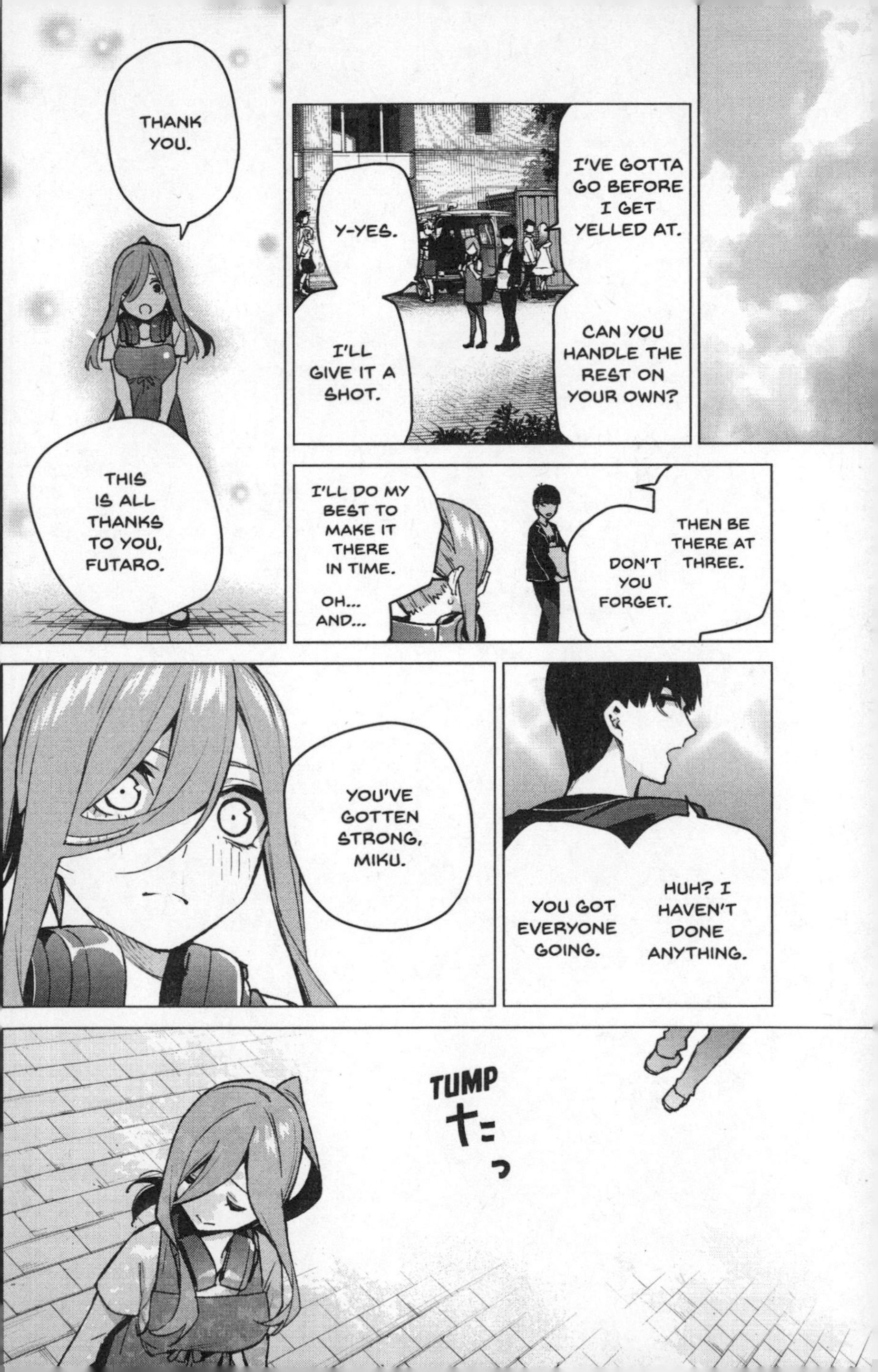
I'VE GOTTA GO BEFORE I GET YELLED AT.
Y-YES.
CAN YOU HANDLE THE REST ON YOUR OWN?
I'LL GIVE IT A SHOT.
THEN BE THERE AT THREE.
DON'T YOU FORGET.
I'LL DO MY BEST TO MAKE IT THERE IN TIME.
OH... AND...
THANK YOU.
THIS IS ALL THANKS TO YOU, FUTARO.
HUH? I HAVEN'T DONE ANYTHING.
YOU GOT EVERYONE GOING.
YOU'VE GOTTEN STRONG, MIKU.
TUMP
たっ

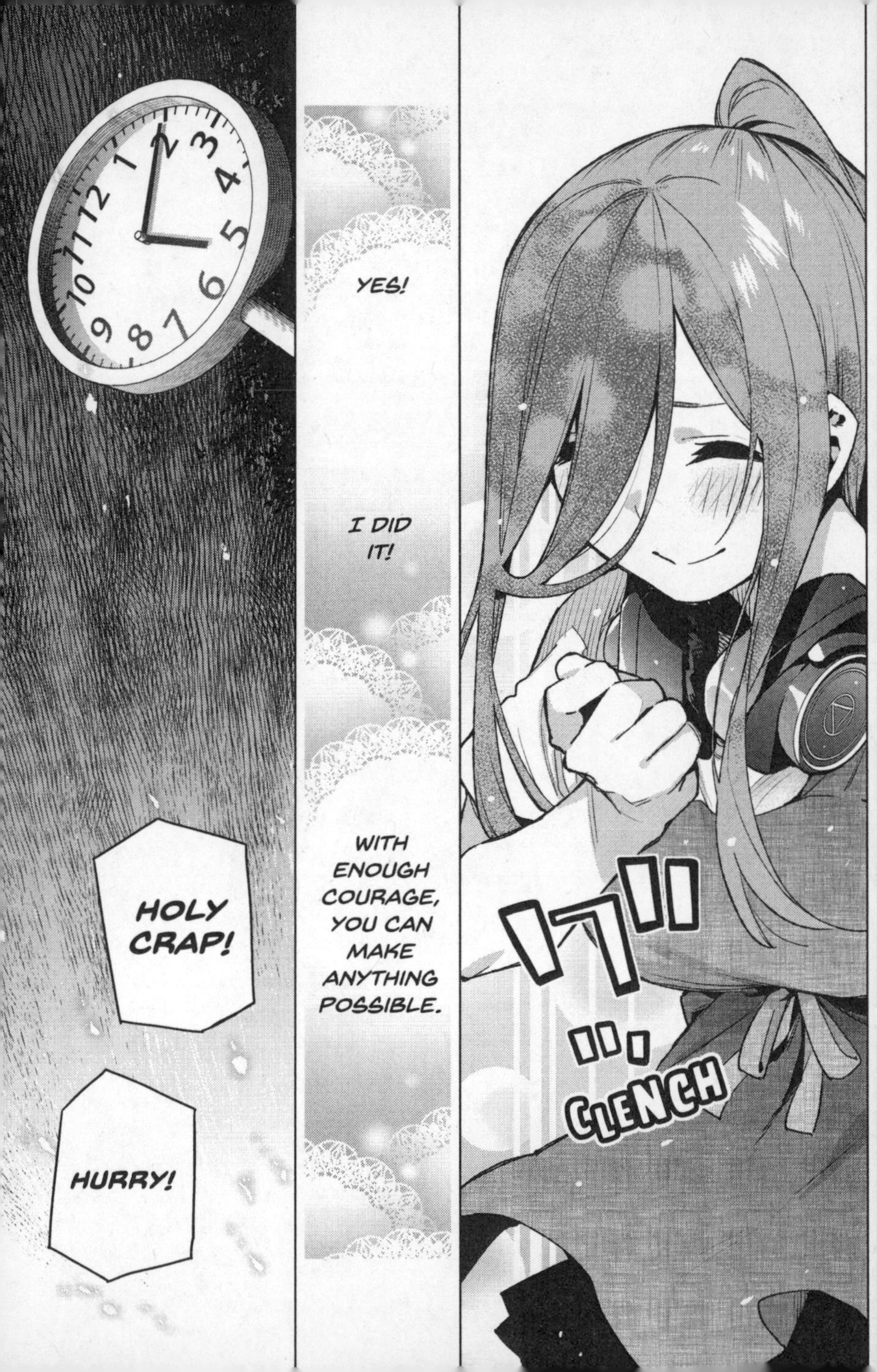
CLENCH
YES!
I DID IT!
WITH ENOUGH COURAGE, YOU CAN MAKE ANYTHING POSSIBLE.
HOLY CRAP!
HURRY!

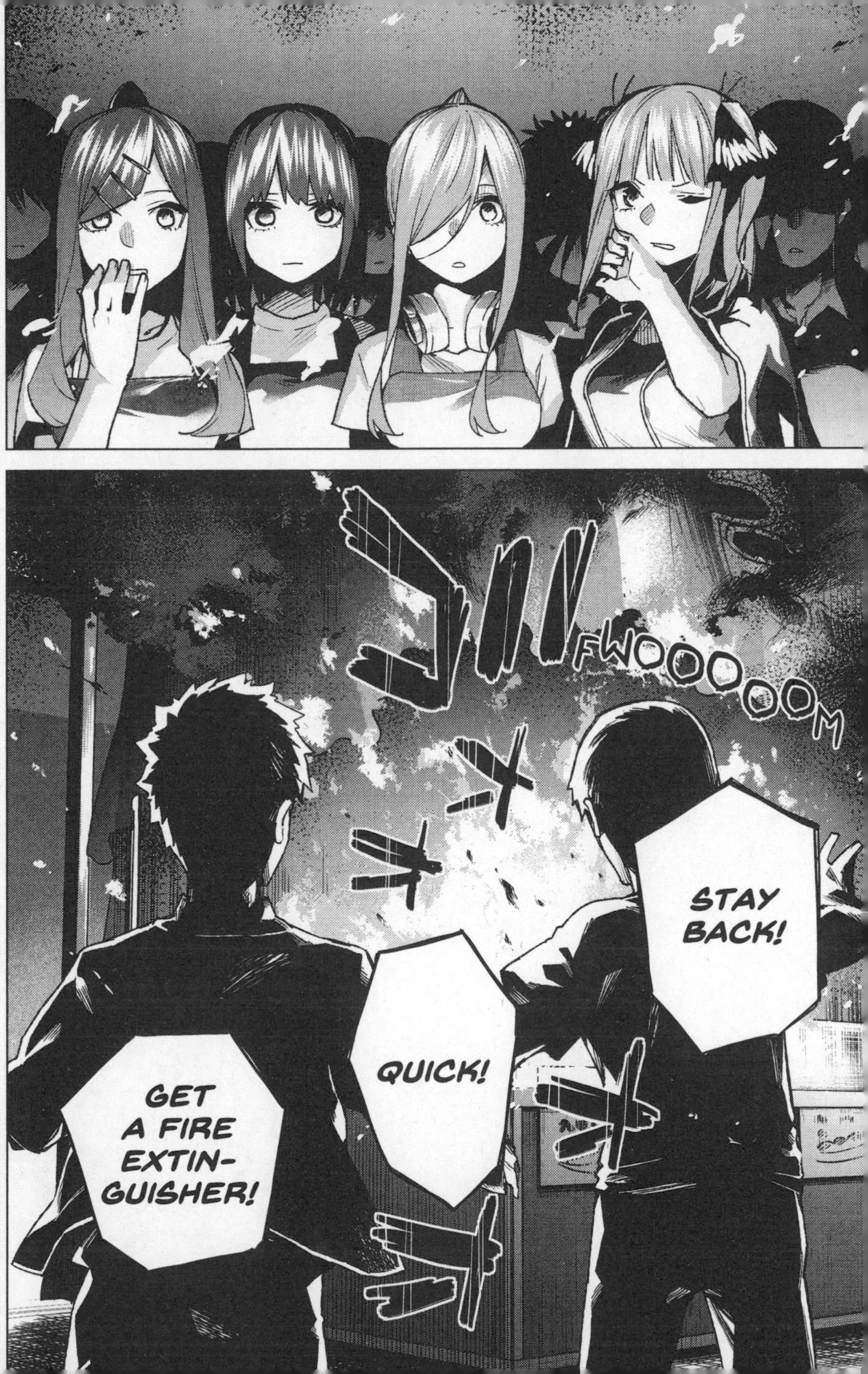
FWOOOOOOM
STAY BACK!
QUICK!
GET A FIRE EXTIN-GUISHER!

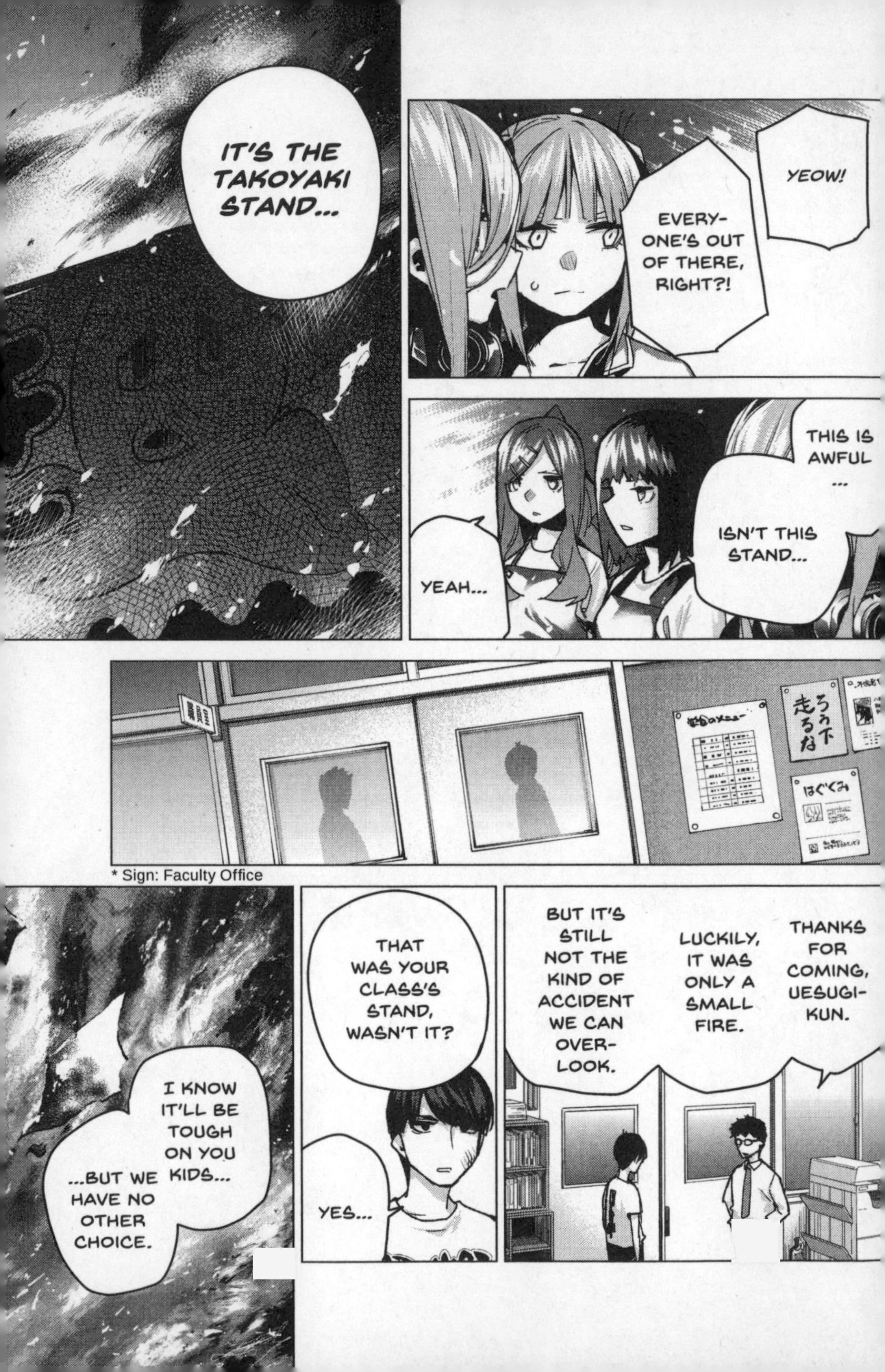
YEOW!
EVERYONE'S OUT OF THERE, RIGHT?!
THIS IS AWFUL ...
ISN'T THIS STAND...
YEAH...
IT'S THE TAKOYAKI STAND...
職員室
ろう下 走るな
はぐくみ
THANKS FOR COMING, UESUGI-KUN.
LUCKILY, IT WAS ONLY A SMALL FIRE.
BUT IT'S STILL NOT THE KIND OF ACCIDENT WE CAN OVERLOOK.
THAT WAS YOUR CLASS'S STAND, WASN'T IT?
YES...
I KNOW IT'LL BE TOUGH ON YOU KIDS...
...BUT WE HAVE NO OTHER CHOICE.
* Sign: Faculty Office

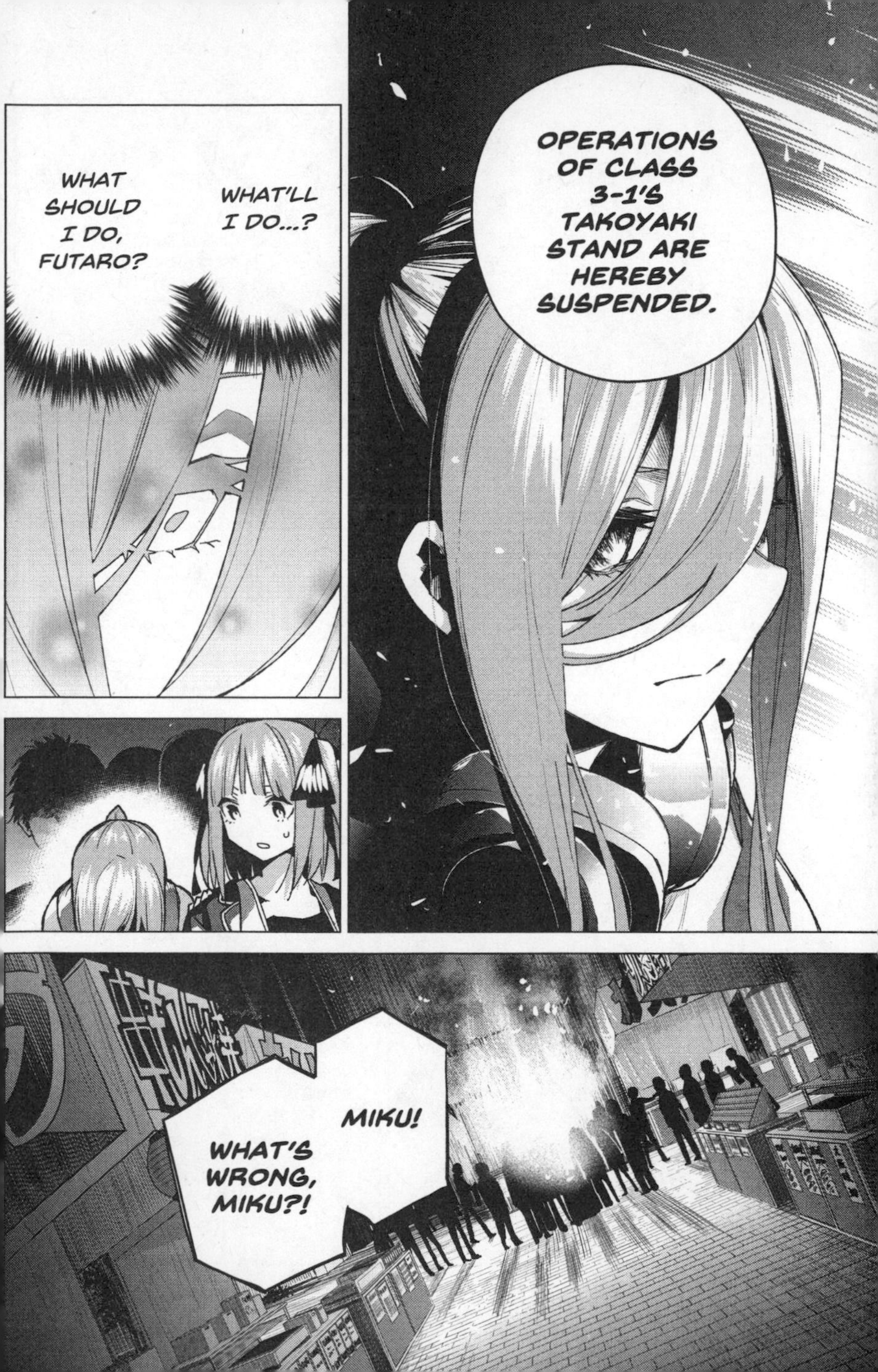
OPERATIONS OF CLASS 3-1'S TAKOYAKI STAND ARE HEREBY SUSPENDED.
WHAT'LL I DO...?
WHAT SHOULD I DO, FUTARO?
MIKU!
WHAT'S WRONG, MIKU?!

CHAPTER 106 IF THE FINAL FESTIVAL WAS MIKU'S ②

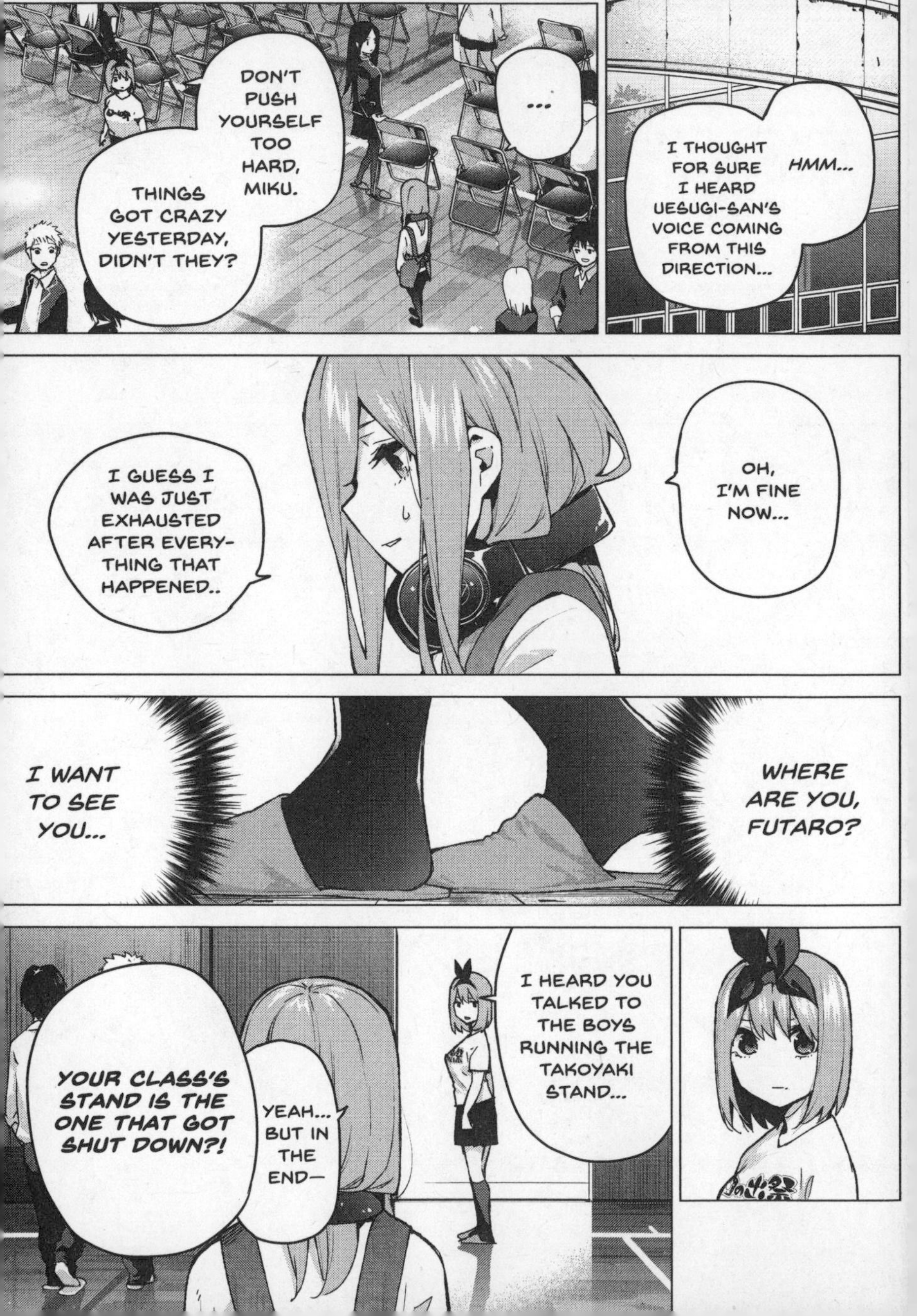
HMM...
I THOUGHT FOR SURE I HEARD UESUGI-SAN'S VOICE COMING FROM THIS DIRECTION...
...
DON'T PUSH YOURSELF TOO HARD, MIKU.
THINGS GOT CRAZY YESTERDAY, DIDN'T THEY?
OH, I'M FINE NOW...
I GUESS I WAS JUST EXHAUSTED AFTER EVERY-THING THAT HAPPENED..
WHERE ARE YOU, FUTARO?
I WANT TO SEE YOU...
I HEARD YOU TALKED TO THE BOYS RUNNING THE TAKOYAKI STAND...
YEAH... BUT IN THE END—
YOUR CLASS'S STAND IS THE ONE THAT GOT SHUT DOWN?!

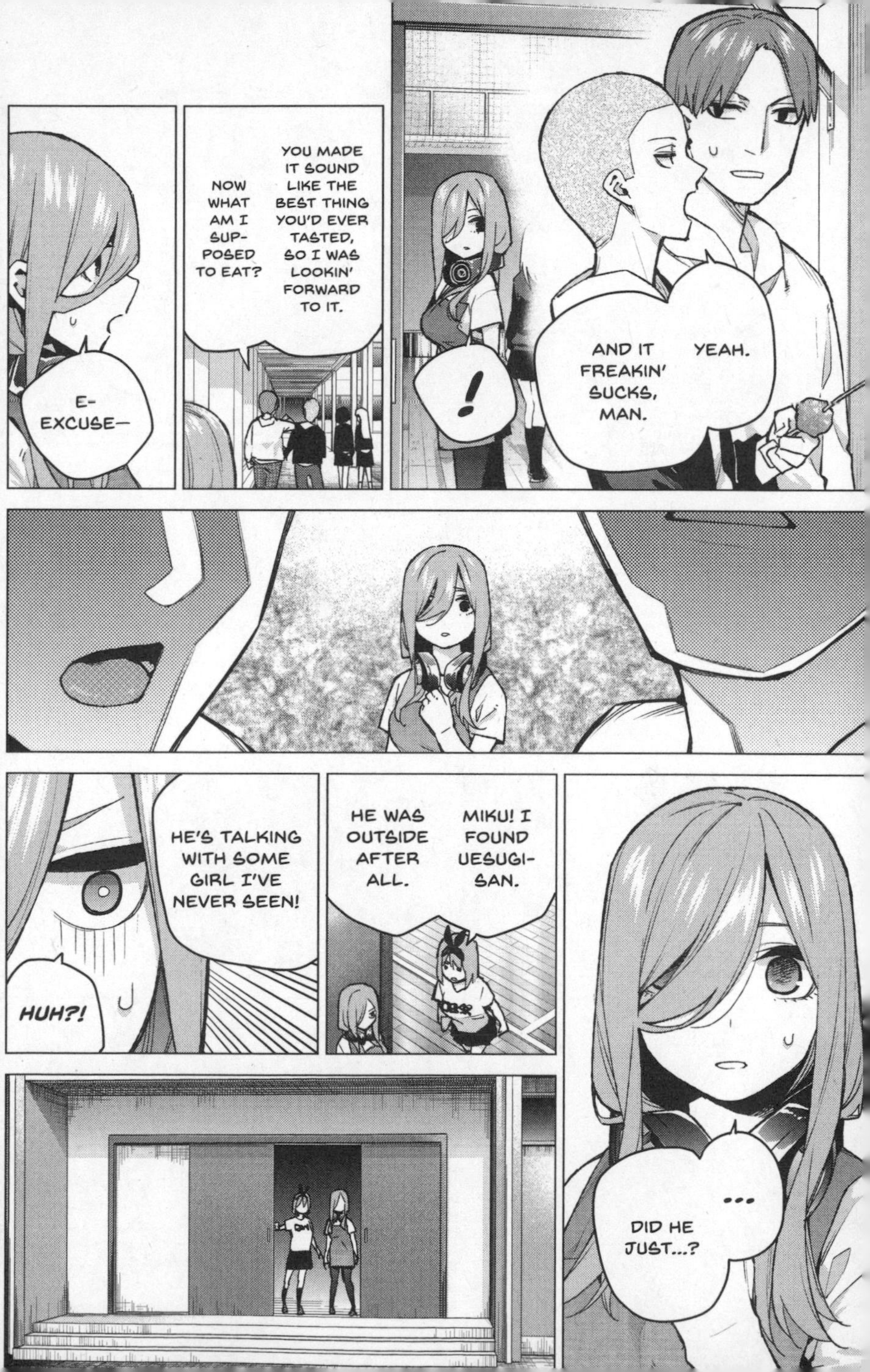
YEAH.
AND IT FREAKIN' SUCKS, MAN.
!
YOU MADE IT SOUND LIKE THE BEST THING YOU'D EVER TASTED, SO I WAS LOOKIN' FORWARD TO IT.
NOW WHAT AM I SUP-POSED TO EAT?
E-EXCUSE—
...
DID HE JUST...?
MIKU! I FOUND UESUGI-SAN.
HE WAS OUTSIDE AFTER ALL.
HE'S TALKING WITH SOME GIRL I'VE NEVER SEEN!
HUH?!

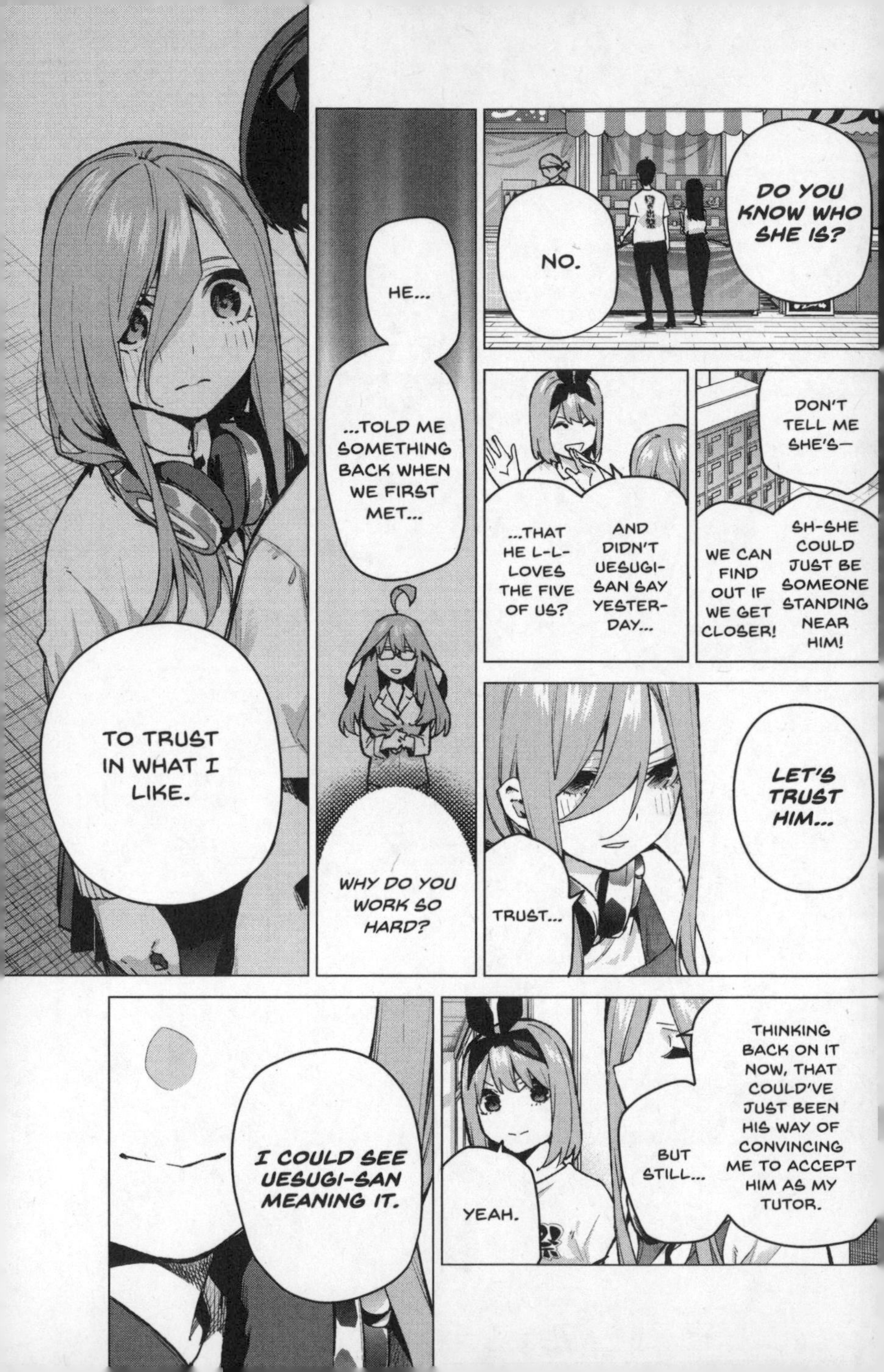
DO YOU KNOW WHO SHE IS?
NO.
DON'T TELL ME SHE'S—
SH-SHE COULD JUST BE SOMEONE STANDING NEAR HIM!
WE CAN FIND OUT IF WE GET CLOSER!
AND DIDN'T UESUGI-SAN SAY YESTER-DAY...
...THAT HE L-L-LOVES THE FIVE OF US?
LET'S TRUST HIM...
TRUST...
HE...
...TOLD ME SOMETHING BACK WHEN WE FIRST MET...
WHY DO YOU WORK SO HARD?
TO TRUST IN WHAT I LIKE.
THINKING BACK ON IT NOW, THAT COULD'VE JUST BEEN HIS WAY OF CONVINCING ME TO ACCEPT HIM AS MY TUTOR.
BUT STILL...
YEAH.
I COULD SEE UESUGI-SAN MEANING IT.

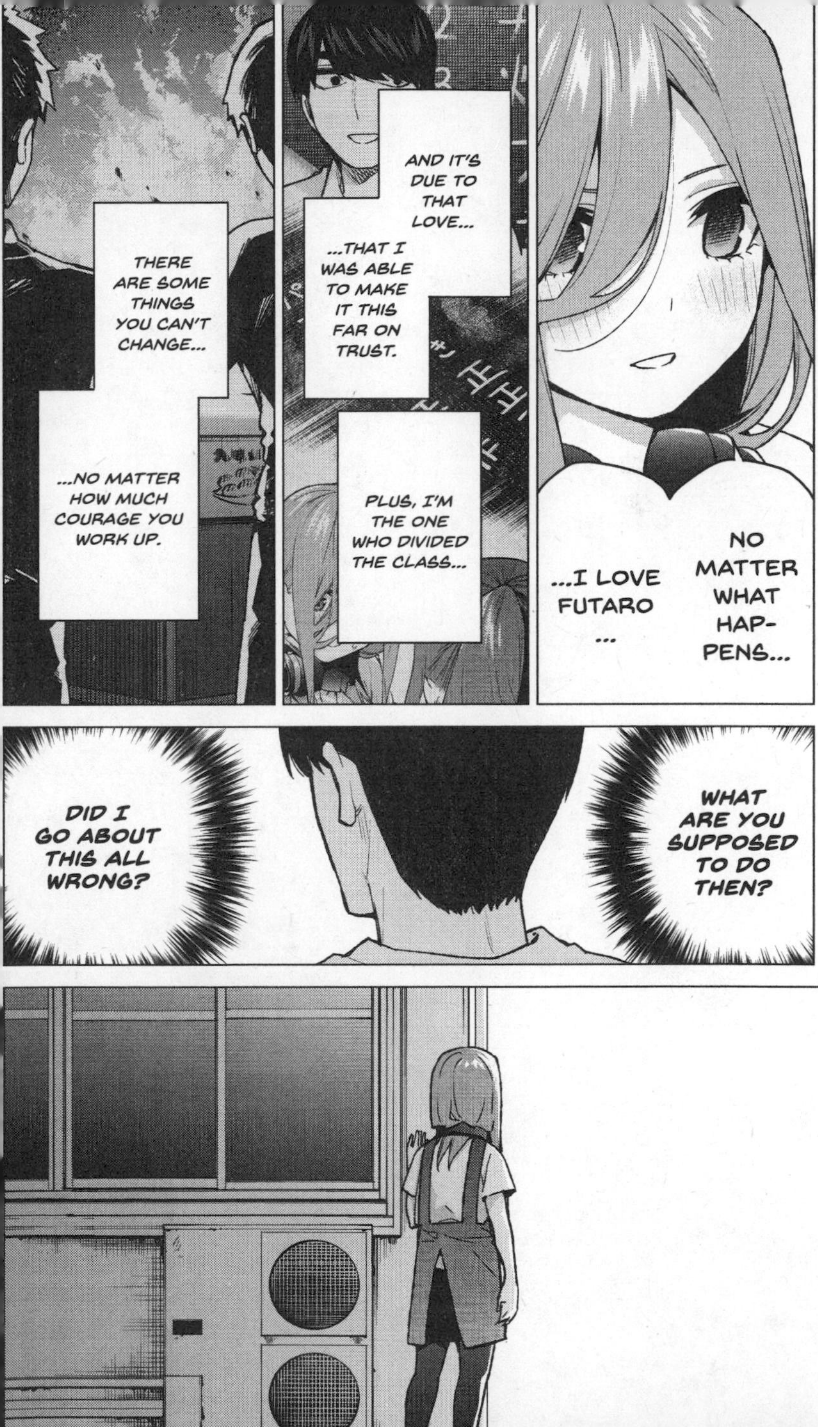
NO MATTER WHAT HAP- PENS...
...I LOVE FUTARO ...
AND IT'S DUE TO THAT LOVE...
...THAT I WAS ABLE TO MAKE IT THIS FAR ON TRUST.
PLUS, I'M THE ONE WHO DIVIDED THE CLASS...
THERE ARE SOME THINGS YOU CAN'T CHANGE...
...NO MATTER HOW MUCH COURAGE YOU WORK UP.
WHAT ARE YOU SUPPOSED TO DO THEN?
DID I GO ABOUT THIS ALL WRONG?

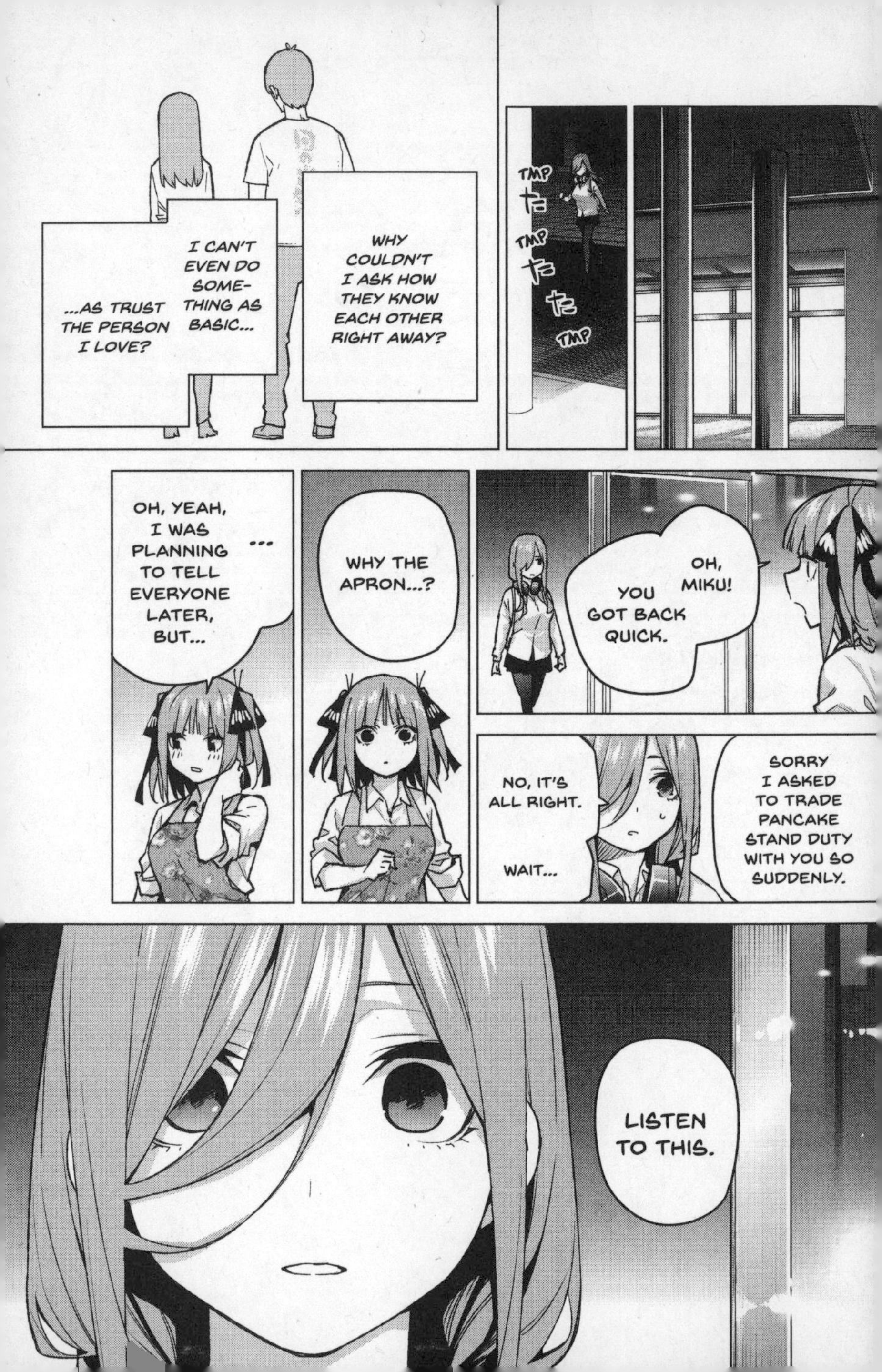
TMP
た
TMP
た
た
TMP
WHY COULDN'T I ASK HOW THEY KNOW EACH OTHER RIGHT AWAY?
I CAN'T EVEN DO SOME-THING AS BASIC...
...AS TRUST THE PERSON I LOVE?
OH, MIKU! YOU GOT BACK QUICK.
SORRY I ASKED TO TRADE PANCAKE STAND DUTY WITH YOU SO SUDDENLY.
NO, IT'S ALL RIGHT.
WAIT...
WHY THE APRON...?
...
OH, YEAH, I WAS PLANNING TO TELL EVERYONE LATER, BUT...
LISTEN TO THIS.

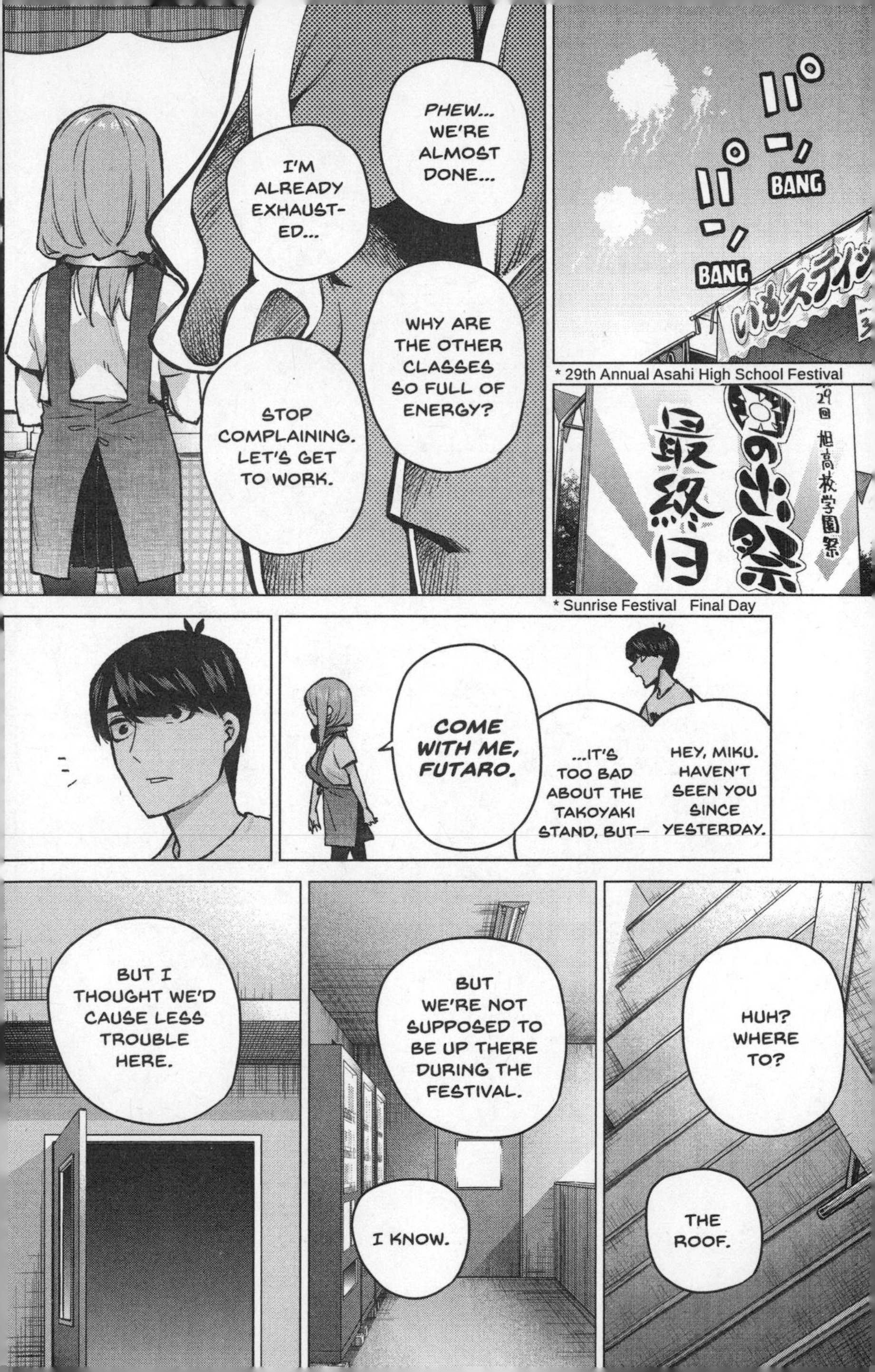
パーン
BANG
パーン
BANG
* 29th Annual Asahi High School Festival
第29回 旭高校学園祭
日の出祭
最終日
* Sunrise Festival Final Day
PHEW... WE'RE ALMOST DONE...
I'M ALREADY EXHAUST-ED...
WHY ARE THE OTHER CLASSES SO FULL OF ENERGY?
STOP COMPLAINING. LET'S GET TO WORK.
HEY, MIKU. HAVEN'T SEEN YOU SINCE YESTERDAY.
...IT'S TOO BAD ABOUT THE TAKOYAKI STAND, BUT—
COME WITH ME, FUTARO.
HUH? WHERE TO?
THE ROOF.
BUT WE'RE NOT SUPPOSED TO BE UP THERE DURING THE FESTIVAL.
I KNOW.
BUT I THOUGHT WE'D CAUSE LESS TROUBLE HERE.

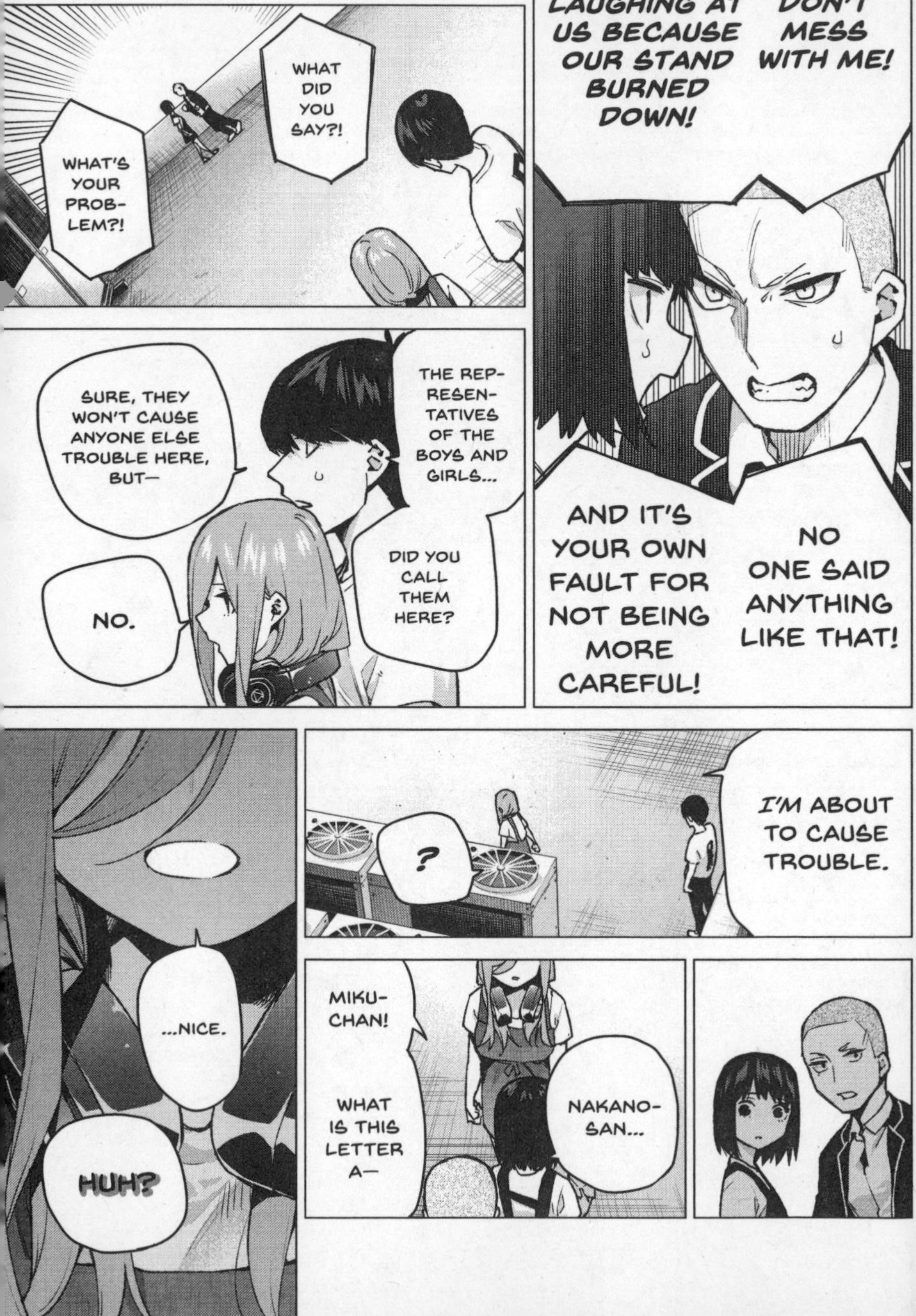
DON'T MESS WITH ME!
I KNOW YOU'RE LAUGHING AT US BECAUSE OUR STAND BURNED DOWN!
NO ONE SAID ANYTHING LIKE THAT!
AND IT'S YOUR OWN FAULT FOR NOT BEING MORE CAREFUL!
WHAT DID YOU SAY?!
WHAT'S YOUR PROB-LEM?!
THE REP-RESEN-TATIVES OF THE BOYS AND GIRLS...
DID YOU CALL THEM HERE?
SURE, THEY WON'T CAUSE ANYONE ELSE TROUBLE HERE, BUT—
NO.
I'M ABOUT TO CAUSE TROUBLE.
?
NAKANO-SAN...
MIKU-CHAN!
WHAT IS THIS LETTER A—
...NICE.
HUH?

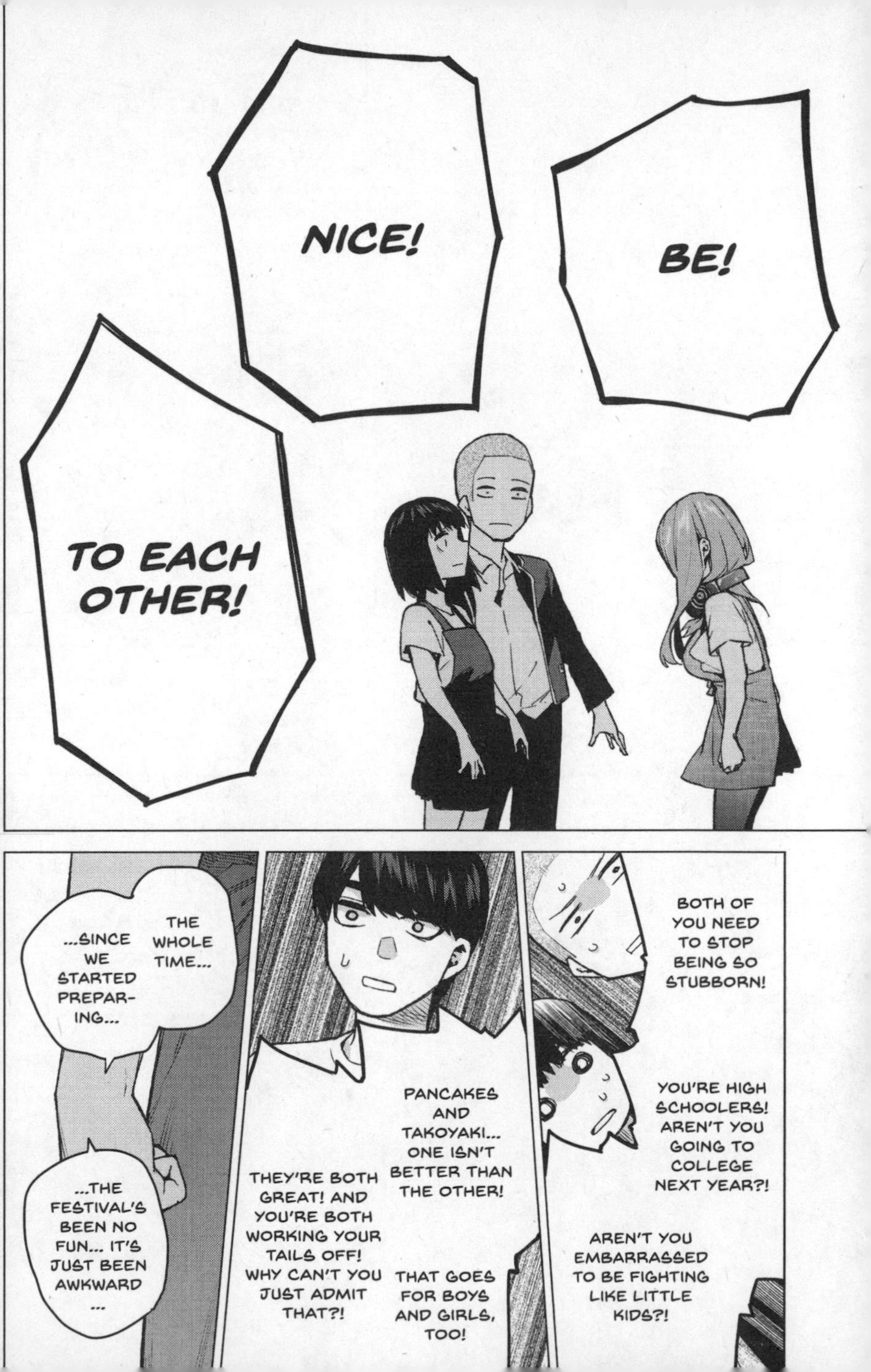
BE!
NICE!
TO EACH OTHER!
BOTH OF YOU NEED TO STOP BEING SO STUBBORN!
YOU'RE HIGH SCHOOLERS! AREN'T YOU GOING TO COLLEGE NEXT YEAR?!
AREN'T YOU EMBARRASSED TO BE FIGHTING LIKE LITTLE KIDS?!
PANCAKES AND TAKOYAKI... ONE ISN'T BETTER THAN THE OTHER!
THEY'RE BOTH GREAT! AND YOU'RE BOTH WORKING YOUR TAILS OFF! WHY CAN'T YOU JUST ADMIT THAT?!
THAT GOES FOR BOYS AND GIRLS, TOO!
THE WHOLE TIME...
...SINCE WE STARTED PREPAR-ING...
...THE FESTIVAL'S BEEN NO FUN... IT'S JUST BEEN AWKWARD...

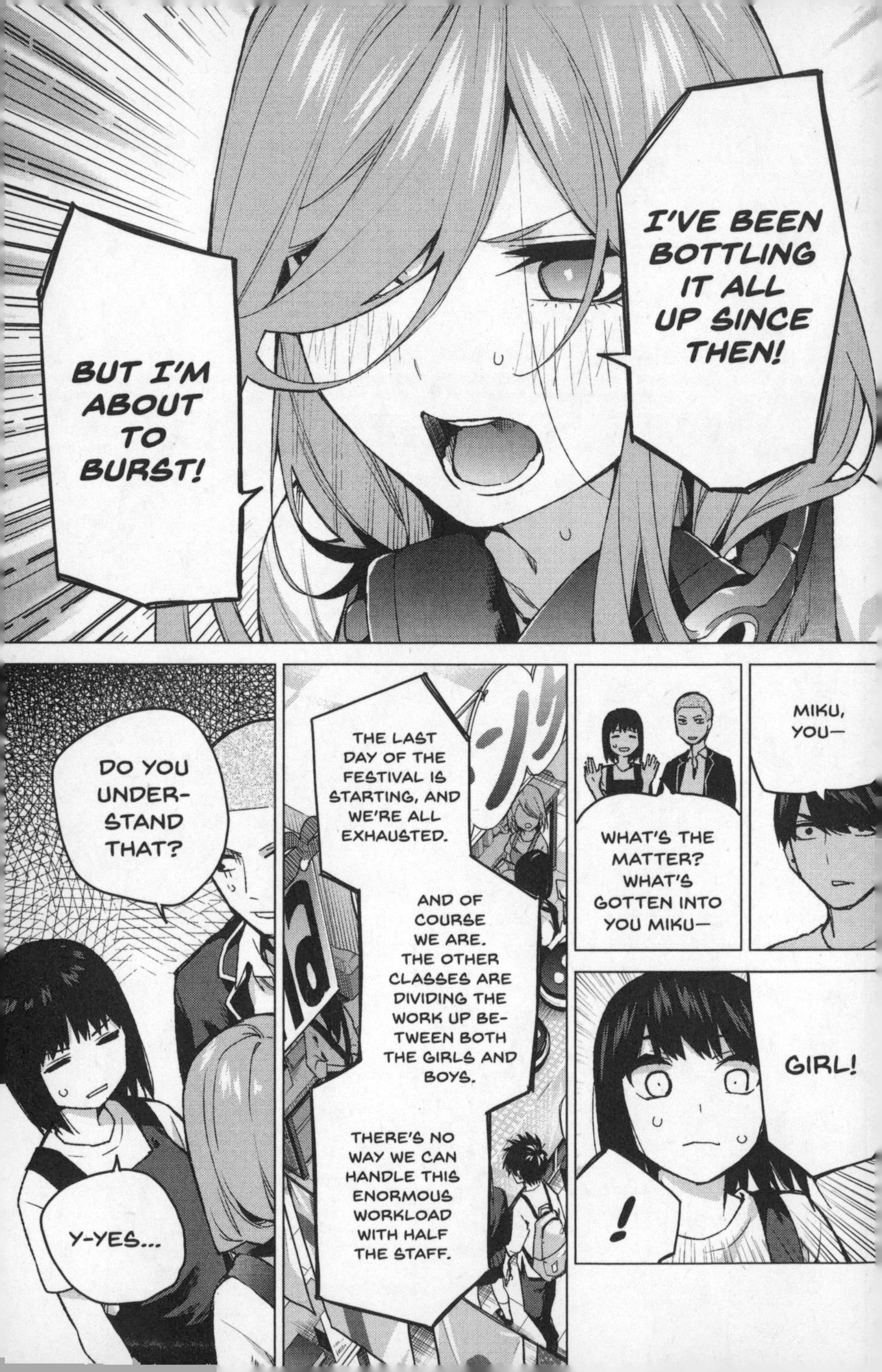
I'VE BEEN BOTTLING IT ALL UP SINCE THEN!
BUT I'M ABOUT TO BURST!
MIKU, YOU—
WHAT'S THE MATTER? WHAT'S GOTTEN INTO YOU MIKU—
GIRL!
!
THE LAST DAY OF THE FESTIVAL IS STARTING, AND WE'RE ALL EXHAUSTED.
AND OF COURSE WE ARE. THE OTHER CLASSES ARE DIVIDING THE WORK UP BE-TWEEN BOTH THE GIRLS AND BOYS.
THERE'S NO WAY WE CAN HANDLE THIS ENORMOUS WORKLOAD WITH HALF THE STAFF.
DO YOU UNDER-STAND THAT?
Y-YES...

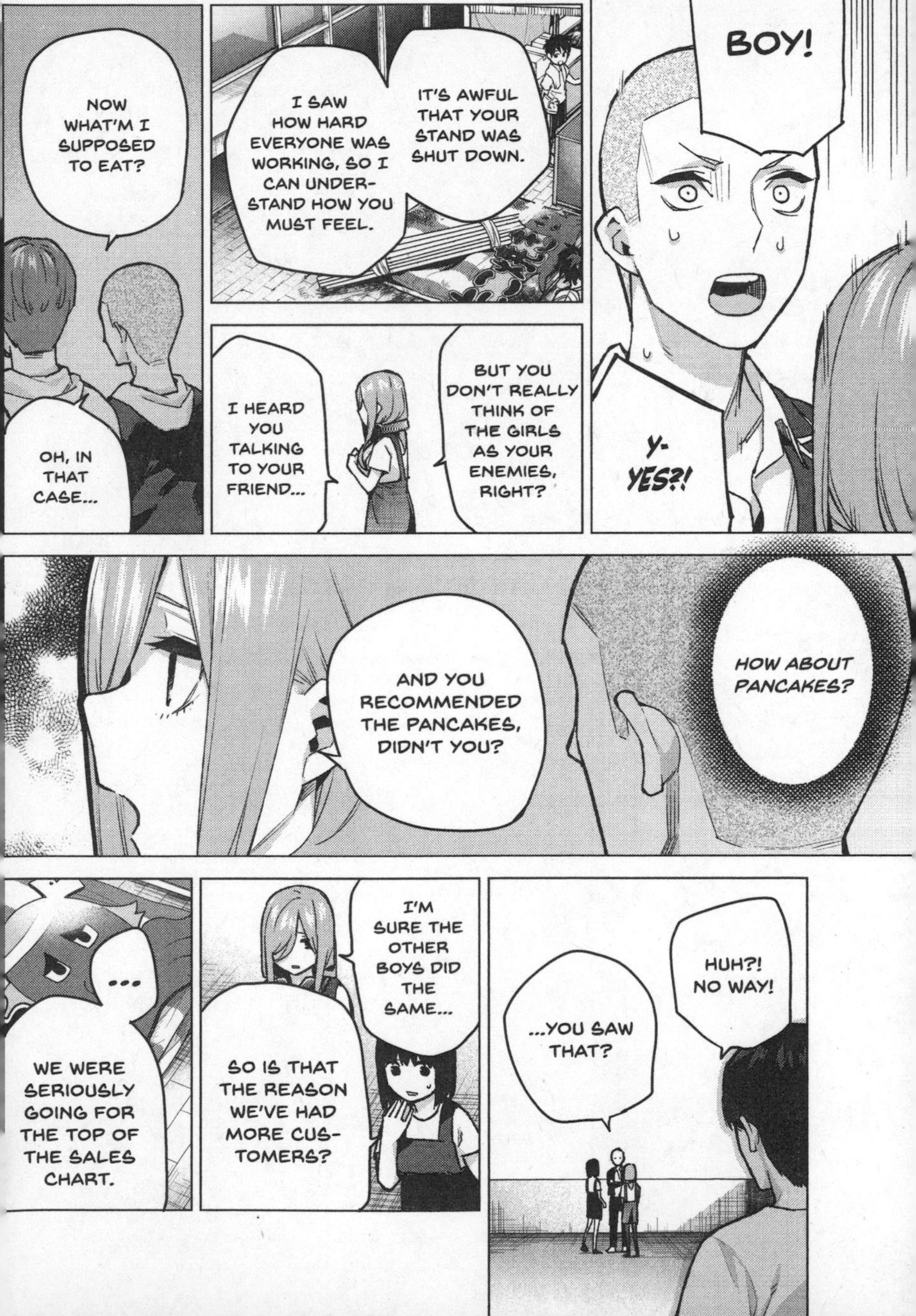
BOY!
Y-YES?!
IT'S AWFUL THAT YOUR STAND WAS SHUT DOWN.
I SAW HOW HARD EVERYONE WAS WORKING, SO I CAN UNDERSTAND HOW YOU MUST FEEL.
BUT YOU DON'T REALLY THINK OF THE GIRLS AS YOUR ENEMIES, RIGHT?
I HEARD YOU TALKING TO YOUR FRIEND...
NOW WHAT'M I SUPPOSED TO EAT?
OH, IN THAT CASE...
HOW ABOUT PANCAKES?
AND YOU RECOMMENDED THE PANCAKES, DIDN'T YOU?
HUH?! NO WAY!
...YOU SAW THAT?
I'M SURE THE OTHER BOYS DID THE SAME...
SO IS THAT THE REASON WE'VE HAD MORE CUSTOMERS?
...
WE WERE SERIOUSLY GOING FOR THE TOP OF THE SALES CHART.

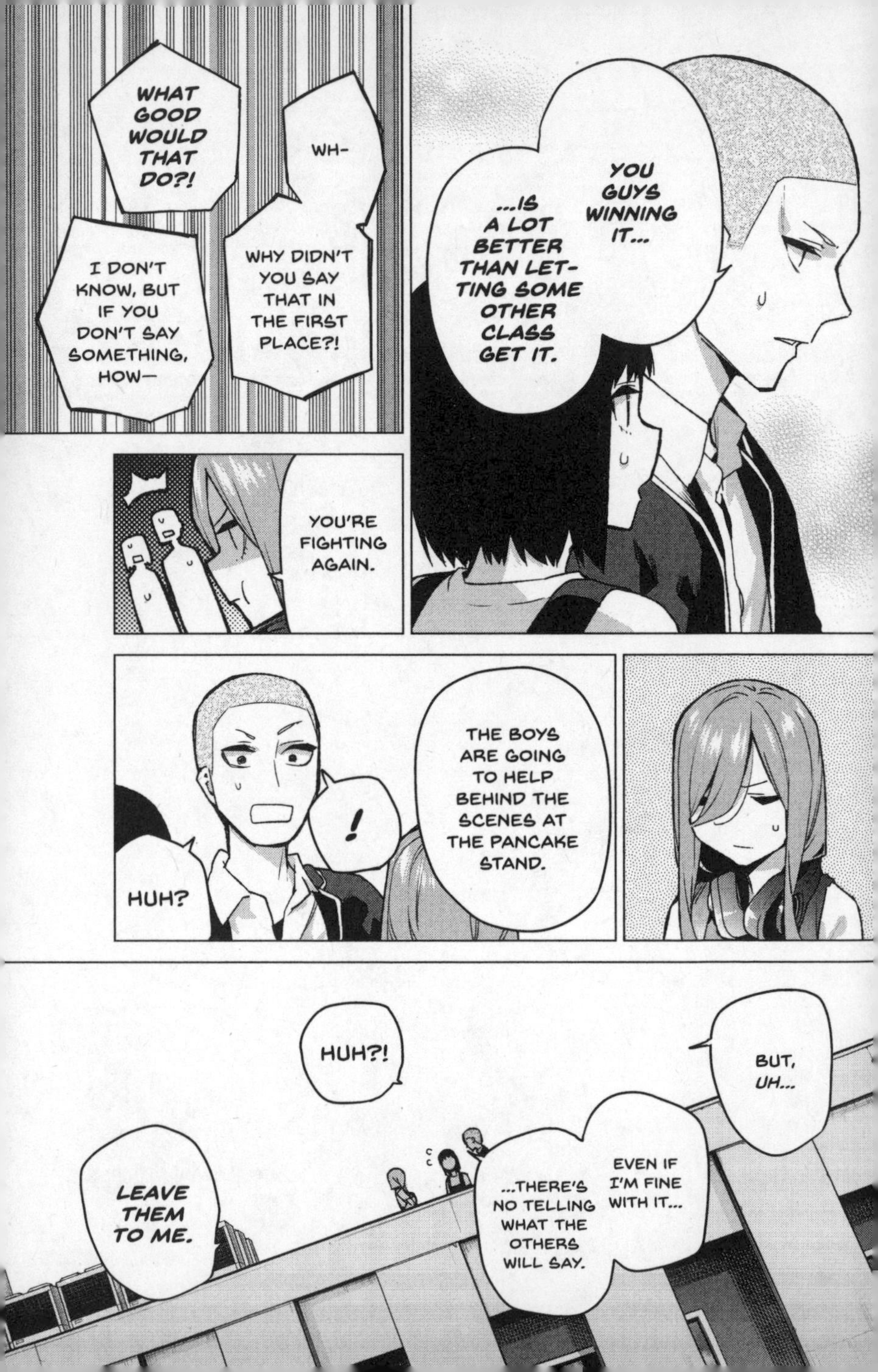
YOU GUYS WINNING IT...
...IS A LOT BETTER THAN LET-TING SOME OTHER CLASS GET IT.
WH-
WHAT GOOD WOULD THAT DO?!
WHY DIDN'T YOU SAY THAT IN THE FIRST PLACE?!
I DON'T KNOW, BUT IF YOU DON'T SAY SOMETHING, HOW—
YOU'RE FIGHTING AGAIN.
THE BOYS ARE GOING TO HELP BEHIND THE SCENES AT THE PANCAKE STAND.
!
HUH?
BUT, UH...
EVEN IF I'M FINE WITH IT...
...THERE'S NO TELLING WHAT THE OTHERS WILL SAY.
HUH?!
LEAVE THEM TO ME.

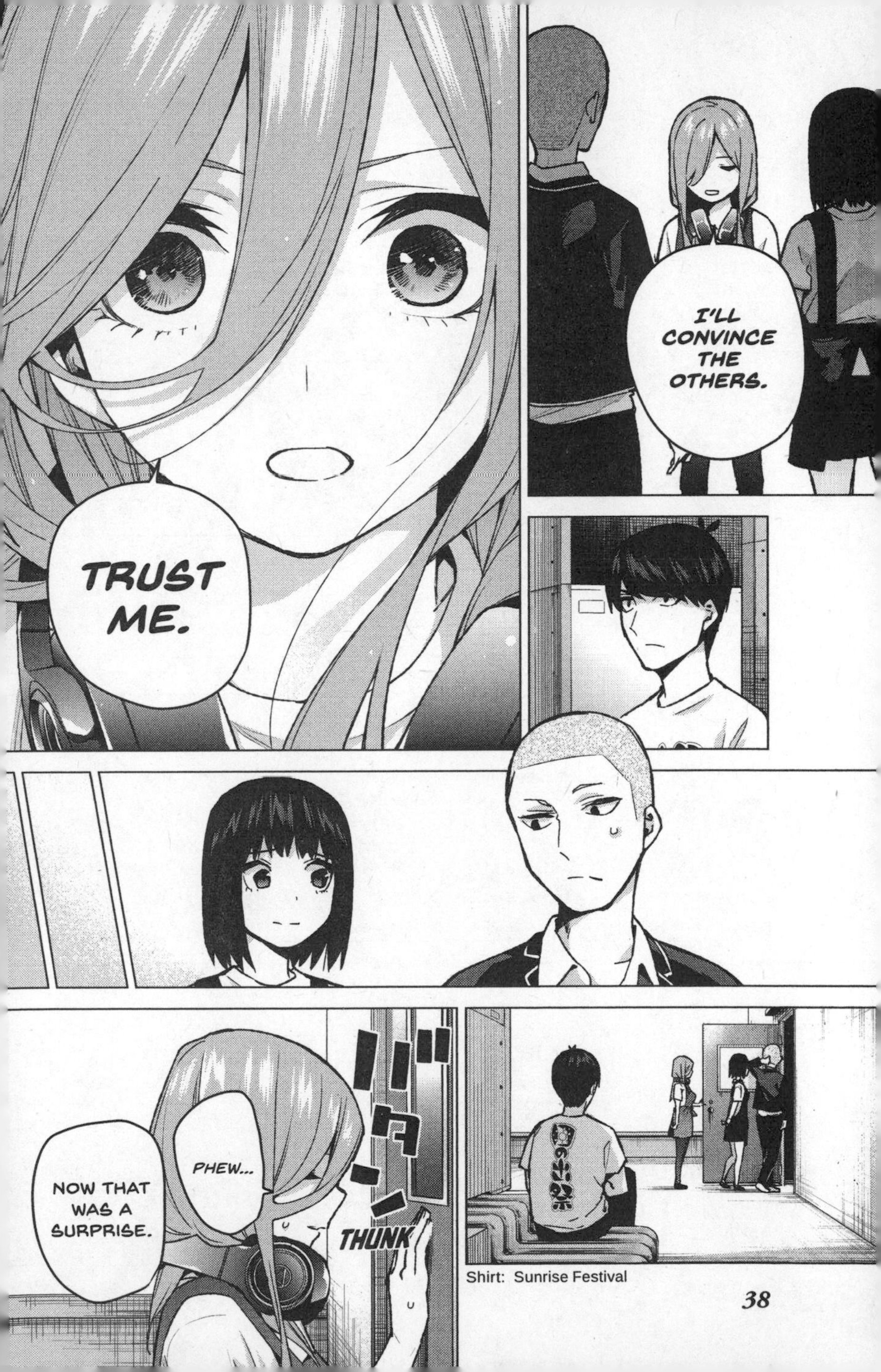
I'LL CONVINCE THE OTHERS.
TRUST ME.
PHEW...
NOW THAT WAS A SURPRISE.
THUNK
Shirt: Sunrise Festival

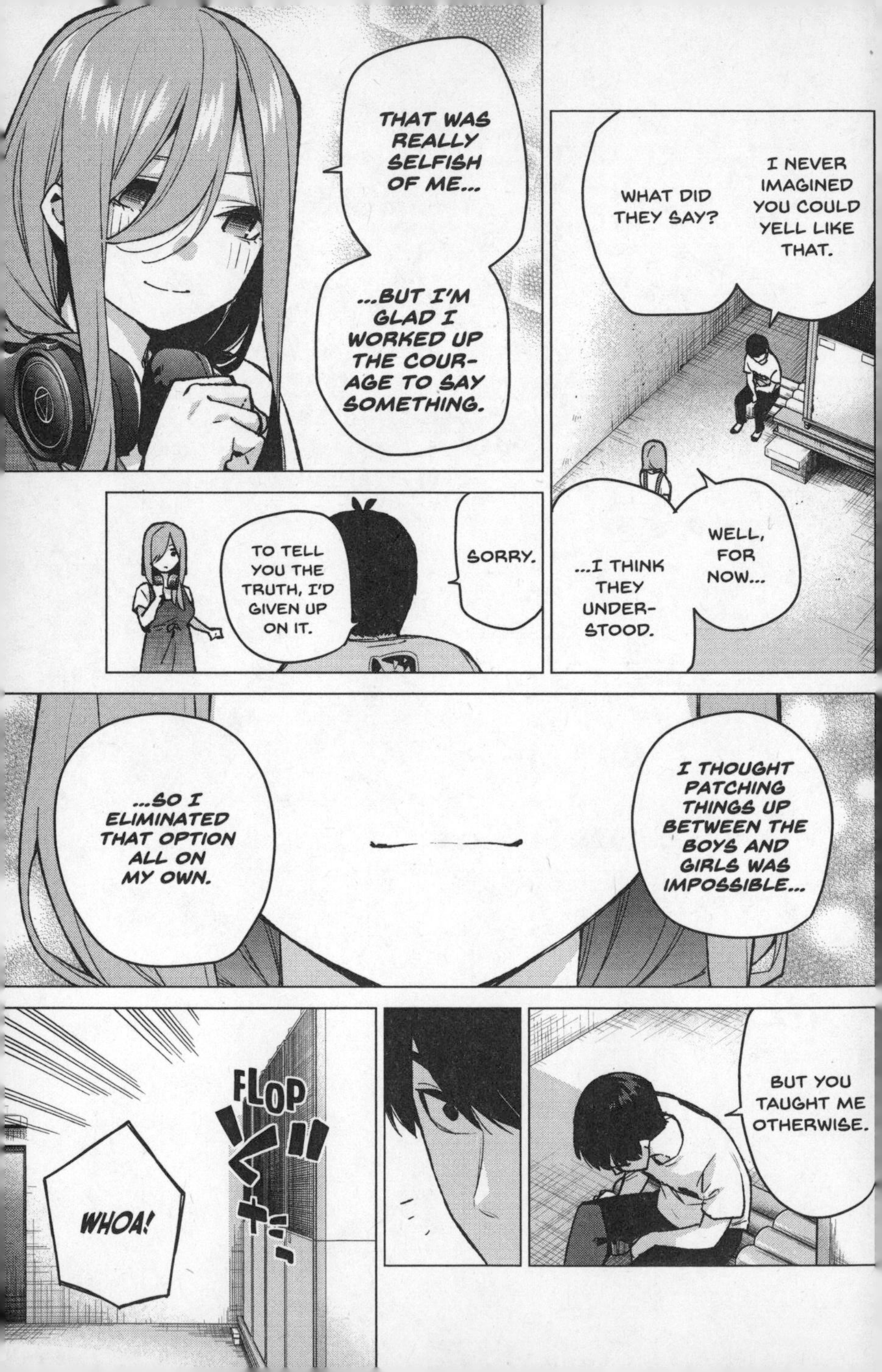
I NEVER IMAGINED YOU COULD YELL LIKE THAT.
WHAT DID THEY SAY?
WELL, FOR NOW...
...I THINK THEY UNDERSTOOD.
THAT WAS REALLY SELFISH OF ME...
...BUT I'M GLAD I WORKED UP THE COURAGE TO SAY SOMETHING.
SORRY.
TO TELL YOU THE TRUTH, I'D GIVEN UP ON IT.
I THOUGHT PATCHING THINGS UP BETWEEN THE BOYS AND GIRLS WAS IMPOSSIBLE...
...SO I ELIMINATED THAT OPTION ALL ON MY OWN.
BUT YOU TAUGHT ME OTHERWISE.
FLOP
WHOA!

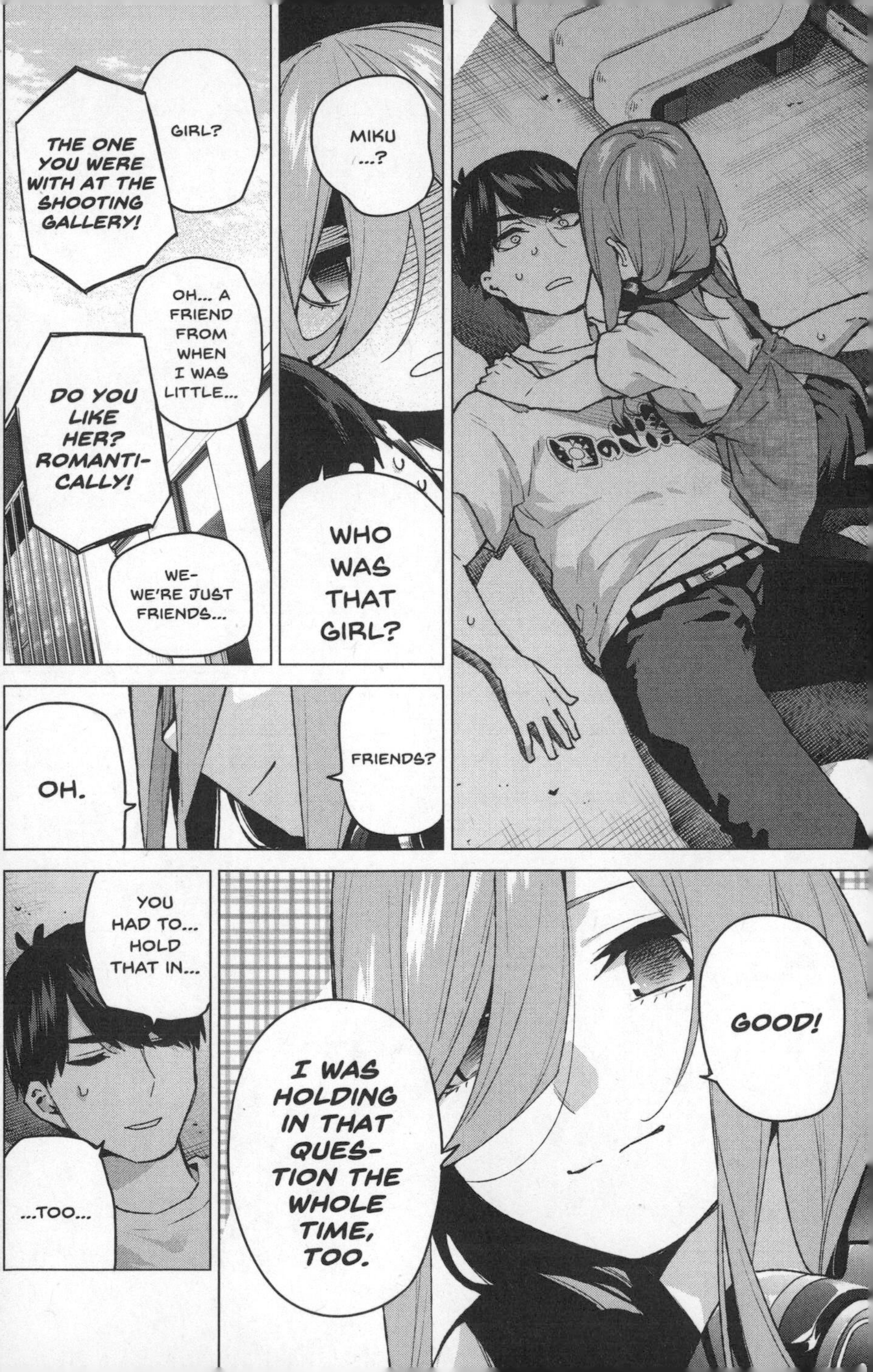
MIKU ...?
WHO WAS THAT GIRL?
GIRL?
THE ONE YOU WERE WITH AT THE SHOOTING GALLERY!
OH... A FRIEND FROM WHEN I WAS LITTLE...
DO YOU LIKE HER? ROMANTICALLY!
WE- WE'RE JUST FRIENDS...
FRIENDS?
OH.
GOOD!
I WAS HOLDING IN THAT QUESTION THE WHOLE TIME, TOO.
YOU HAD TO... HOLD THAT IN...
...TOO...

DON'T HOLD BACK ANY-THING ON MY ACCOUNT.
I WANT TO KISS YOU.
OH...
OKAY.
THEN...
HUH?
I KNOW I TOLD YOU NOT TO HOLD BACK...
...BUT I DON'T SEE HOW THAT FOLLOWS.
PLUS—
OH, SORRY.

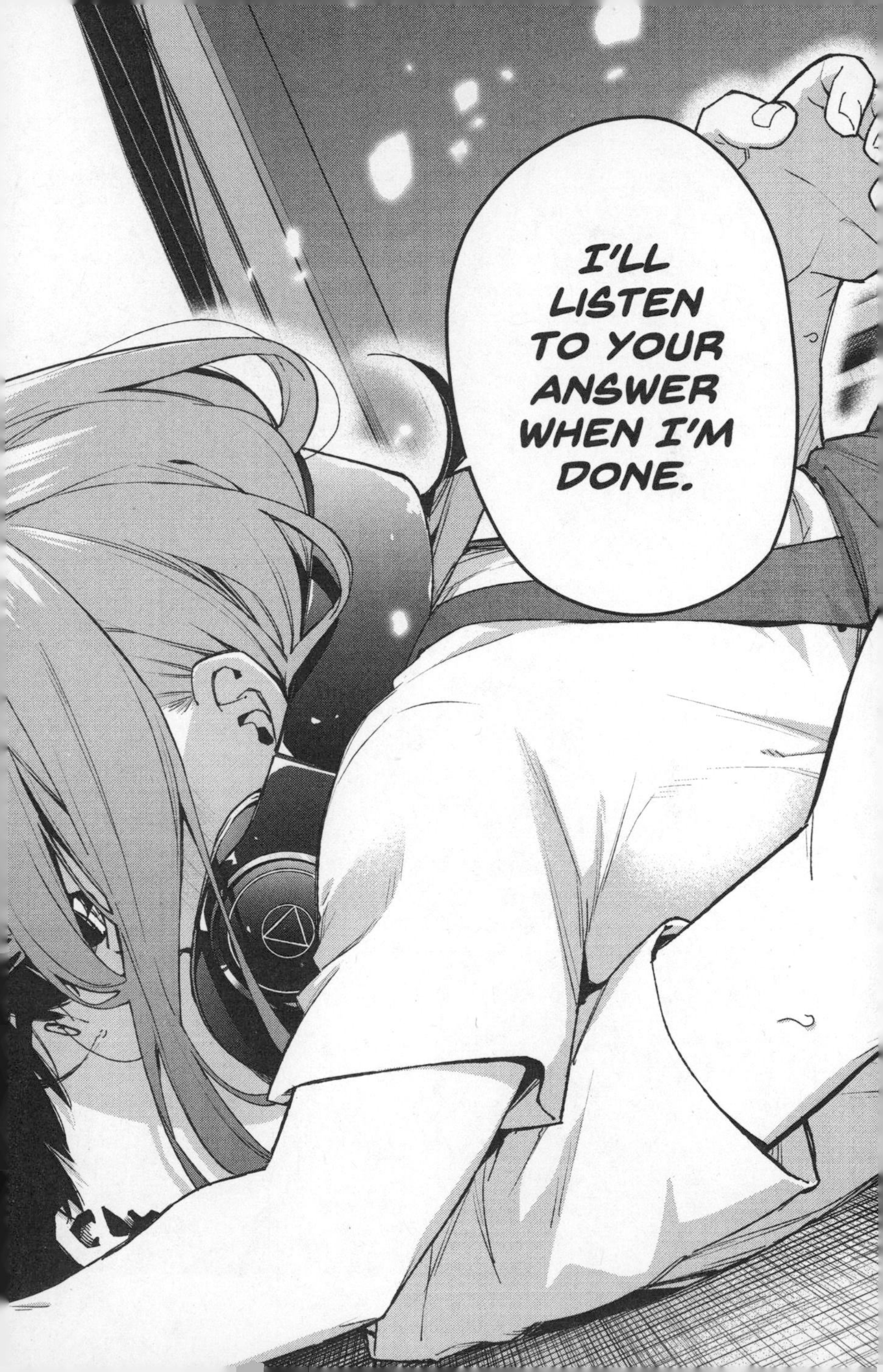
I'LL LISTEN TO YOUR ANSWER WHEN I'M DONE.

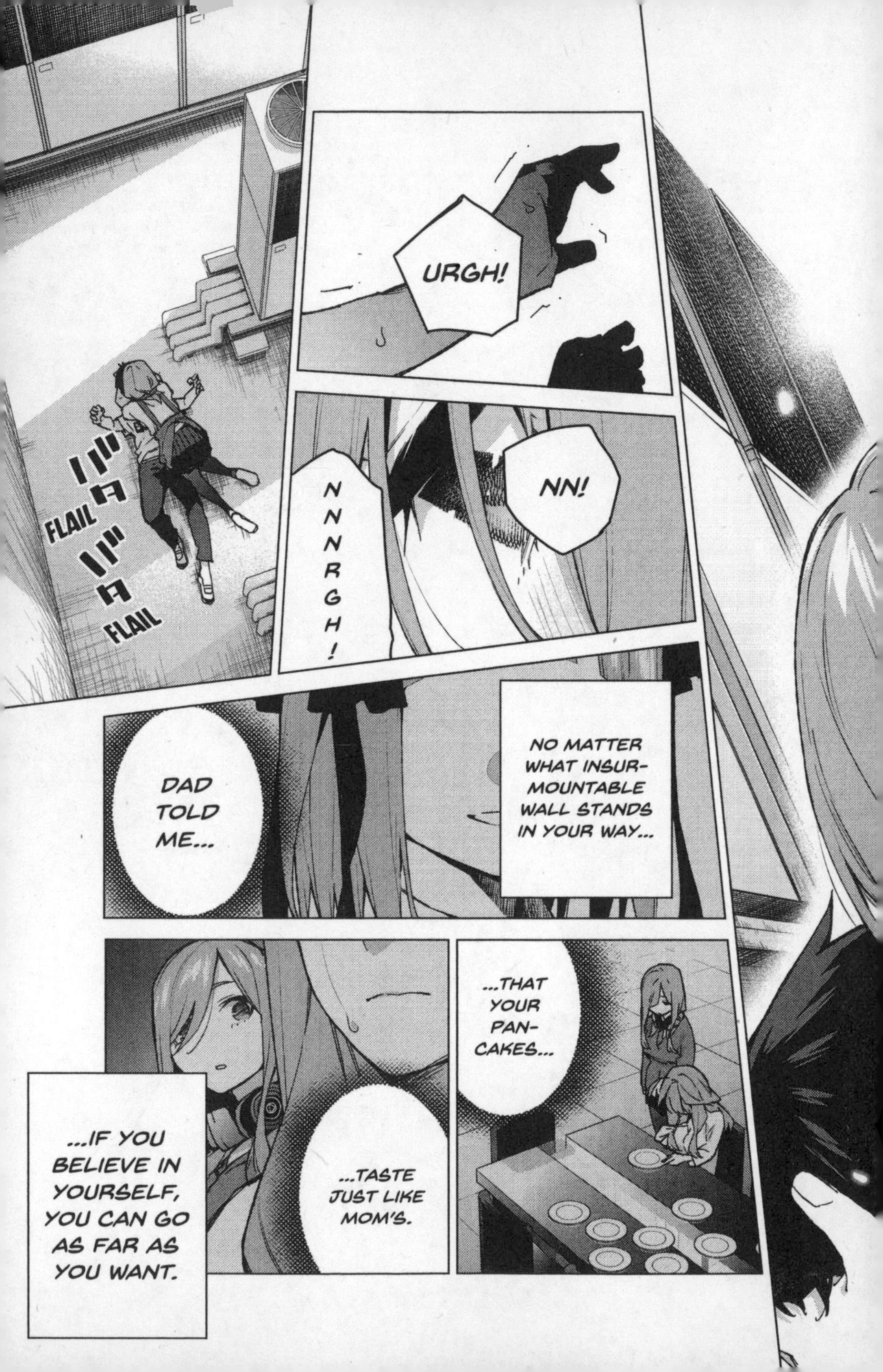
URGH!
NN!
NNNRGH!
バタバタ
FLAIL
FLAIL
NO MATTER WHAT INSUR-MOUNTABLE WALL STANDS IN YOUR WAY...
DAD TOLD ME...
...THAT YOUR PAN-CAKES...
...TASTE JUST LIKE MOM'S.
...IF YOU BELIEVE IN YOURSELF, YOU CAN GO AS FAR AS YOU WANT.

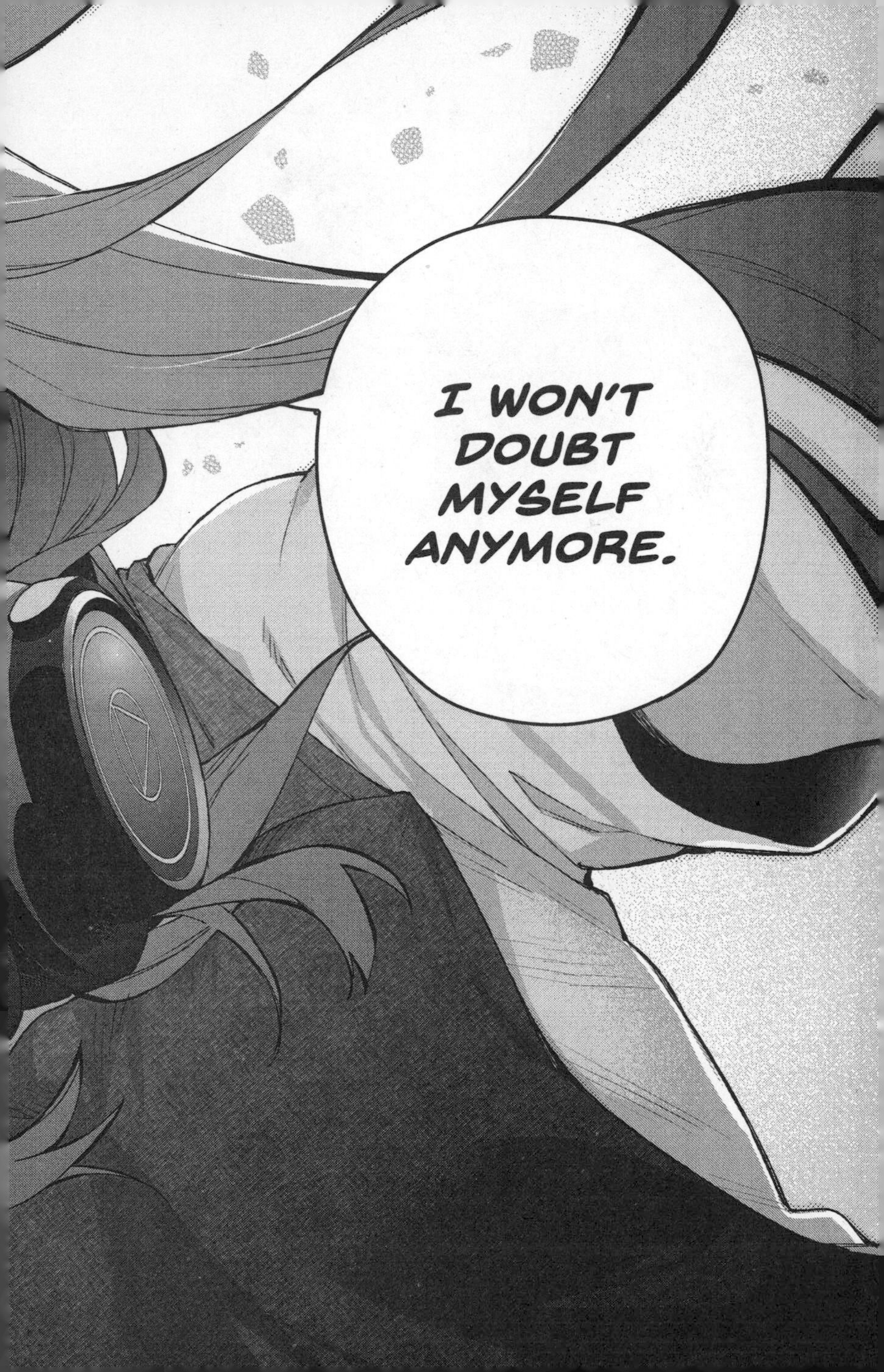
I WON'T DOUBT MYSELF ANYMORE.

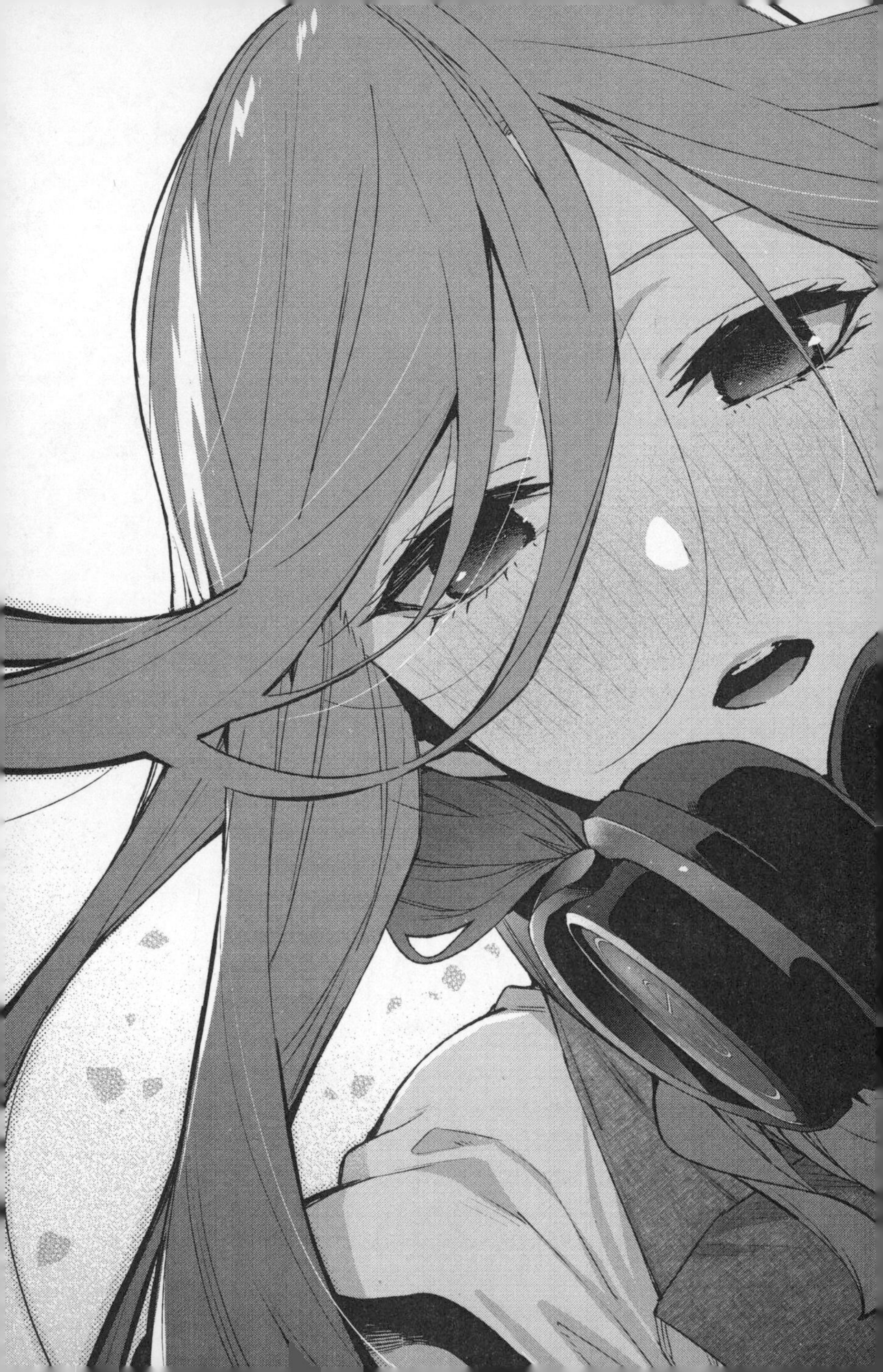

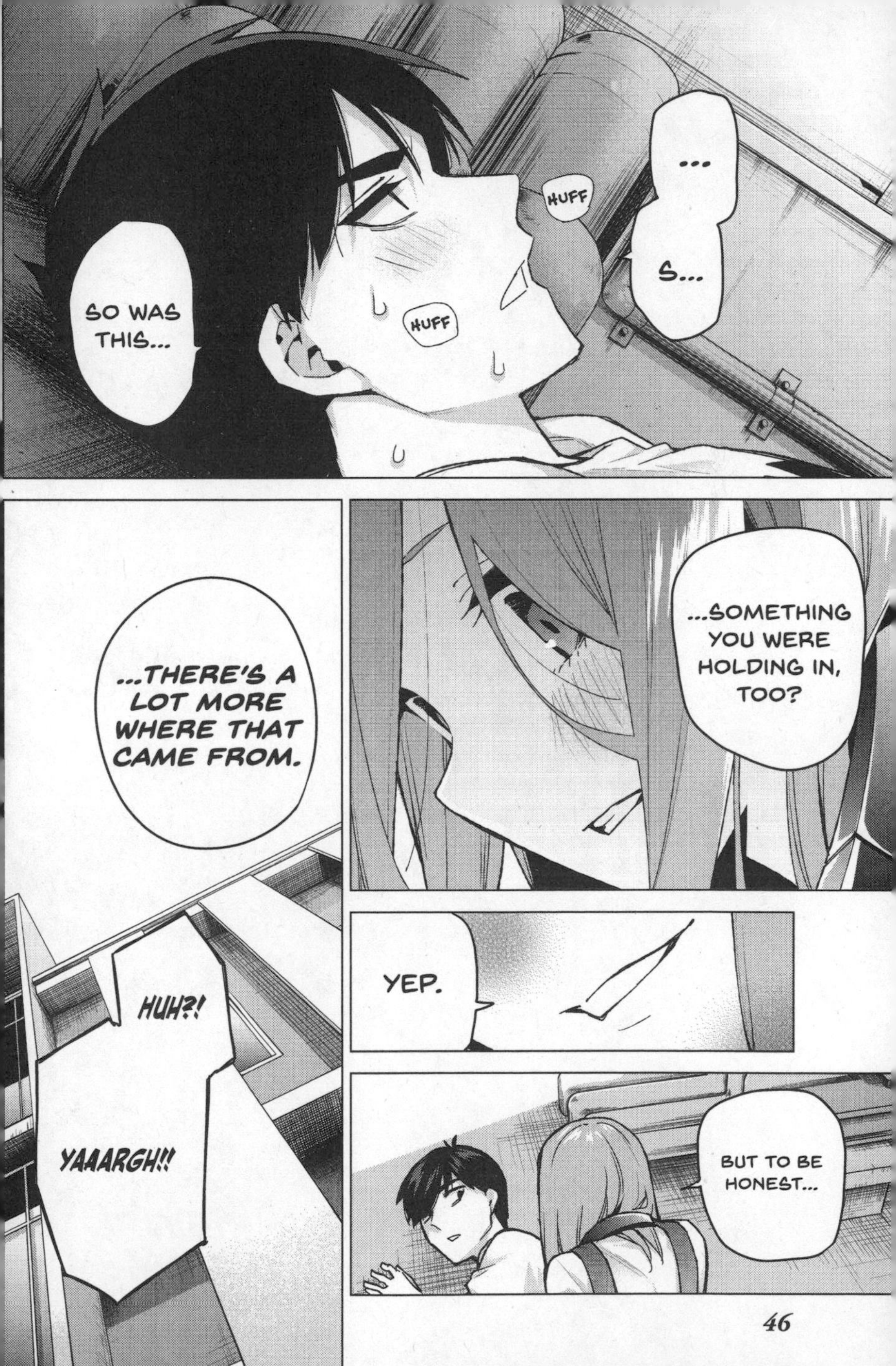
...
S...
HUFF
HUFF
SO WAS THIS...
...SOMETHING YOU WERE HOLDING IN, TOO?
YEP.
BUT TO BE HONEST...
...THERE'S A LOT MORE WHERE THAT CAME FROM.
HUH?!
YAAARGH!!

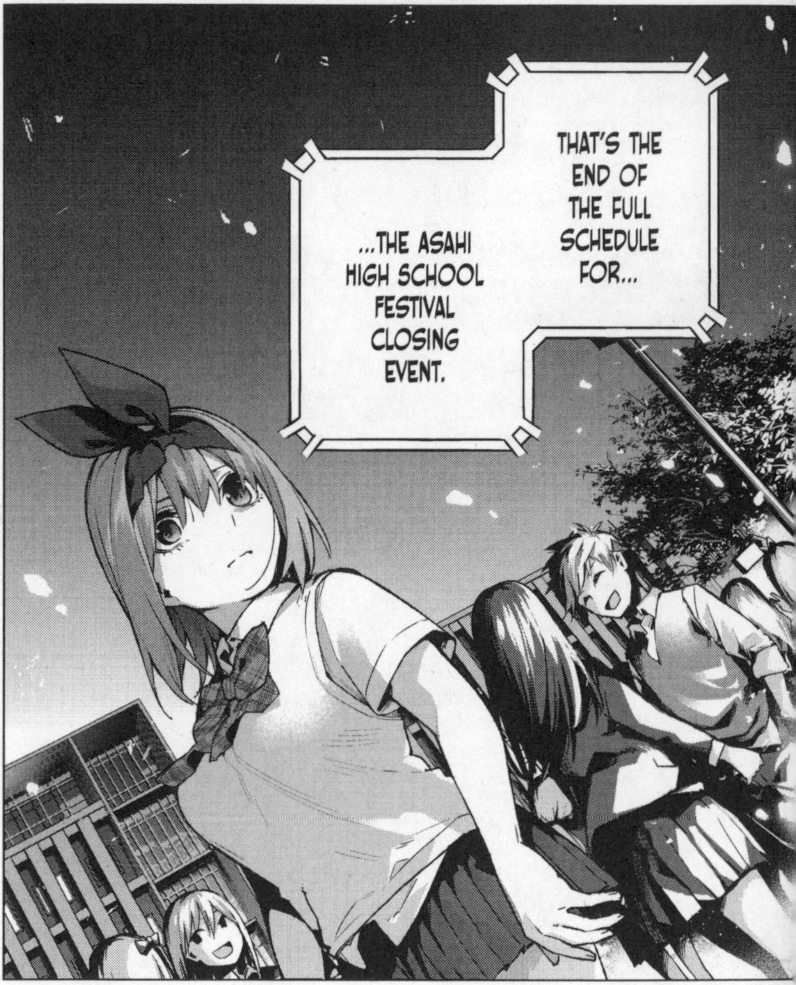
THAT'S THE END OF THE FULL SCHEDULE FOR...
...THE ASAHI HIGH SCHOOL FESTIVAL CLOSING EVENT.

CHAPTER 107 IF THE FINAL FESTIVAL WAS YOTSUBA'S ①

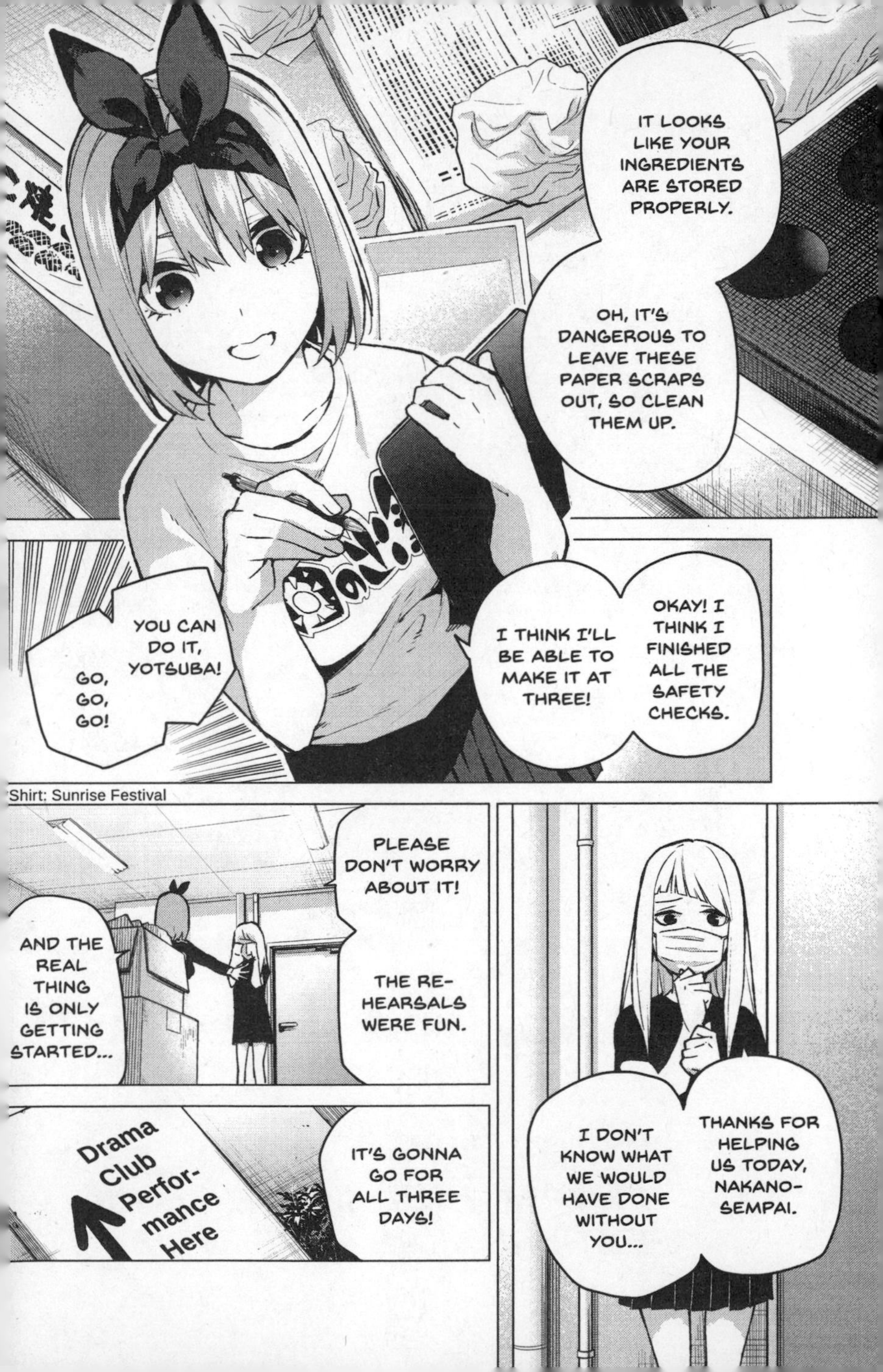
IT LOOKS LIKE YOUR INGREDIENTS ARE STORED PROPERLY.
OH, IT'S DANGEROUS TO LEAVE THESE PAPER SCRAPS OUT, SO CLEAN THEM UP.
OKAY! I THINK I FINISHED ALL THE SAFETY CHECKS.
I THINK I'LL BE ABLE TO MAKE IT AT THREE!
YOU CAN DO IT, YOTSUBA!
GO, GO, GO!
Shirt: Sunrise Festival
THANKS FOR HELPING US TODAY, NAKANO-SEMPAI.
I DON'T KNOW WHAT WE WOULD HAVE DONE WITHOUT YOU...
PLEASE DON'T WORRY ABOUT IT!
THE RE-HEARSALS WERE FUN.
AND THE REAL THING IS ONLY GETTING STARTED...
IT'S GONNA GO FOR ALL THREE DAYS!
Drama Club Perfor-mance Here

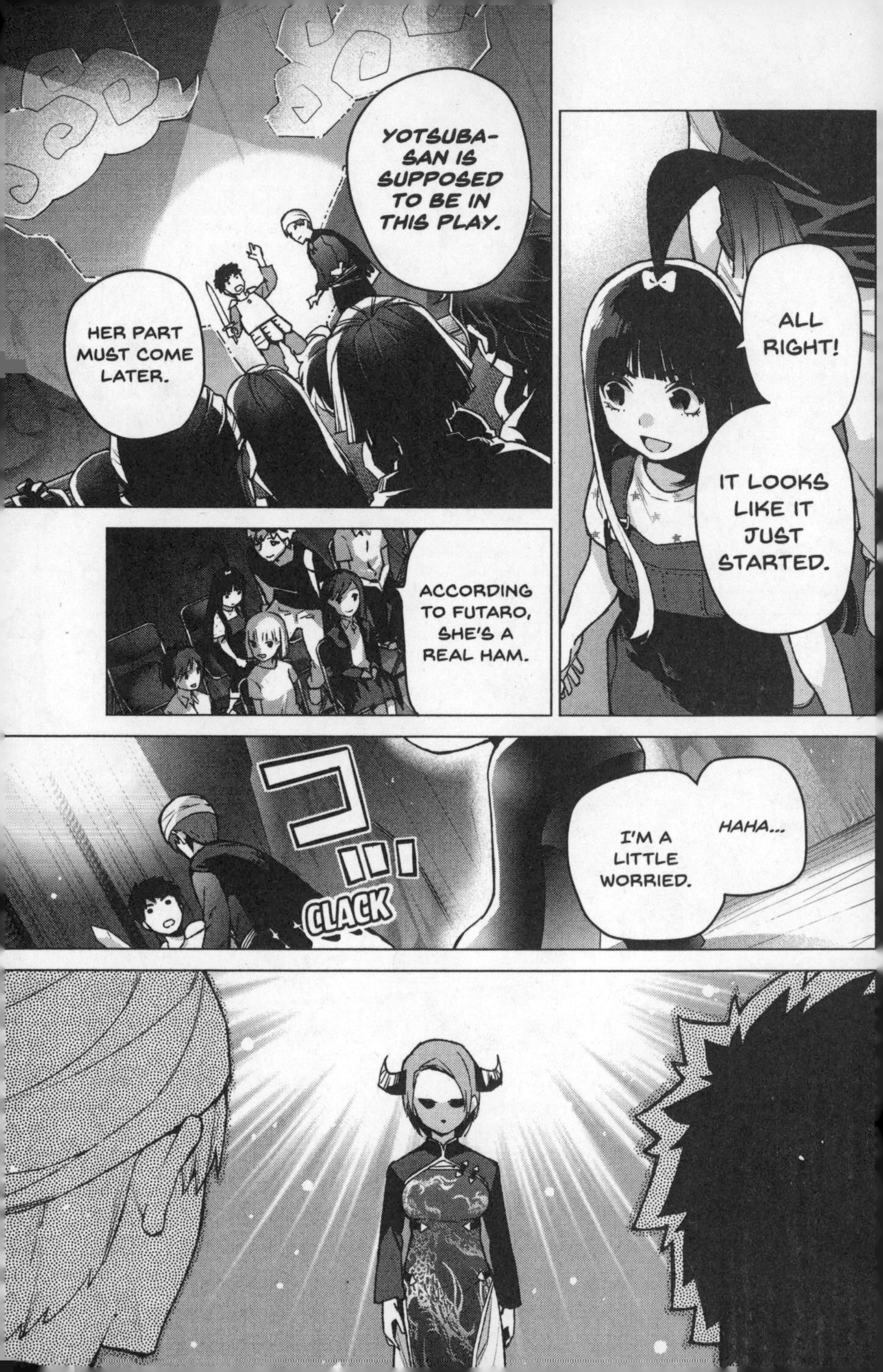
ALL RIGHT!
IT LOOKS LIKE IT JUST STARTED.
YOTSUBA-SAN IS SUPPOSED TO BE IN THIS PLAY.
HER PART MUST COME LATER.
ACCORDING TO FUTARO, SHE'S A REAL HAM.
HAHA...
I'M A LITTLE WORRIED.
CLACK

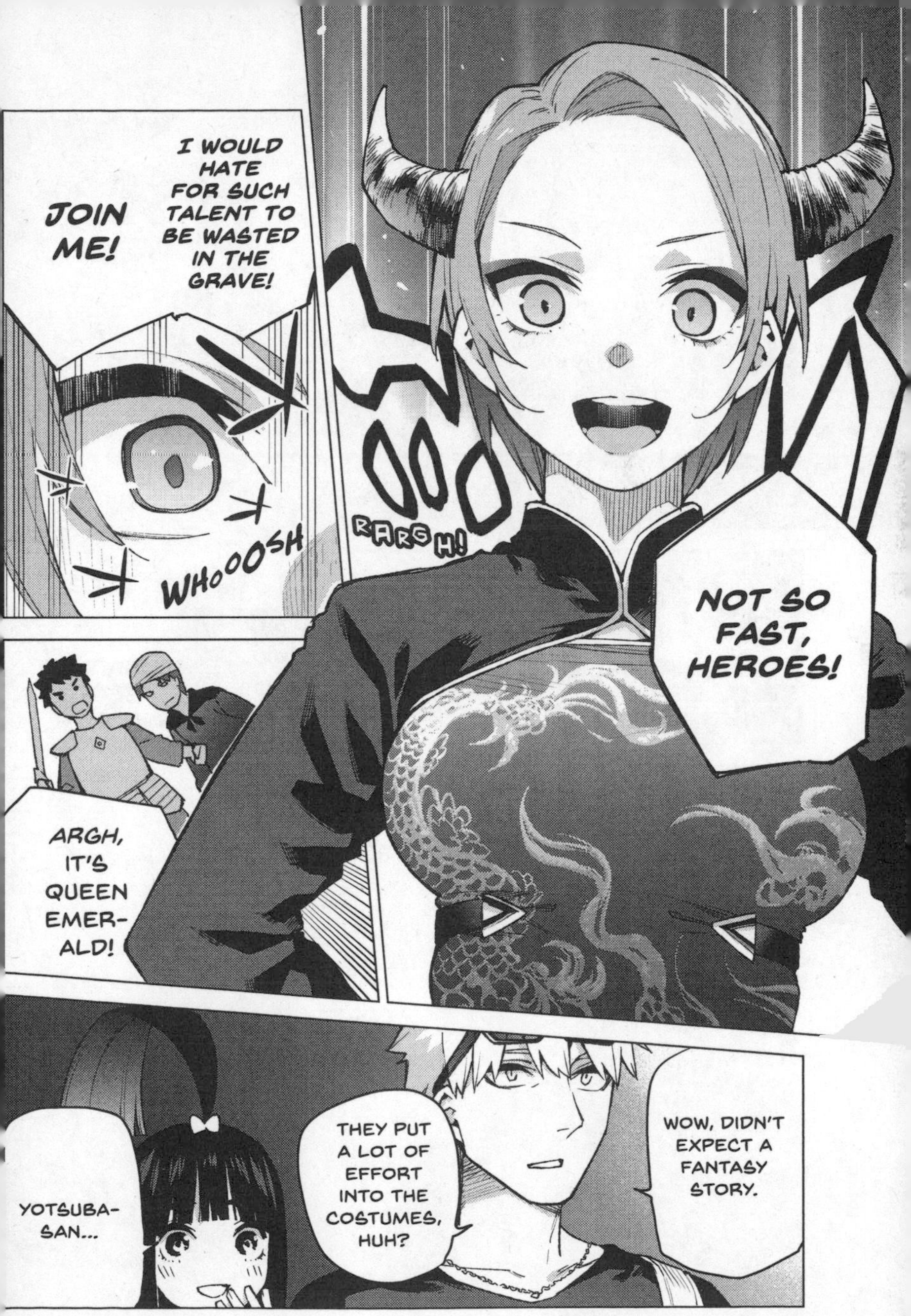
RARGH!
NOT SO FAST, HEROES!
I WOULD HATE FOR SUCH TALENT TO BE WASTED IN THE GRAVE!
JOIN ME!
WHOOOSH
ARGH, IT'S QUEEN EMER-ALD!
WOW, DIDN'T EXPECT A FANTASY STORY.
THEY PUT A LOT OF EFFORT INTO THE COSTUMES, HUH?
YOTSUBA-SAN...

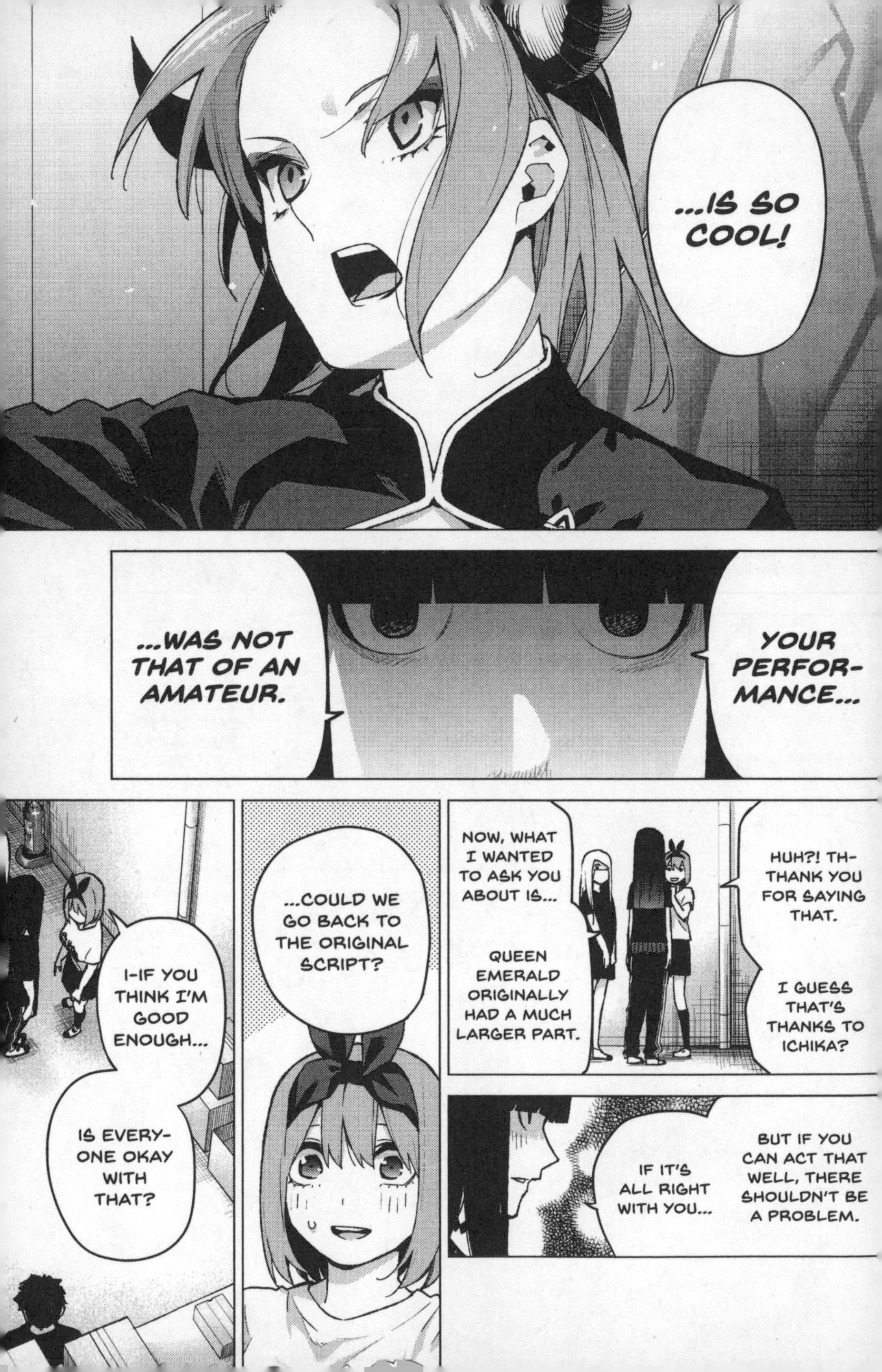
...IS SO COOL!
YOUR PERFORMANCE...
...WAS NOT THAT OF AN AMATEUR.
HUH?! TH-THANK YOU FOR SAYING THAT.
I GUESS THAT'S THANKS TO ICHIKA?
NOW, WHAT I WANTED TO ASK YOU ABOUT IS...
QUEEN EMERALD ORIGINALLY HAD A MUCH LARGER PART.
BUT IF YOU CAN ACT THAT WELL, THERE SHOULDN'T BE A PROBLEM.
IF IT'S ALL RIGHT WITH YOU...
...COULD WE GO BACK TO THE ORIGINAL SCRIPT?
I-IF YOU THINK I'M GOOD ENOUGH...
IS EVERYONE OKAY WITH THAT?

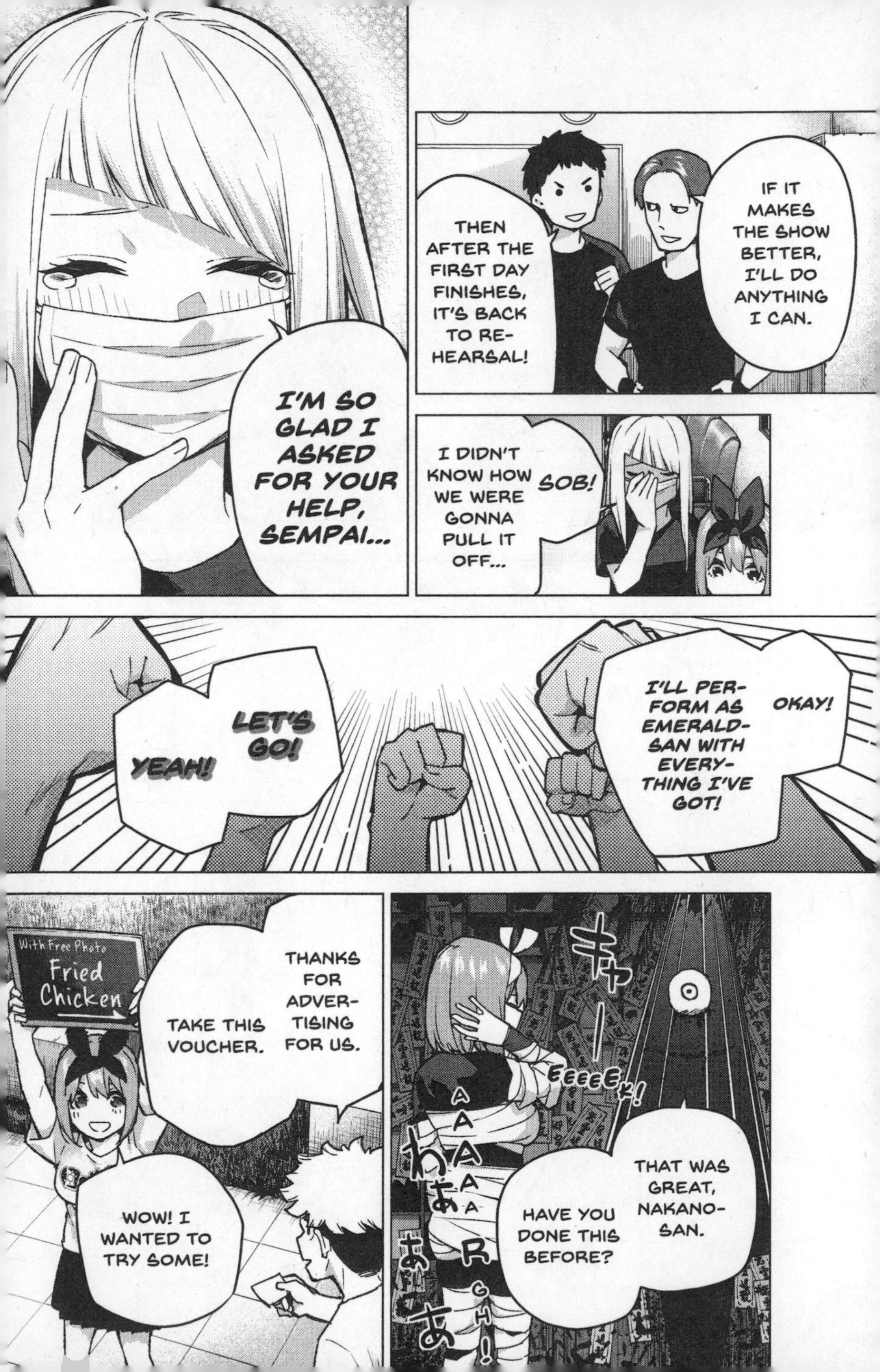
IF IT MAKES THE SHOW BETTER, I'LL DO ANYTHING I CAN.
THEN AFTER THE FIRST DAY FINISHES, IT'S BACK TO RE-HEARSAL!
SOB!
I DIDN'T KNOW HOW WE WERE GONNA PULL IT OFF...
I'M SO GLAD I ASKED FOR YOUR HELP, SEMPAI...
OKAY!
I'LL PER-FORM AS EMERALD-SAN WITH EVERY-THING I'VE GOT!
LET'S GO!
YEAH!
キャー
EEEEEK!
THAT WAS GREAT, NAKANO-SAN.
HAVE YOU DONE THIS BEFORE?
AAAARGH!
THANKS FOR ADVER-TISING FOR US.
TAKE THIS VOUCHER.
With Free Photo
Fried Chicken
WOW! I WANTED TO TRY SOME!

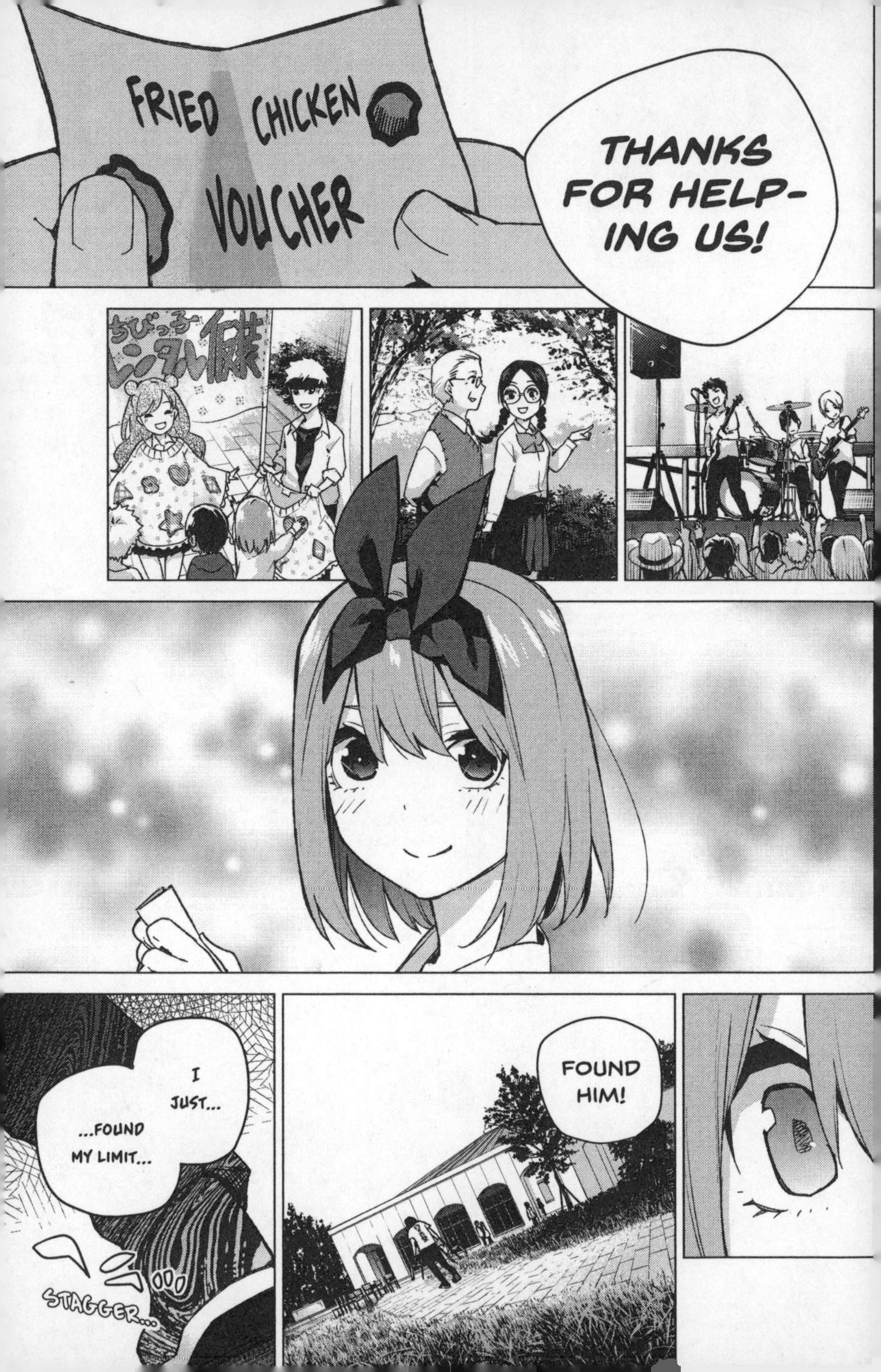
THANKS FOR HELP-ING US!
FRIED CHICKEN VOUCHER
FOUND HIM!
I JUST...
...FOUND MY LIMIT...
STAGGER...

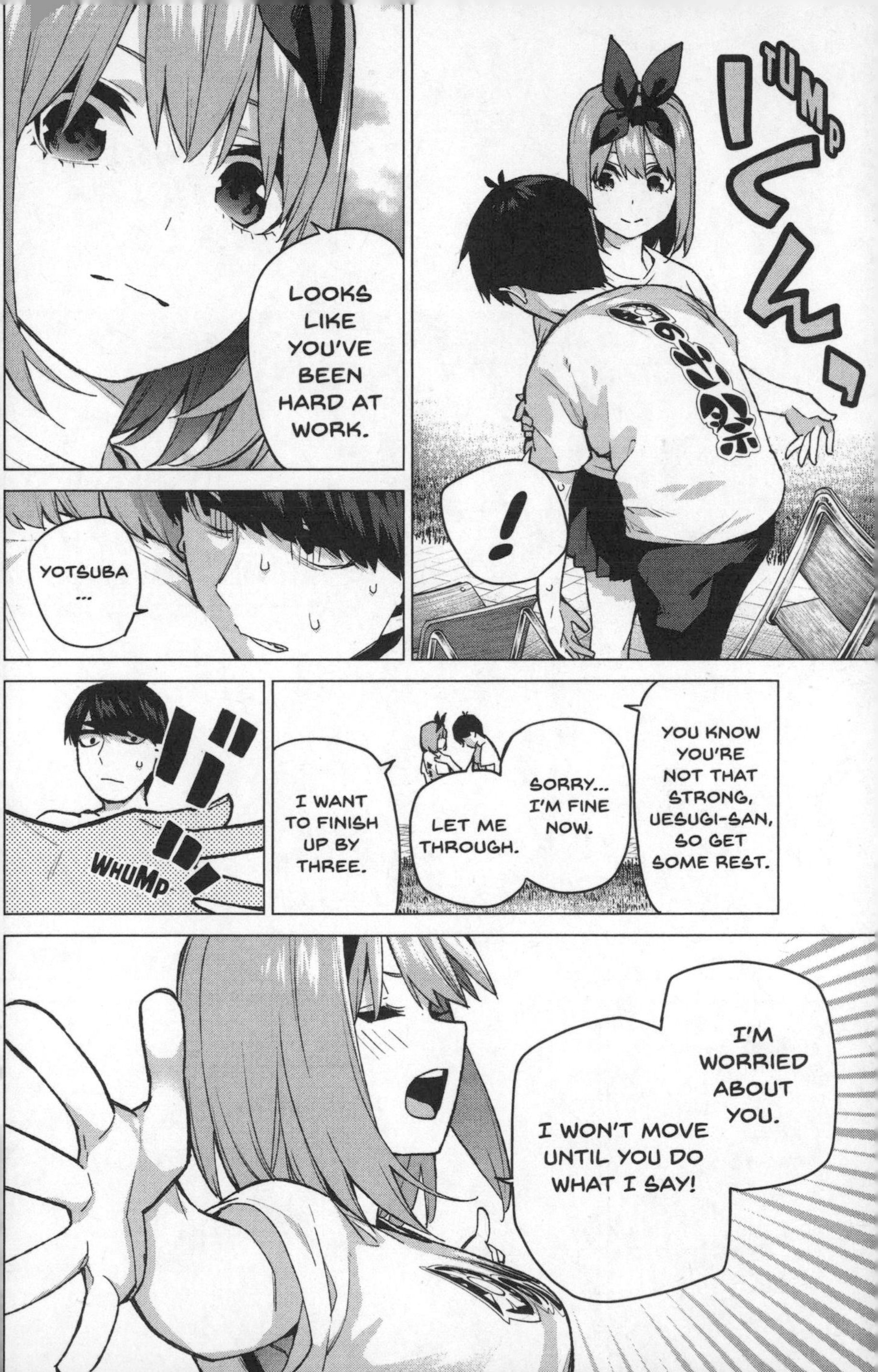
TUMP
!
LOOKS LIKE YOU'VE BEEN HARD AT WORK.
YOTSUBA ...
YOU KNOW YOU'RE NOT THAT STRONG, UESUGI-SAN, SO GET SOME REST.
SORRY... I'M FINE NOW.
LET ME THROUGH.
I WANT TO FINISH UP BY THREE.
WHUMP
I'M WORRIED ABOUT YOU.
I WON'T MOVE UNTIL YOU DO WHAT I SAY!

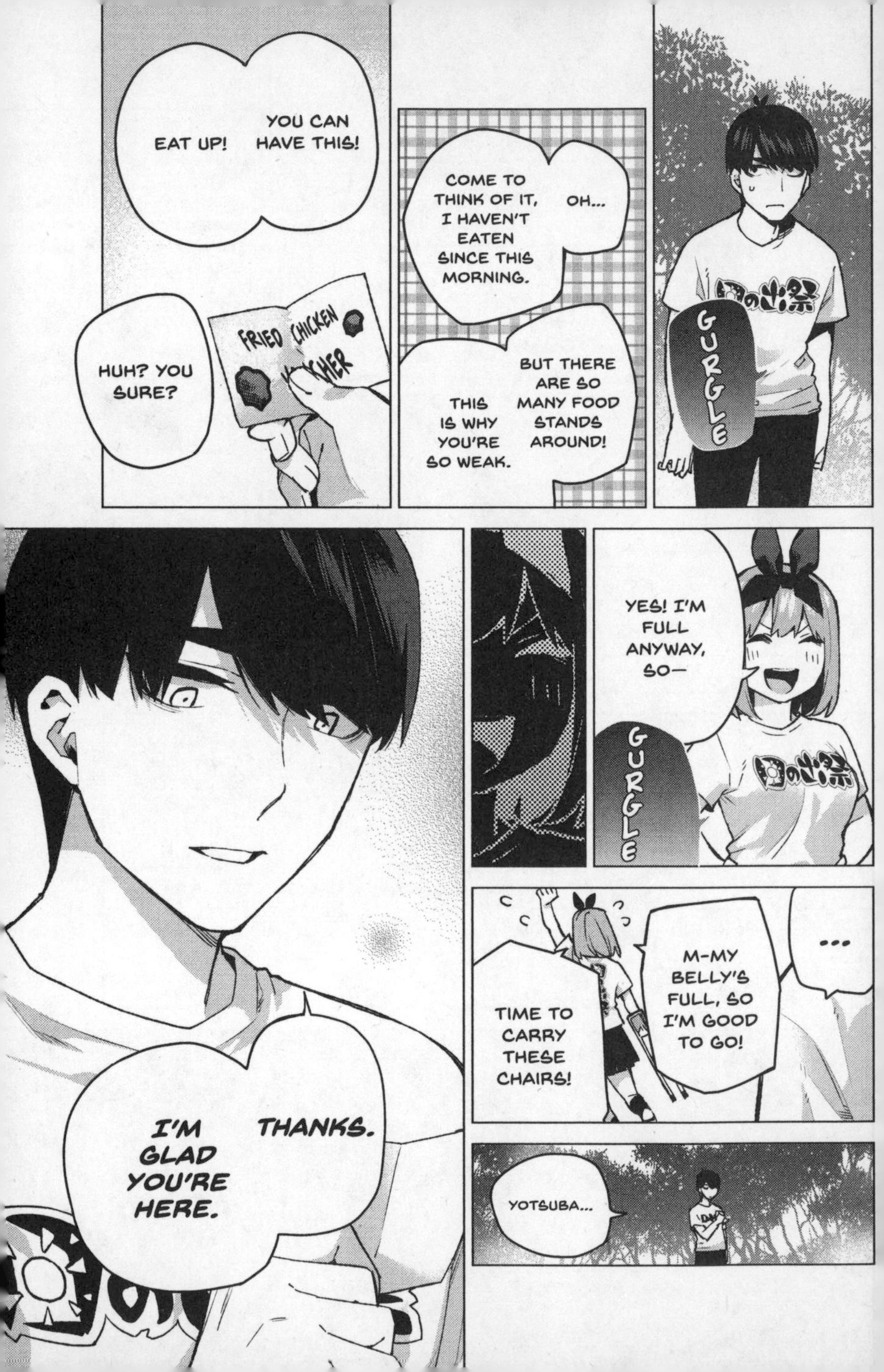
GURGLE
OH...
COME TO THINK OF IT, I HAVEN'T EATEN SINCE THIS MORNING.
BUT THERE ARE SO MANY FOOD STANDS AROUND!
THIS IS WHY YOU'RE SO WEAK.
YOU CAN HAVE THIS!
EAT UP!
FRIED CHICKEN
HUH? YOU SURE?
YES! I'M FULL ANYWAY, SO—
GURGLE
...
M-MY BELLY'S FULL, SO I'M GOOD TO GO!
TIME TO CARRY THESE CHAIRS!
YOTSUBA...
THANKS.
I'M GLAD YOU'RE HERE.

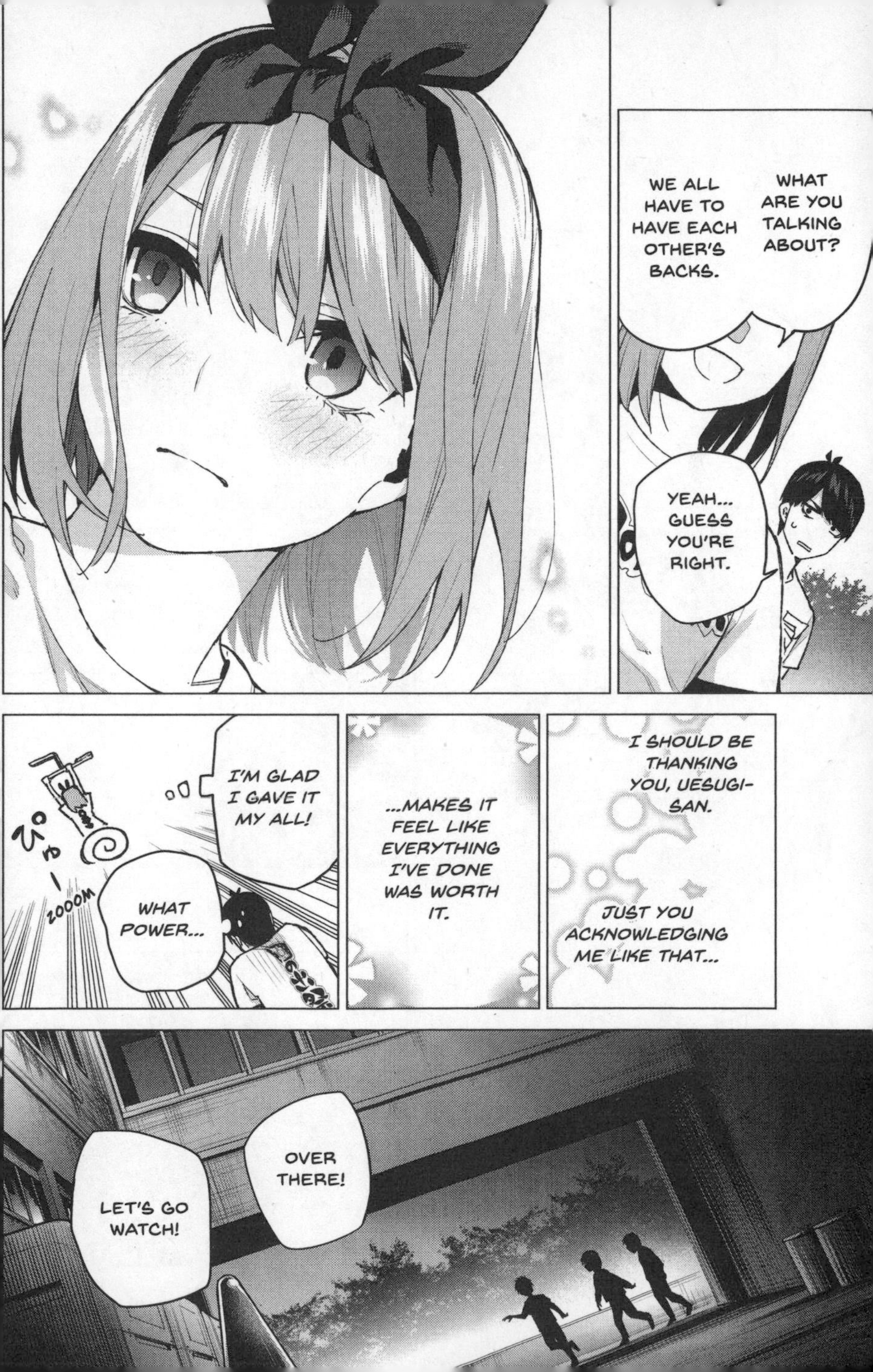
WHAT ARE YOU TALKING ABOUT?
WE ALL HAVE TO HAVE EACH OTHER'S BACKS.
YEAH... GUESS YOU'RE RIGHT.
I SHOULD BE THANKING YOU, UESUGI-SAN.
JUST YOU ACKNOWLEDGING ME LIKE THAT...
...MAKES IT FEEL LIKE EVERYTHING I'VE DONE WAS WORTH IT.
I'M GLAD I GAVE IT MY ALL!
WHAT POWER...
ZOOOM
OVER THERE!
LET'S GO WATCH!

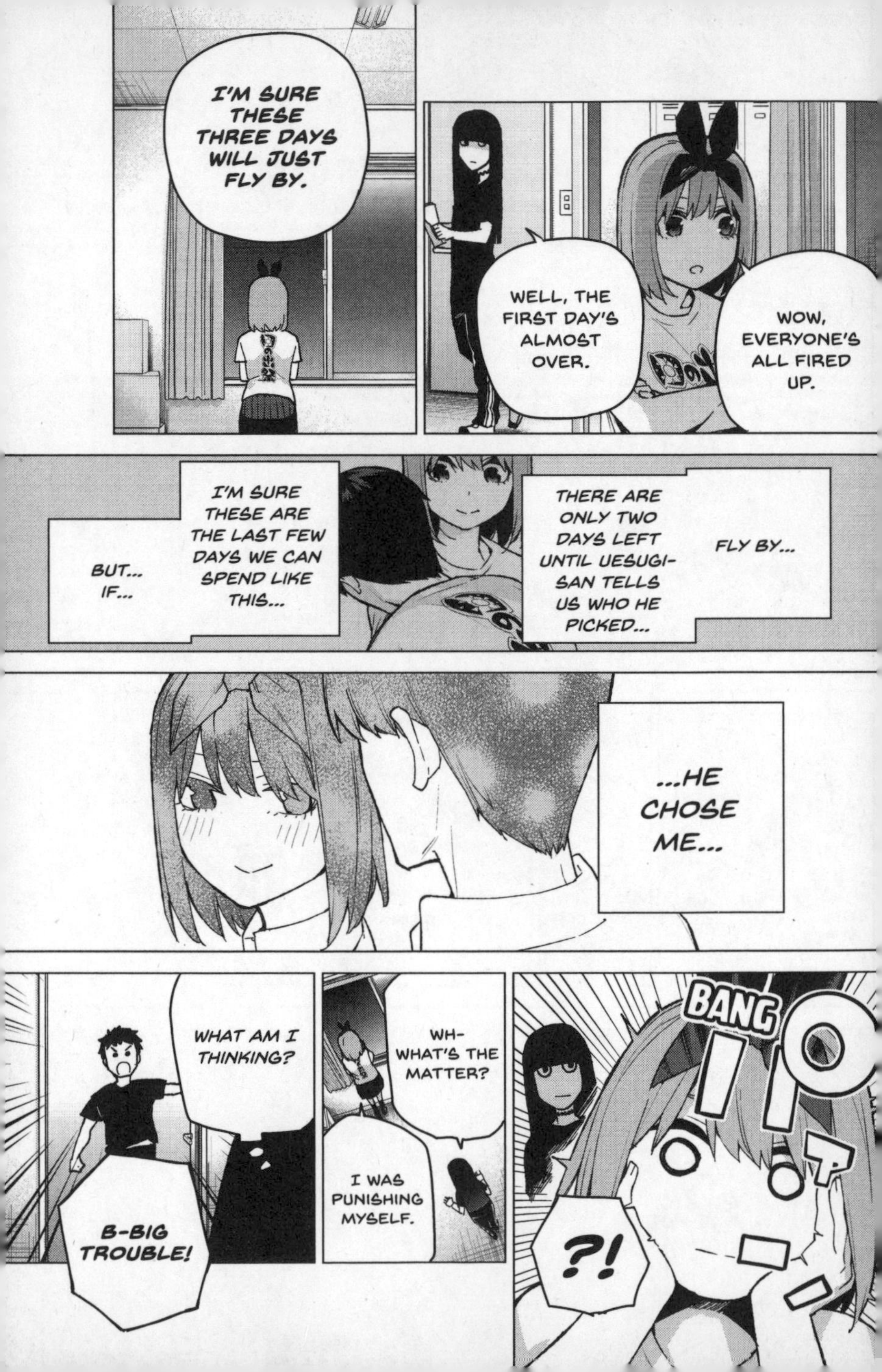
WOW, EVERYONE'S ALL FIRED UP.
WELL, THE FIRST DAY'S ALMOST OVER.
I'M SURE THESE THREE DAYS WILL JUST FLY BY.
FLY BY...
THERE ARE ONLY TWO DAYS LEFT UNTIL UESUGI-SAN TELLS US WHO HE PICKED...
I'M SURE THESE ARE THE LAST FEW DAYS WE CAN SPEND LIKE THIS...
BUT... IF...
...HE CHOSE ME...
BANG
?!
WH- WHAT'S THE MATTER?
I WAS PUNISHING MYSELF.
WHAT AM I THINKING?
B-BIG TROUBLE!

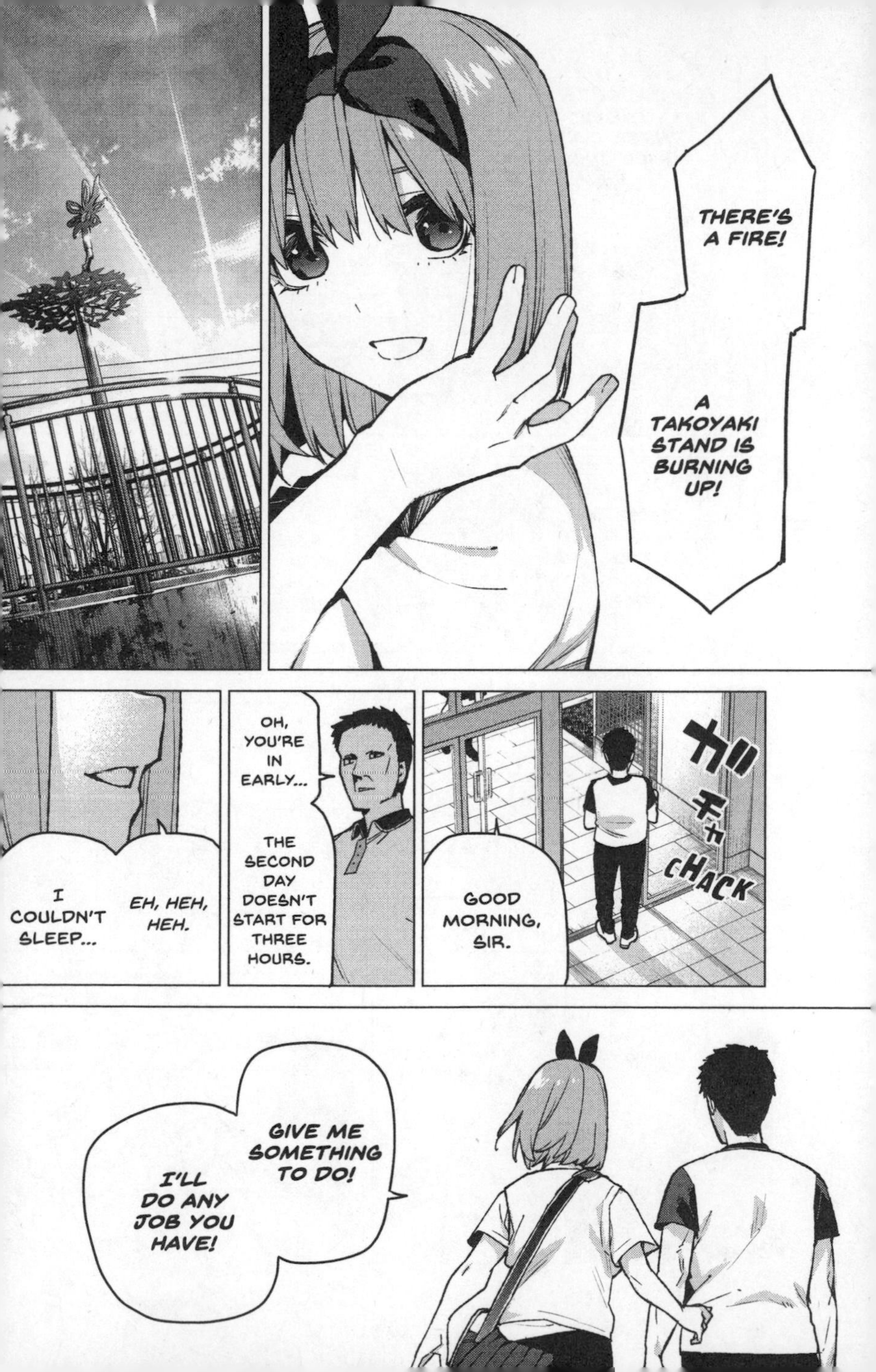
THERE'S A FIRE!
A TAKOYAKI STAND IS BURNING UP!
ガチャ
CHACK
GOOD MORNING, SIR.
OH, YOU'RE IN EARLY...
THE SECOND DAY DOESN'T START FOR THREE HOURS.
I COULDN'T SLEEP... EH, HEH, HEH.
GIVE ME SOMETHING TO DO!
I'LL DO ANY JOB YOU HAVE!

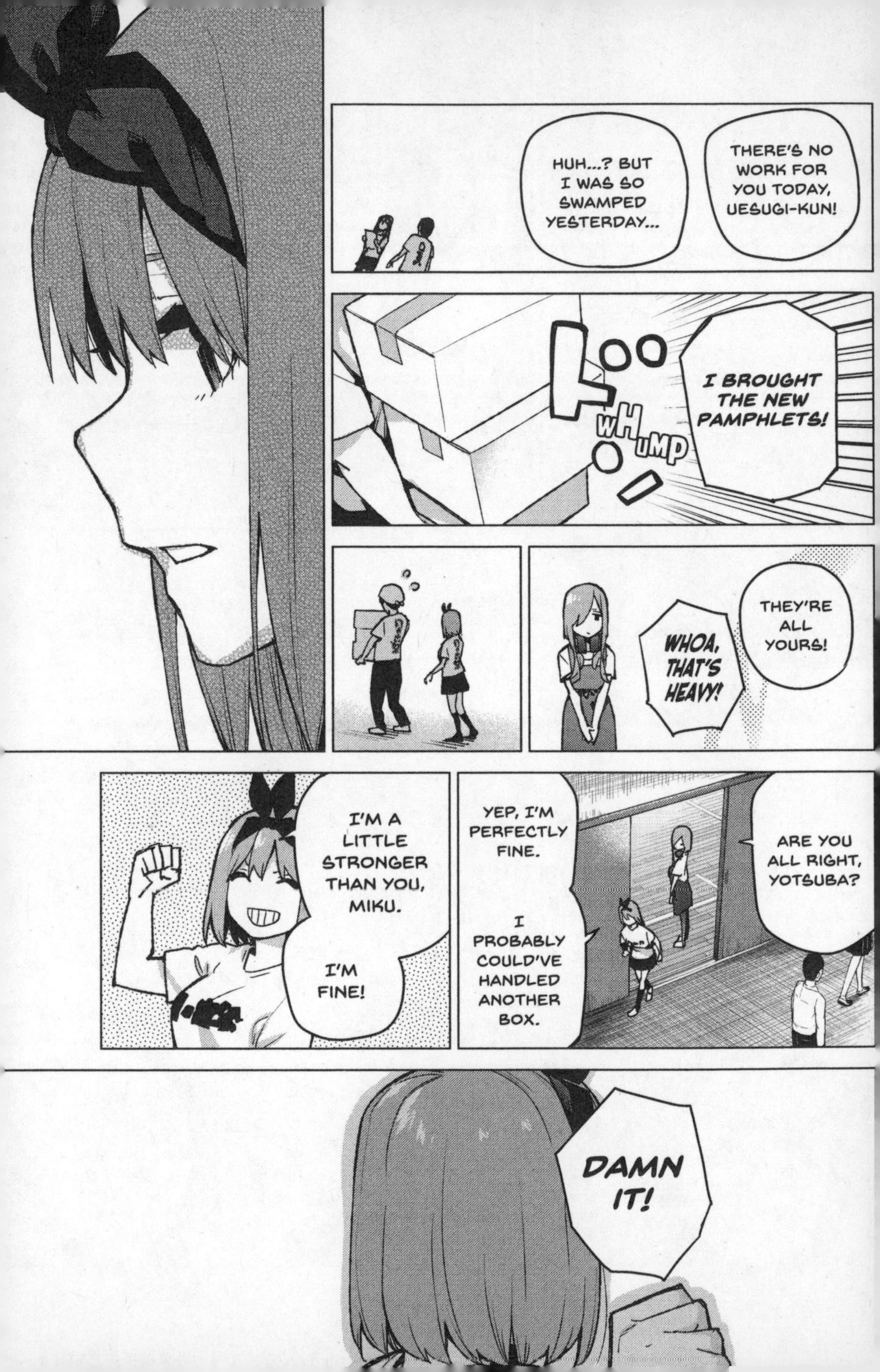
THERE'S NO WORK FOR YOU TODAY, UESUGI-KUN!
HUH...? BUT I WAS SO SWAMPED YESTERDAY...
I BROUGHT THE NEW PAMPHLETS!
wHUMP
THEY'RE ALL YOURS!
WHOA, THAT'S HEAVY!
ARE YOU ALL RIGHT, YOTSUBA?
YEP, I'M PERFECTLY FINE.
I PROBABLY COULD'VE HANDLED ANOTHER BOX.
I'M A LITTLE STRONGER THAN YOU, MIKU.
I'M FINE!
DAMN IT!

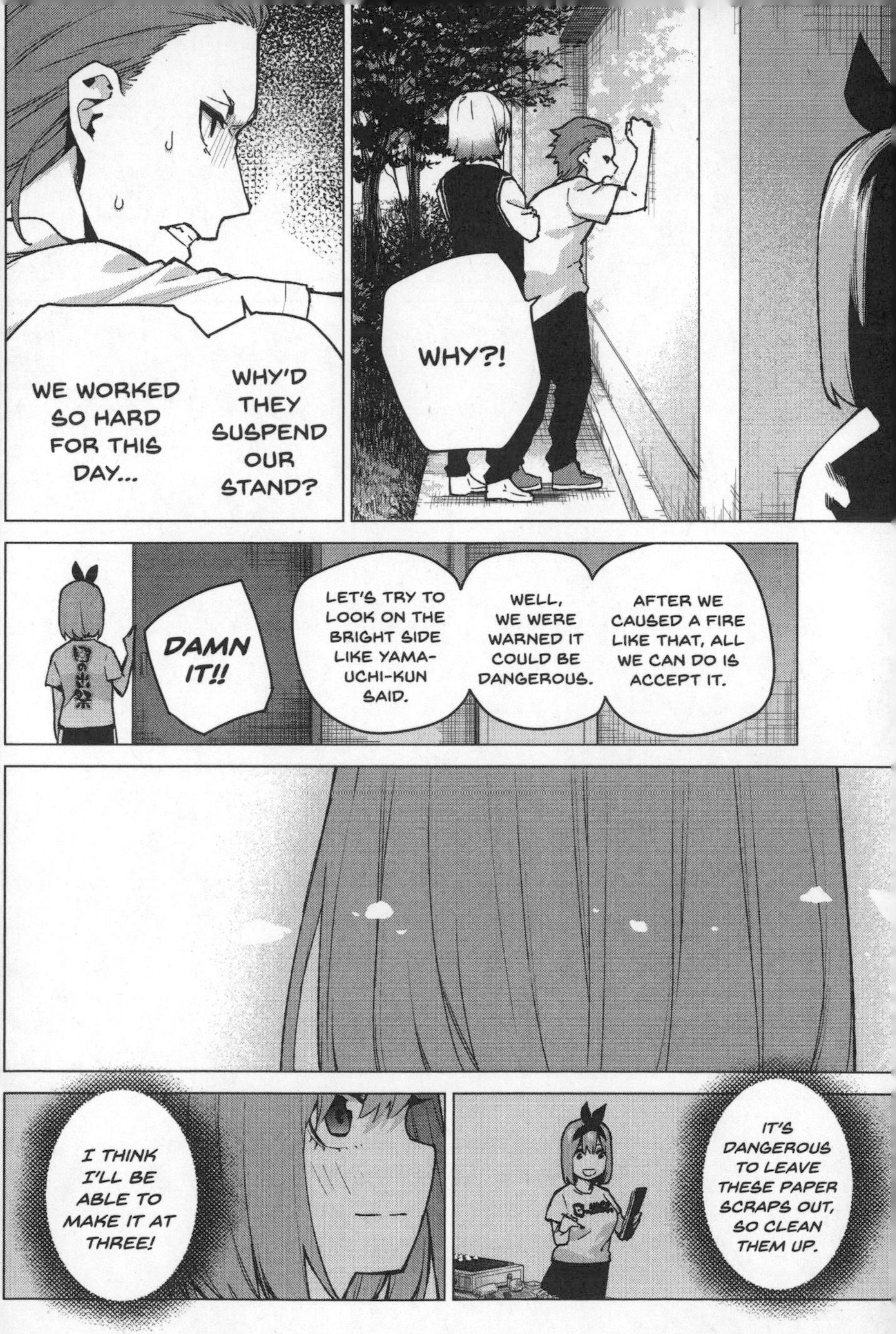
WHY?!
WHY'D THEY SUSPEND OUR STAND?
WE WORKED SO HARD FOR THIS DAY...
AFTER WE CAUSED A FIRE LIKE THAT, ALL WE CAN DO IS ACCEPT IT.
WELL, WE WERE WARNED IT COULD BE DANGEROUS.
LET'S TRY TO LOOK ON THE BRIGHT SIDE LIKE YAMA-UCHI-KUN SAID.
DAMN IT!!
IT'S DANGEROUS TO LEAVE THESE PAPER SCRAPS OUT, SO CLEAN THEM UP.
I THINK I'LL BE ABLE TO MAKE IT AT THREE!

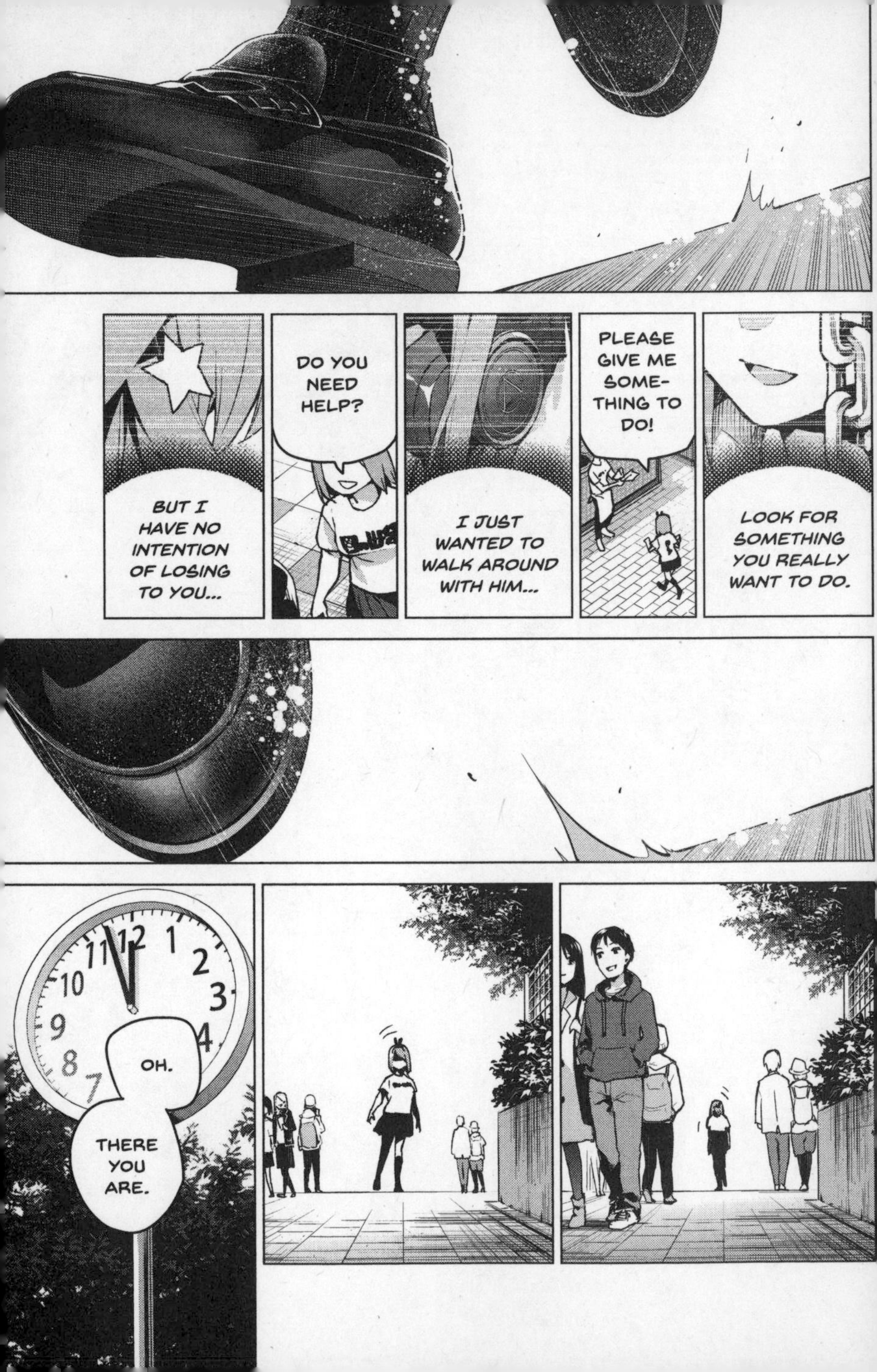
LOOK FOR SOMETHING YOU REALLY WANT TO DO.
PLEASE GIVE ME SOME-THING TO DO!
I JUST WANTED TO WALK AROUND WITH HIM...
DO YOU NEED HELP?
BUT I HAVE NO INTENTION OF LOSING TO YOU...
OH.
THERE YOU ARE.

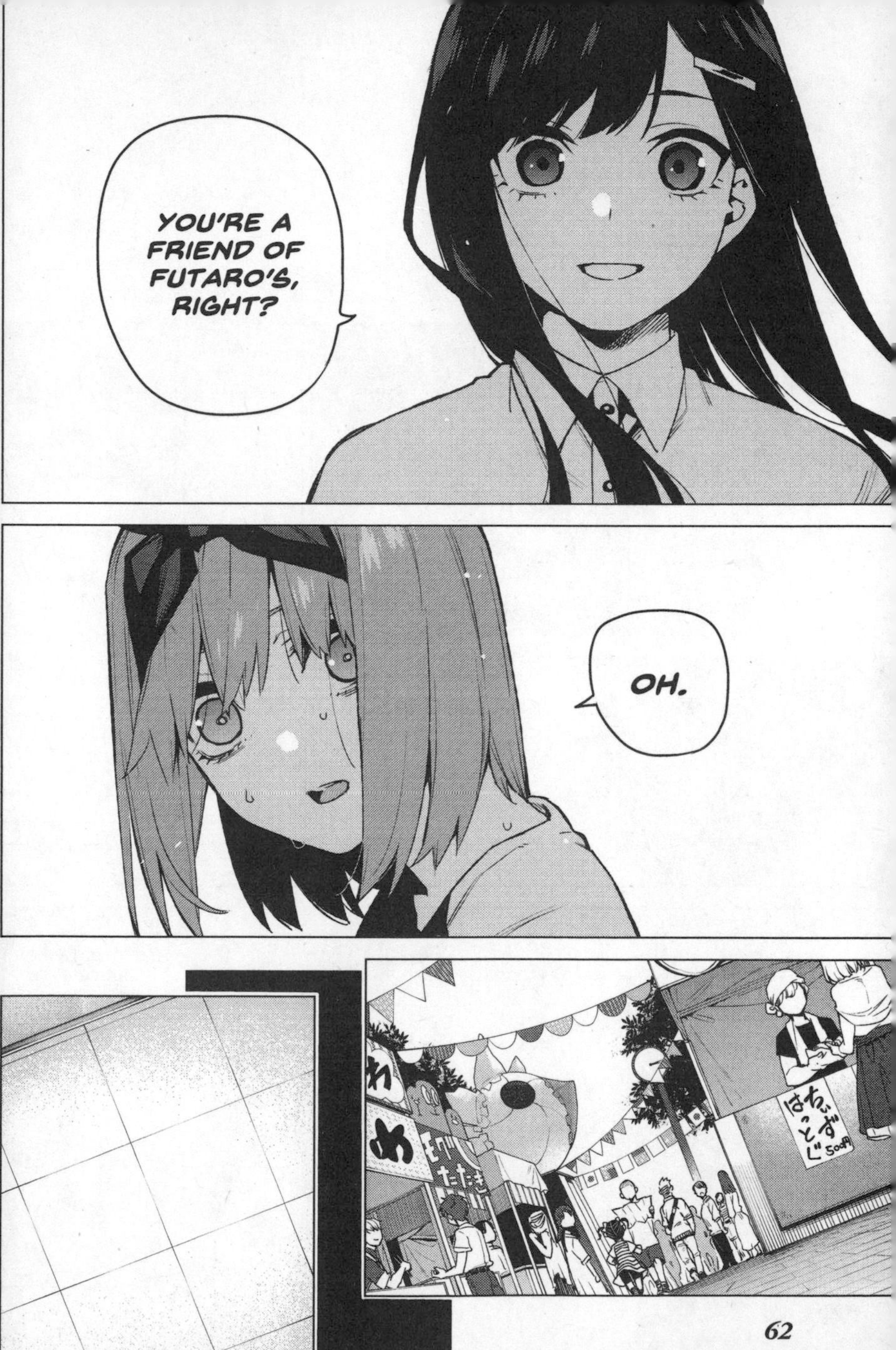
YOU'RE A FRIEND OF FUTARO'S, RIGHT?
OH.

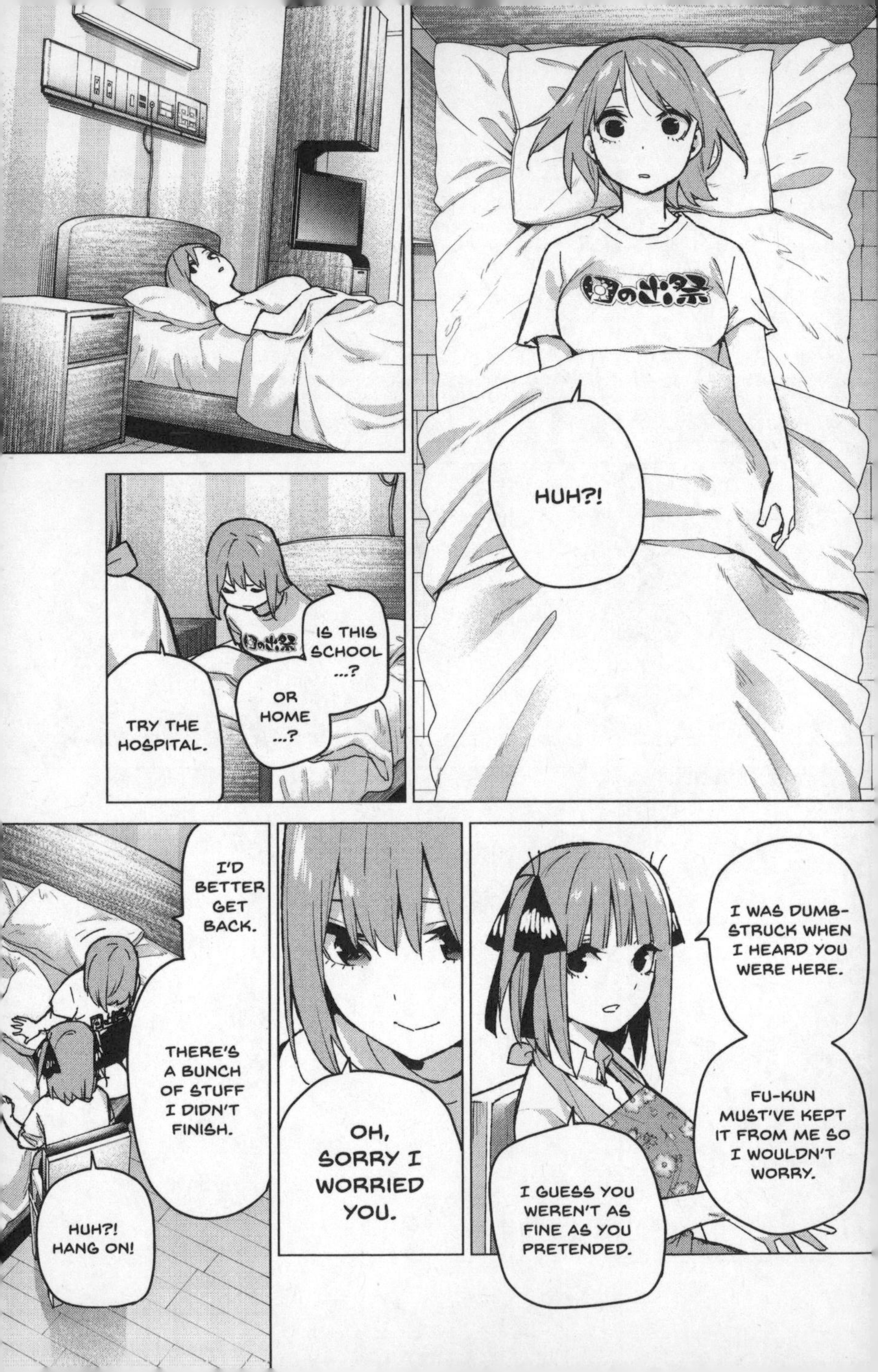
HUH?!
IS THIS SCHOOL ...?
OR HOME ...?
TRY THE HOSPITAL.
I WAS DUMB-STRUCK WHEN I HEARD YOU WERE HERE.
FU-KUN MUST'VE KEPT IT FROM ME SO I WOULDN'T WORRY.
I GUESS YOU WEREN'T AS FINE AS YOU PRETENDED.
OH, SORRY I WORRIED YOU.
I'D BETTER GET BACK.
THERE'S A BUNCH OF STUFF I DIDN'T FINISH.
HUH?! HANG ON!

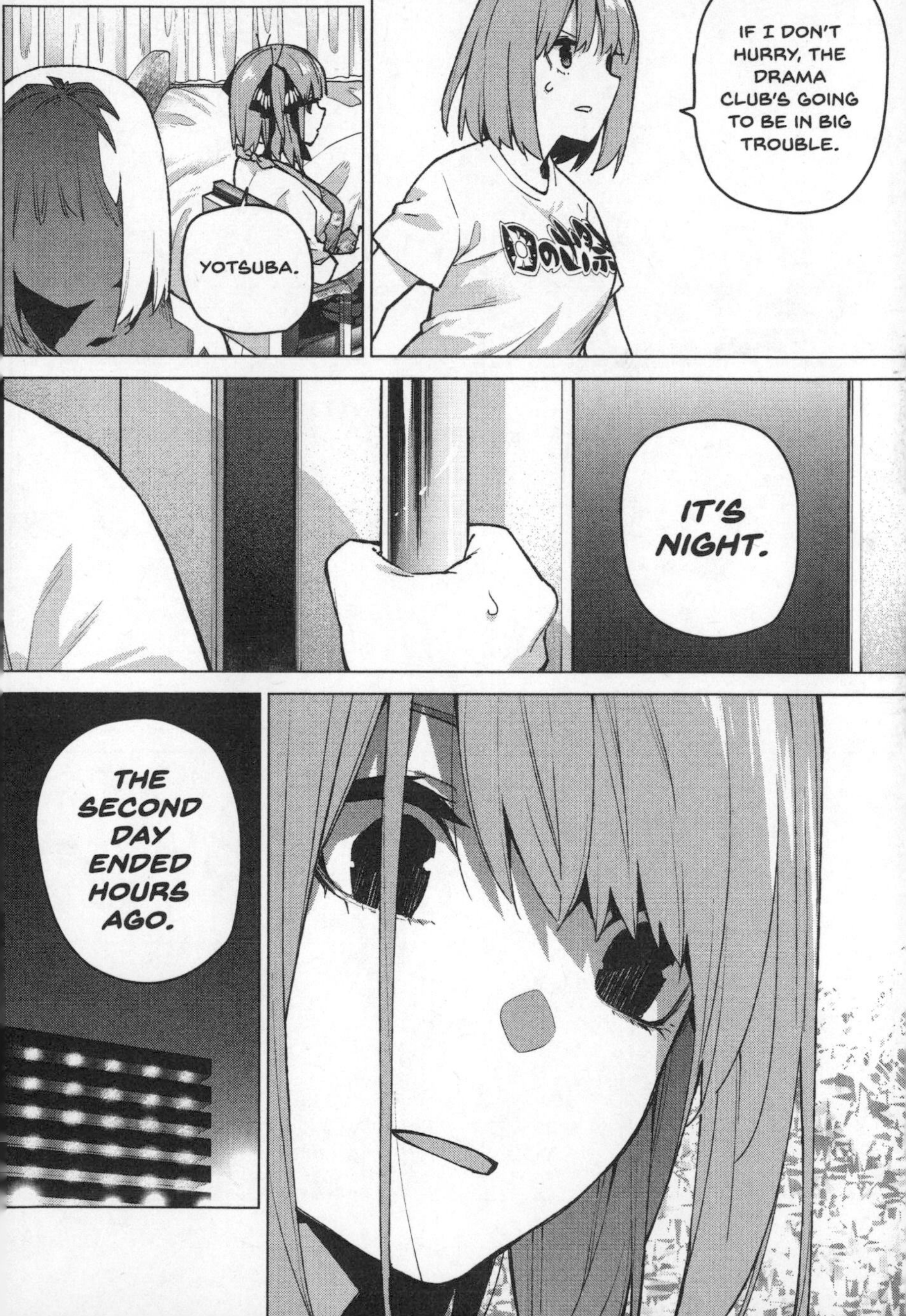
IF I DON'T HURRY, THE DRAMA CLUB'S GOING TO BE IN BIG TROUBLE.
YOTSUBA.
IT'S NIGHT.
THE SECOND DAY ENDED HOURS AGO.

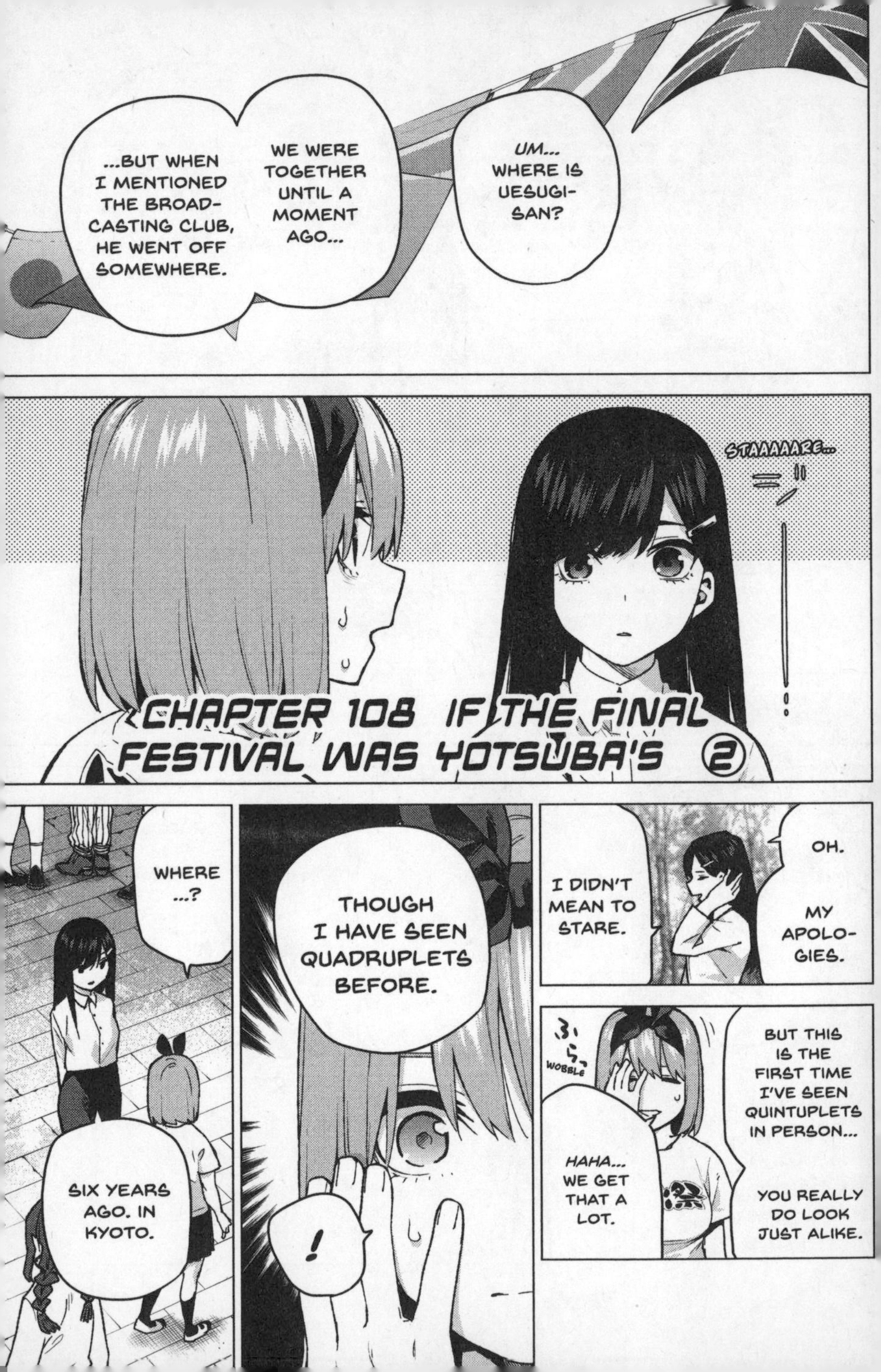
UM... WHERE IS UESUGI-SAN?
WE WERE TOGETHER UNTIL A MOMENT AGO...
...BUT WHEN I MENTIONED THE BROAD-CASTING CLUB, HE WENT OFF SOMEWHERE.
STAAAAARE...
CHAPTER 108 IF THE FINAL FESTIVAL WAS YOTSUBA'S ②
OH.
MY APOLOGIES.
I DIDN'T MEAN TO STARE.
BUT THIS IS THE FIRST TIME I'VE SEEN QUINTUPLETS IN PERSON...
YOU REALLY DO LOOK JUST ALIKE.
ふらっ
WOBBLE
HAHA... WE GET THAT A LOT.
THOUGH I HAVE SEEN QUADRUPLETS BEFORE.
!
WHERE ...?
SIX YEARS AGO. IN KYOTO.

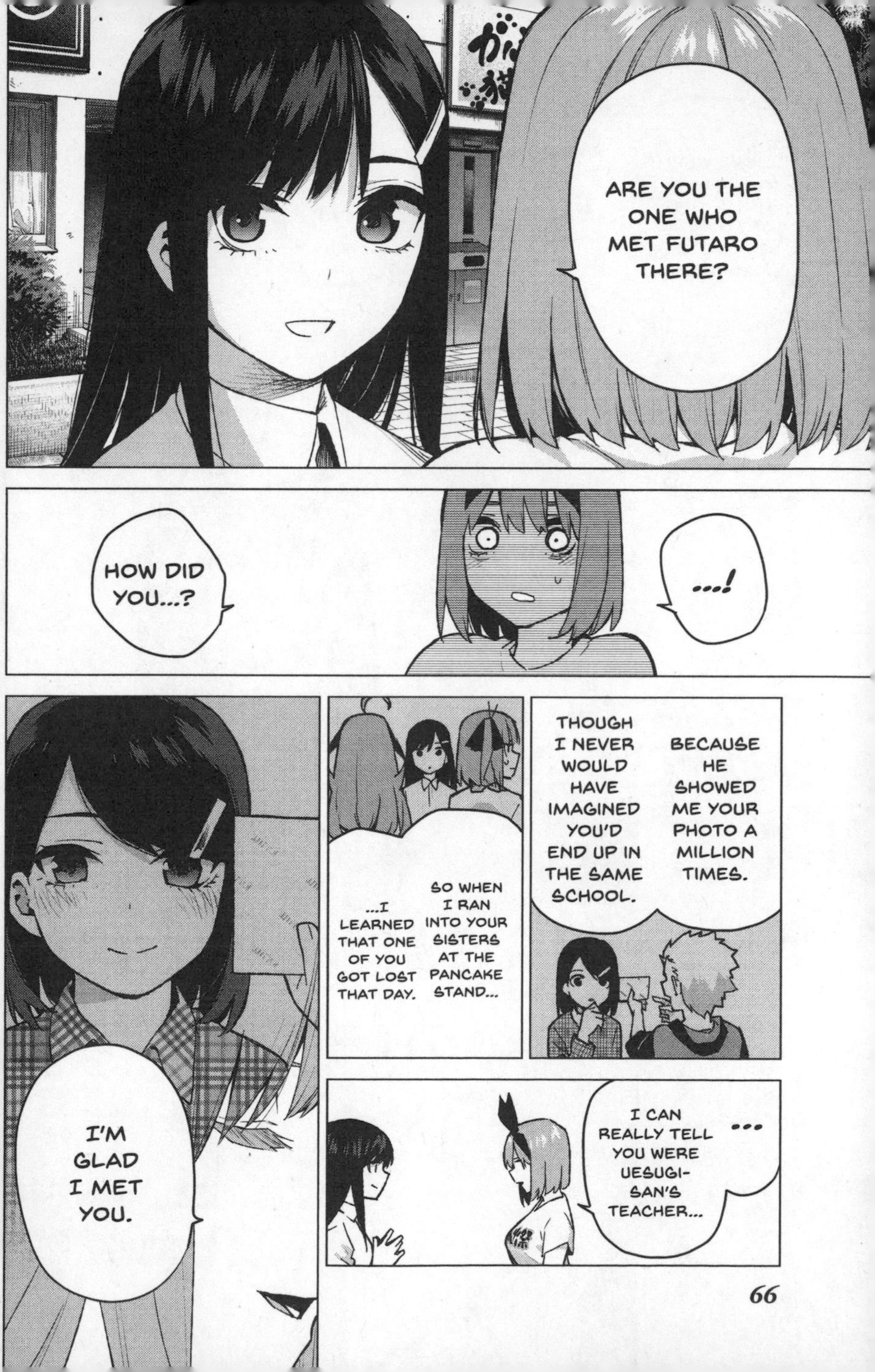
ARE YOU THE ONE WHO MET FUTARO THERE?
...!
HOW DID YOU...?
BECAUSE HE SHOWED ME YOUR PHOTO A MILLION TIMES.
THOUGH I NEVER WOULD HAVE IMAGINED YOU'D END UP IN THE SAME SCHOOL.
SO WHEN I RAN INTO YOUR SISTERS AT THE PANCAKE STAND...
...I LEARNED THAT ONE OF YOU GOT LOST THAT DAY.
...
I CAN REALLY TELL YOU WERE UESUGI-SAN'S TEACHER...
I'M GLAD I MET YOU.

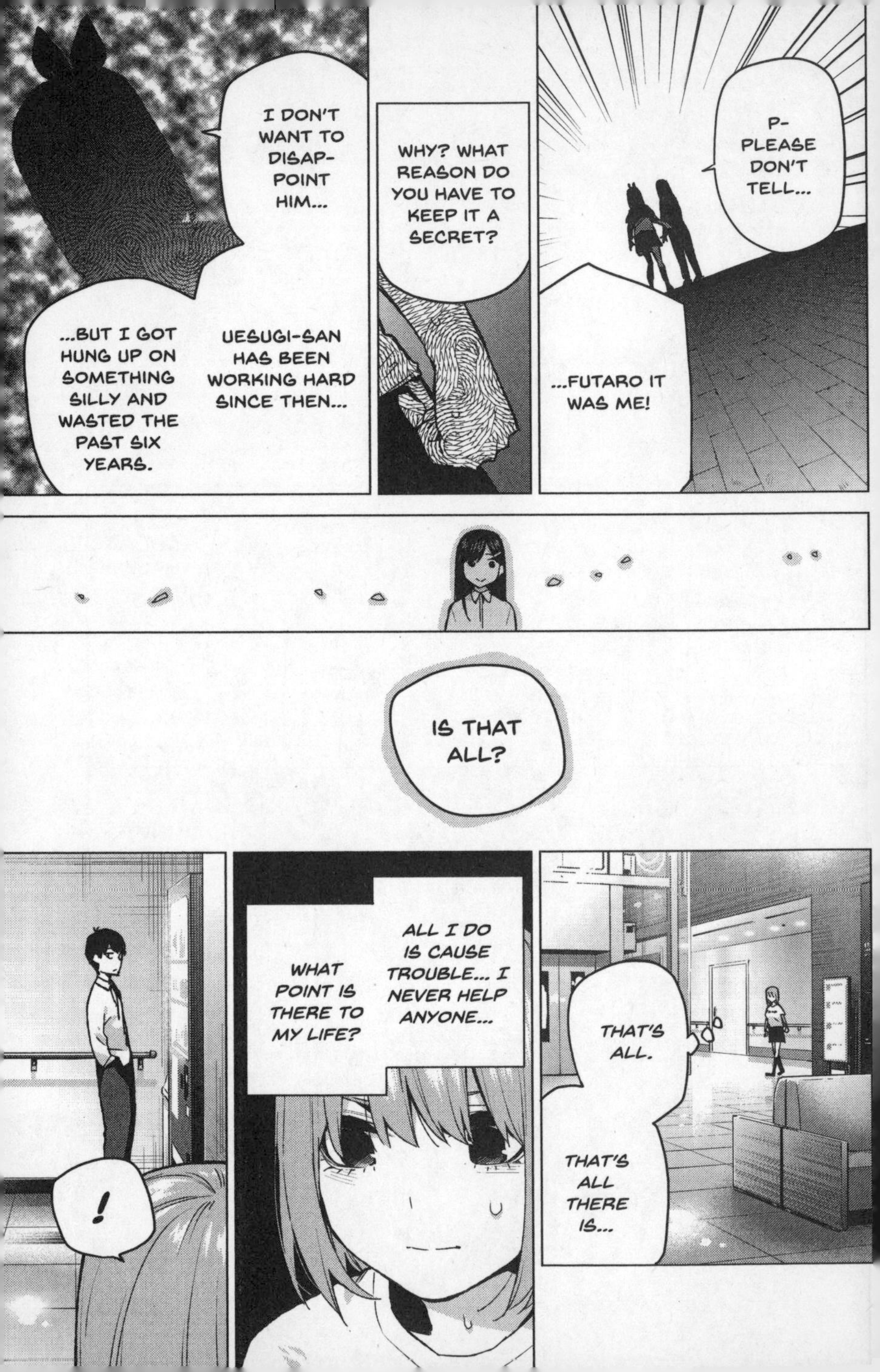
P- PLEASE DON'T TELL...
...FUTARO IT WAS ME!
WHY? WHAT REASON DO YOU HAVE TO KEEP IT A SECRET?
I DON'T WANT TO DISAP- POINT HIM...
UESUGI-SAN HAS BEEN WORKING HARD SINCE THEN...
...BUT I GOT HUNG UP ON SOMETHING SILLY AND WASTED THE PAST SIX YEARS.
IS THAT ALL?
THAT'S ALL.
THAT'S ALL THERE IS...
ALL I DO IS CAUSE TROUBLE... I NEVER HELP ANYONE...
WHAT POINT IS THERE TO MY LIFE?
!

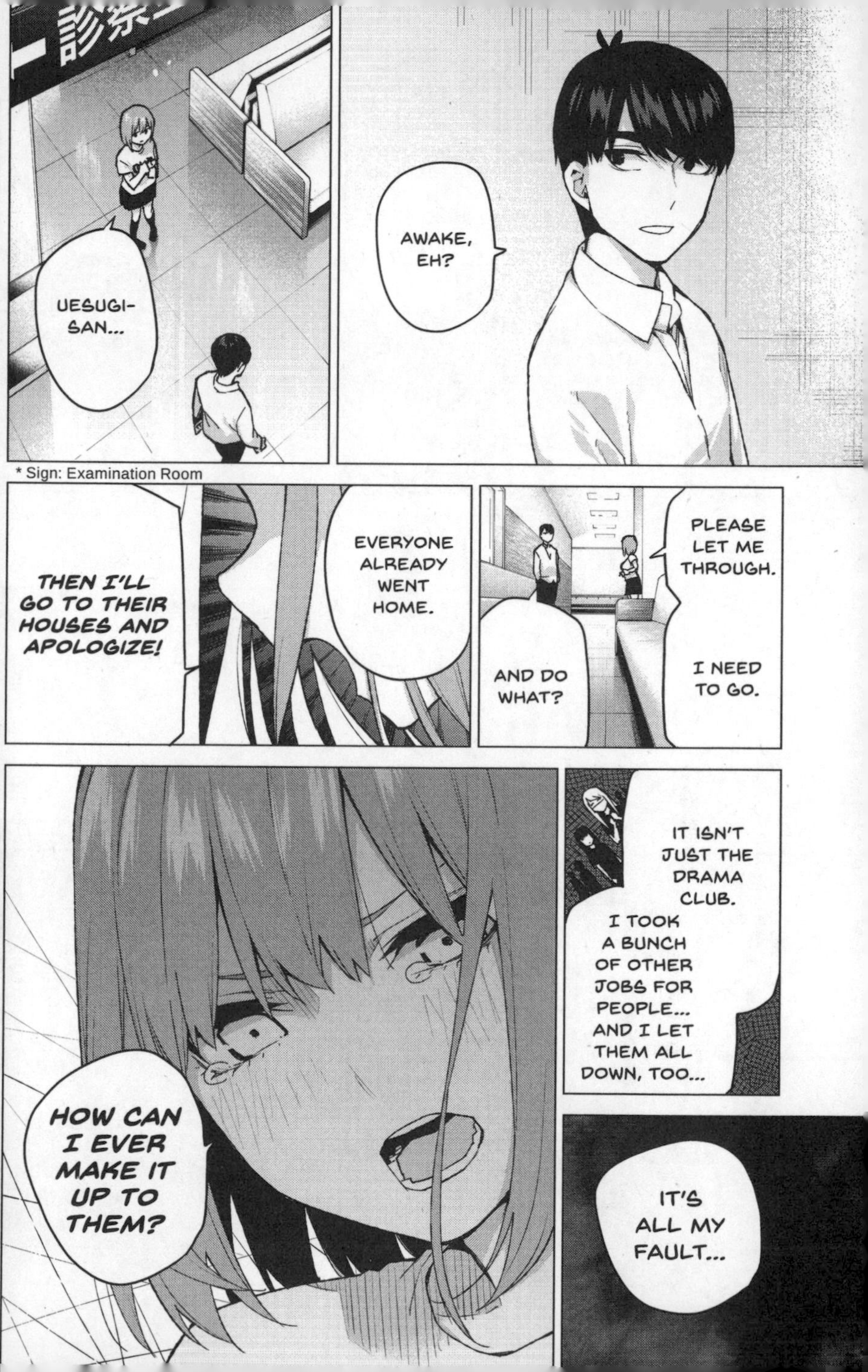
AWAKE, EH?
UESUGI-SAN...
診察
PLEASE LET ME THROUGH.
I NEED TO GO.
AND DO WHAT?
EVERYONE ALREADY WENT HOME.
THEN I'LL GO TO THEIR HOUSES AND APOLOGIZE!
IT ISN'T JUST THE DRAMA CLUB.
I TOOK A BUNCH OF OTHER JOBS FOR PEOPLE... AND I LET THEM ALL DOWN, TOO...
IT'S ALL MY FAULT...
HOW CAN I EVER MAKE IT UP TO THEM?
* Sign: Examination Room

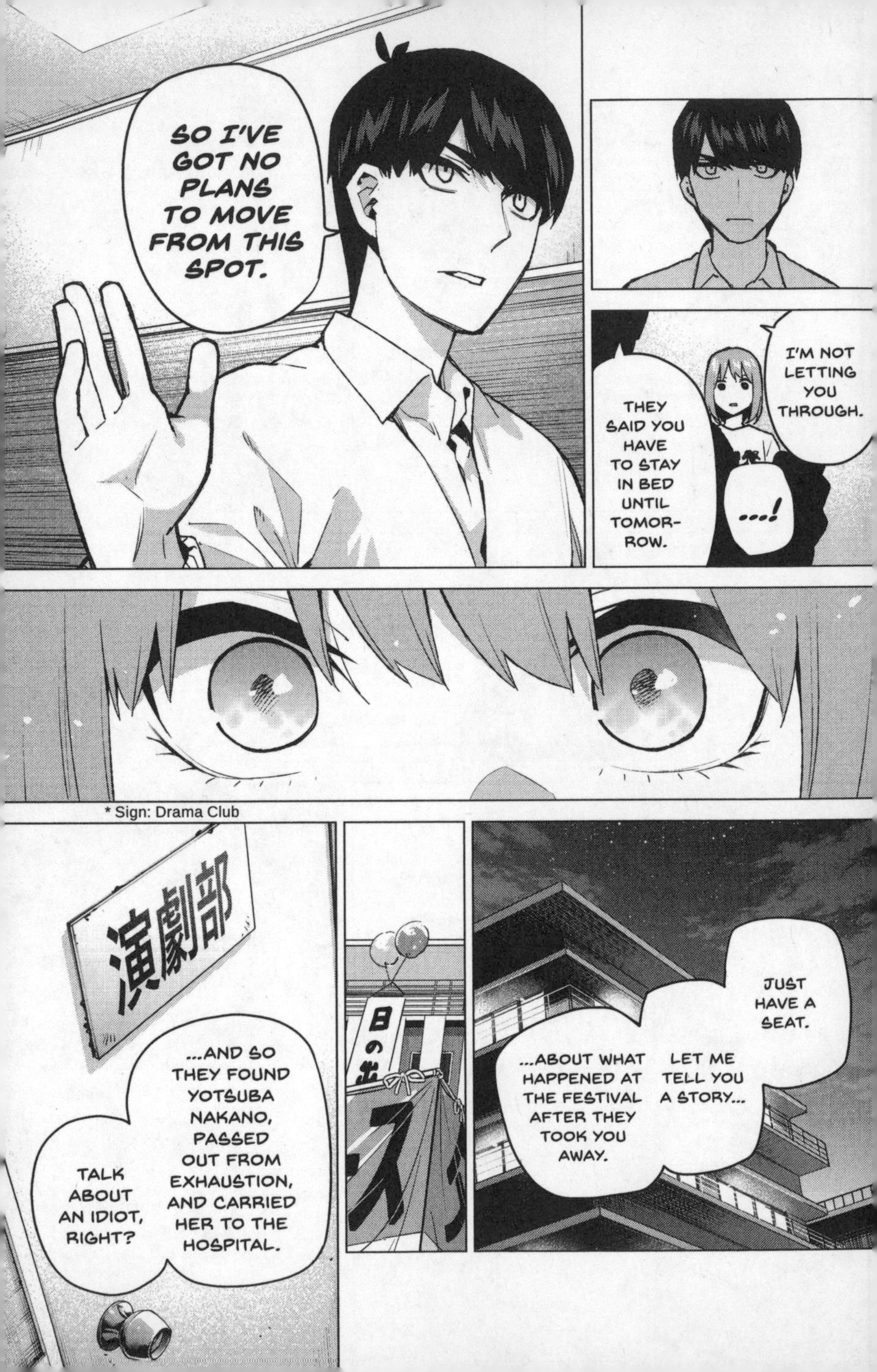
I'M NOT LETTING YOU THROUGH.
THEY SAID YOU HAVE TO STAY IN BED UNTIL TOMORROW.
...!
SO I'VE GOT NO PLANS TO MOVE FROM THIS SPOT.
JUST HAVE A SEAT.
LET ME TELL YOU A STORY...
...ABOUT WHAT HAPPENED AT THE FESTIVAL AFTER THEY TOOK YOU AWAY.
演劇部
...AND SO THEY FOUND YOTSUBA NAKANO, PASSED OUT FROM EXHAUSTION, AND CARRIED HER TO THE HOSPITAL.
TALK ABOUT AN IDIOT, RIGHT?
* Sign: Drama Club

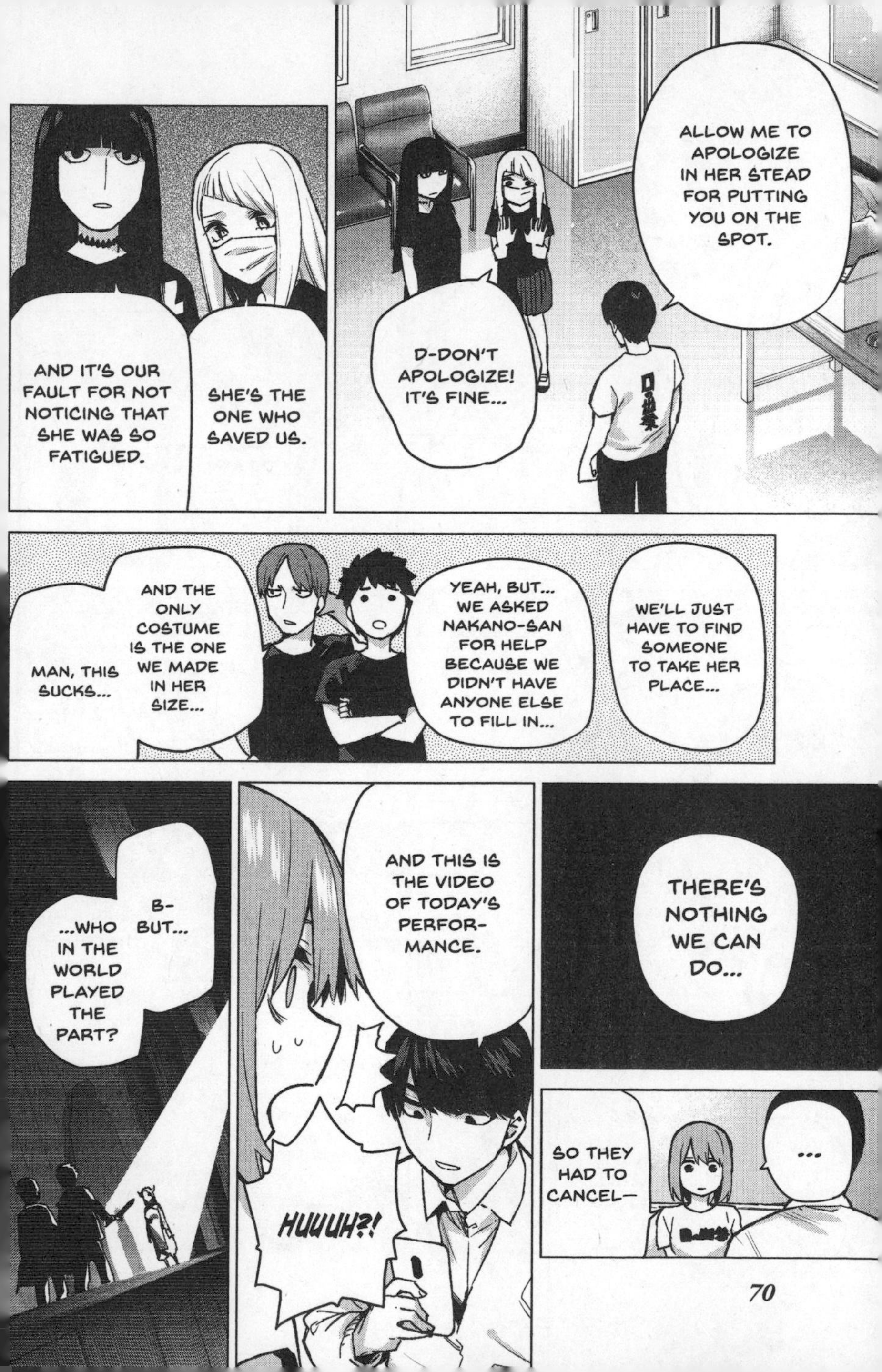
ALLOW ME TO APOLOGIZE IN HER STEAD FOR PUTTING YOU ON THE SPOT.
D-DON'T APOLOGIZE! IT'S FINE...
SHE'S THE ONE WHO SAVED US.
AND IT'S OUR FAULT FOR NOT NOTICING THAT SHE WAS SO FATIGUED.
WE'LL JUST HAVE TO FIND SOMEONE TO TAKE HER PLACE...
YEAH, BUT... WE ASKED NAKANO-SAN FOR HELP BECAUSE WE DIDN'T HAVE ANYONE ELSE TO FILL IN...
AND THE ONLY COSTUME IS THE ONE WE MADE IN HER SIZE...
MAN, THIS SUCKS...
THERE'S NOTHING WE CAN DO...
...
SO THEY HAD TO CANCEL—
AND THIS IS THE VIDEO OF TODAY'S PERFORMANCE.
HUUUH?!
B-BUT...
...WHO IN THE WORLD PLAYED THE PART?

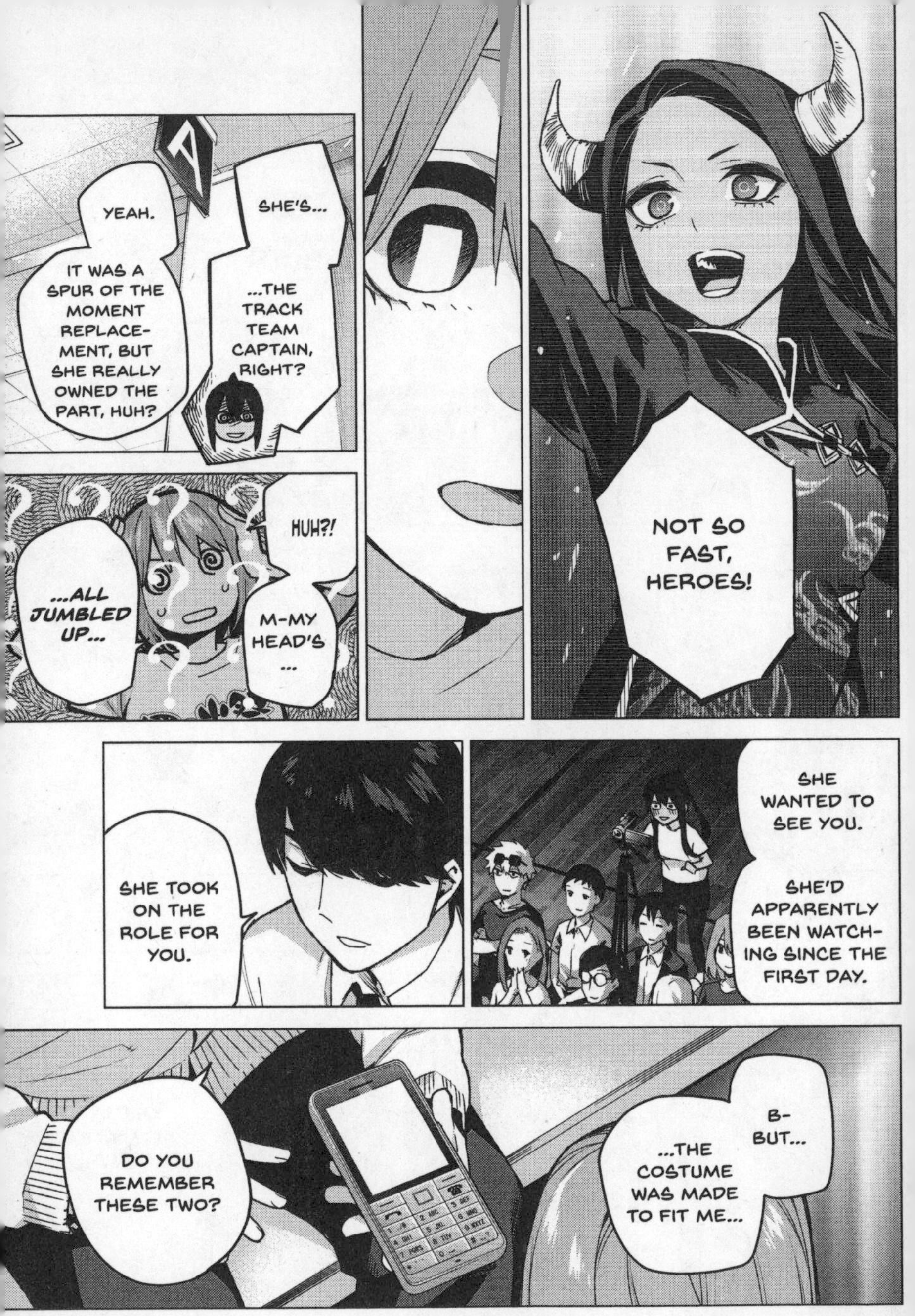
NOT SO FAST, HEROES!
SHE'S...
...THE TRACK TEAM CAPTAIN, RIGHT?
YEAH.
IT WAS A SPUR OF THE MOMENT REPLACEMENT, BUT SHE REALLY OWNED THE PART, HUH?
HUH?!
M-MY HEAD'S ...
...ALL JUMBLED UP...
SHE WANTED TO SEE YOU.
SHE'D APPARENTLY BEEN WATCHING SINCE THE FIRST DAY.
SHE TOOK ON THE ROLE FOR YOU.
B-BUT...
...THE COSTUME WAS MADE TO FIT ME...
DO YOU REMEMBER THESE TWO?

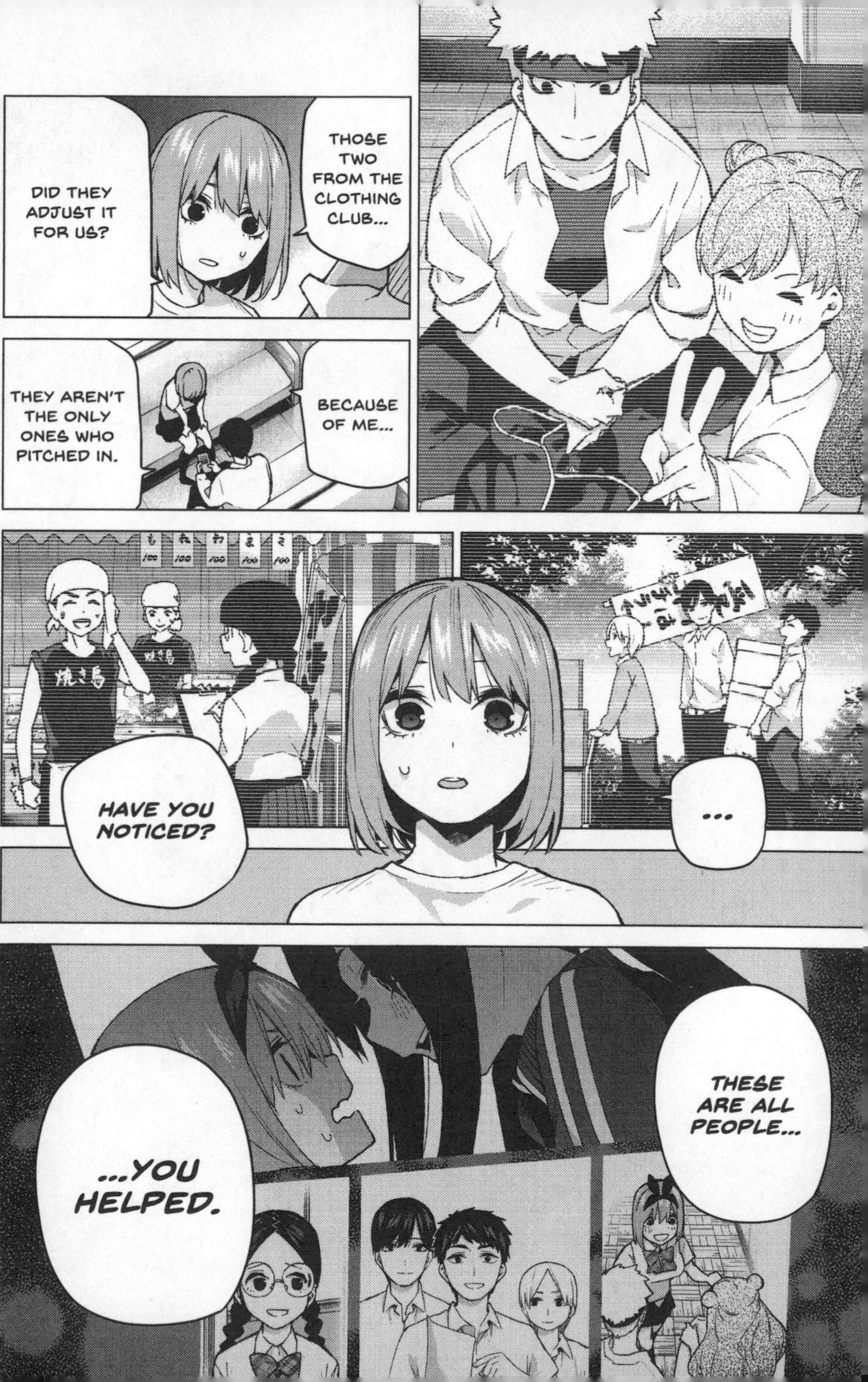
THOSE TWO FROM THE CLOTHING CLUB...
DID THEY ADJUST IT FOR US?
BECAUSE OF ME...
THEY AREN'T THE ONLY ONES WHO PITCHED IN.
...
HAVE YOU NOTICED?
THESE ARE ALL PEOPLE...
...YOU HELPED.

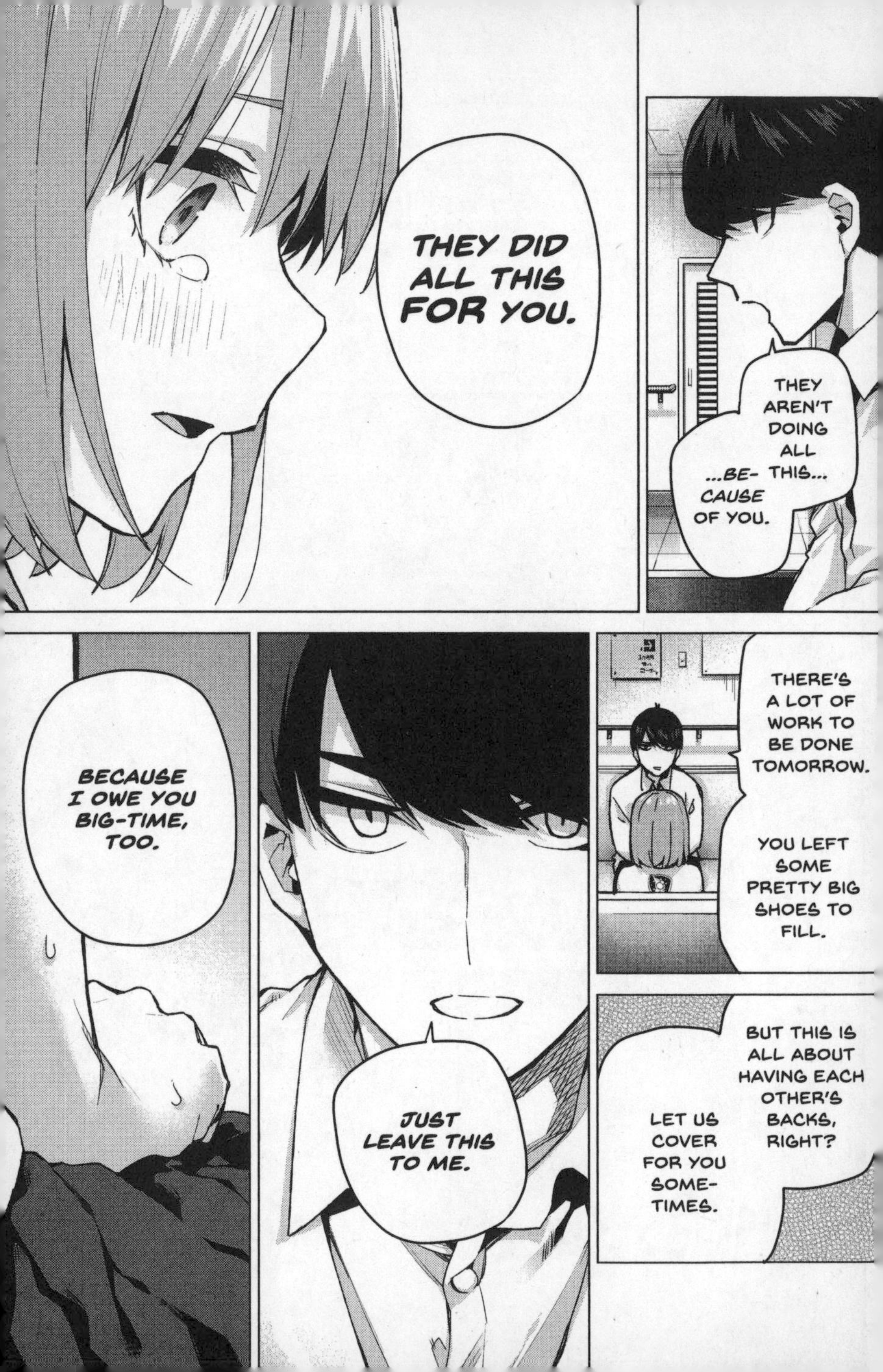
THEY AREN'T DOING ALL THIS...
...BE-CAUSE OF YOU.
THEY DID ALL THIS FOR YOU.
THERE'S A LOT OF WORK TO BE DONE TOMORROW.
YOU LEFT SOME PRETTY BIG SHOES TO FILL.
BUT THIS IS ALL ABOUT HAVING EACH OTHER'S BACKS, RIGHT?
LET US COVER FOR YOU SOME-TIMES.
JUST LEAVE THIS TO ME.
BECAUSE I OWE YOU BIG-TIME, TOO.

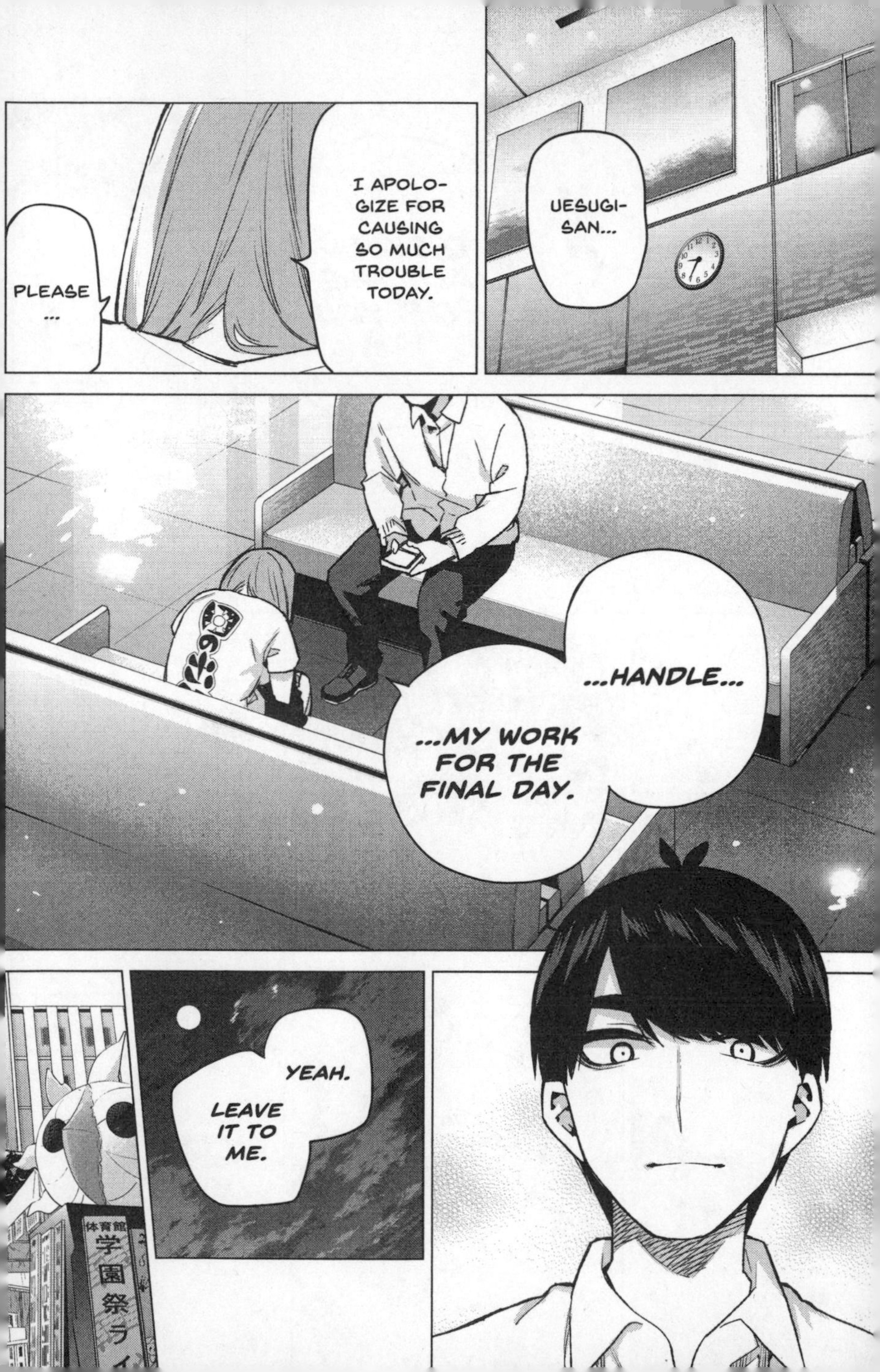
UESUGI-SAN...
I APOLOGIZE FOR CAUSING SO MUCH TROUBLE TODAY.
PLEASE ...
...HANDLE...
...MY WORK FOR THE FINAL DAY.
YEAH.
LEAVE IT TO ME.
体育館
学園祭ライ

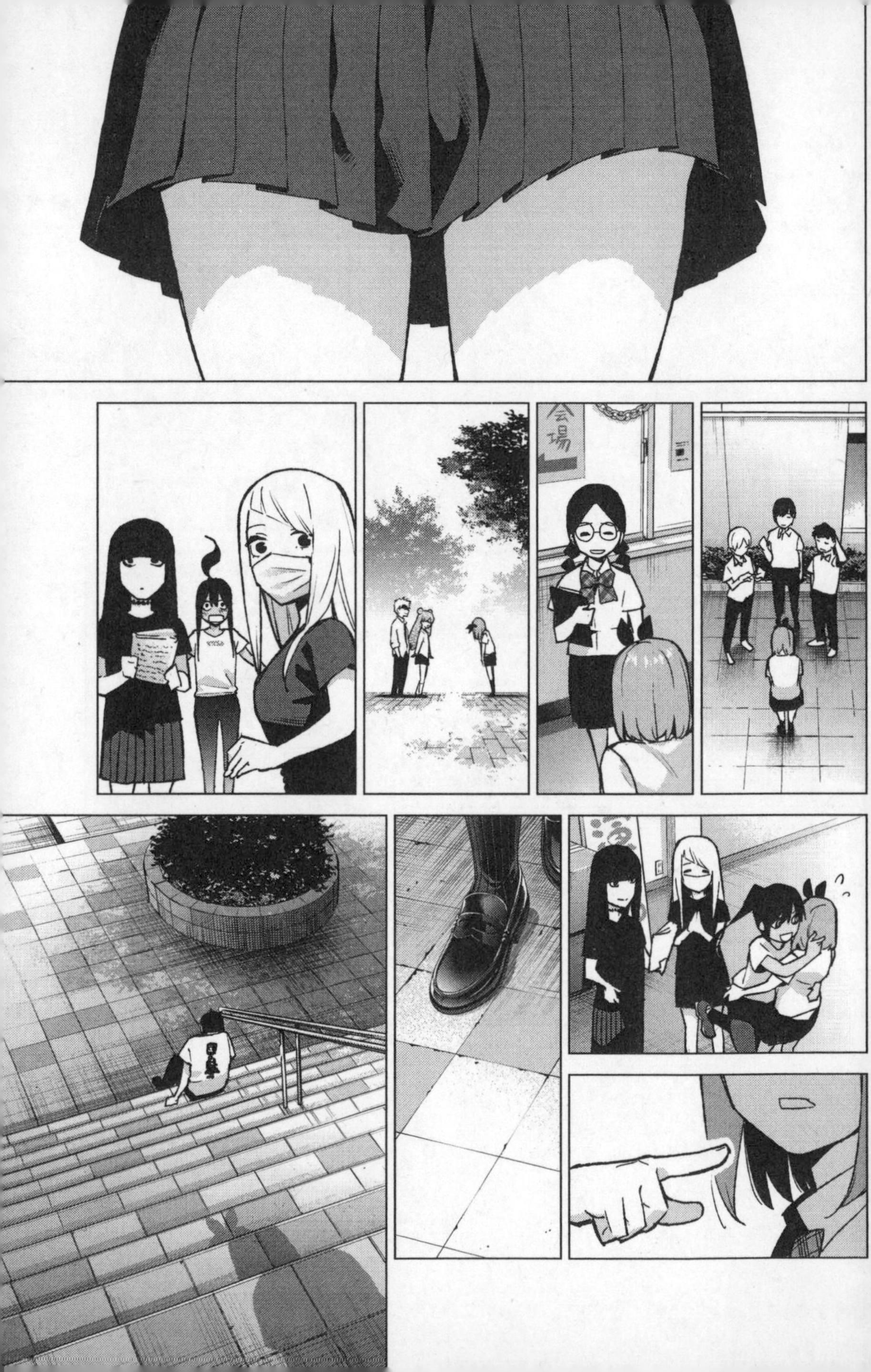
会場

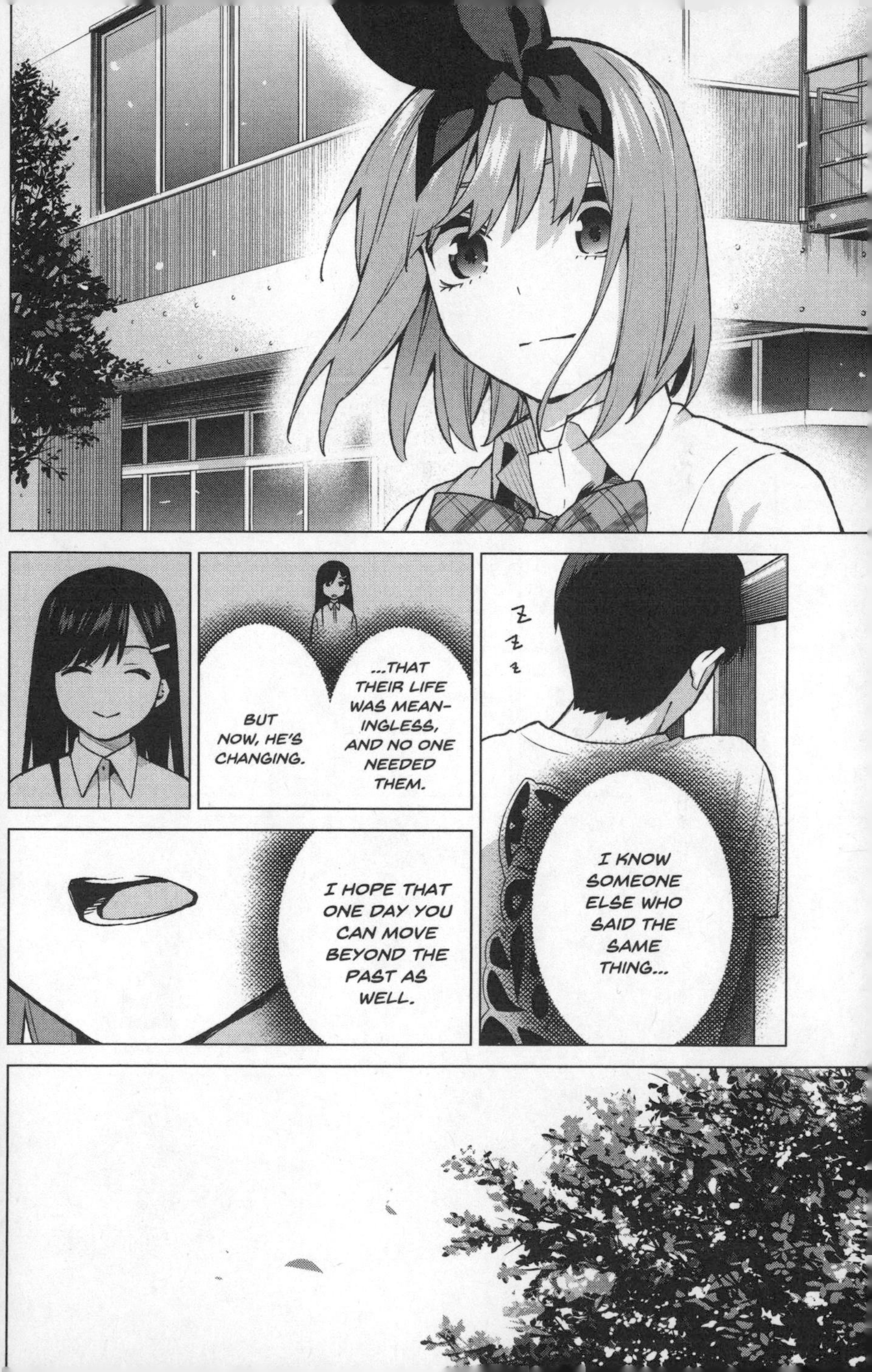
Z Z z
I KNOW SOMEONE ELSE WHO SAID THE SAME THING...
...THAT THEIR LIFE WAS MEANINGLESS, AND NO ONE NEEDED THEM.
BUT NOW, HE'S CHANGING.
I HOPE THAT ONE DAY YOU CAN MOVE BEYOND THE PAST AS WELL.

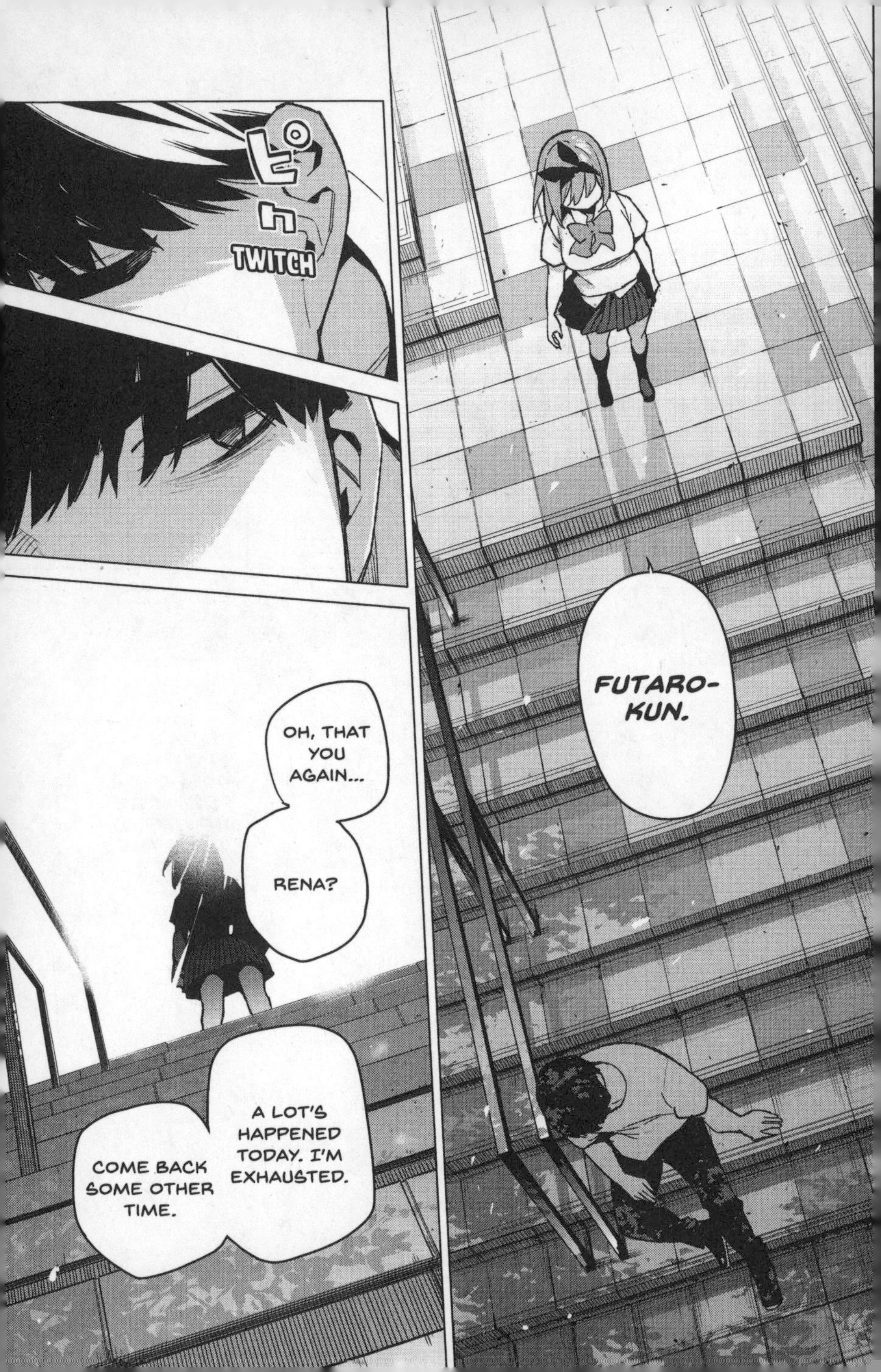
FUTARO-KUN.
TWITCH
OH, THAT YOU AGAIN...
RENA?
A LOT'S HAPPENED TODAY. I'M EXHAUSTED.
COME BACK SOME OTHER TIME.

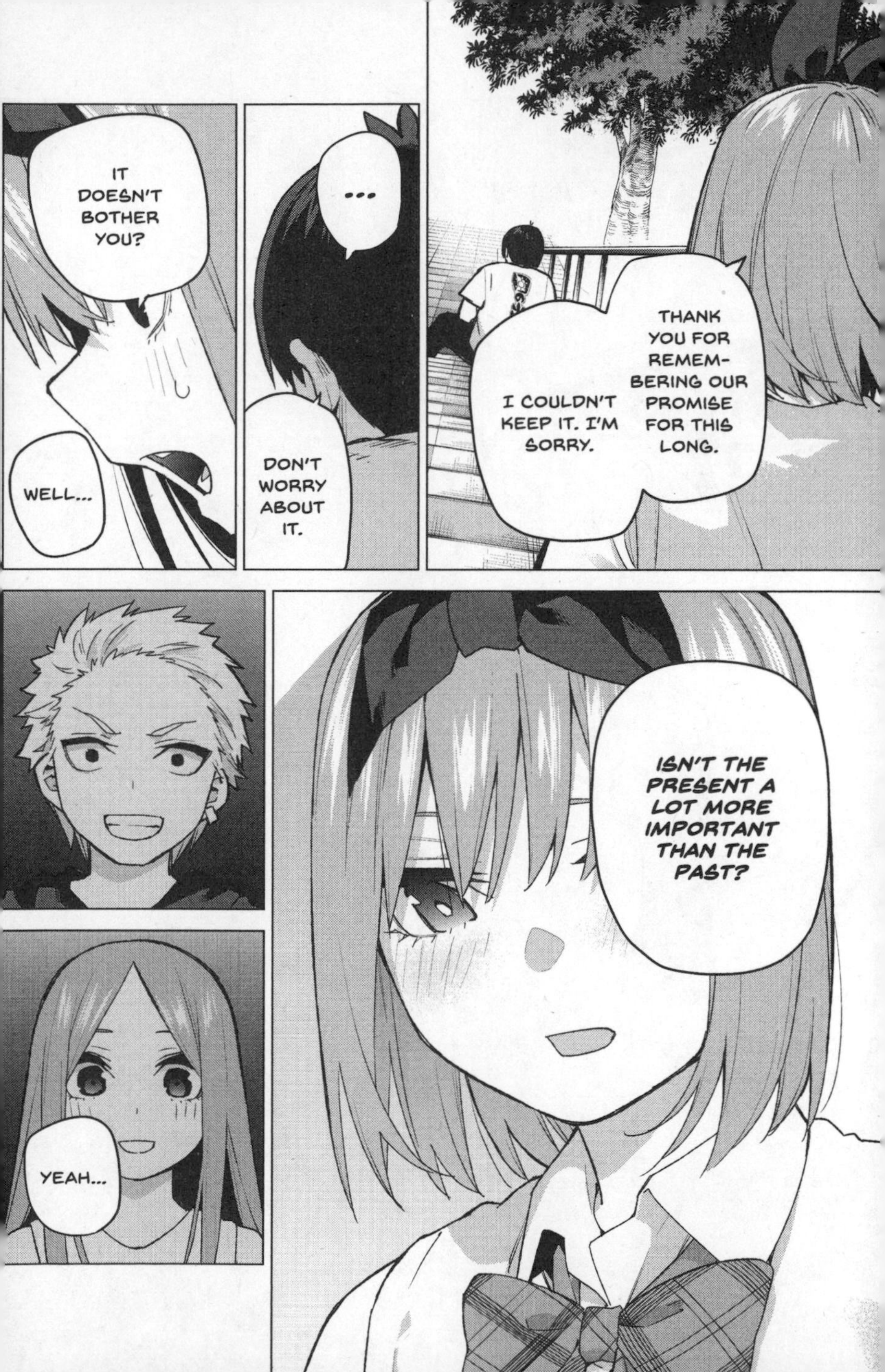
THANK YOU FOR REMEM-BERING OUR PROMISE FOR THIS LONG.
I COULDN'T KEEP IT. I'M SORRY.
...
DON'T WORRY ABOUT IT.
IT DOESN'T BOTHER YOU?
WELL...
ISN'T THE PRESENT A LOT MORE IMPORTANT THAN THE PAST?
YEAH...

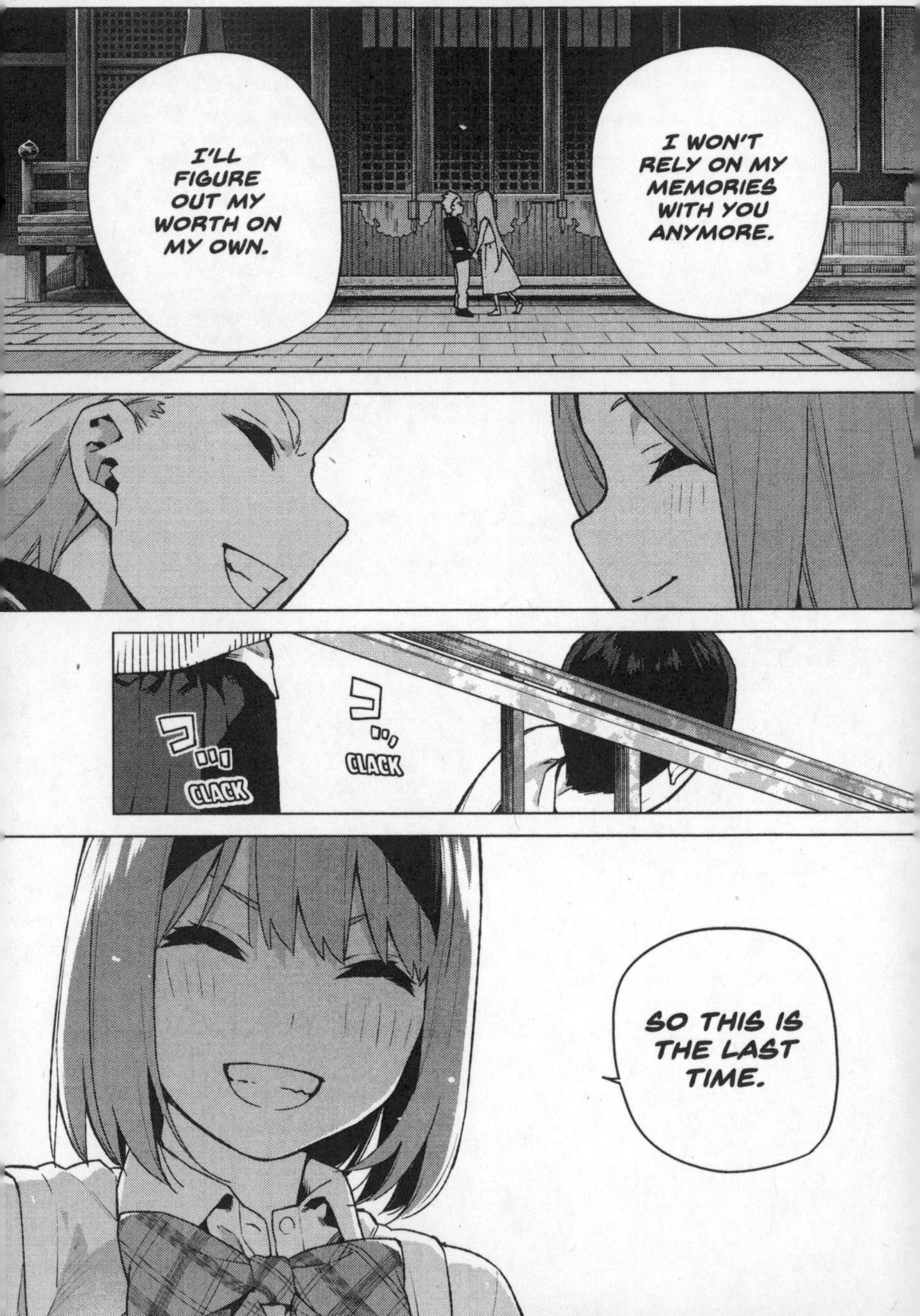
I WON'T RELY ON MY MEMORIES WITH YOU ANYMORE.
I'LL FIGURE OUT MY WORTH ON MY OWN.
CLACK
CLACK
SO THIS IS THE LAST TIME.

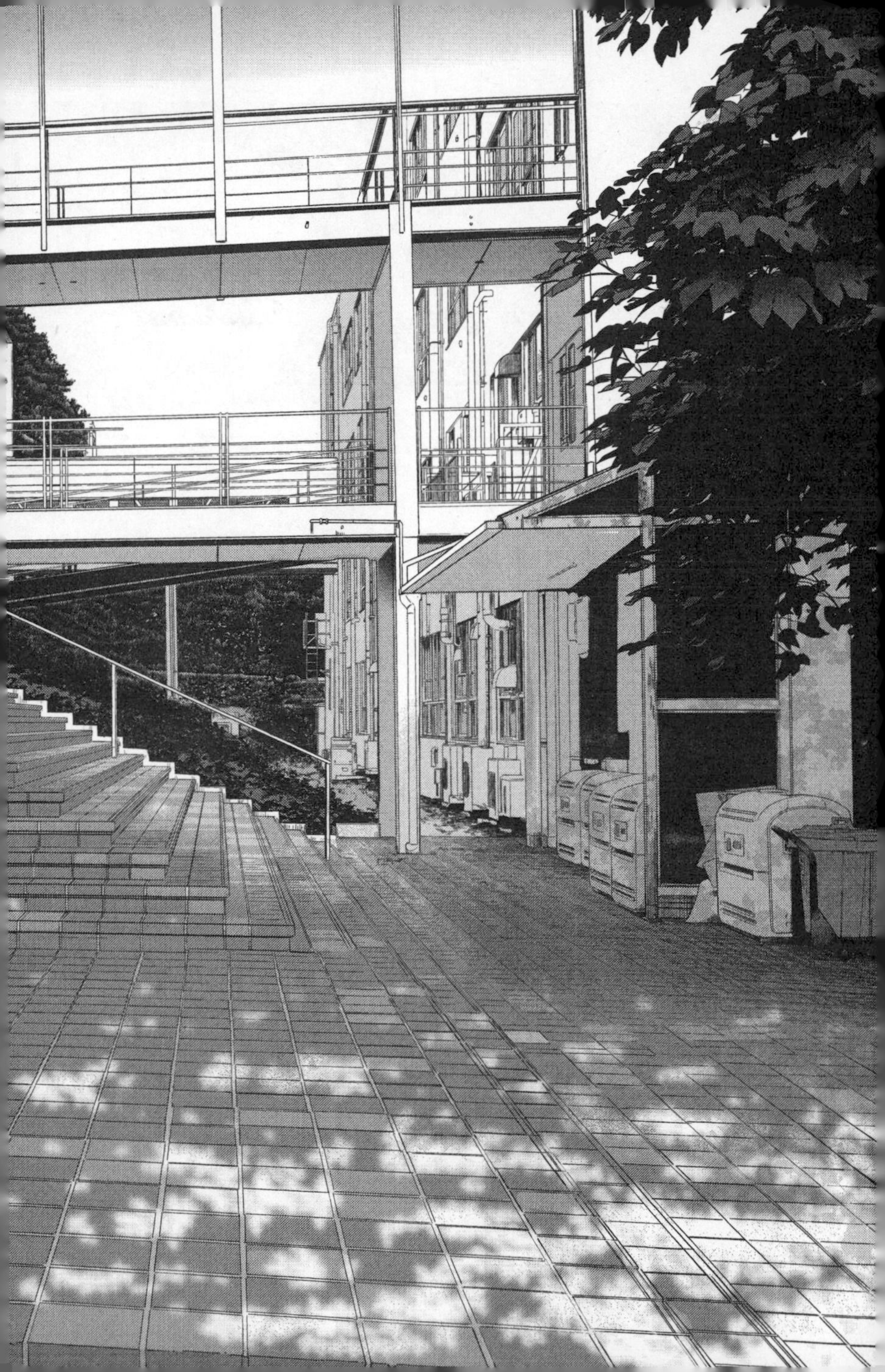

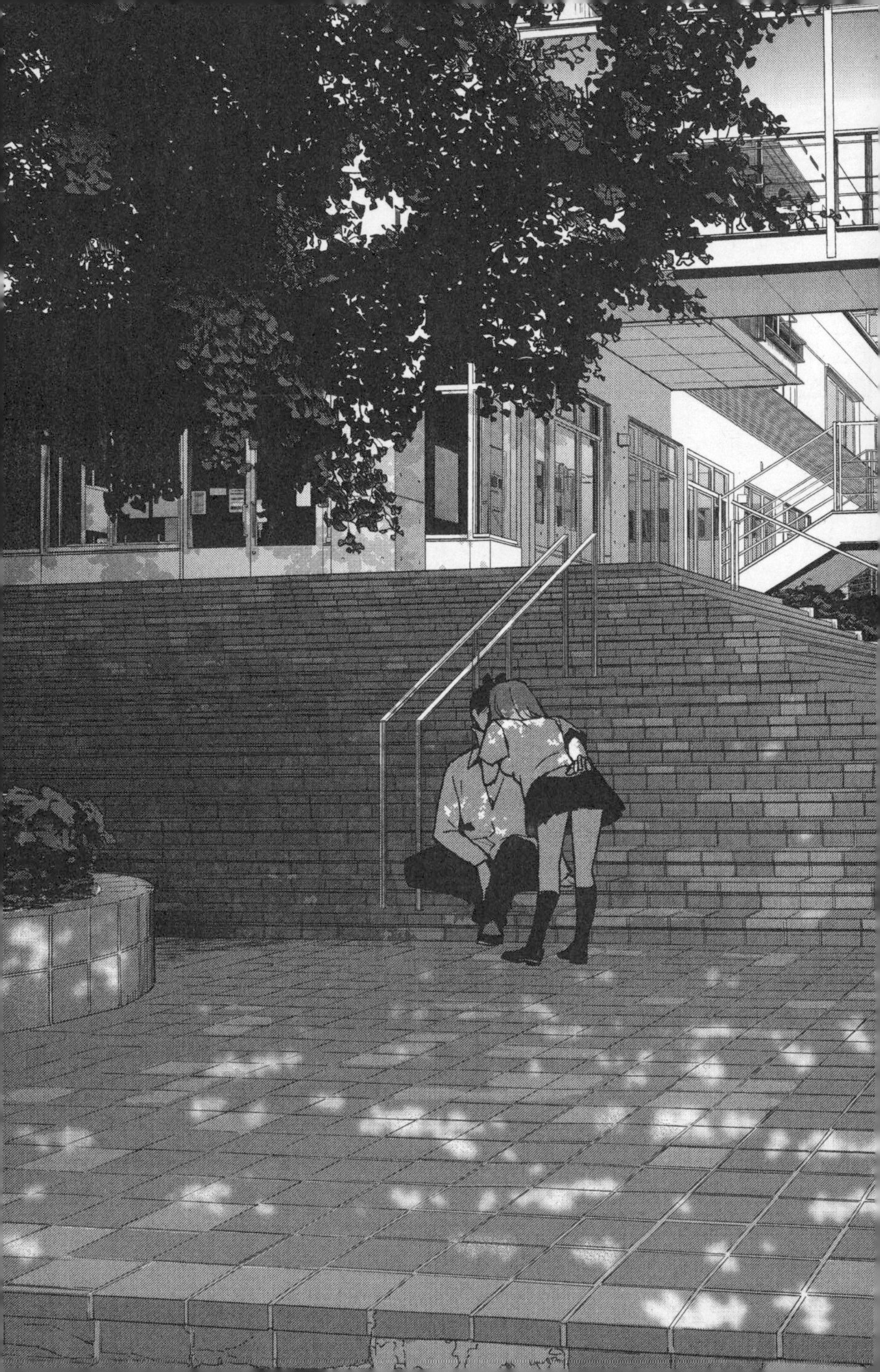

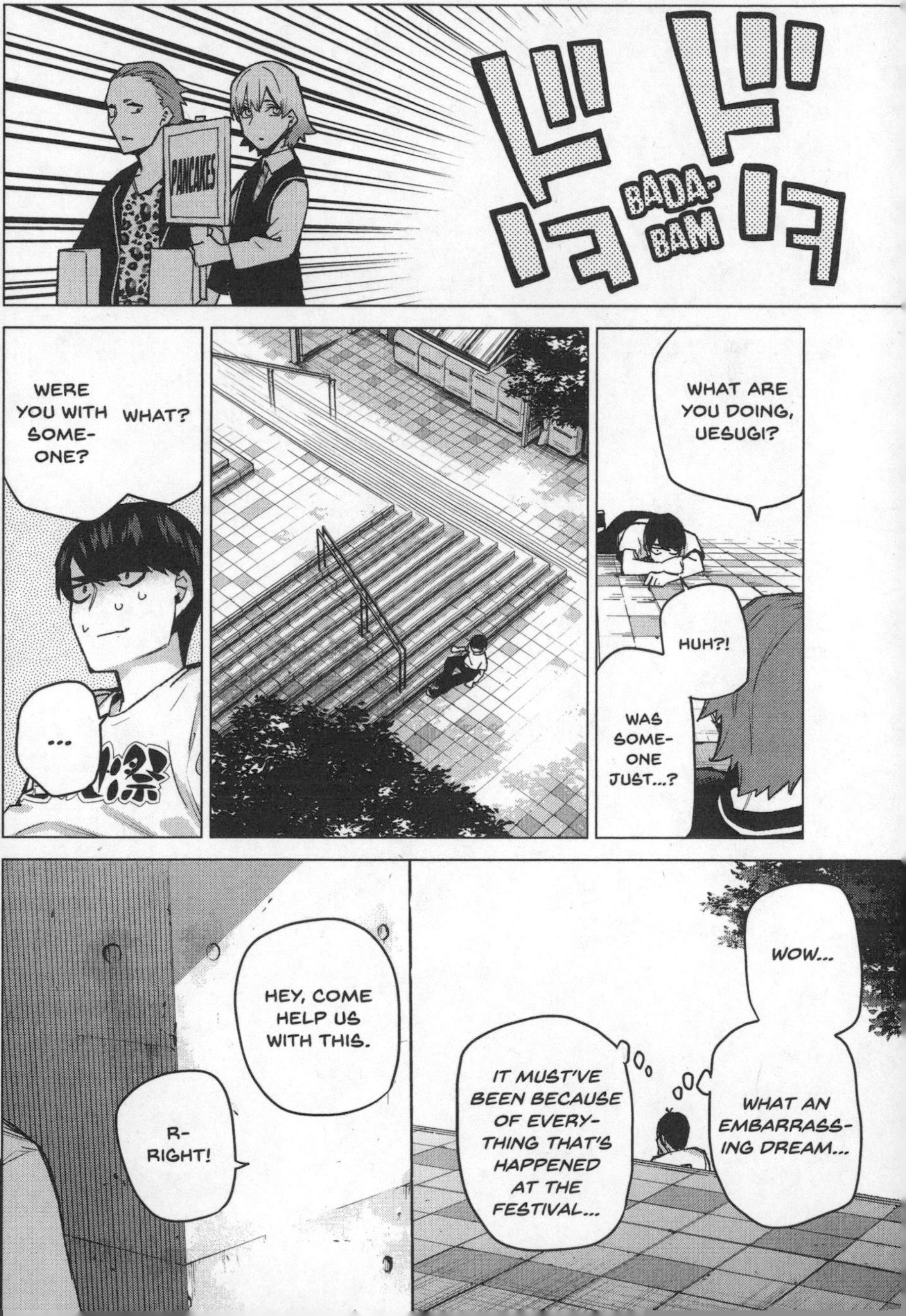
PANCAKES
BADA-BAM
WHAT ARE YOU DOING, UESUGI?
HUH?!
WAS SOME-ONE JUST...?
WHAT?
WERE YOU WITH SOME-ONE?
...
WOW...
WHAT AN EMBARRASS-ING DREAM...
IT MUST'VE BEEN BECAUSE OF EVERY-THING THAT'S HAPPENED AT THE FESTIVAL...
HEY, COME HELP US WITH THIS.
R-RIGHT!

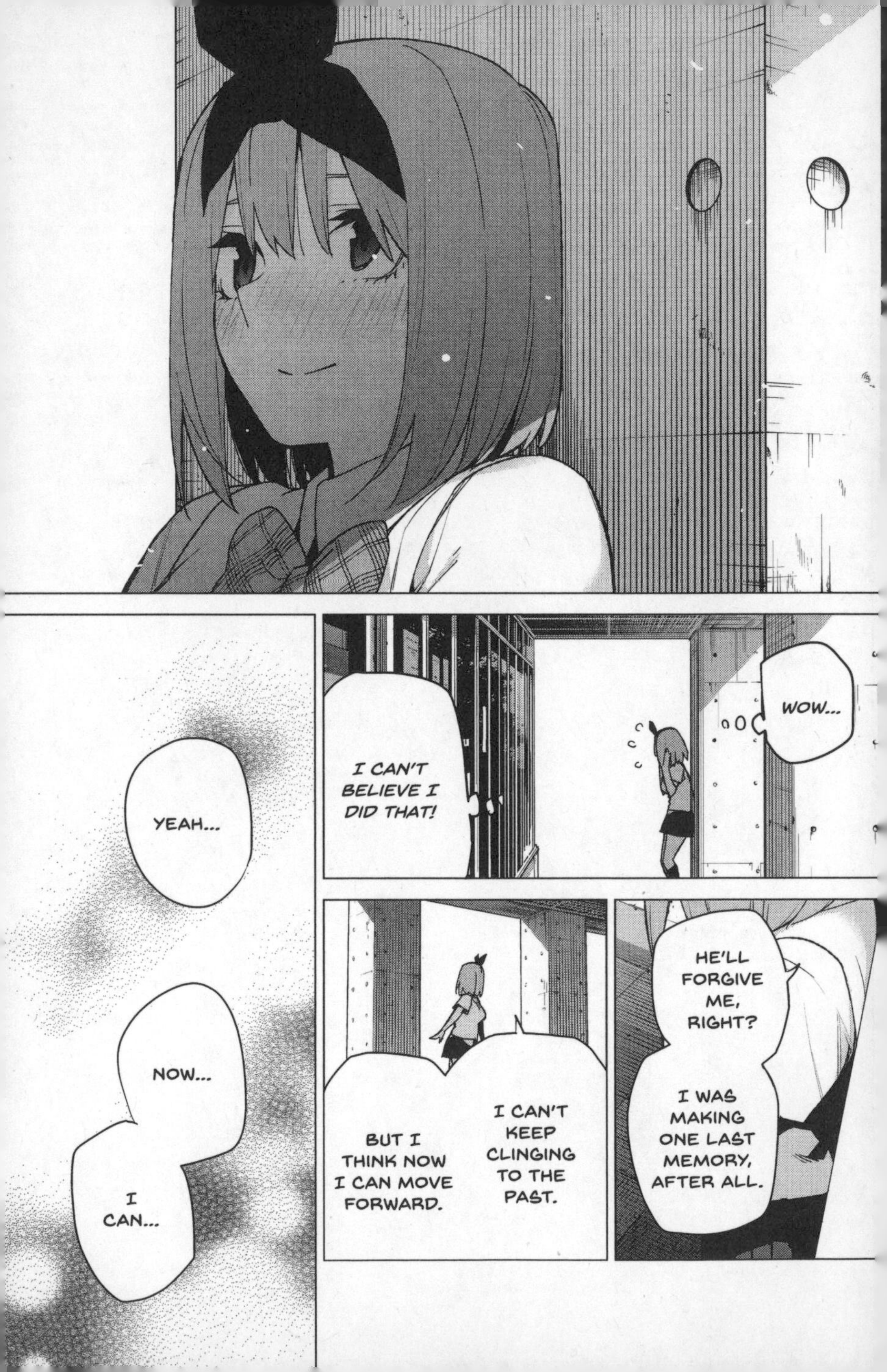
WOW...
I CAN'T BELIEVE I DID THAT!
HE'LL FORGIVE ME, RIGHT?
I WAS MAKING ONE LAST MEMORY, AFTER ALL.
I CAN'T KEEP CLINGING TO THE PAST.
BUT I THINK NOW I CAN MOVE FORWARD.
YEAH...
NOW...
I CAN...

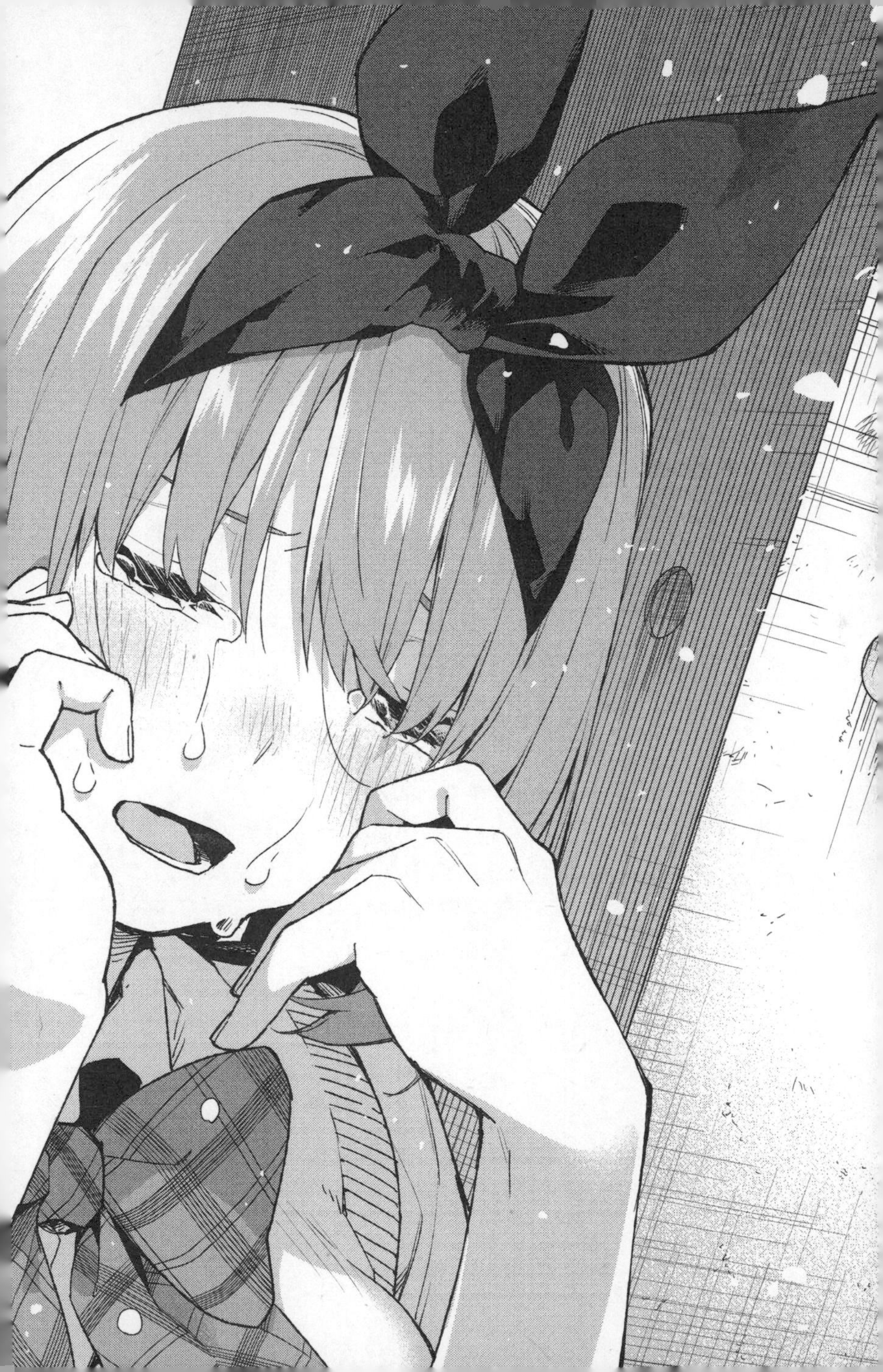

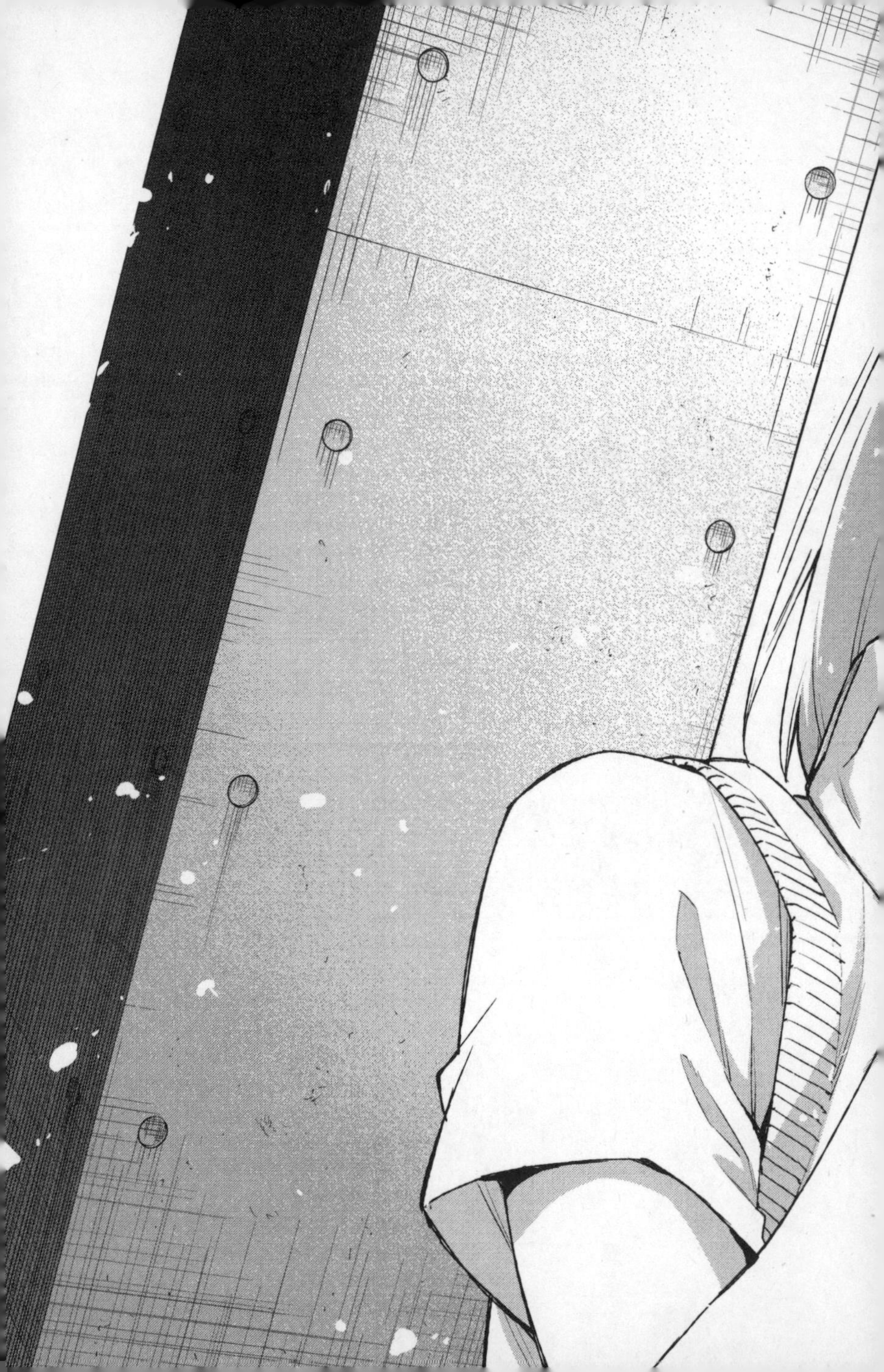

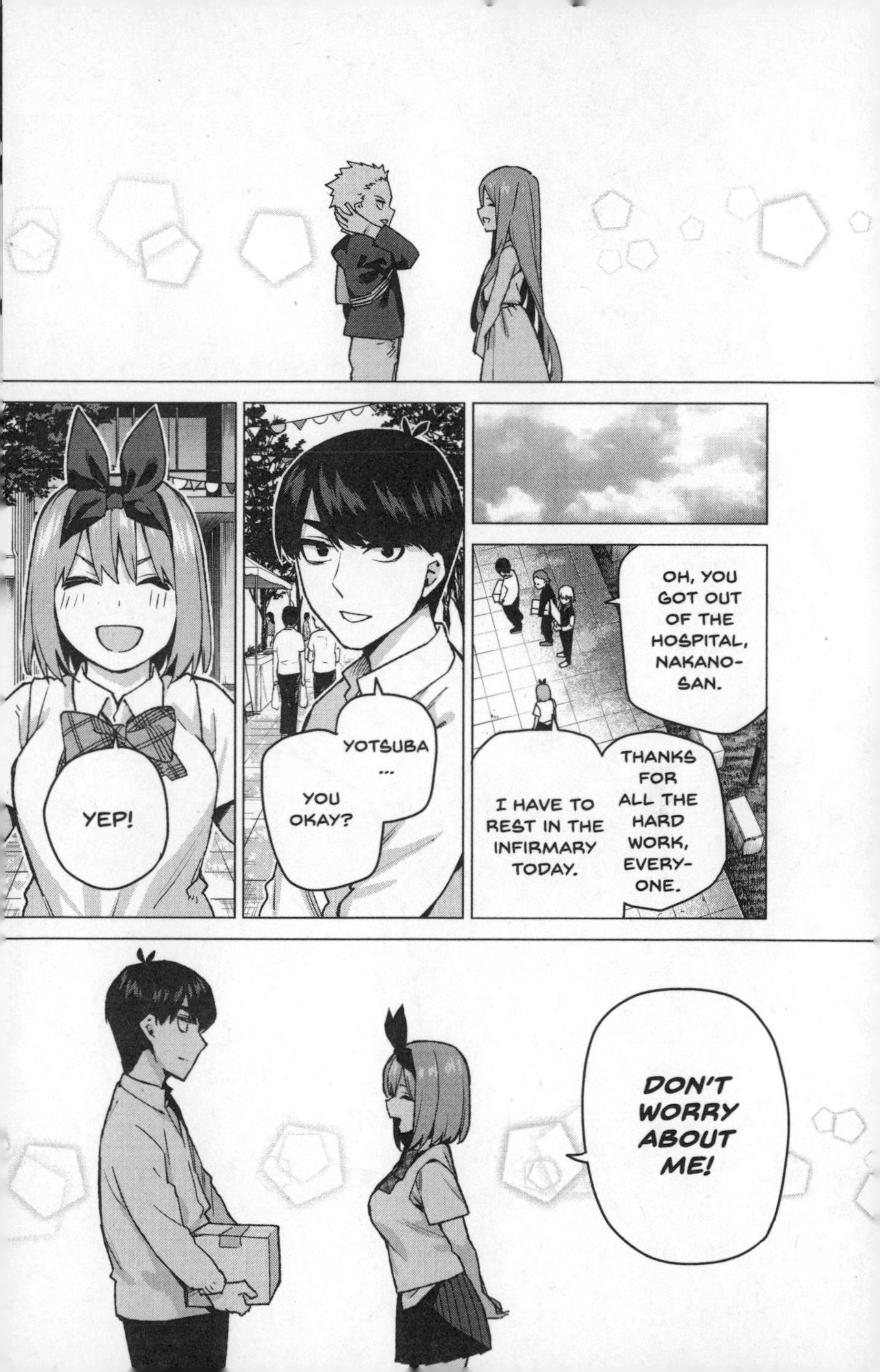
OH, YOU GOT OUT OF THE HOSPITAL, NAKANO-SAN.
THANKS FOR ALL THE HARD WORK, EVERYONE.
I HAVE TO REST IN THE INFIRMARY TODAY.
YOTSUBA ... YOU OKAY?
YEP!
DON'T WORRY ABOUT ME!

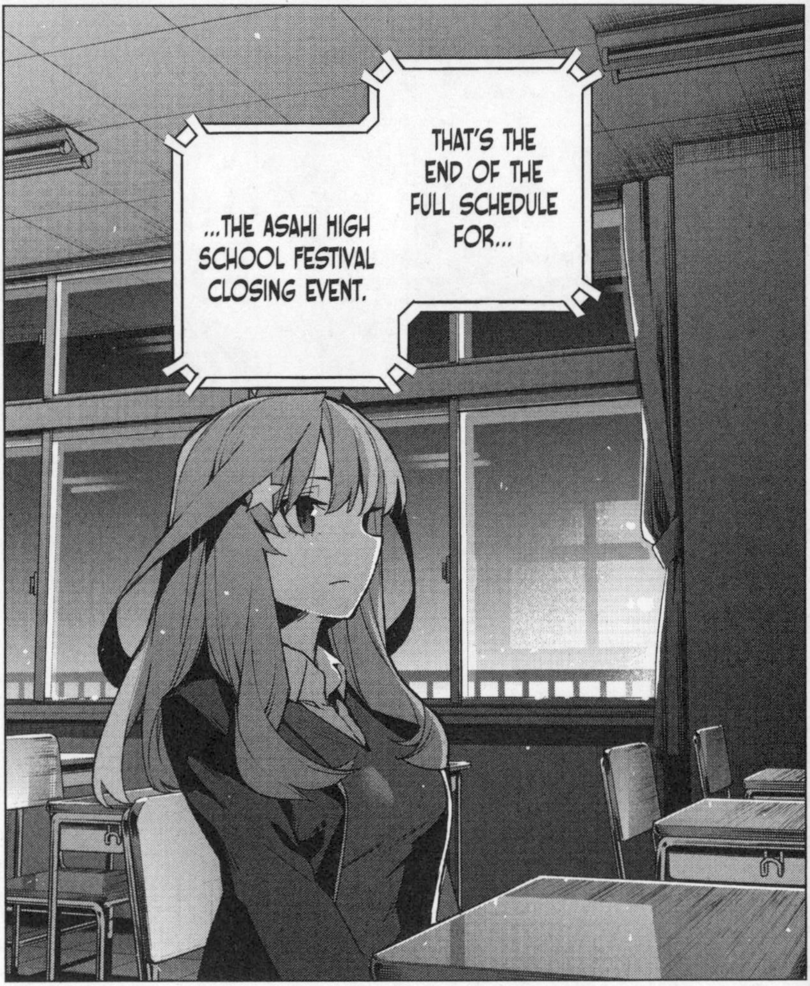
THAT'S THE END OF THE FULL SCHEDULE FOR...
...THE ASAHI HIGH SCHOOL FESTIVAL CLOSING EVENT.

CHAPTER 109 IF THE FINAL FESTIVAL WAS ITSUKI'S ①

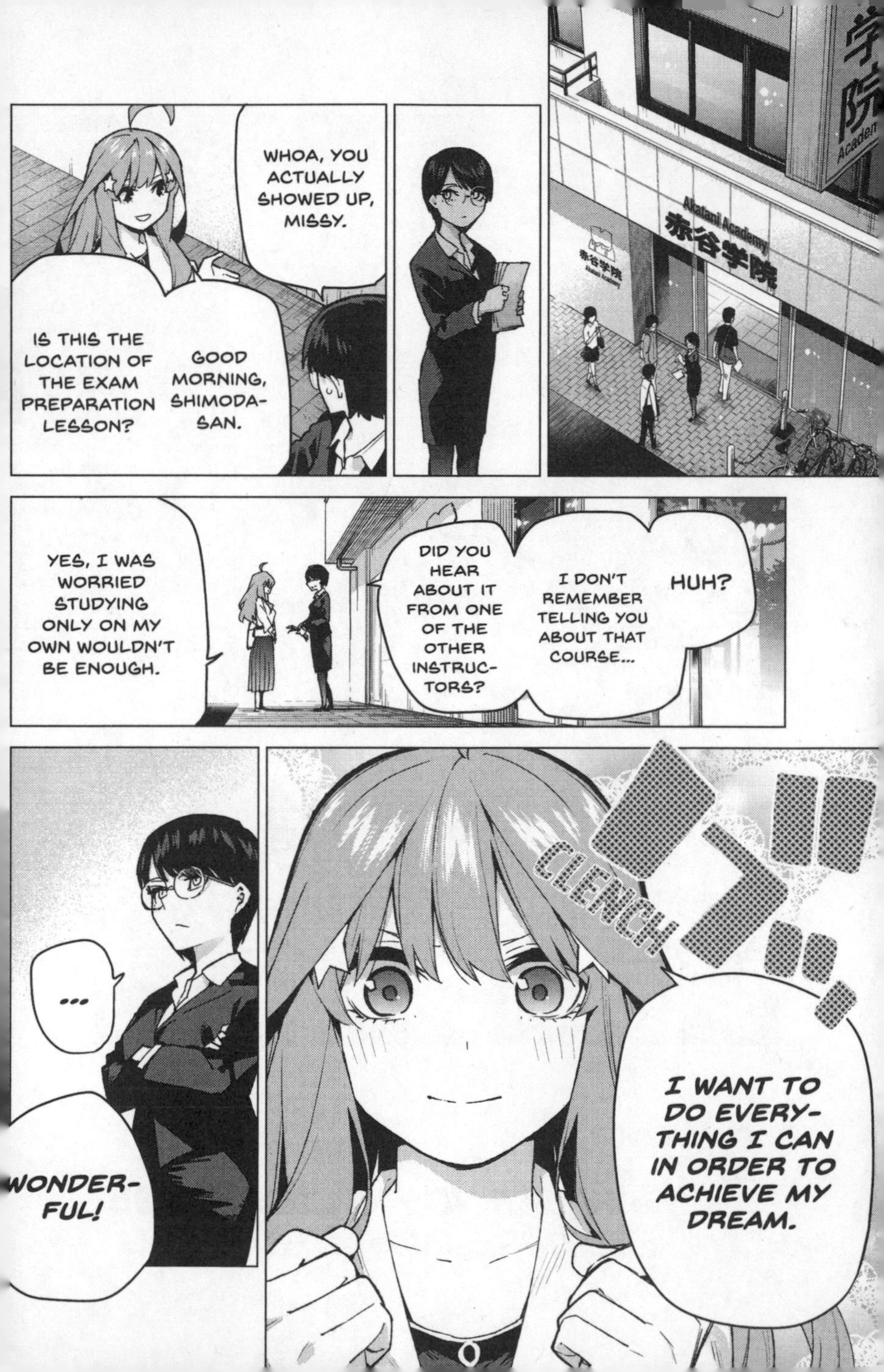

Akatani Academy
赤谷学院
赤谷学院
Akatani Academy
WHOA, YOU ACTUALLY SHOWED UP, MISSY.
GOOD MORNING, SHIMODA-SAN.
IS THIS THE LOCATION OF THE EXAM PREPARATION LESSON?
HUH?
I DON'T REMEMBER TELLING YOU ABOUT THAT COURSE...
DID YOU HEAR ABOUT IT FROM ONE OF THE OTHER INSTRUCTORS?
YES, I WAS WORRIED STUDYING ONLY ON MY OWN WOULDN'T BE ENOUGH.
CLENCH
I WANT TO DO EVERYTHING I CAN IN ORDER TO ACHIEVE MY DREAM.
...
WONDERFUL!

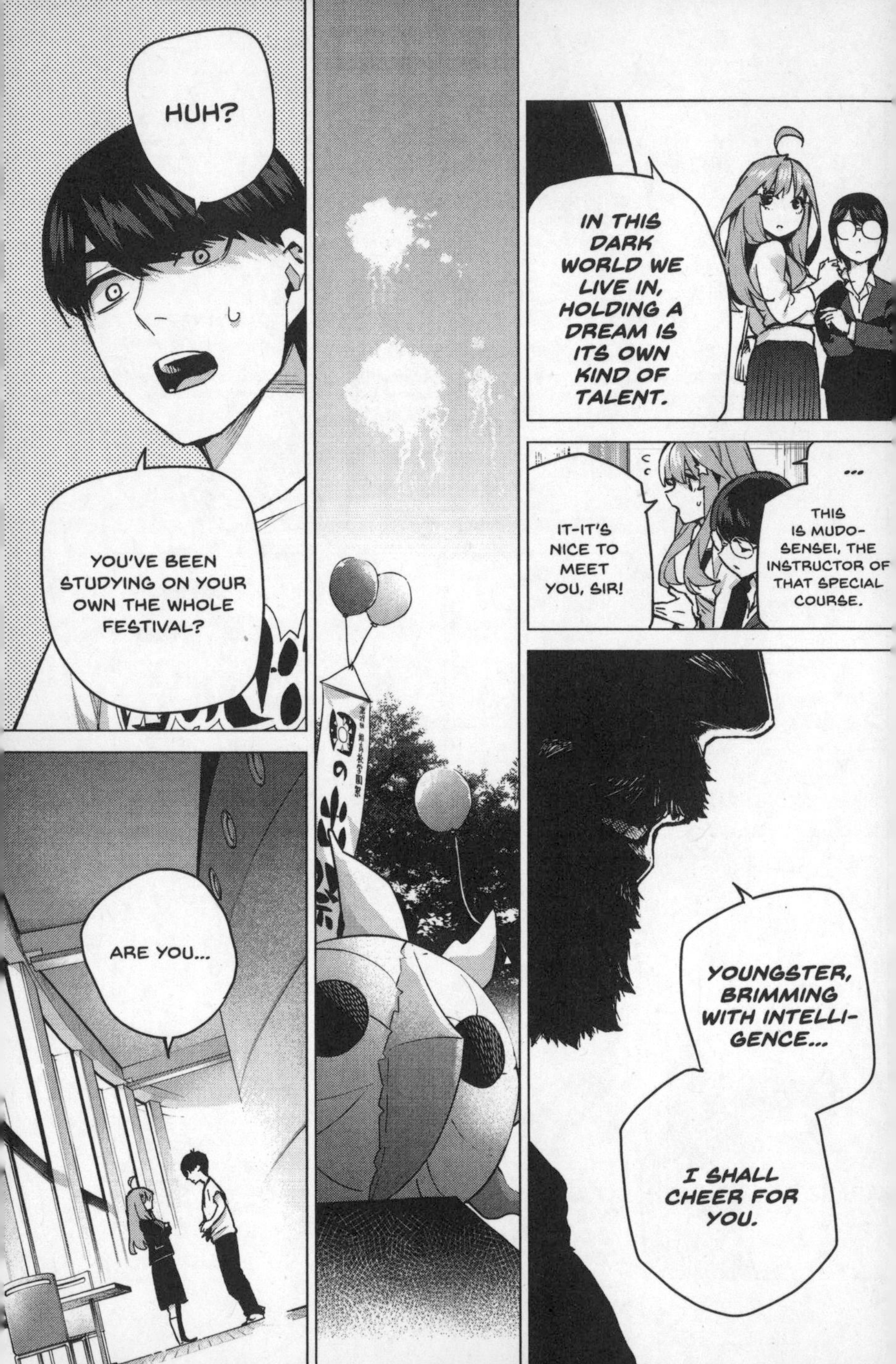
IN THIS DARK WORLD WE LIVE IN, HOLDING A DREAM IS ITS OWN KIND OF TALENT.
...
THIS IS MUDO-SENSEI, THE INSTRUCTOR OF THAT SPECIAL COURSE.
IT-IT'S NICE TO MEET YOU, SIR!
YOUNGSTER, BRIMMING WITH INTELLI-GENCE...
I SHALL CHEER FOR YOU.
HUH?
YOU'VE BEEN STUDYING ON YOUR OWN THE WHOLE FESTIVAL?
ARE YOU...

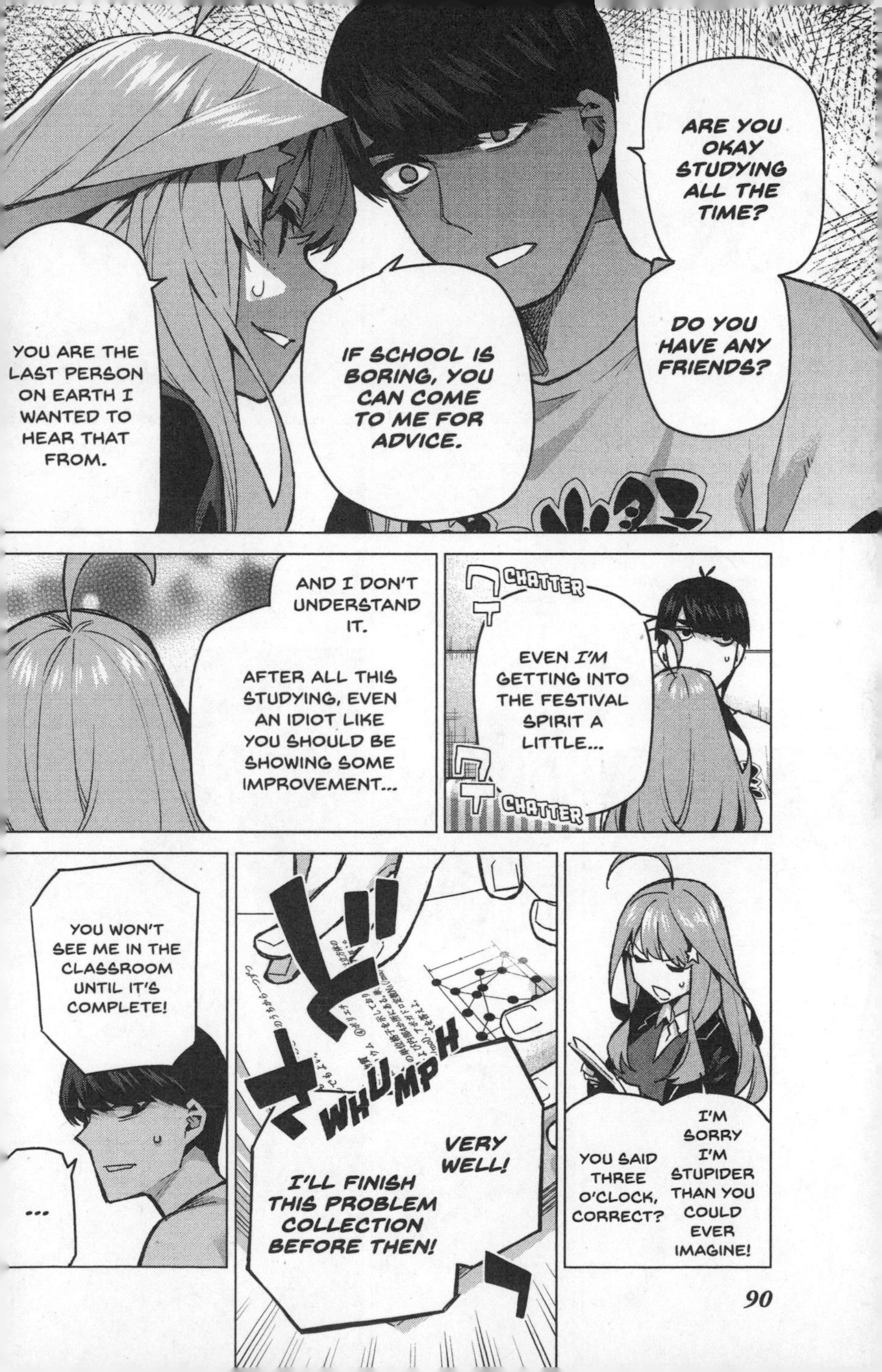
ARE YOU OKAY STUDYING ALL THE TIME?
DO YOU HAVE ANY FRIENDS?
IF SCHOOL IS BORING, YOU CAN COME TO ME FOR ADVICE.
YOU ARE THE LAST PERSON ON EARTH I WANTED TO HEAR THAT FROM.
CHATTER
EVEN *I'M* GETTING INTO THE FESTIVAL SPIRIT A LITTLE...
CHATTER
AND I DON'T UNDERSTAND IT.
AFTER ALL THIS STUDYING, EVEN AN IDIOT LIKE YOU SHOULD BE SHOWING SOME IMPROVEMENT...
I'M SORRY I'M STUPIDER THAN YOU COULD EVER IMAGINE!
YOU SAID THREE O'CLOCK, CORRECT?
WHUMPH
VERY WELL!
I'LL FINISH THIS PROBLEM COLLECTION BEFORE THEN!
YOU WON'T SEE ME IN THE CLASSROOM UNTIL IT'S COMPLETE!
...

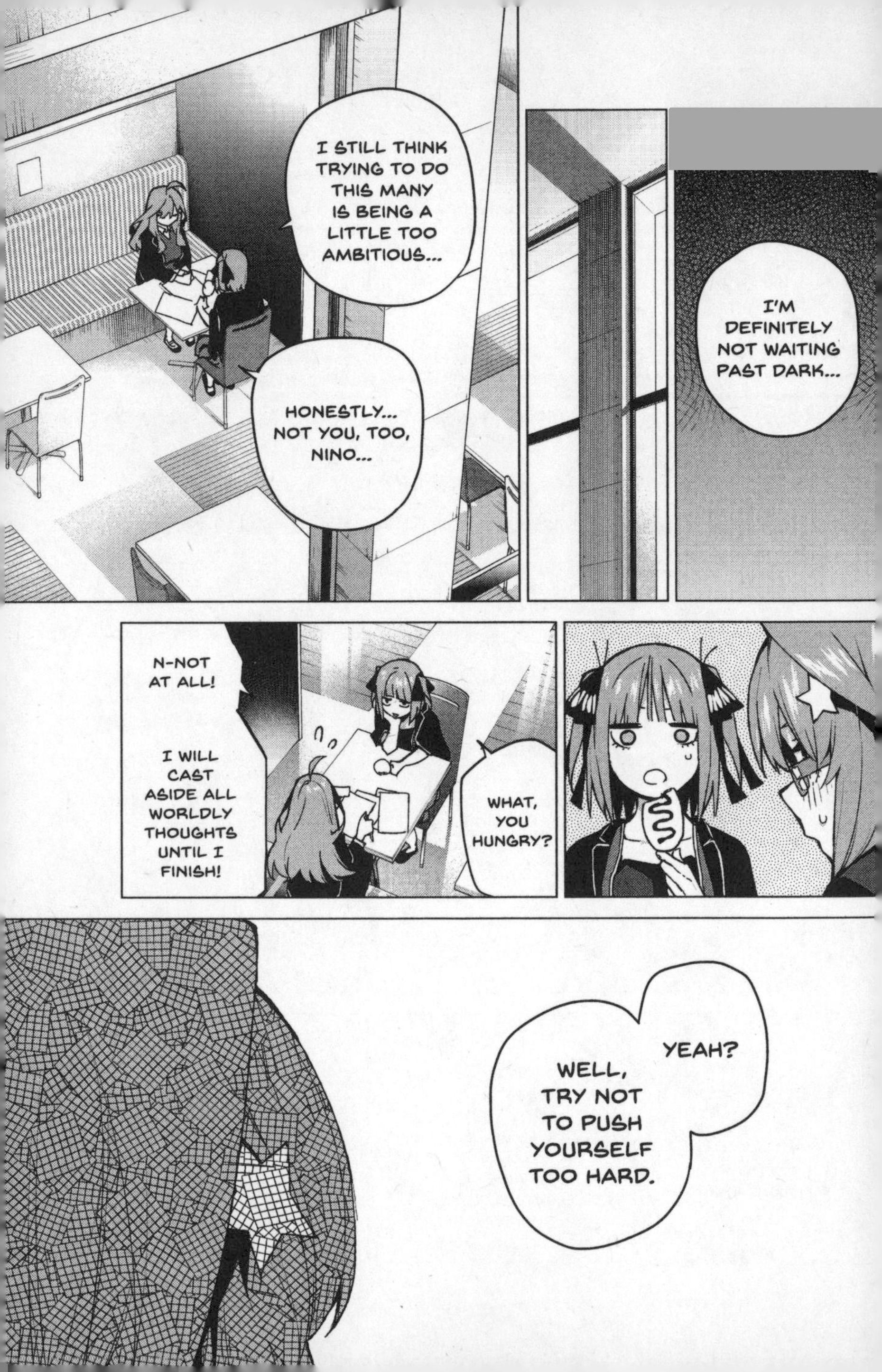
I'M DEFINITELY NOT WAITING PAST DARK...
I STILL THINK TRYING TO DO THIS MANY IS BEING A LITTLE TOO AMBITIOUS...
HONESTLY... NOT YOU, TOO, NINO...
WHAT, YOU HUNGRY?
N-NOT AT ALL!
I WILL CAST ASIDE ALL WORLDLY THOUGHTS UNTIL I FINISH!
YEAH? WELL, TRY NOT TO PUSH YOURSELF TOO HARD.

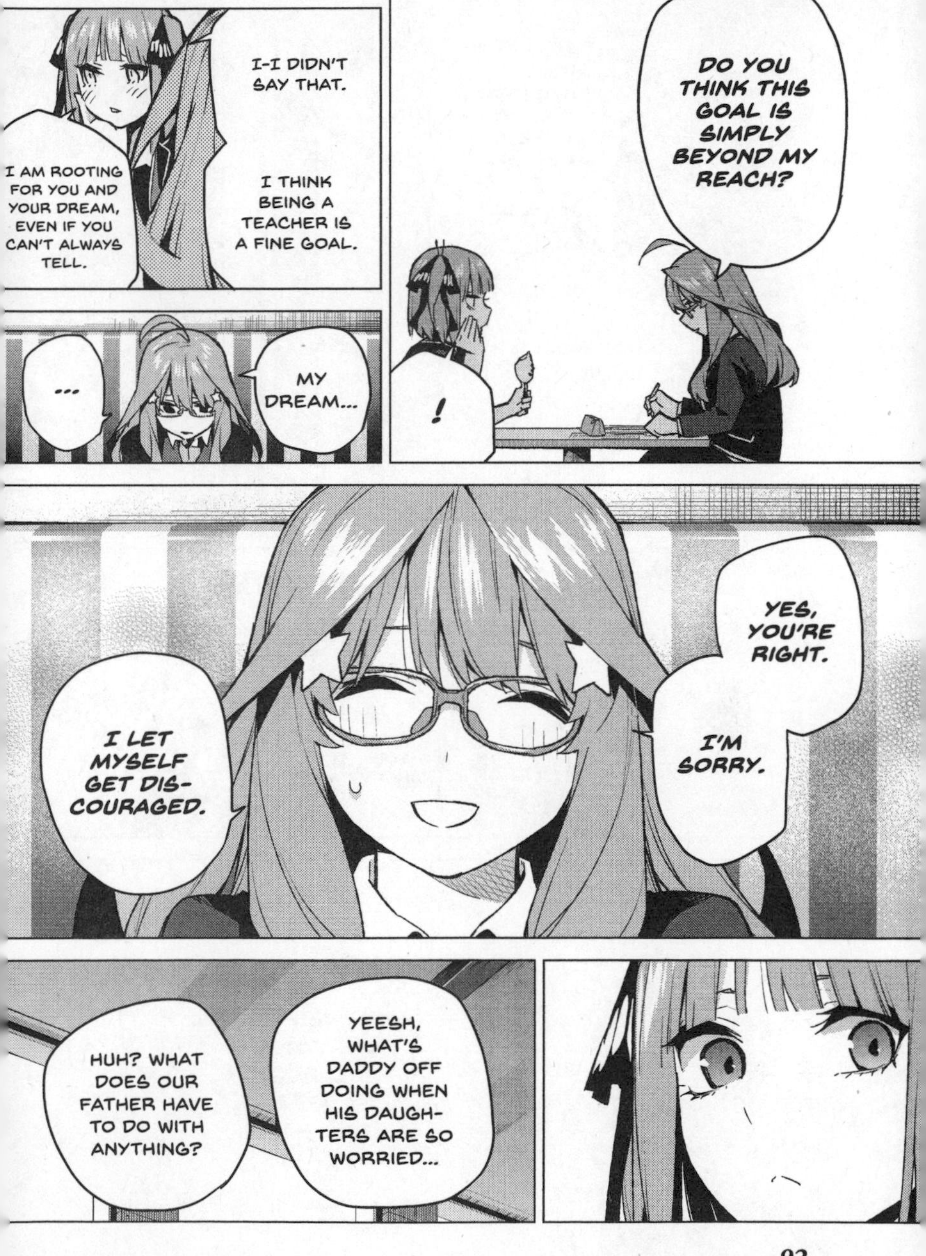
DO YOU THINK THIS GOAL IS SIMPLY BEYOND MY REACH?
!
I-I DIDN'T SAY THAT.
I THINK BEING A TEACHER IS A FINE GOAL.
I AM ROOTING FOR YOU AND YOUR DREAM, EVEN IF YOU CAN'T ALWAYS TELL.
MY DREAM...
...
YES, YOU'RE RIGHT.
I'M SORRY.
I LET MYSELF GET DISCOURAGED.
YEESH, WHAT'S DADDY OFF DOING WHEN HIS DAUGHTERS ARE SO WORRIED...
HUH? WHAT DOES OUR FATHER HAVE TO DO WITH ANYTHING?

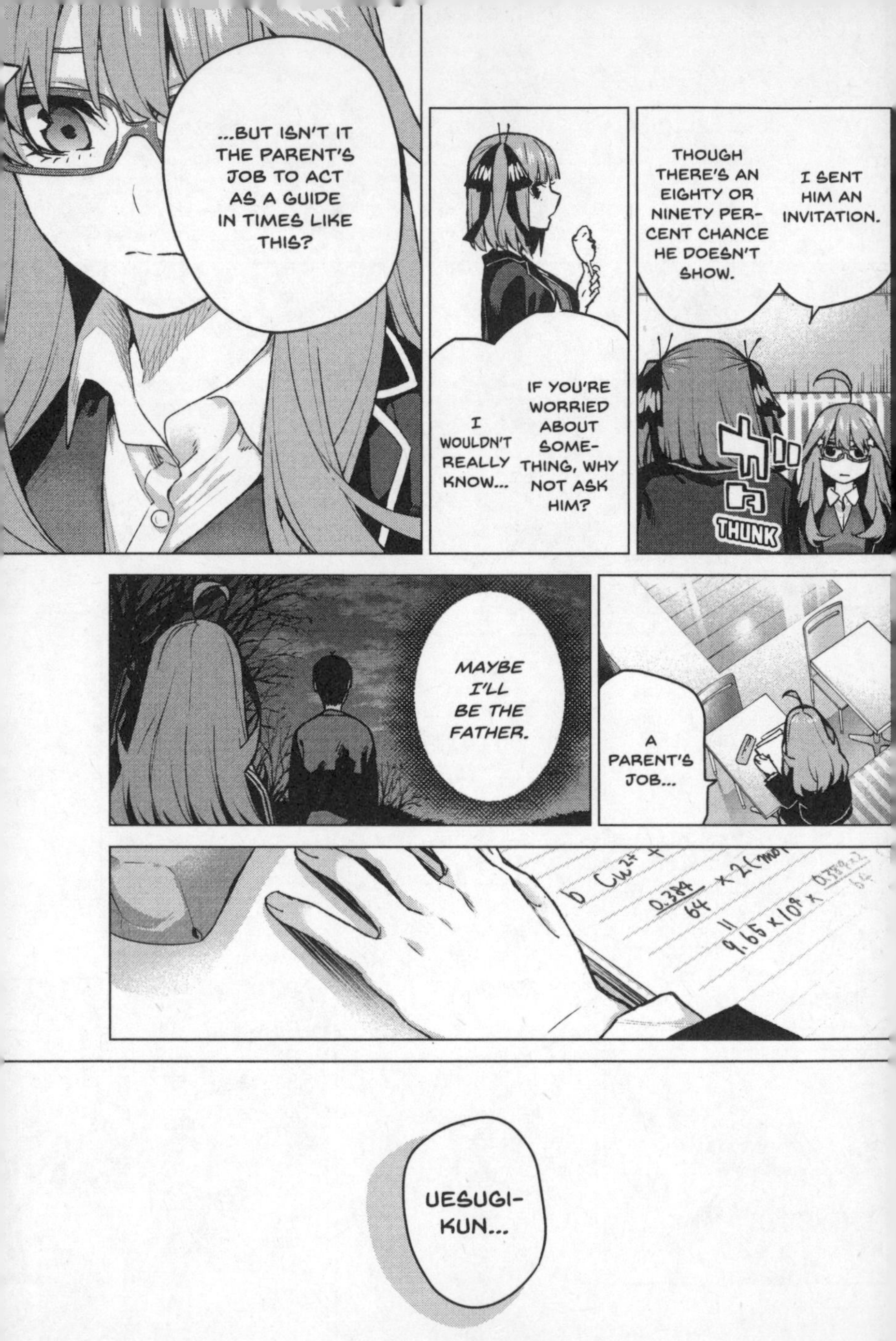
I SENT HIM AN INVITATION.
THOUGH THERE'S AN EIGHTY OR NINETY PERCENT CHANCE HE DOESN'T SHOW.
THUNK
IF YOU'RE WORRIED ABOUT SOMETHING, WHY NOT ASK HIM?
I WOULDN'T REALLY KNOW...
...BUT ISN'T IT THE PARENT'S JOB TO ACT AS A GUIDE IN TIMES LIKE THIS?
A PARENT'S JOB...
MAYBE I'LL BE THE FATHER.
UESUGI-KUN...

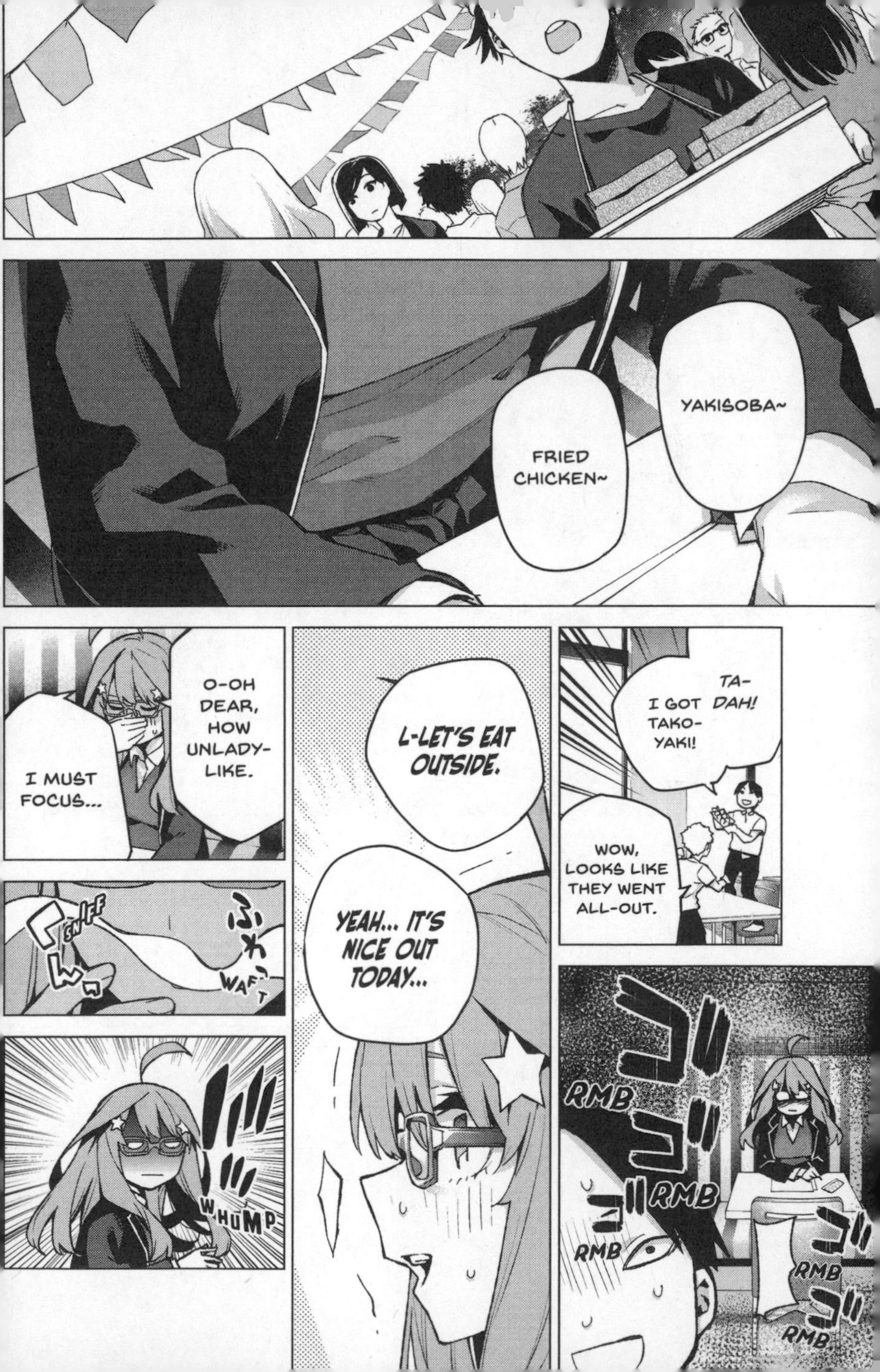

YAKISOBA~
FRIED CHICKEN~
TA-DAH!
I GOT TAKO-YAKI!
WOW, LOOKS LIKE THEY WENT ALL-OUT.
RMB
RMB
RMB
RMB
RMB
L-LET'S EAT OUTSIDE.
YEAH... IT'S NICE OUT TODAY...
O-OH DEAR, HOW UNLADY-LIKE.
I MUST FOCUS...
SNIFF
ふわ
WAFT
WHUMP

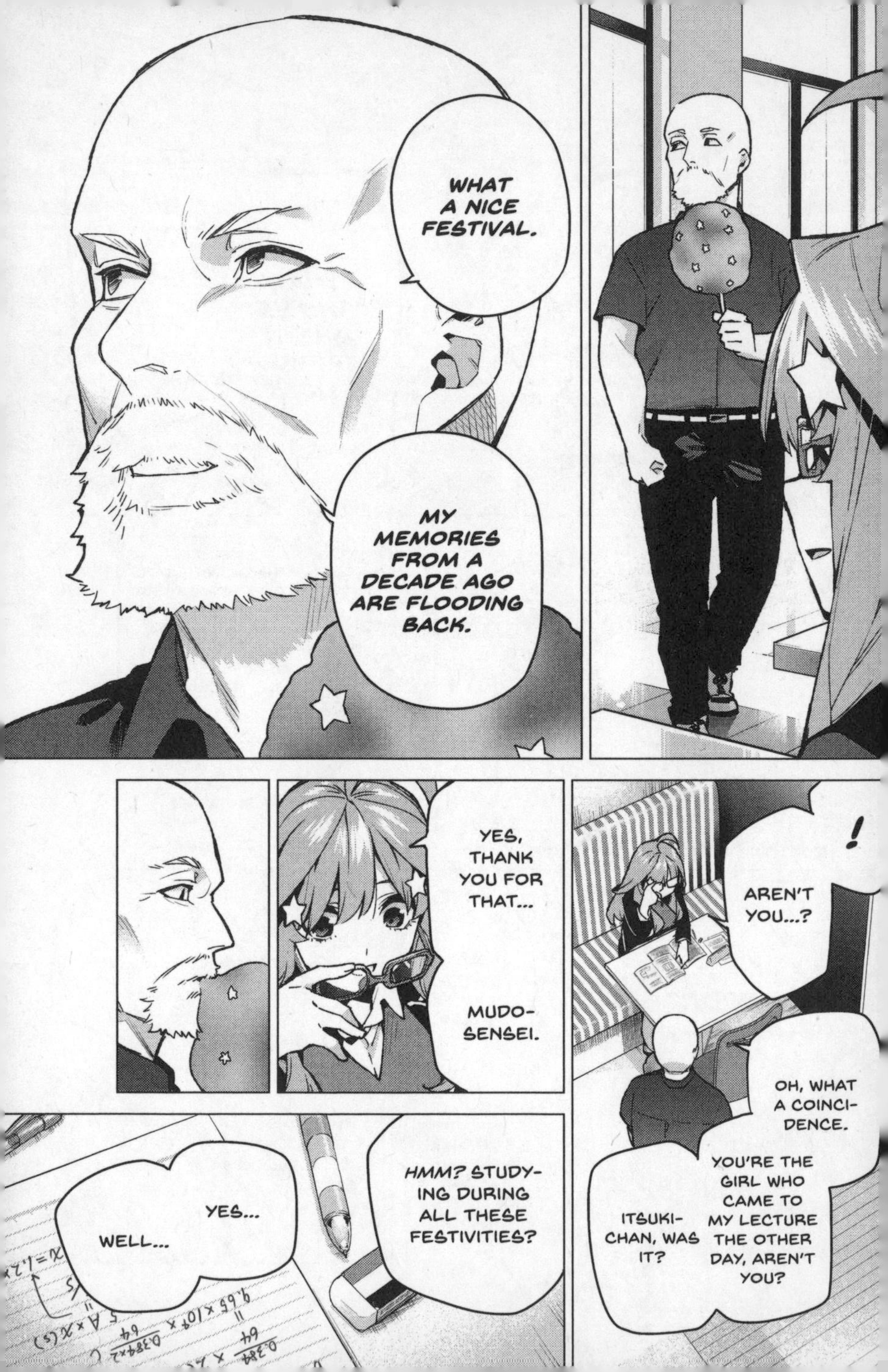
WHAT A NICE FESTIVAL.
MY MEMORIES FROM A DECADE AGO ARE FLOODING BACK.
!
AREN'T YOU...?
OH, WHAT A COINCIDENCE.
YOU'RE THE GIRL WHO CAME TO MY LECTURE THE OTHER DAY, AREN'T YOU?
ITSUKI-CHAN, WAS IT?
YES, THANK YOU FOR THAT...
MUDO-SENSEI.
HMM? STUDYING DURING ALL THESE FESTIVITIES?
YES...
WELL...

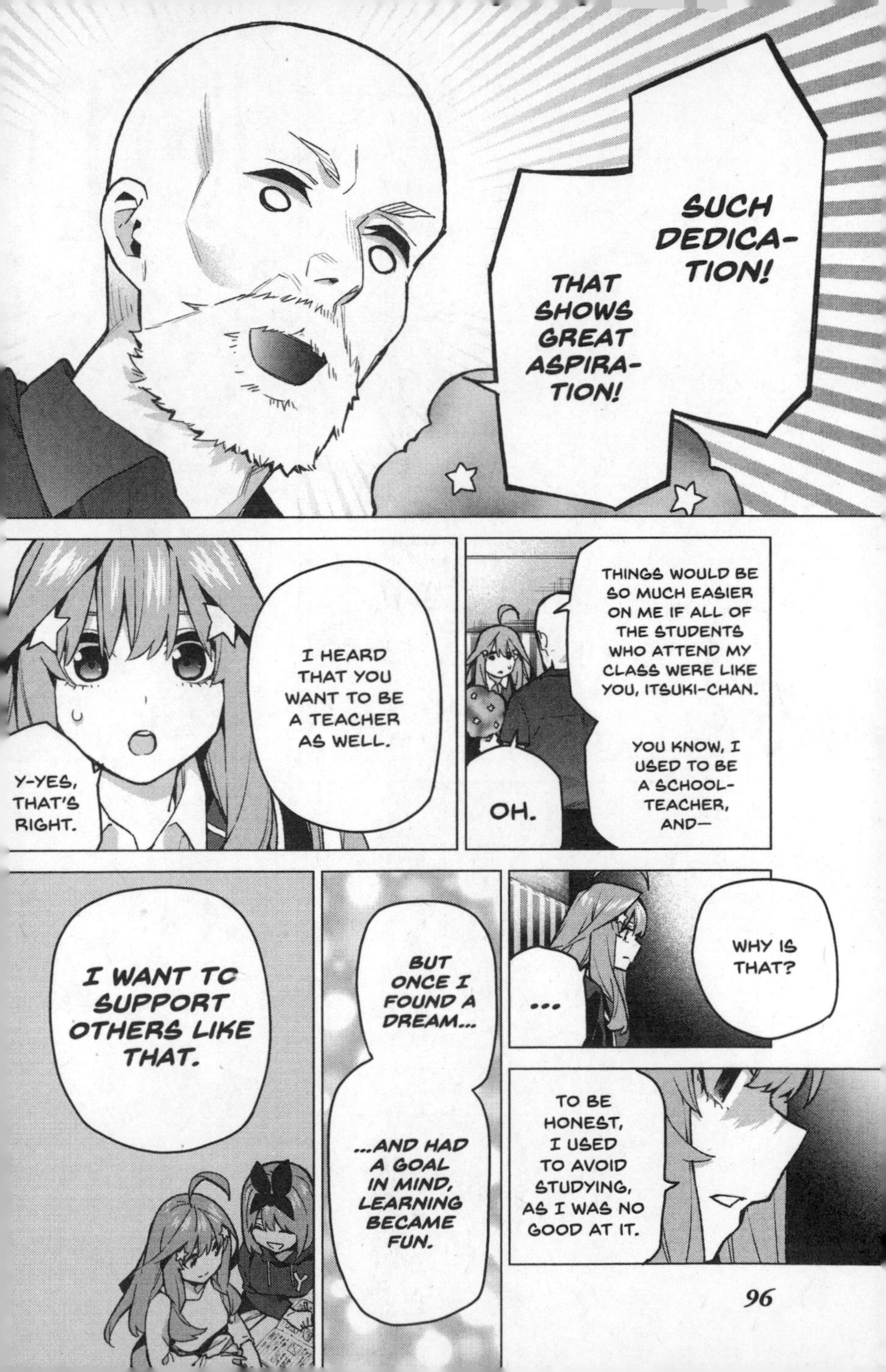
SUCH DEDICATION!
THAT SHOWS GREAT ASPIRATION!
THINGS WOULD BE SO MUCH EASIER ON ME IF ALL OF THE STUDENTS WHO ATTEND MY CLASS WERE LIKE YOU, ITSUKI-CHAN.
YOU KNOW, I USED TO BE A SCHOOL-TEACHER, AND—
OH.
I HEARD THAT YOU WANT TO BE A TEACHER AS WELL.
Y-YES, THAT'S RIGHT.
WHY IS THAT?
...
TO BE HONEST, I USED TO AVOID STUDYING, AS I WAS NO GOOD AT IT.
BUT ONCE I FOUND A DREAM...
...AND HAD A GOAL IN MIND, LEARNING BECAME FUN.
I WANT TO SUPPORT OTHERS LIKE THAT.

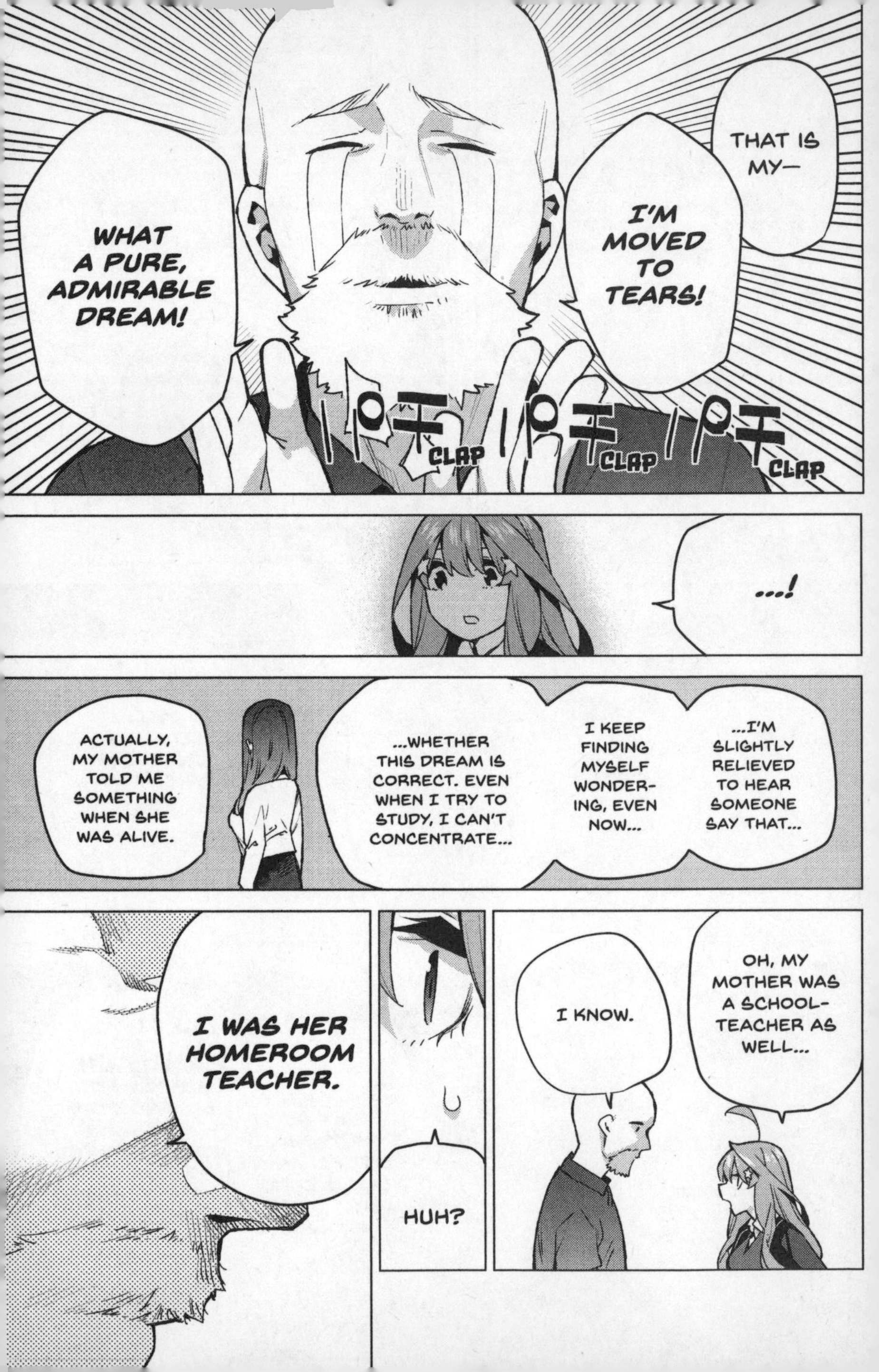

THAT IS MY—
I'M MOVED TO TEARS!
WHAT A PURE, ADMIRABLE DREAM!
CLAP
CLAP
CLAP
...!
...I'M SLIGHTLY RELIEVED TO HEAR SOMEONE SAY THAT...
I KEEP FINDING MYSELF WONDERING, EVEN NOW...
...WHETHER THIS DREAM IS CORRECT. EVEN WHEN I TRY TO STUDY, I CAN'T CONCENTRATE...
ACTUALLY, MY MOTHER TOLD ME SOMETHING WHEN SHE WAS ALIVE.
OH, MY MOTHER WAS A SCHOOL-TEACHER AS WELL...
I KNOW.
HUH?
I WAS HER HOMEROOM TEACHER.

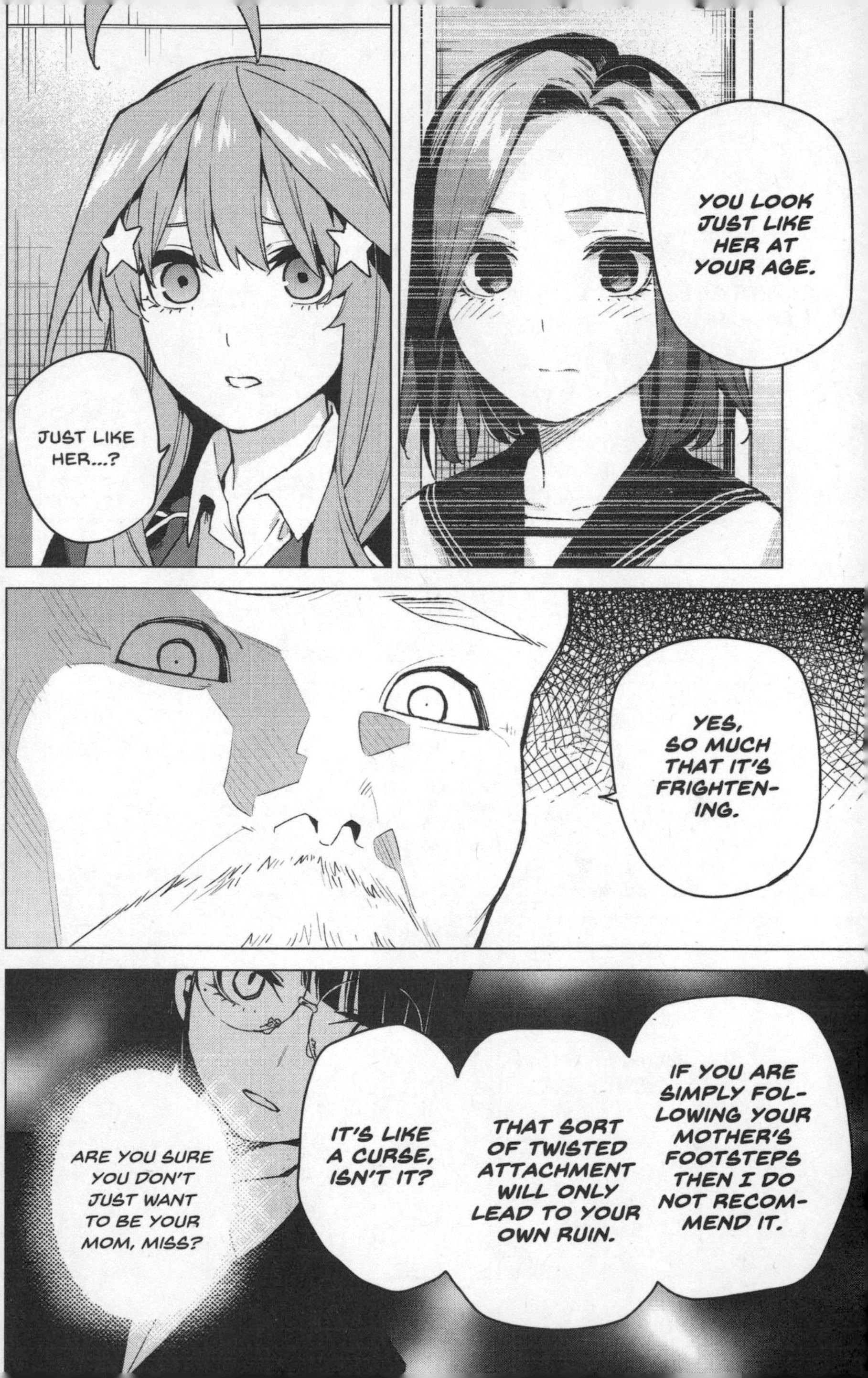
YOU LOOK JUST LIKE HER AT YOUR AGE.
JUST LIKE HER...?
YES, SO MUCH THAT IT'S FRIGHTEN-ING.
IF YOU ARE SIMPLY FOL-LOWING YOUR MOTHER'S FOOTSTEPS THEN I DO NOT RECOM-MEND IT.
THAT SORT OF TWISTED ATTACHMENT WILL ONLY LEAD TO YOUR OWN RUIN.
IT'S LIKE A CURSE, ISN'T IT?
ARE YOU SURE YOU DON'T JUST WANT TO BE YOUR MOM, MISS?

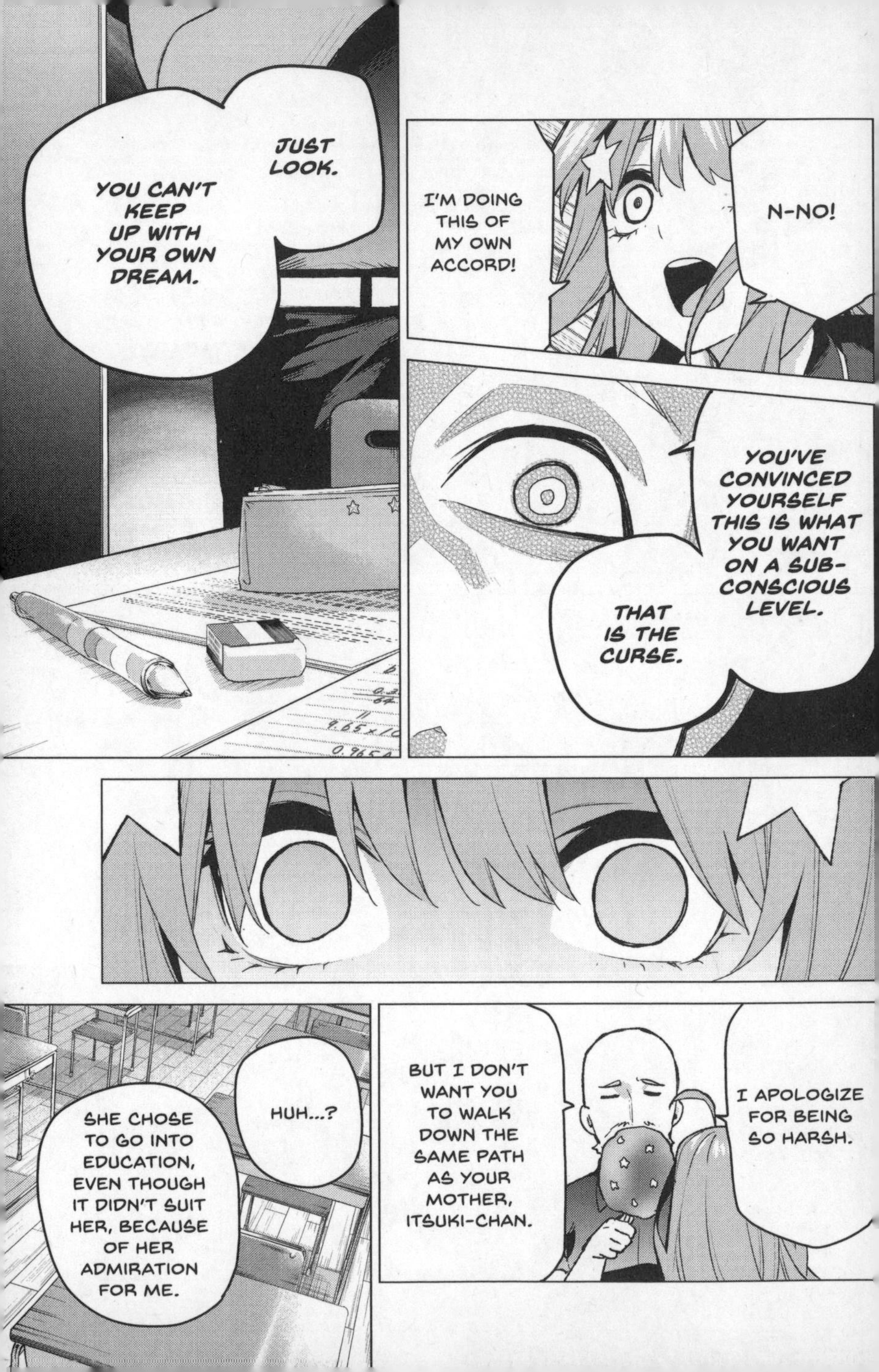
N-NO!
I'M DOING THIS OF MY OWN ACCORD!
YOU'VE CONVINCED YOURSELF THIS IS WHAT YOU WANT ON A SUB-CONSCIOUS LEVEL.
THAT IS THE CURSE.
JUST LOOK.
YOU CAN'T KEEP UP WITH YOUR OWN DREAM.
I APOLOGIZE FOR BEING SO HARSH.
BUT I DON'T WANT YOU TO WALK DOWN THE SAME PATH AS YOUR MOTHER, ITSUKI-CHAN.
HUH...?
SHE CHOSE TO GO INTO EDUCATION, EVEN THOUGH IT DIDN'T SUIT HER, BECAUSE OF HER ADMIRATION FOR ME.

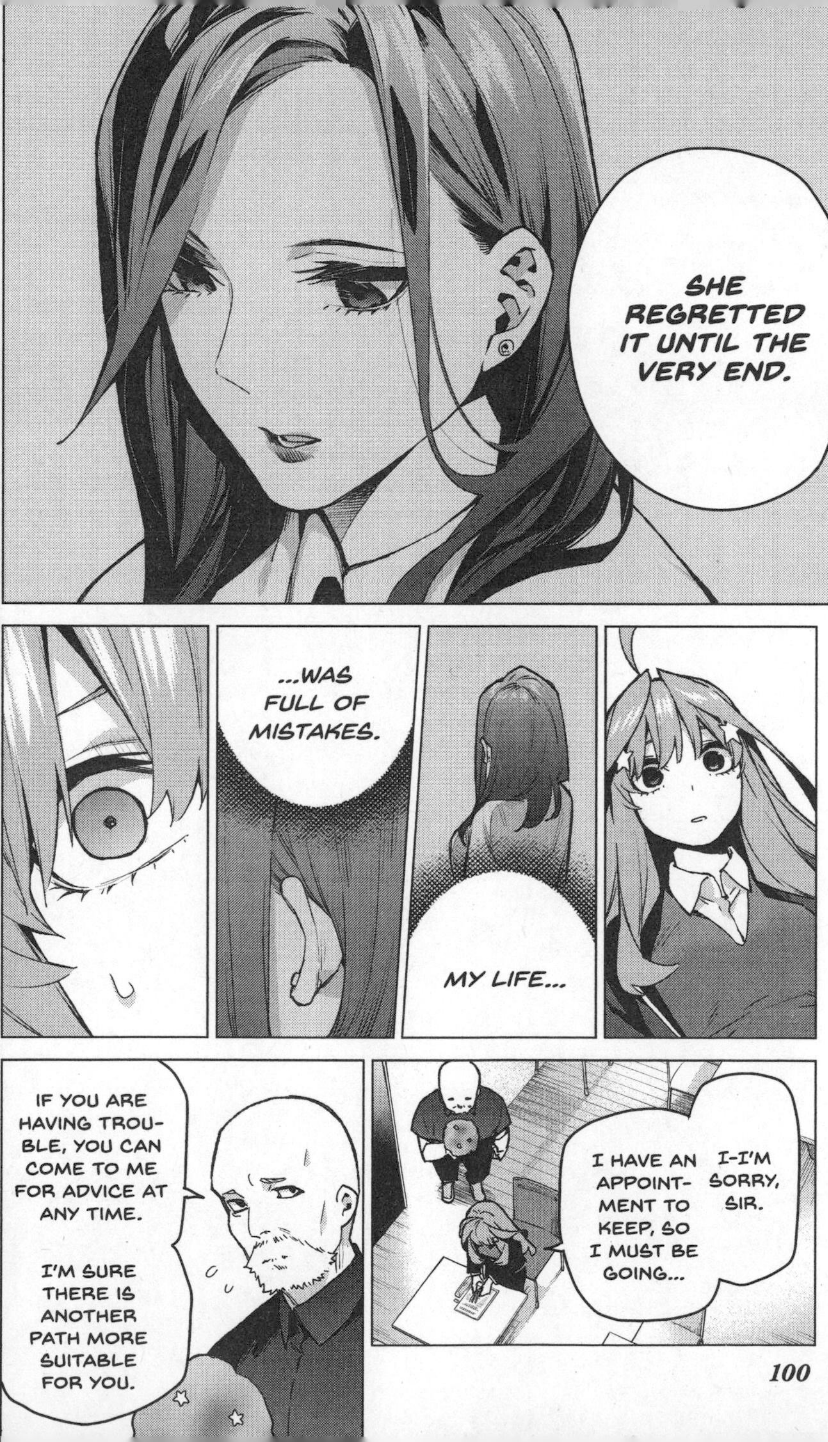
SHE REGRETTED IT UNTIL THE VERY END.
MY LIFE...
...WAS FULL OF MISTAKES.
I-I'M SORRY, SIR.
I HAVE AN APPOINT-MENT TO KEEP, SO I MUST BE GOING...
IF YOU ARE HAVING TROU-BLE, YOU CAN COME TO ME FOR ADVICE AT ANY TIME.
I'M SURE THERE IS ANOTHER PATH MORE SUITABLE FOR YOU.

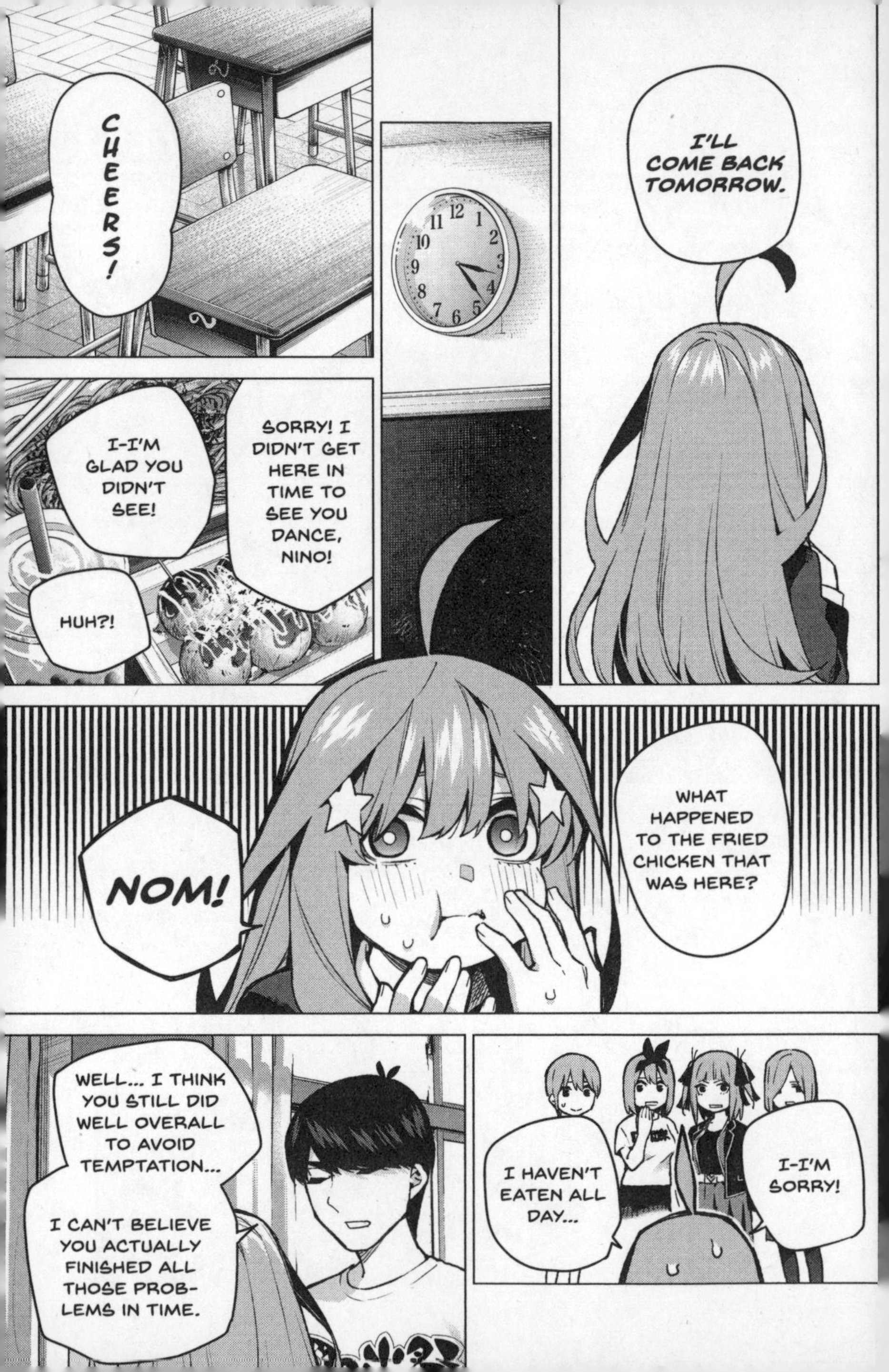
I'LL COME BACK TOMORROW.
CHEERS!
SORRY! I DIDN'T GET HERE IN TIME TO SEE YOU DANCE, NINO!
I-I'M GLAD YOU DIDN'T SEE!
HUH?!
WHAT HAPPENED TO THE FRIED CHICKEN THAT WAS HERE?
NOM!
I-I'M SORRY!
I HAVEN'T EATEN ALL DAY...
WELL... I THINK YOU STILL DID WELL OVERALL TO AVOID TEMPTATION...
I CAN'T BELIEVE YOU ACTUALLY FINISHED ALL THOSE PROB-LEMS IN TIME.

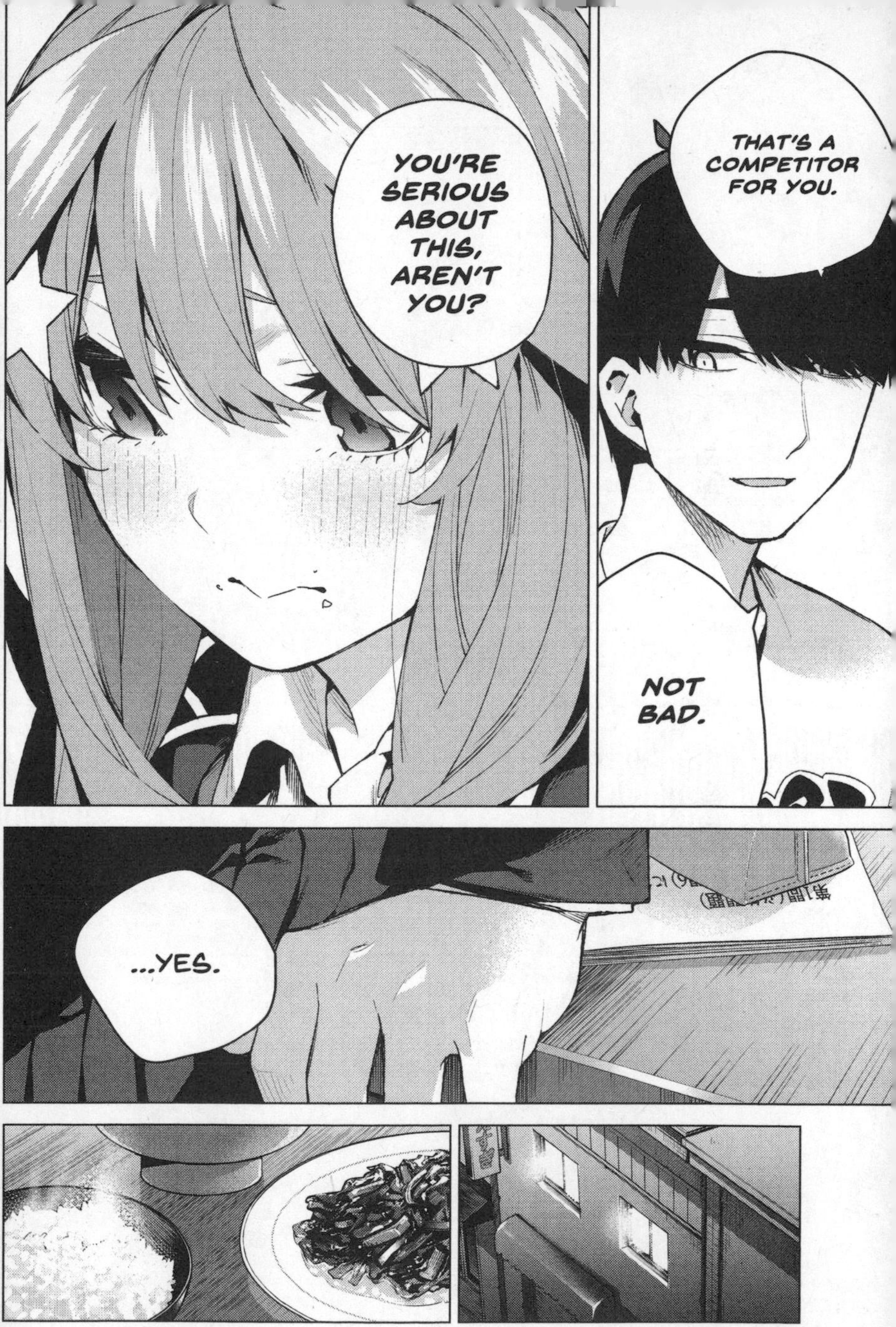
THAT'S A COMPETITOR FOR YOU.
NOT BAD.
YOU'RE SERIOUS ABOUT THIS, AREN'T YOU?
...YES.

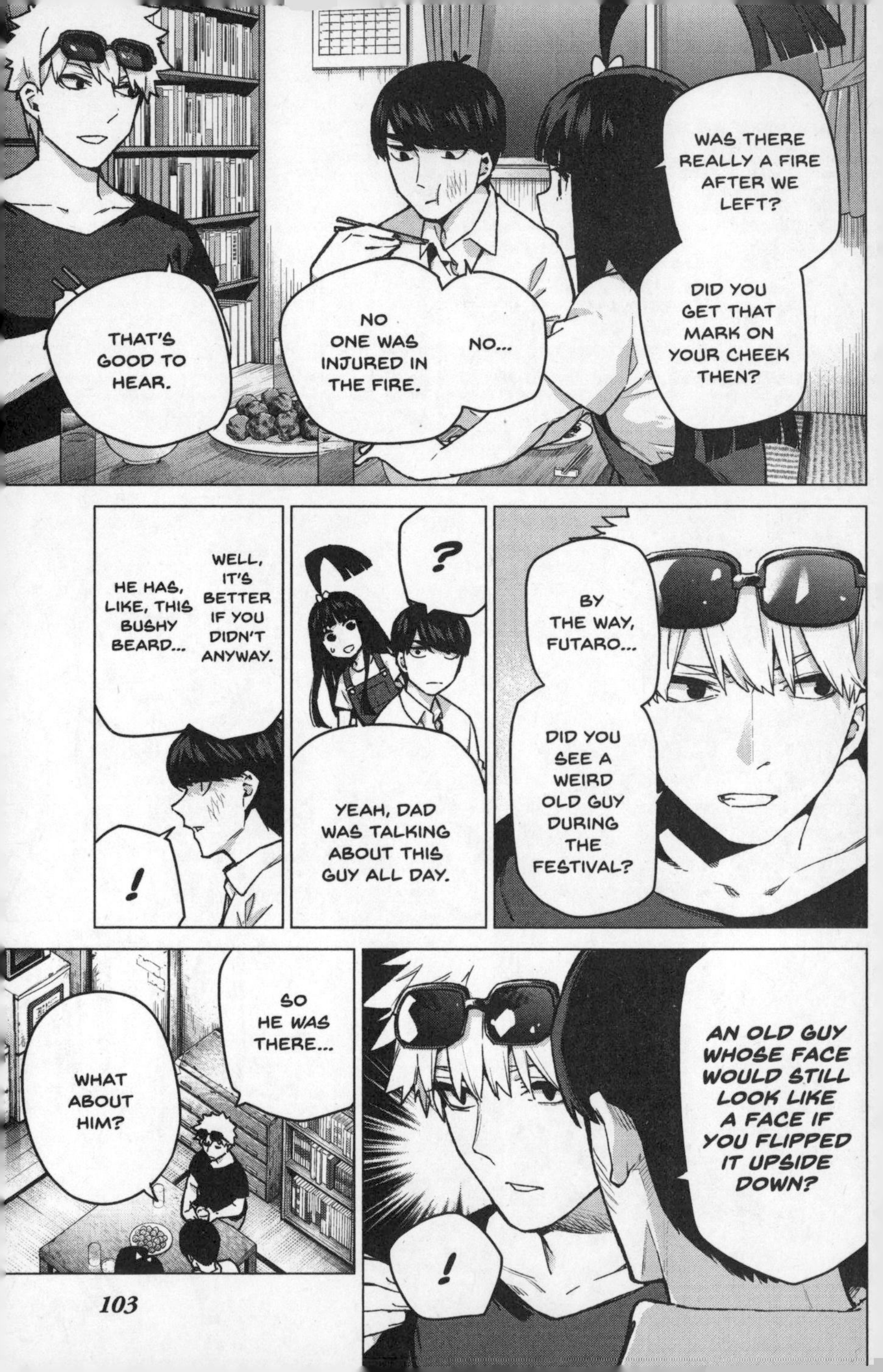
WAS THERE REALLY A FIRE AFTER WE LEFT?
DID YOU GET THAT MARK ON YOUR CHEEK THEN?
NO...
NO ONE WAS INJURED IN THE FIRE.
THAT'S GOOD TO HEAR.
BY THE WAY, FUTARO...
DID YOU SEE A WEIRD OLD GUY DURING THE FESTIVAL?
?
YEAH, DAD WAS TALKING ABOUT THIS GUY ALL DAY.
WELL, IT'S BETTER IF YOU DIDN'T ANYWAY.
HE HAS, LIKE, THIS BUSHY BEARD...
!
AN OLD GUY WHOSE FACE WOULD STILL LOOK LIKE A FACE IF YOU FLIPPED IT UPSIDE DOWN?
!
SO HE WAS THERE...
WHAT ABOUT HIM?

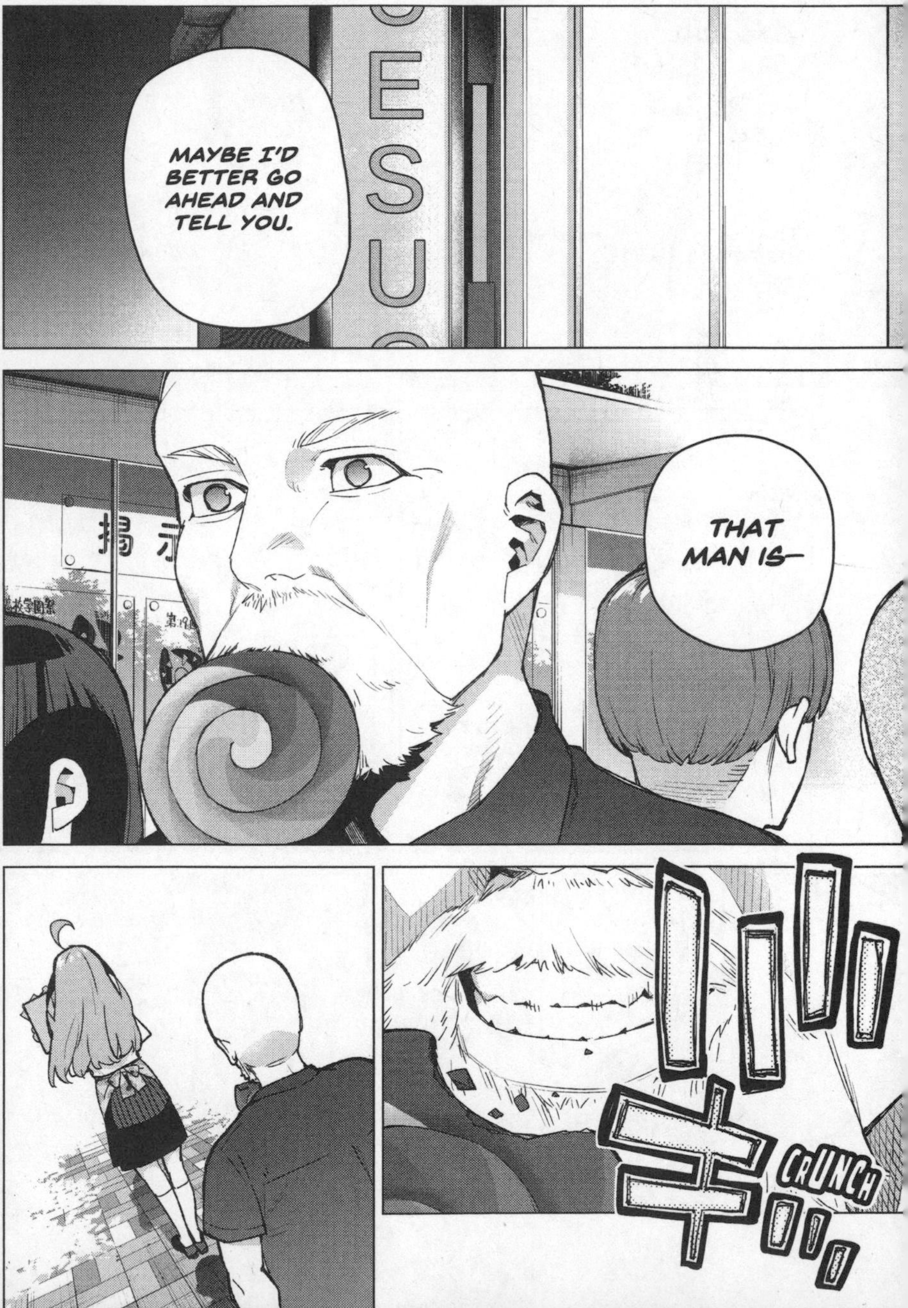
MAYBE I'D BETTER GO AHEAD AND TELL YOU.
THAT MAN IS—
CRUNCH

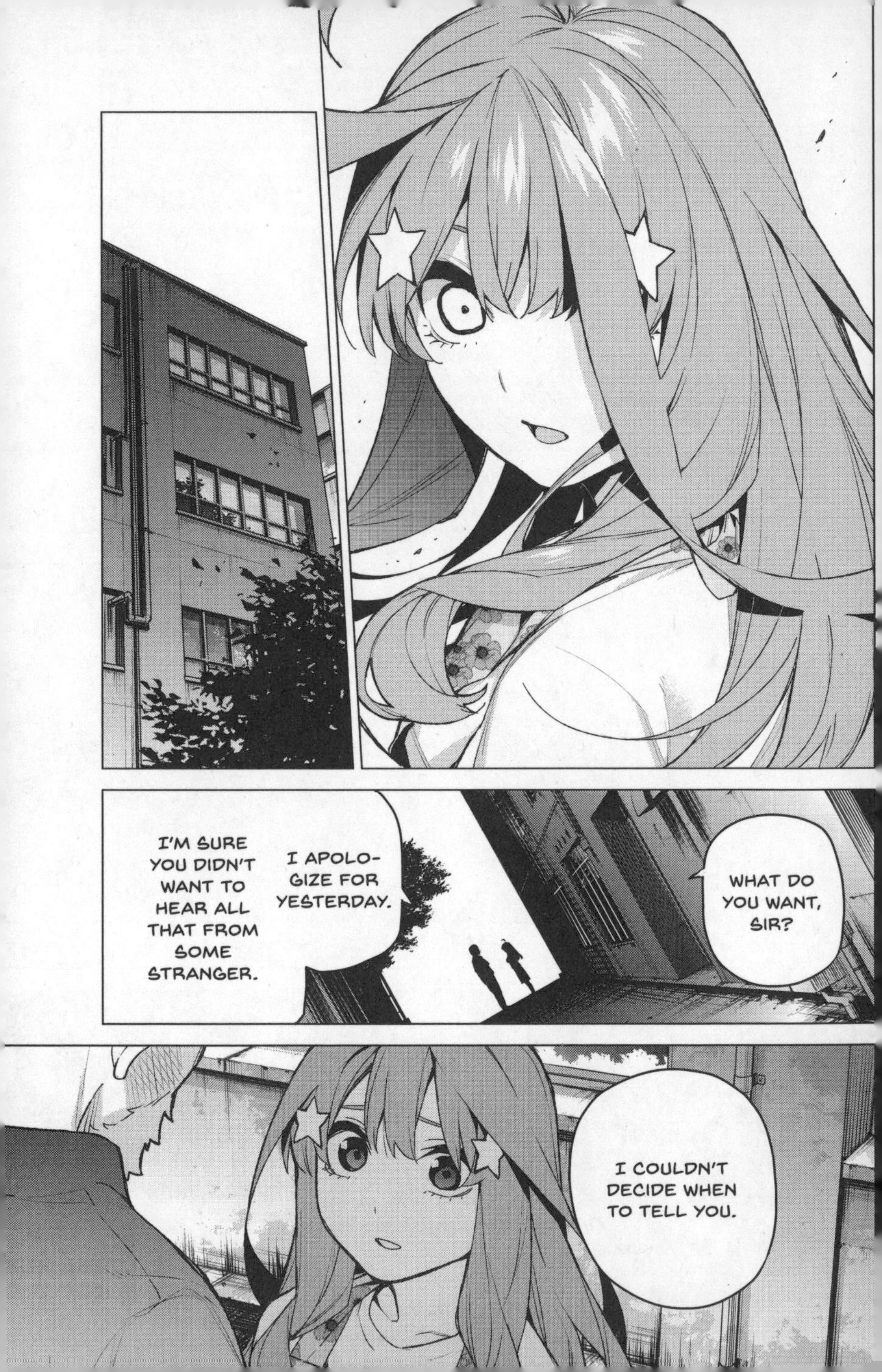
WHAT DO YOU WANT, SIR?
I APOLOGIZE FOR YESTERDAY.
I'M SURE YOU DIDN'T WANT TO HEAR ALL THAT FROM SOME STRANGER.
I COULDN'T DECIDE WHEN TO TELL YOU.

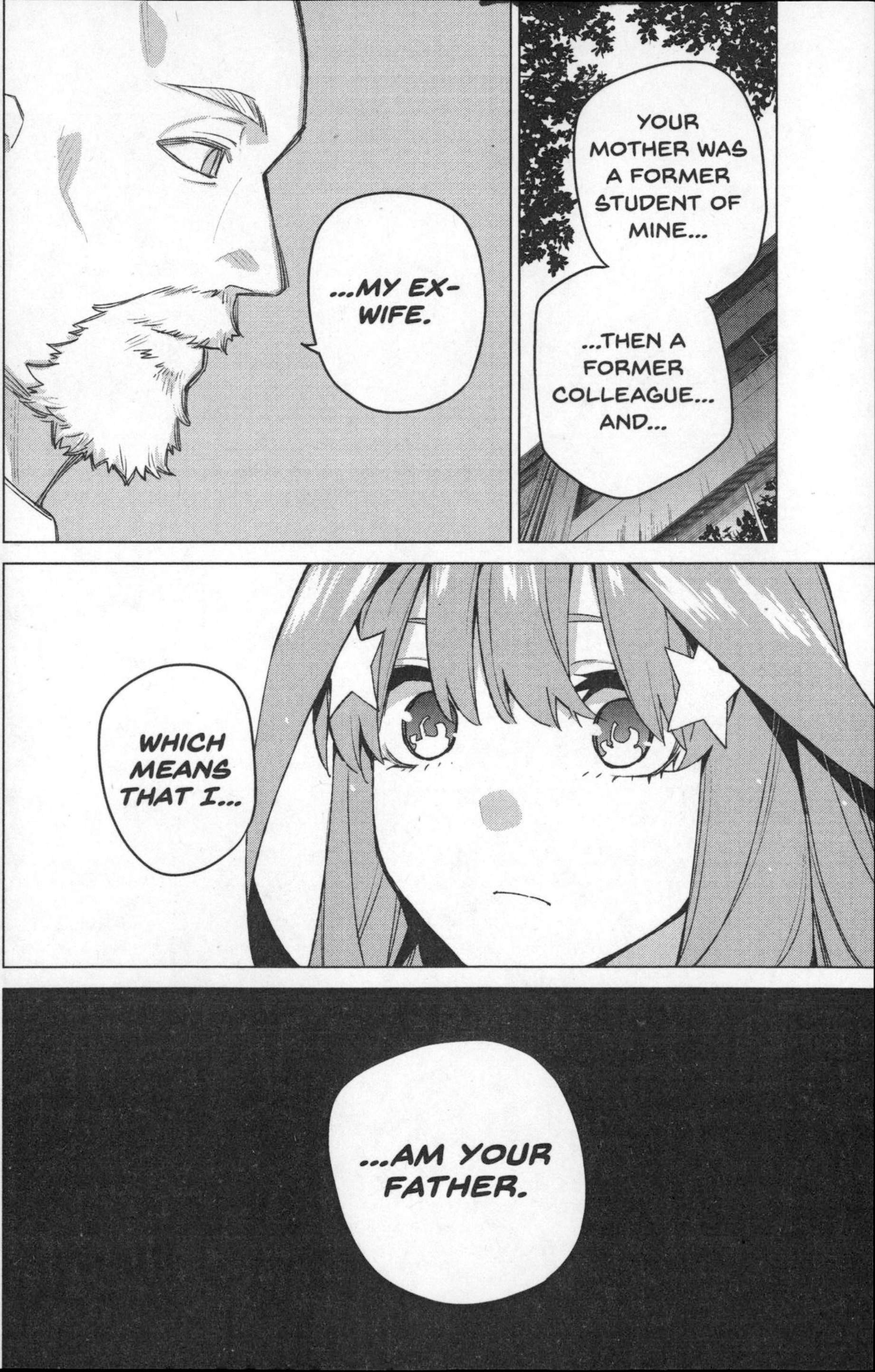
YOUR MOTHER WAS A FORMER STUDENT OF MINE...
...THEN A FORMER COLLEAGUE... AND...
...MY EX-WIFE.
WHICH MEANS THAT I...
...AM YOUR FATHER.

CHAPTER 110 IF THE FINAL FESTIVAL WAS ITSUKI'S ②

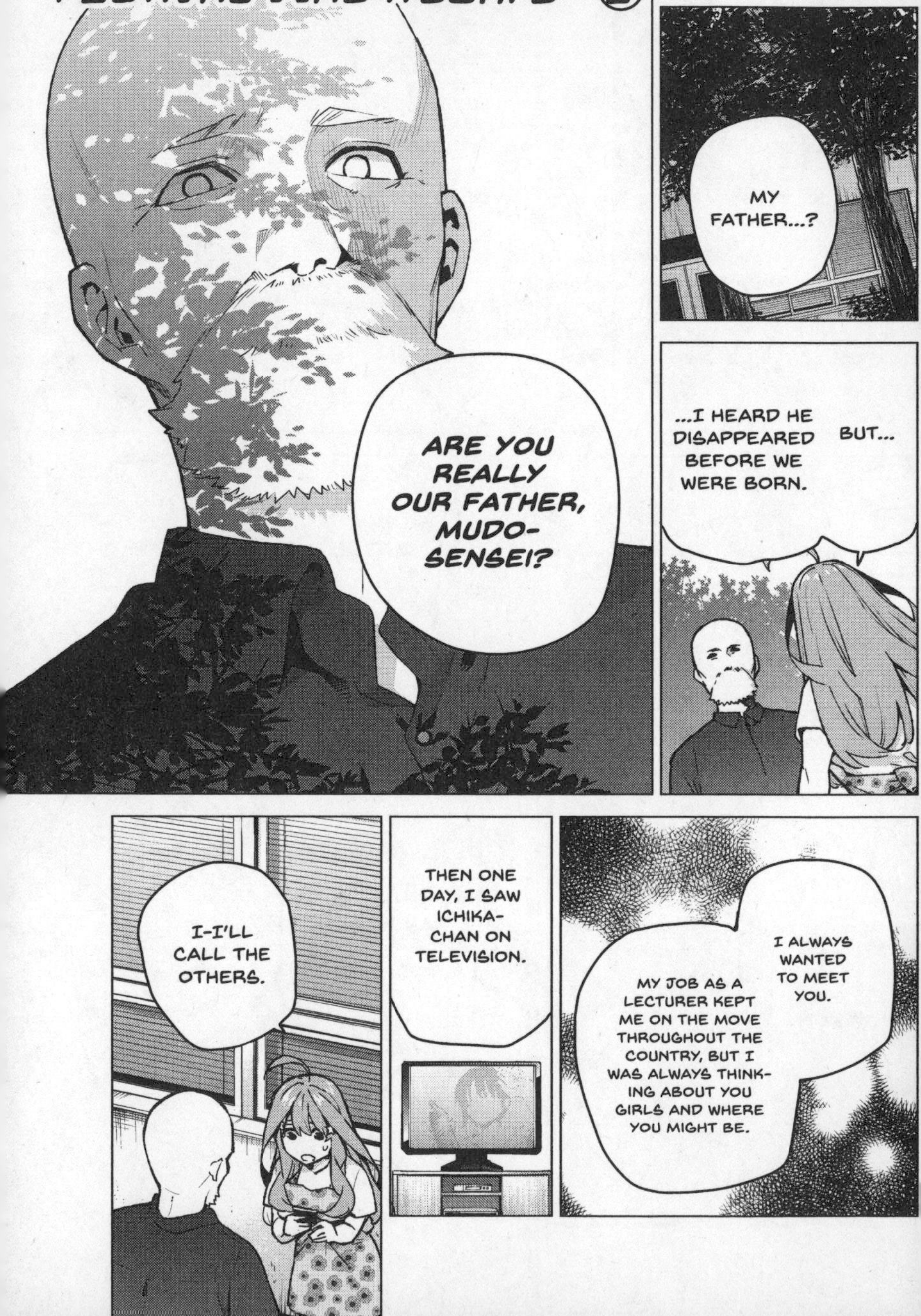
MY FATHER...?
BUT...
...I HEARD HE DISAPPEARED BEFORE WE WERE BORN.
ARE YOU REALLY OUR FATHER, MUDO-SENSEI?
I ALWAYS WANTED TO MEET YOU.
MY JOB AS A LECTURER KEPT ME ON THE MOVE THROUGHOUT THE COUNTRY, BUT I WAS ALWAYS THINKING ABOUT YOU GIRLS AND WHERE YOU MIGHT BE.
THEN ONE DAY, I SAW ICHIKA-CHAN ON TELEVISION.
I-I'LL CALL THE OTHERS.

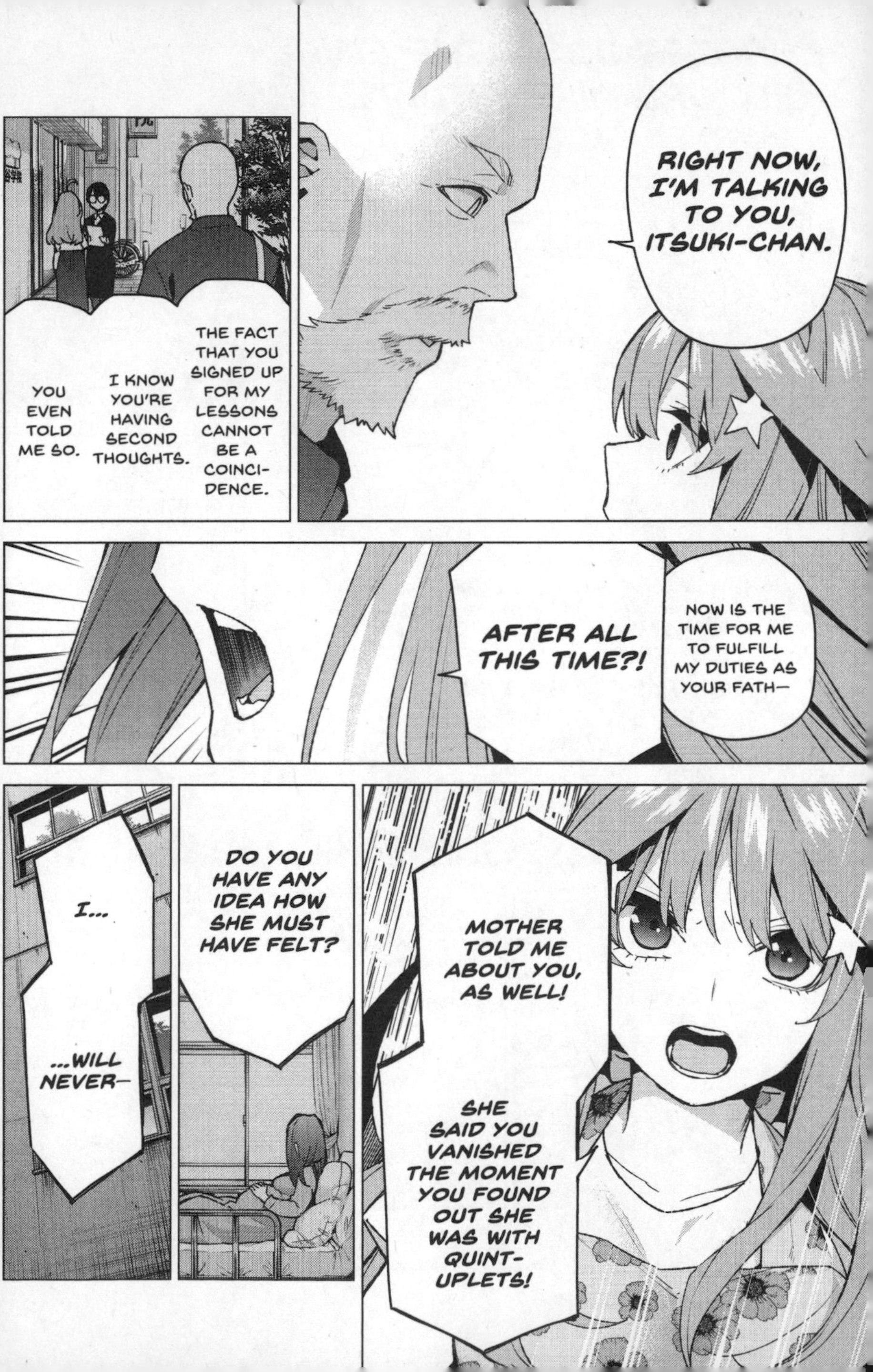
RIGHT NOW, I'M TALKING TO YOU, ITSUKI-CHAN.
THE FACT THAT YOU SIGNED UP FOR MY LESSONS CANNOT BE A COINCIDENCE.
I KNOW YOU'RE HAVING SECOND THOUGHTS.
YOU EVEN TOLD ME SO.
NOW IS THE TIME FOR ME TO FULFILL MY DUTIES AS YOUR FATH—
AFTER ALL THIS TIME?!
MOTHER TOLD ME ABOUT YOU, AS WELL!
SHE SAID YOU VANISHED THE MOMENT YOU FOUND OUT SHE WAS WITH QUINT-UPLETS!
DO YOU HAVE ANY IDEA HOW SHE MUST HAVE FELT?
I...
...WILL NEVER—

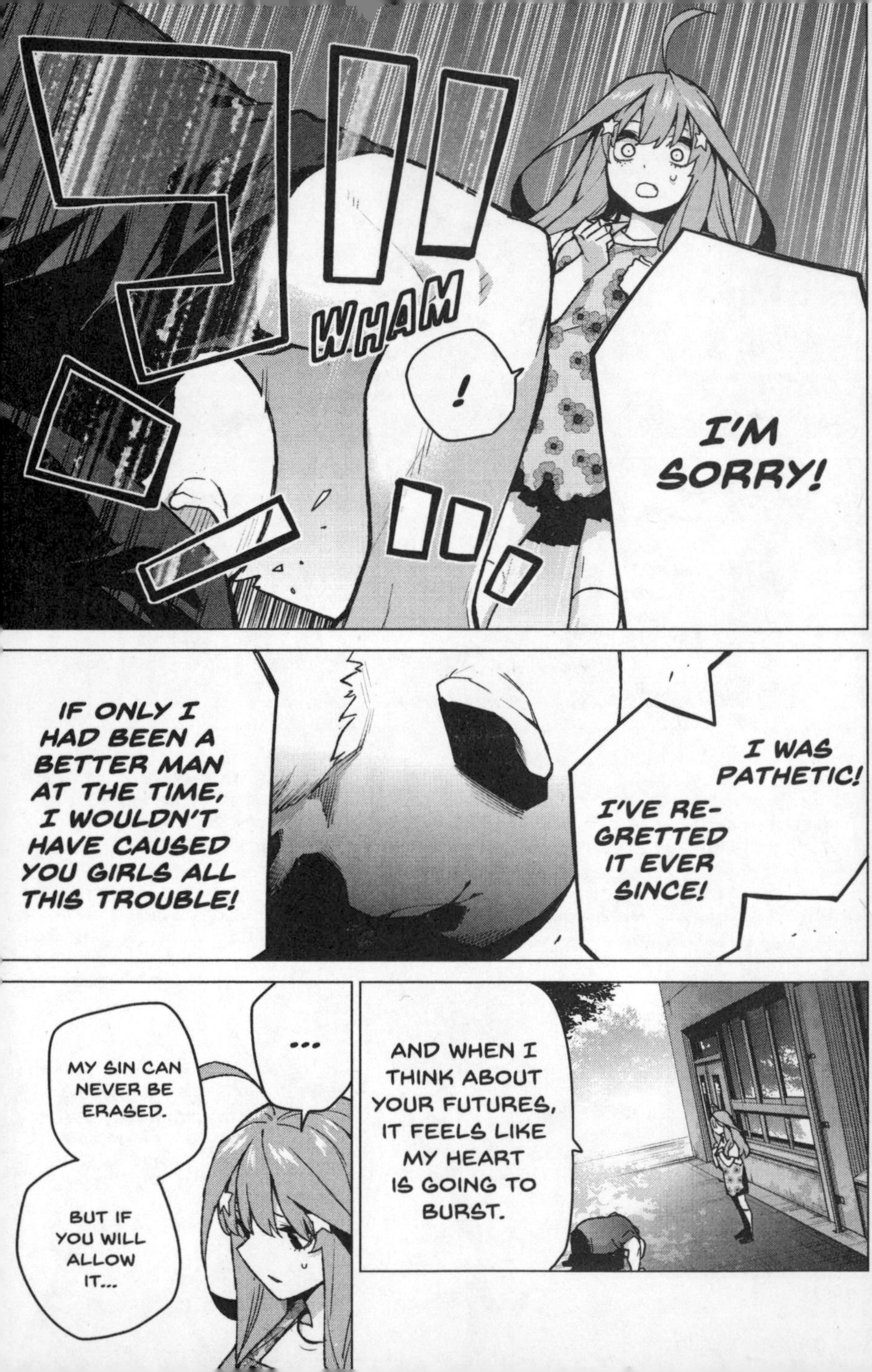
I'M SORRY!
WHAM
!
I WAS PATHETIC!
I'VE RE-GRETTED IT EVER SINCE!
IF ONLY I HAD BEEN A BETTER MAN AT THE TIME, I WOULDN'T HAVE CAUSED YOU GIRLS ALL THIS TROUBLE!
AND WHEN I THINK ABOUT YOUR FUTURES, IT FEELS LIKE MY HEART IS GOING TO BURST.
...
MY SIN CAN NEVER BE ERASED.
BUT IF YOU WILL ALLOW IT...

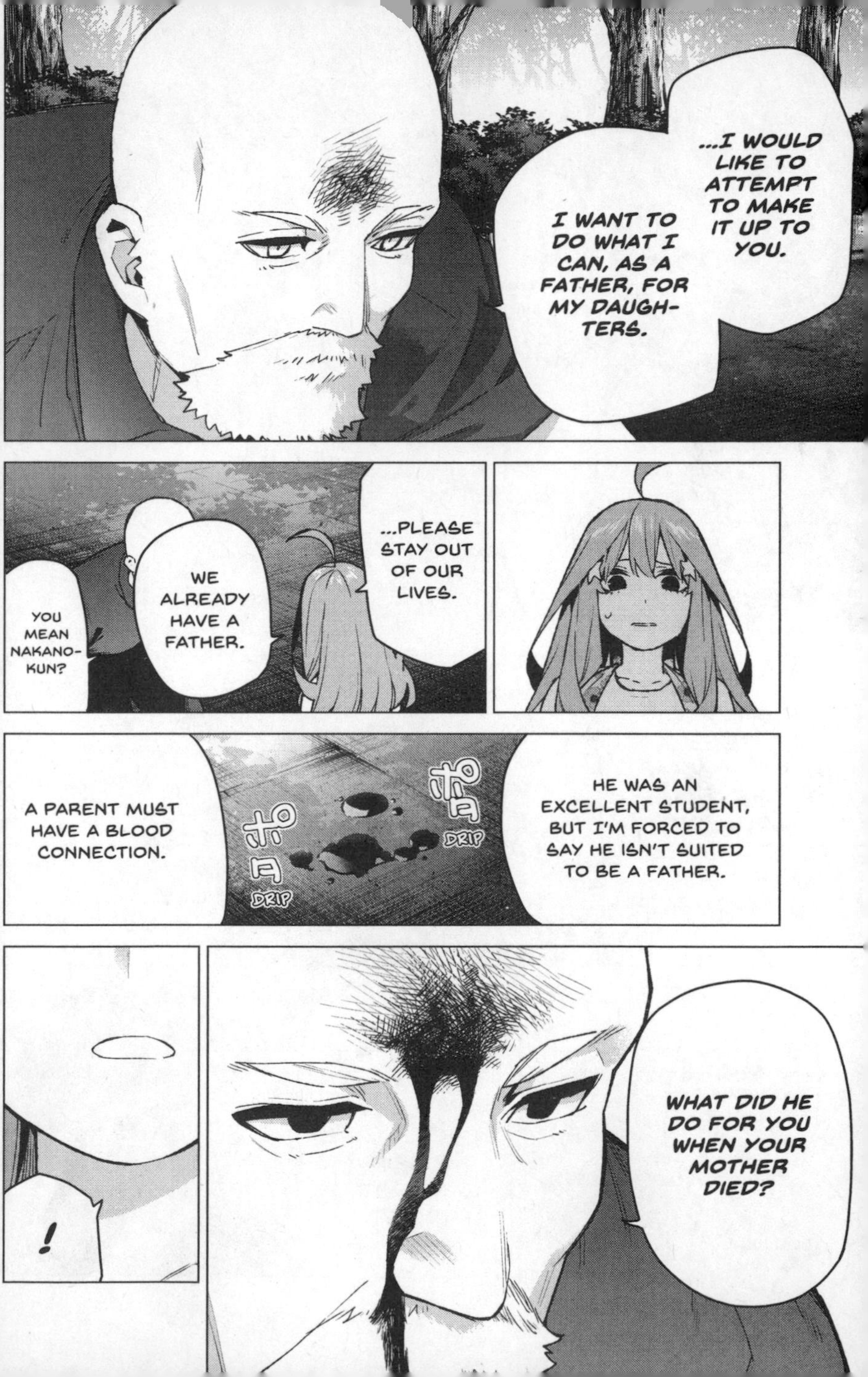
...I WOULD LIKE TO ATTEMPT TO MAKE IT UP TO YOU.
I WANT TO DO WHAT I CAN, AS A FATHER, FOR MY DAUGHTERS.
...PLEASE STAY OUT OF OUR LIVES.
WE ALREADY HAVE A FATHER.
YOU MEAN NAKANO-KUN?
HE WAS AN EXCELLENT STUDENT, BUT I'M FORCED TO SAY HE ISN'T SUITED TO BE A FATHER.
ポタ DRIP
ポタ DRIP
A PARENT MUST HAVE A BLOOD CONNECTION.
WHAT DID HE DO FOR YOU WHEN YOUR MOTHER DIED?
!

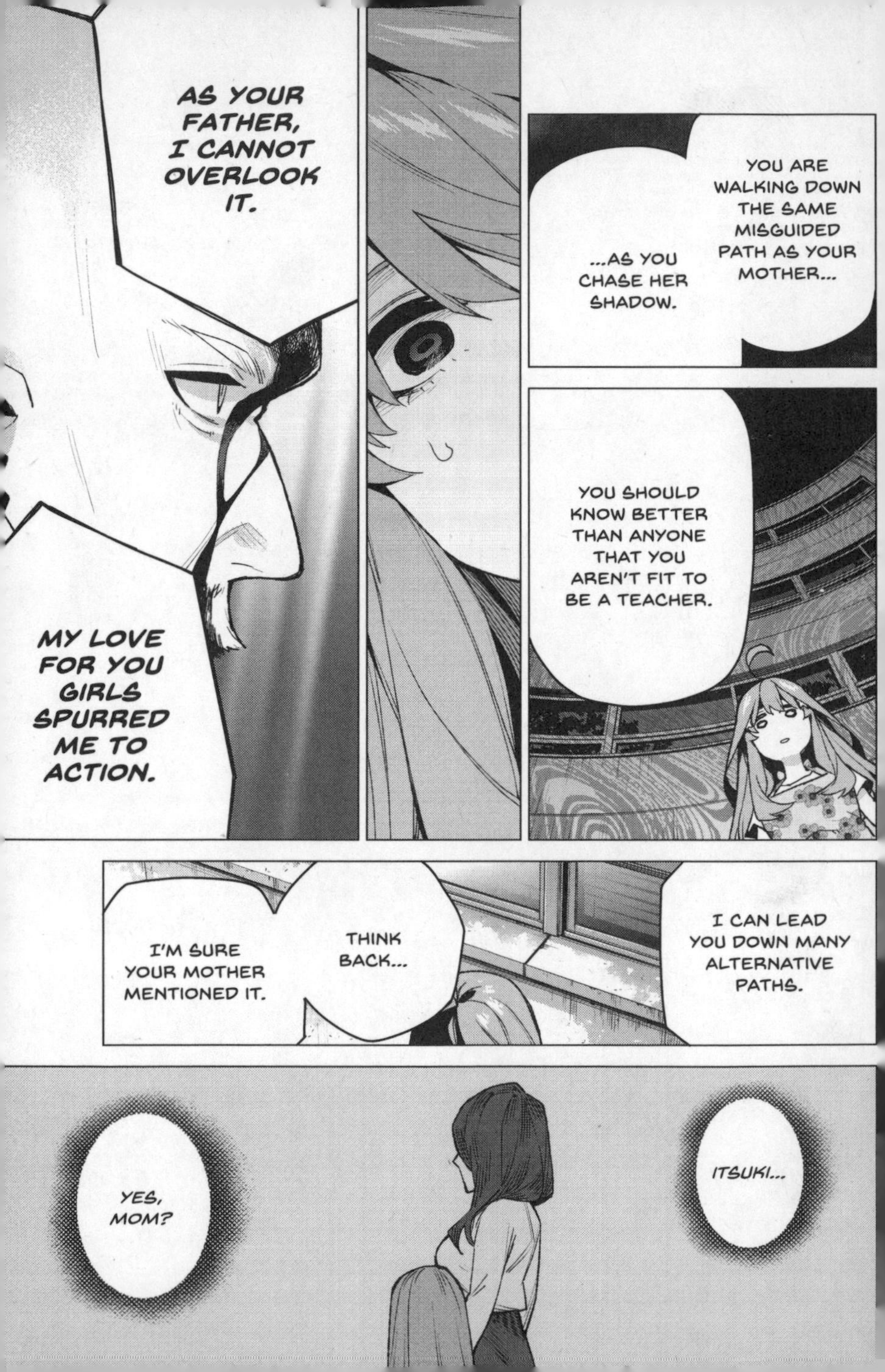
YOU ARE WALKING DOWN THE SAME MISGUIDED PATH AS YOUR MOTHER...
...AS YOU CHASE HER SHADOW.
YOU SHOULD KNOW BETTER THAN ANYONE THAT YOU AREN'T FIT TO BE A TEACHER.
AS YOUR FATHER, I CANNOT OVERLOOK IT.
MY LOVE FOR YOU GIRLS SPURRED ME TO ACTION.
I CAN LEAD YOU DOWN MANY ALTERNATIVE PATHS.
THINK BACK...
I'M SURE YOUR MOTHER MENTIONED IT.
ITSUKI...
YES, MOM?

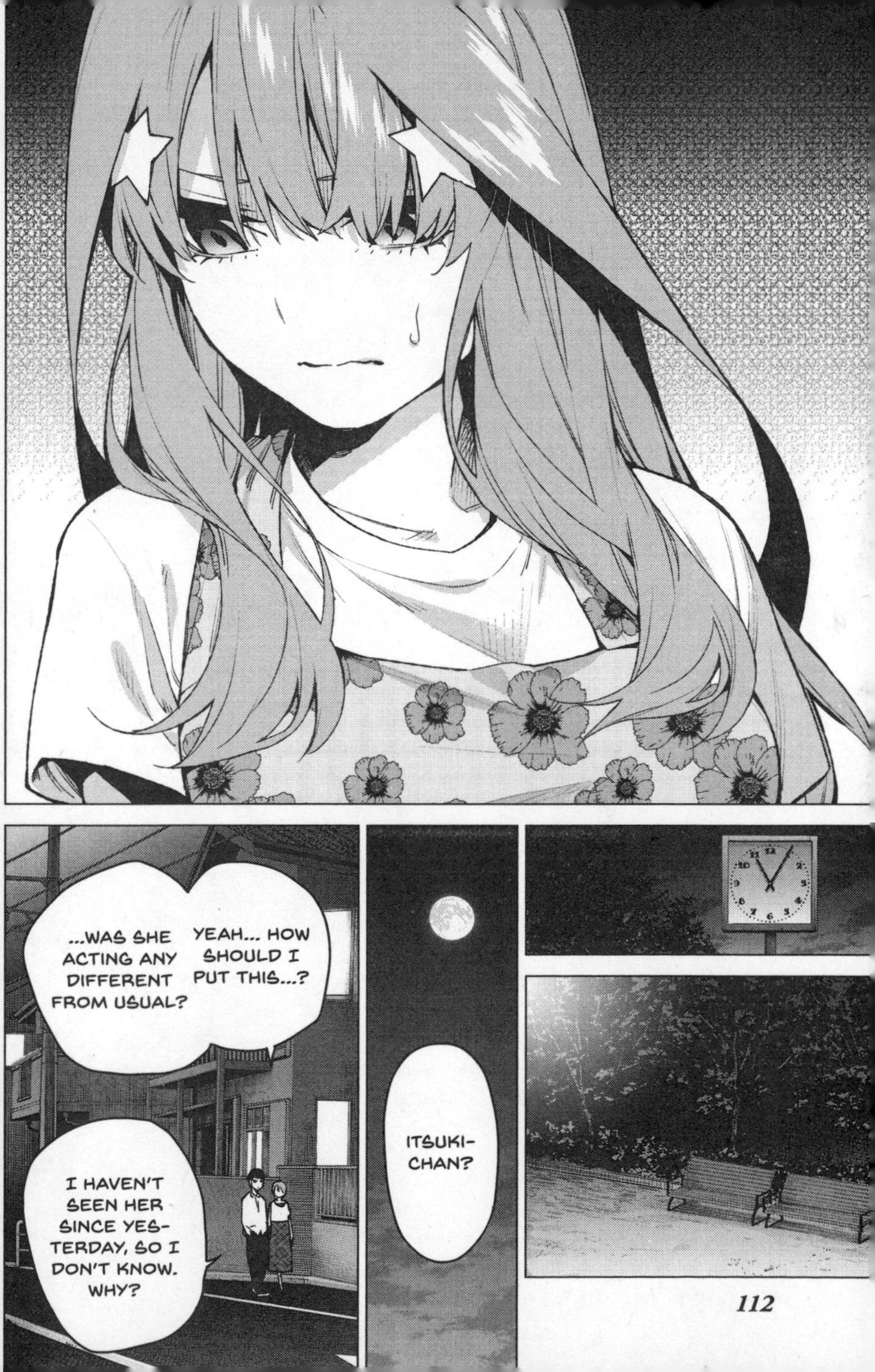
ITSUKI-CHAN?
YEAH... HOW SHOULD I PUT THIS...?
...WAS SHE ACTING ANY DIFFERENT FROM USUAL?
I HAVEN'T SEEN HER SINCE YES-TERDAY, SO I DON'T KNOW. WHY?

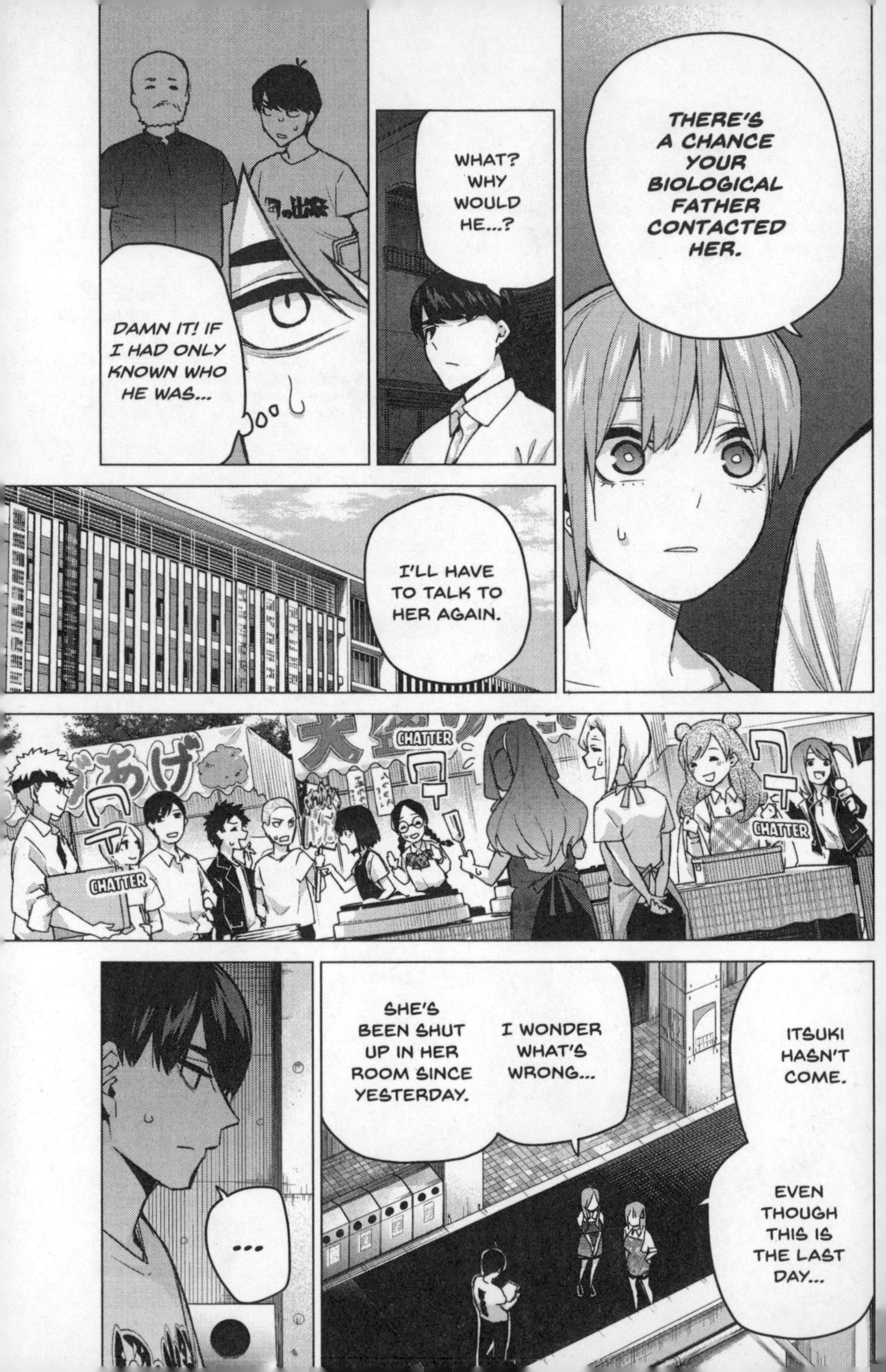
THERE'S A CHANCE YOUR BIOLOGICAL FATHER CONTACTED HER.
WHAT? WHY WOULD HE...?
DAMN IT! IF I HAD ONLY KNOWN WHO HE WAS...
I'LL HAVE TO TALK TO HER AGAIN.
CHATTER
CHATTER
CHATTER
ITSUKI HASN'T COME.
EVEN THOUGH THIS IS THE LAST DAY...
I WONDER WHAT'S WRONG...
SHE'S BEEN SHUT UP IN HER ROOM SINCE YESTERDAY.
...

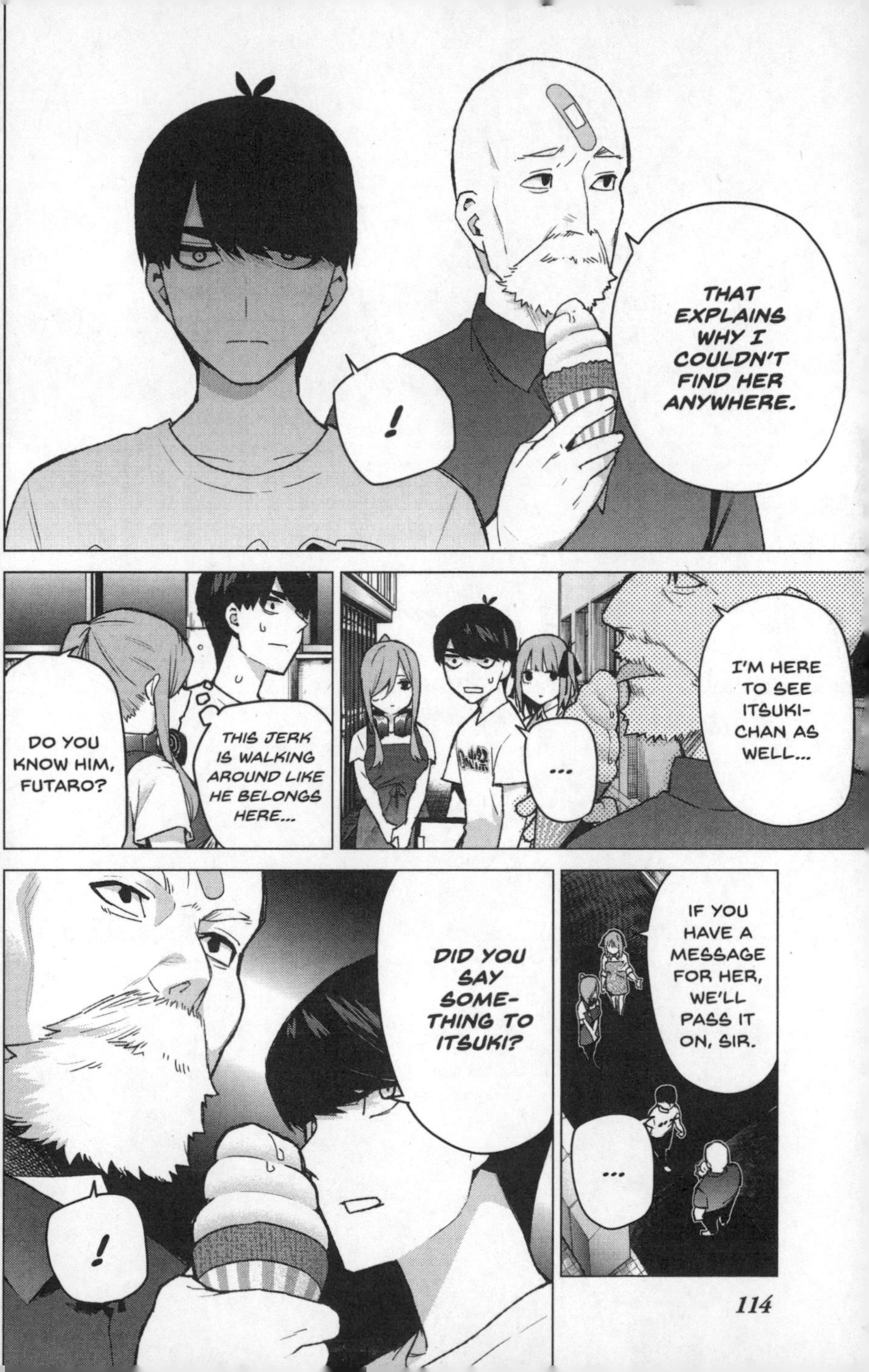
THAT EXPLAINS WHY I COULDN'T FIND HER ANYWHERE.
!
I'M HERE TO SEE ITSUKI-CHAN AS WELL...
...
THIS JERK IS WALKING AROUND LIKE HE BELONGS HERE...
DO YOU KNOW HIM, FUTARO?
IF YOU HAVE A MESSAGE FOR HER, WE'LL PASS IT ON, SIR.
...
DID YOU SAY SOMETHING TO ITSUKI?
!

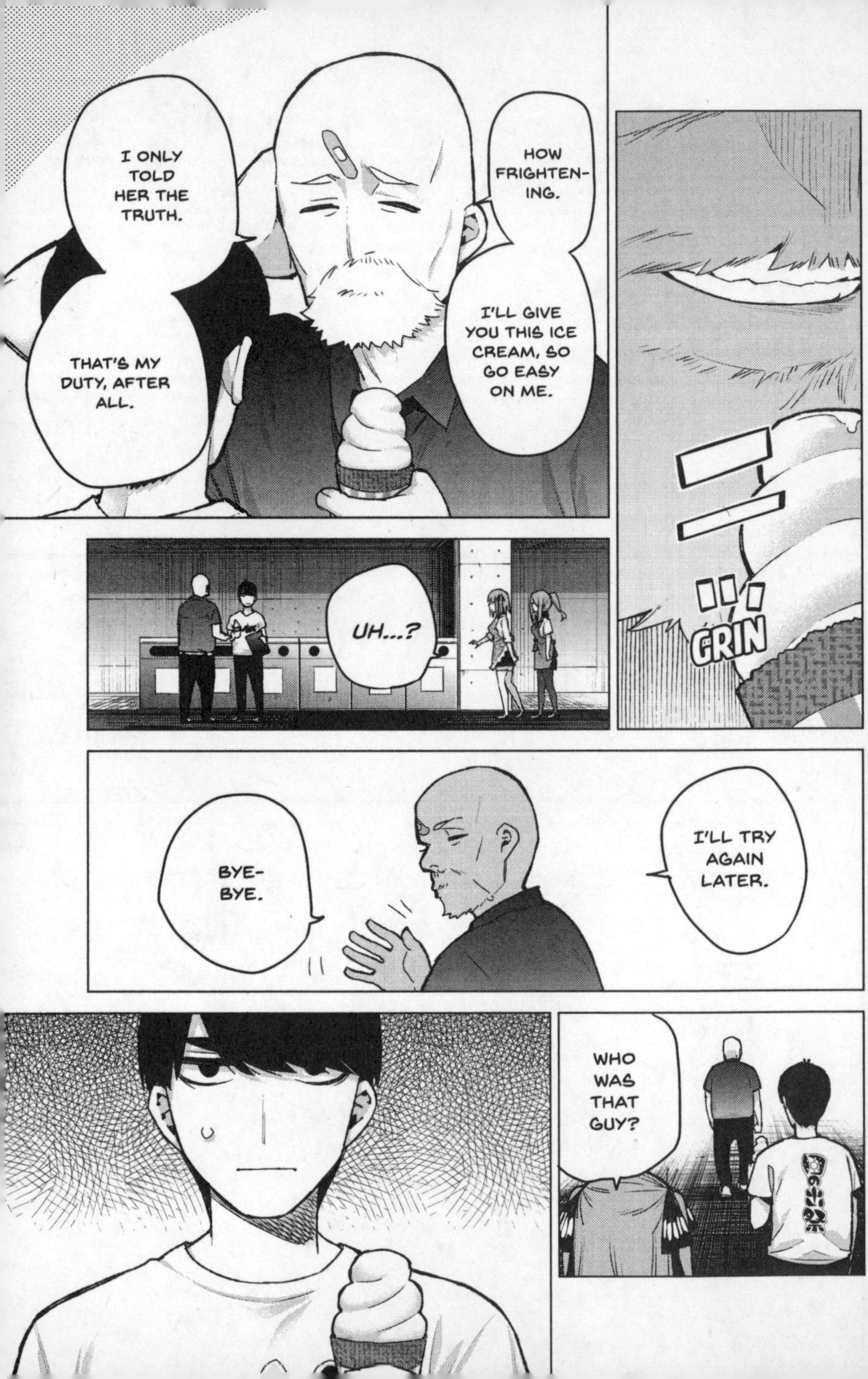
HOW FRIGHTENING.
I'LL GIVE YOU THIS ICE CREAM, SO GO EASY ON ME.
I ONLY TOLD HER THE TRUTH.
THAT'S MY DUTY, AFTER ALL.
GRIN
UH...?
I'LL TRY AGAIN LATER.
BYE-BYE.
WHO WAS THAT GUY?

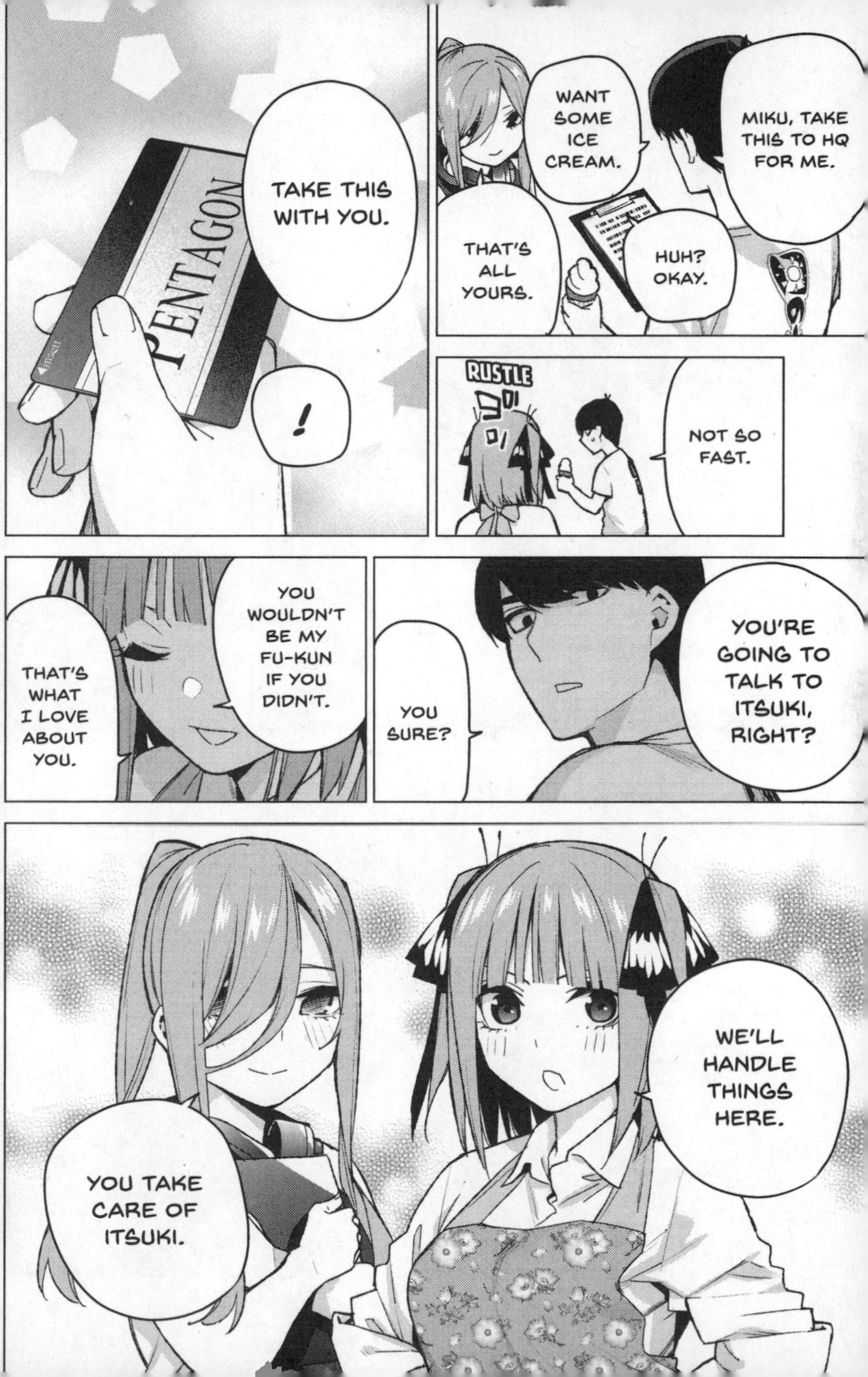
MIKU, TAKE THIS TO HQ FOR ME.
WANT SOME ICE CREAM.
HUH? OKAY.
THAT'S ALL YOURS.
NOT SO FAST.
RUSTLE
TAKE THIS WITH YOU.
PENTAGON
!
YOU'RE GOING TO TALK TO ITSUKI, RIGHT?
YOU SURE?
YOU WOULDN'T BE MY FU-KUN IF YOU DIDN'T.
THAT'S WHAT I LOVE ABOUT YOU.
WE'LL HANDLE THINGS HERE.
YOU TAKE CARE OF ITSUKI.

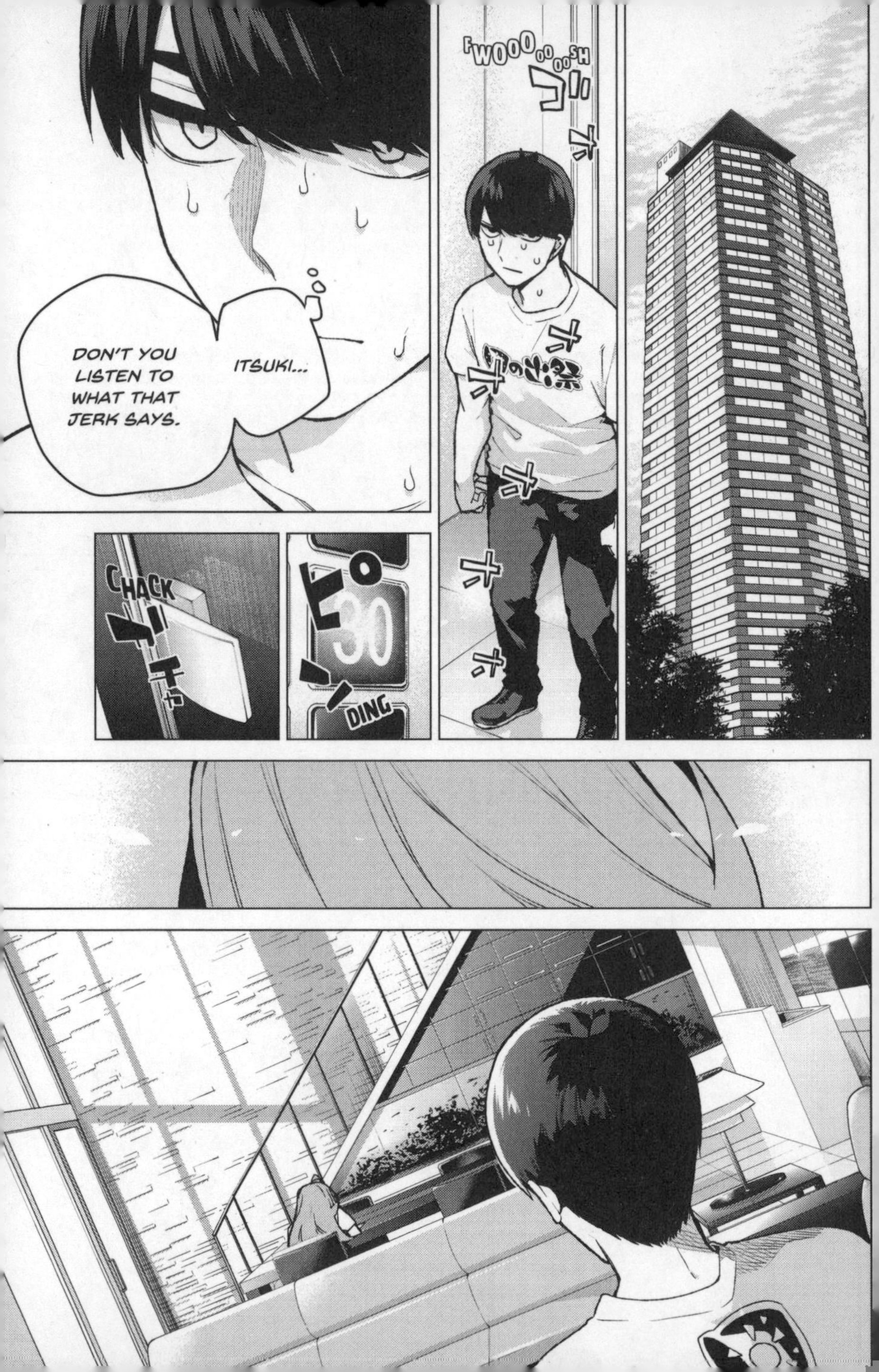
FWOOOOOOOSH
ITSUKI...
DON'T YOU LISTEN TO WHAT THAT JERK SAYS.
DING
CHACK

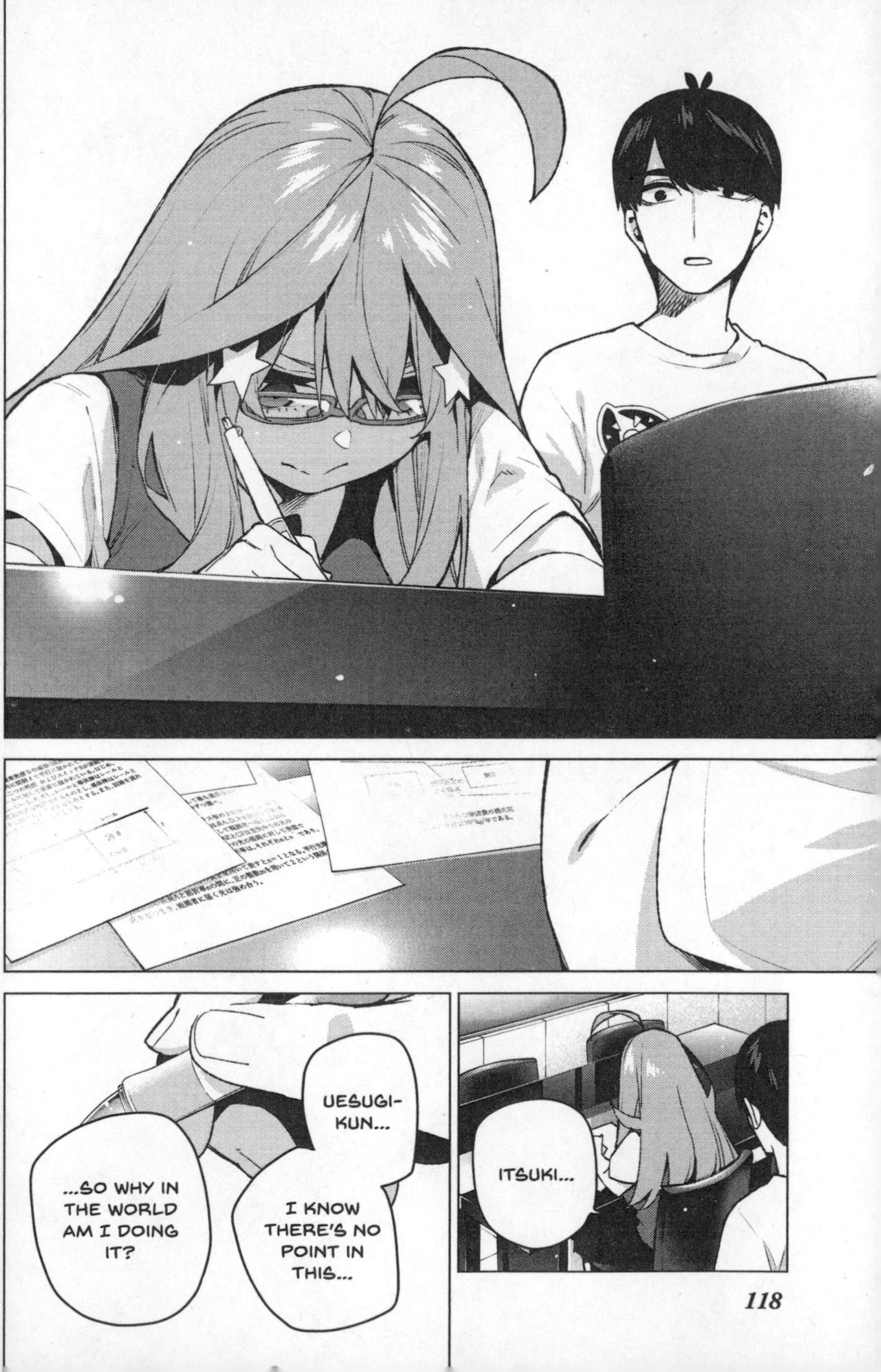
ITSUKI...
UESUGI-KUN...
I KNOW THERE'S NO POINT IN THIS...
...SO WHY IN THE WORLD AM I DOING IT?

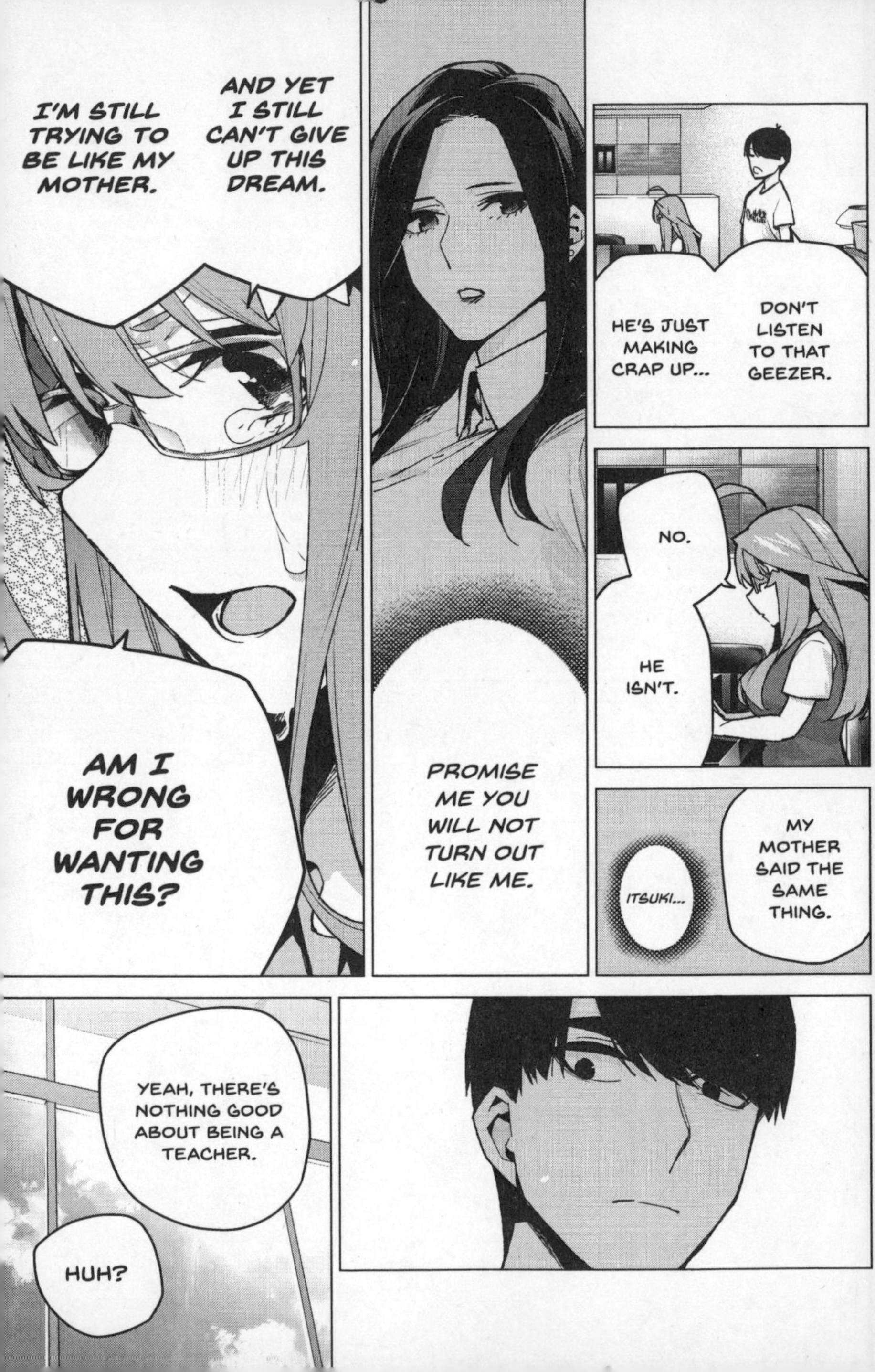
DON'T LISTEN TO THAT GEEZER.
HE'S JUST MAKING CRAP UP...
NO.
HE ISN'T.
MY MOTHER SAID THE SAME THING.
ITSUKI...
PROMISE ME YOU WILL NOT TURN OUT LIKE ME.
AND YET I STILL CAN'T GIVE UP THIS DREAM.
I'M STILL TRYING TO BE LIKE MY MOTHER.
AM I WRONG FOR WANTING THIS?
YEAH, THERE'S NOTHING GOOD ABOUT BEING A TEACHER.
HUH?

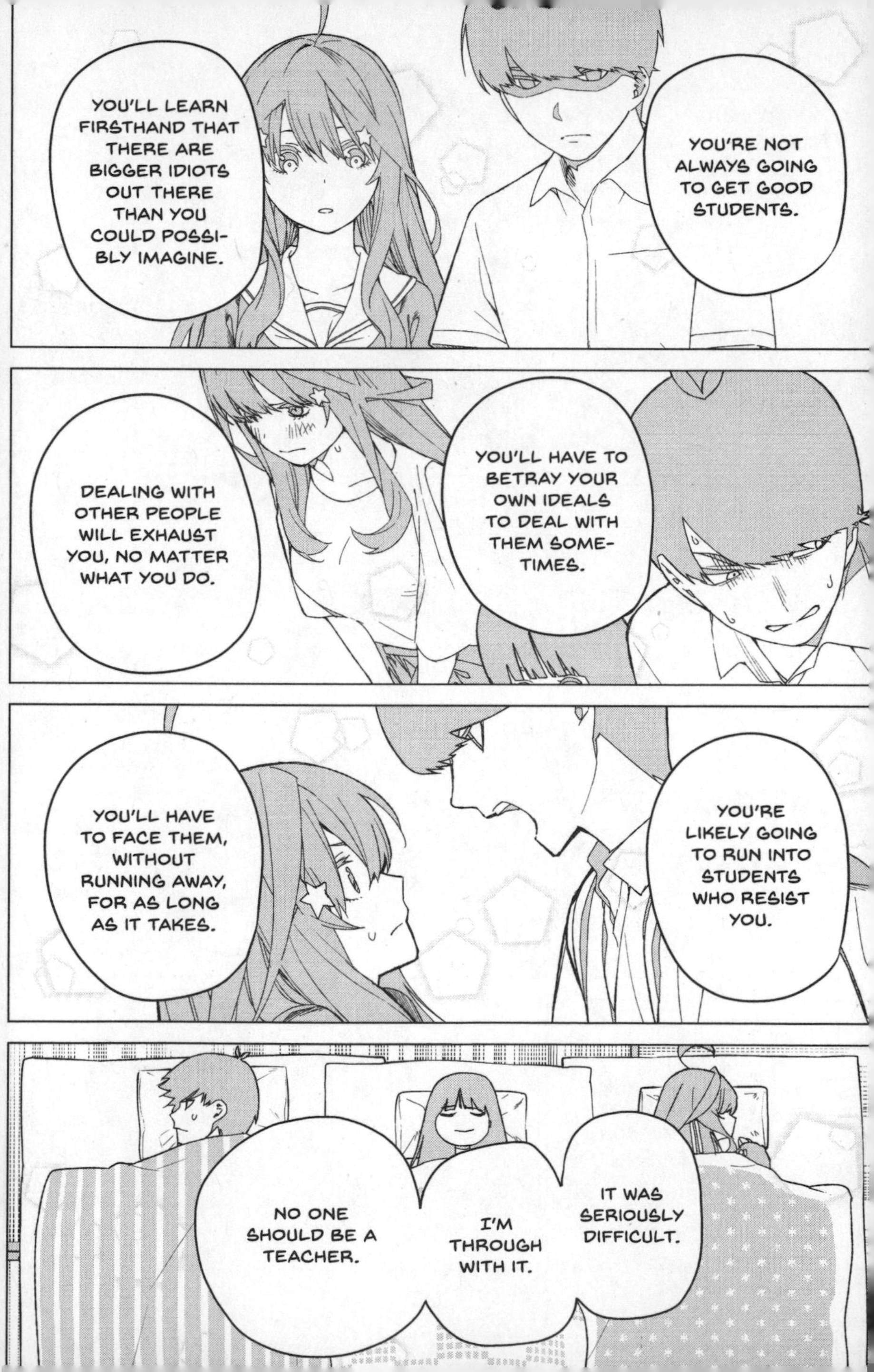
YOU'RE NOT ALWAYS GOING TO GET GOOD STUDENTS.
YOU'LL LEARN FIRSTHAND THAT THERE ARE BIGGER IDIOTS OUT THERE THAN YOU COULD POSSI-BLY IMAGINE.
YOU'LL HAVE TO BETRAY YOUR OWN IDEALS TO DEAL WITH THEM SOME-TIMES.
DEALING WITH OTHER PEOPLE WILL EXHAUST YOU, NO MATTER WHAT YOU DO.
YOU'RE LIKELY GOING TO RUN INTO STUDENTS WHO RESIST YOU.
YOU'LL HAVE TO FACE THEM, WITHOUT RUNNING AWAY, FOR AS LONG AS IT TAKES.
IT WAS SERIOUSLY DIFFICULT.
I'M THROUGH WITH IT.
NO ONE SHOULD BE A TEACHER.

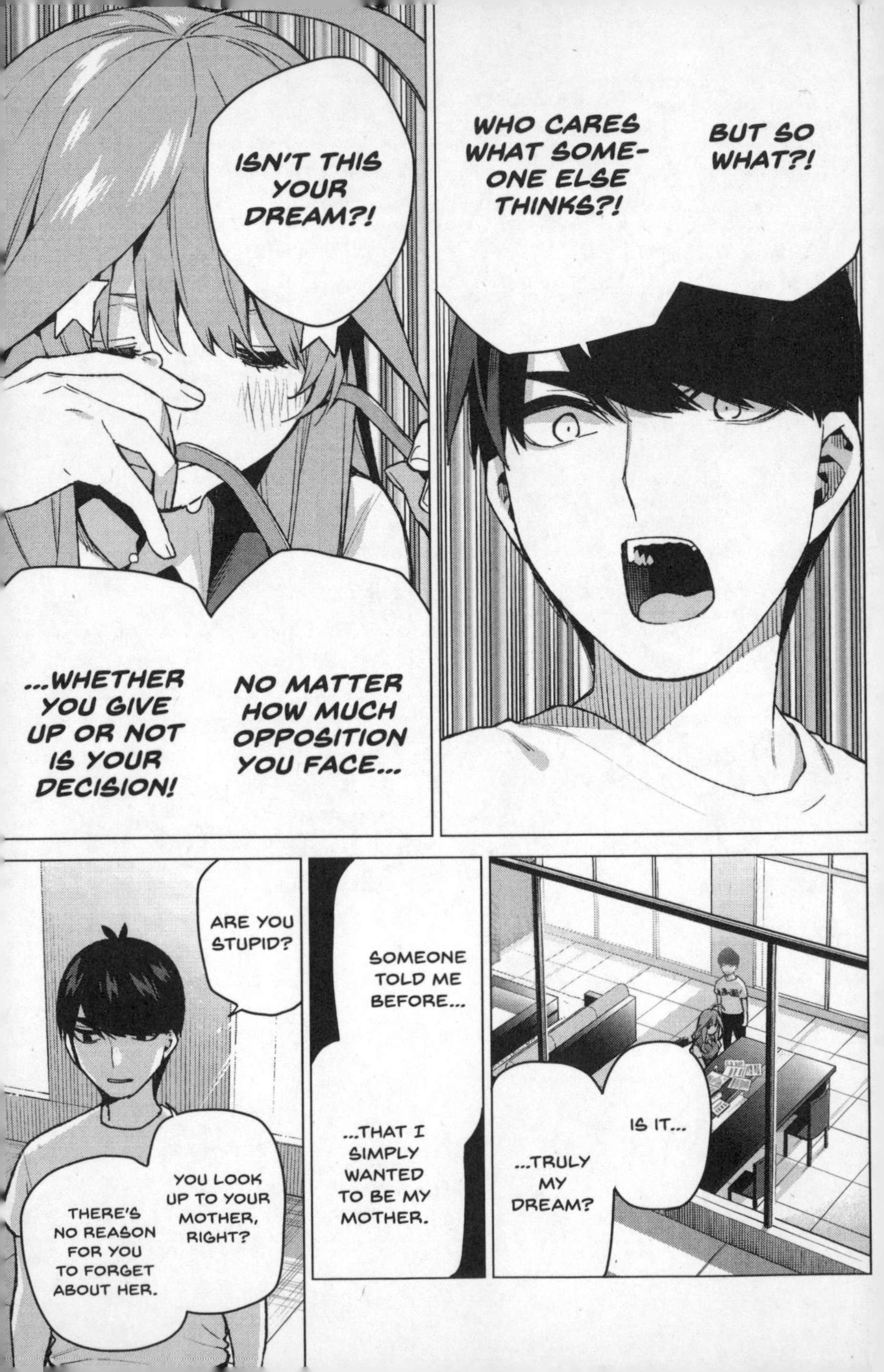
BUT SO WHAT?!
WHO CARES WHAT SOME-ONE ELSE THINKS?!
ISN'T THIS YOUR DREAM?!
NO MATTER HOW MUCH OPPOSITION YOU FACE...
...WHETHER YOU GIVE UP OR NOT IS YOUR DECISION!
IS IT...
...TRULY MY DREAM?
SOMEONE TOLD ME BEFORE...
...THAT I SIMPLY WANTED TO BE MY MOTHER.
ARE YOU STUPID?
YOU LOOK UP TO YOUR MOTHER, RIGHT?
THERE'S NO REASON FOR YOU TO FORGET ABOUT HER.

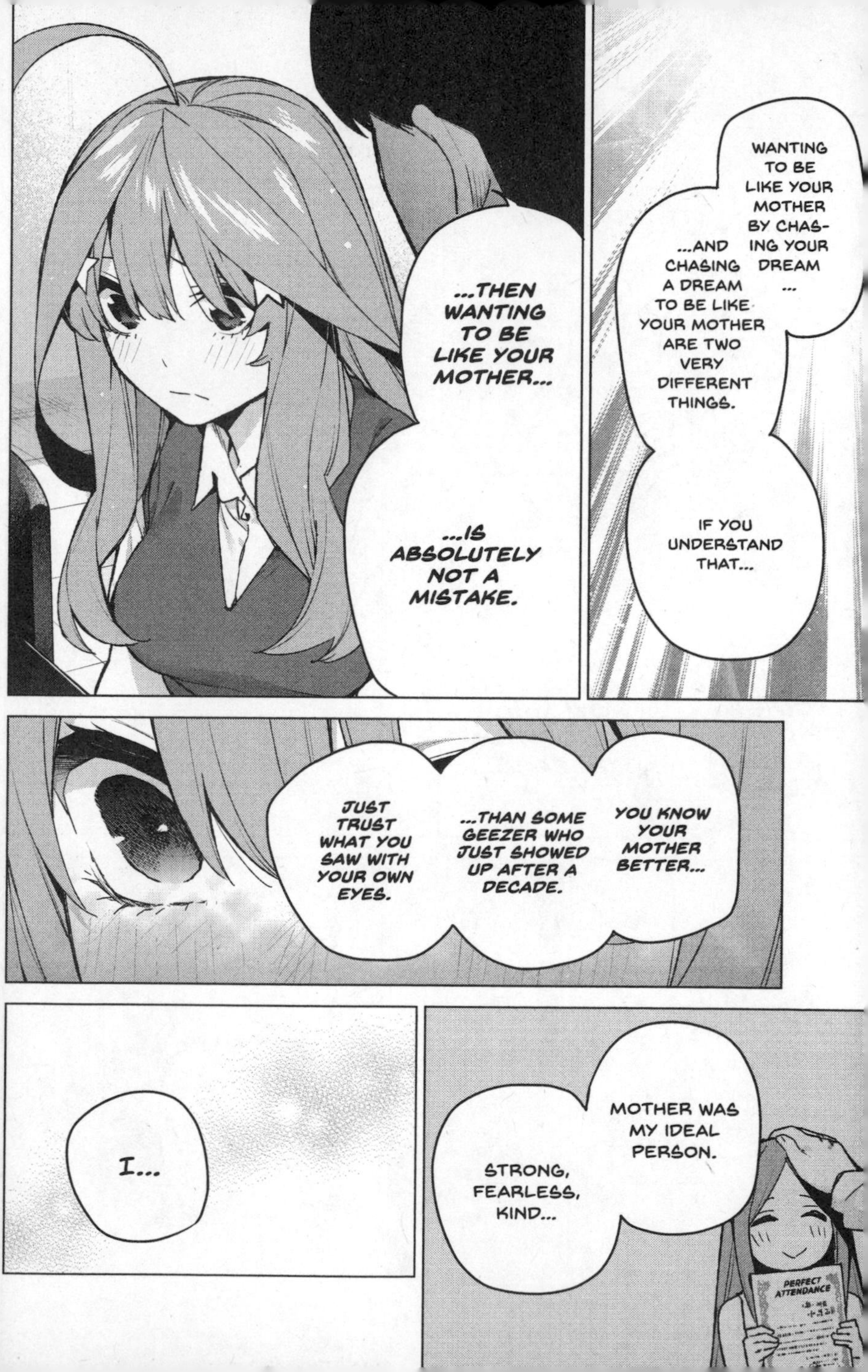
WANTING TO BE LIKE YOUR MOTHER BY CHASING YOUR DREAM...
...AND CHASING A DREAM TO BE LIKE YOUR MOTHER ARE TWO VERY DIFFERENT THINGS.
IF YOU UNDERSTAND THAT...
...THEN WANTING TO BE LIKE YOUR MOTHER...
...IS ABSOLUTELY NOT A MISTAKE.
YOU KNOW YOUR MOTHER BETTER...
...THAN SOME GEEZER WHO JUST SHOWED UP AFTER A DECADE.
JUST TRUST WHAT YOU SAW WITH YOUR OWN EYES.
MOTHER WAS MY IDEAL PERSON.
STRONG, FEARLESS, KIND...
PERFECT ATTENDANCE
I...

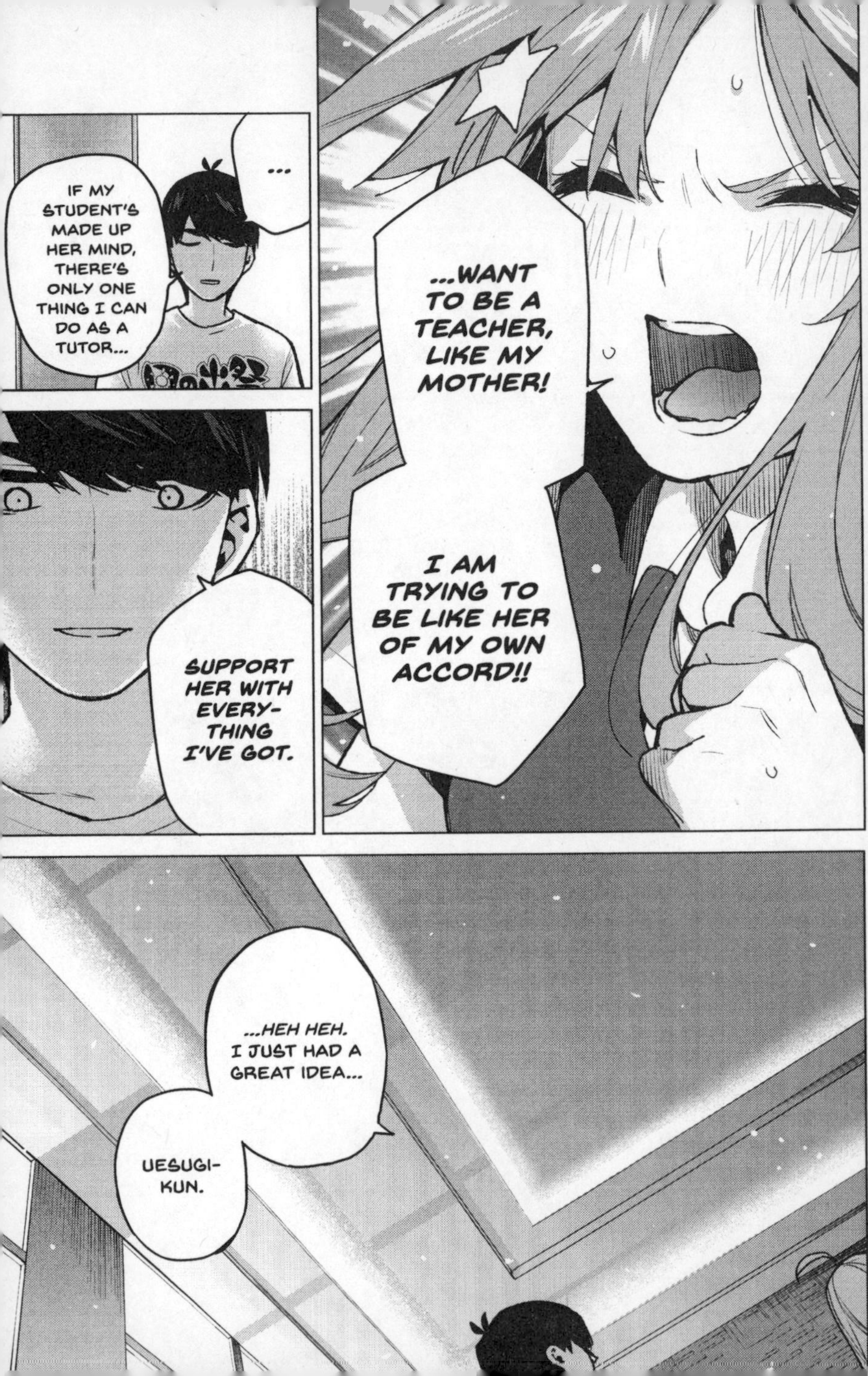
...WANT TO BE A TEACHER, LIKE MY MOTHER!
I AM TRYING TO BE LIKE HER OF MY OWN ACCORD!!
...
IF MY STUDENT'S MADE UP HER MIND, THERE'S ONLY ONE THING I CAN DO AS A TUTOR...
SUPPORT HER WITH EVERY-THING I'VE GOT.
...HEH HEH. I JUST HAD A GREAT IDEA...
UESUGI-KUN.

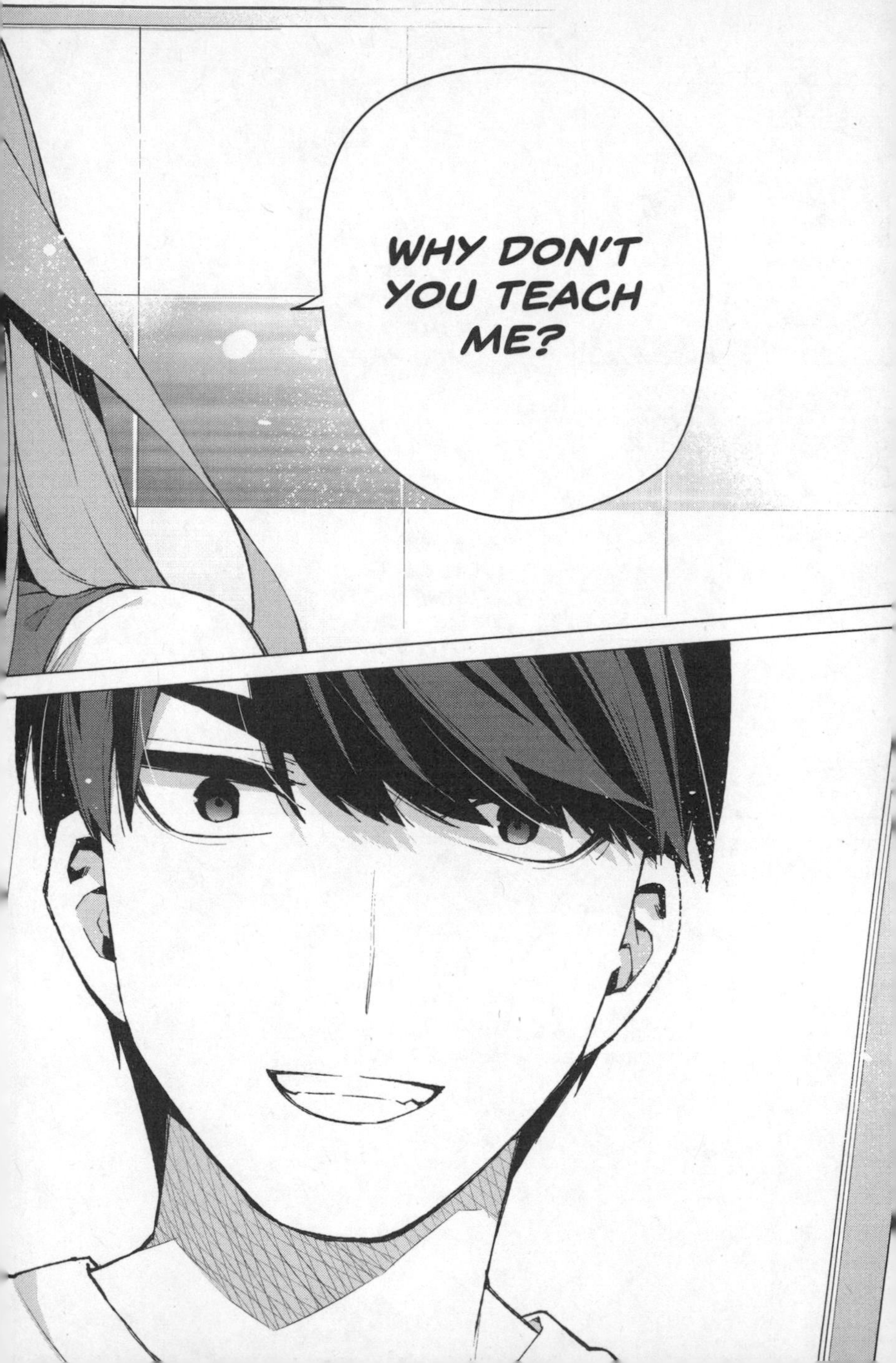
WHY DON'T YOU TEACH ME?

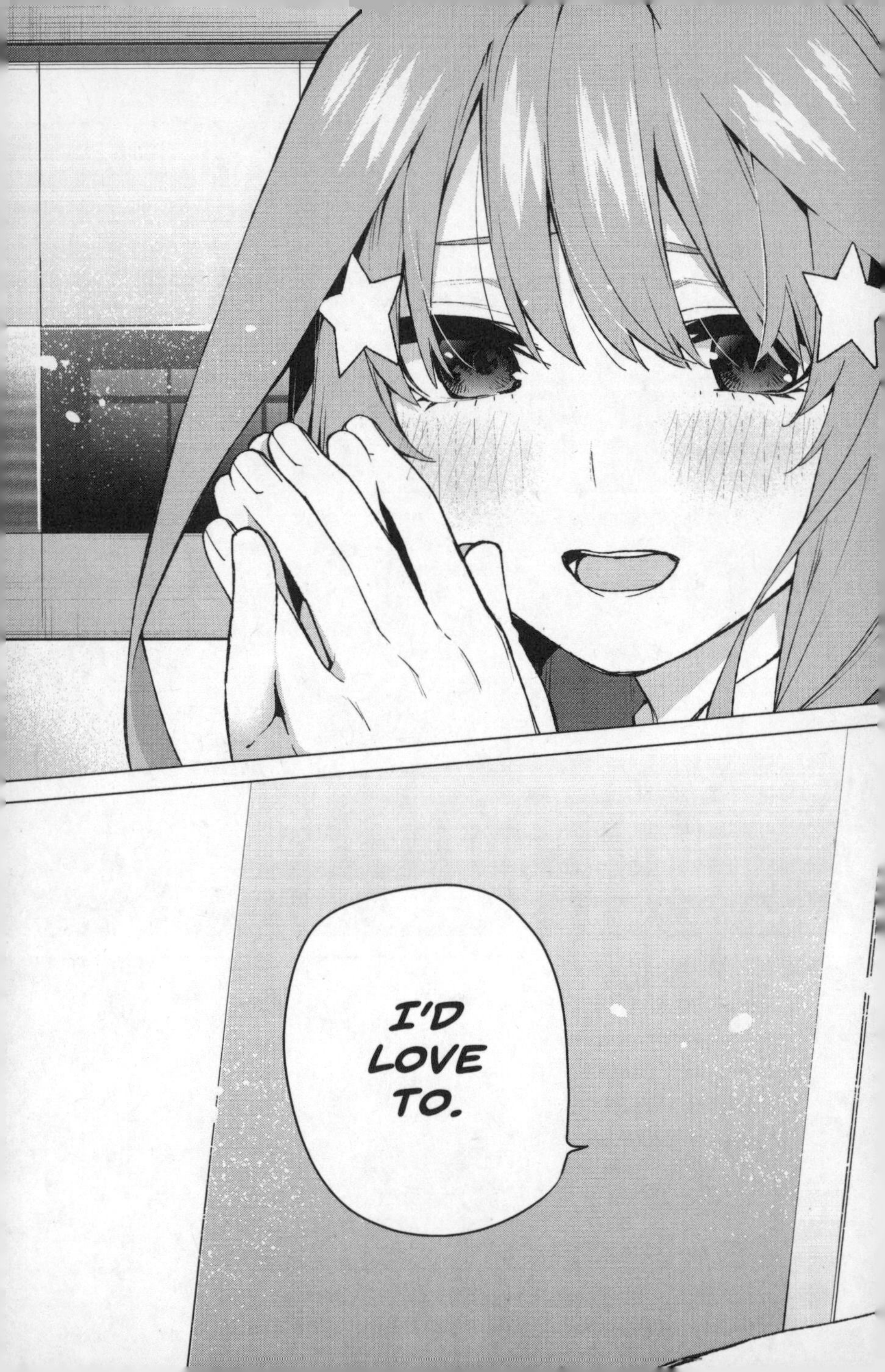
I'D LOVE TO.

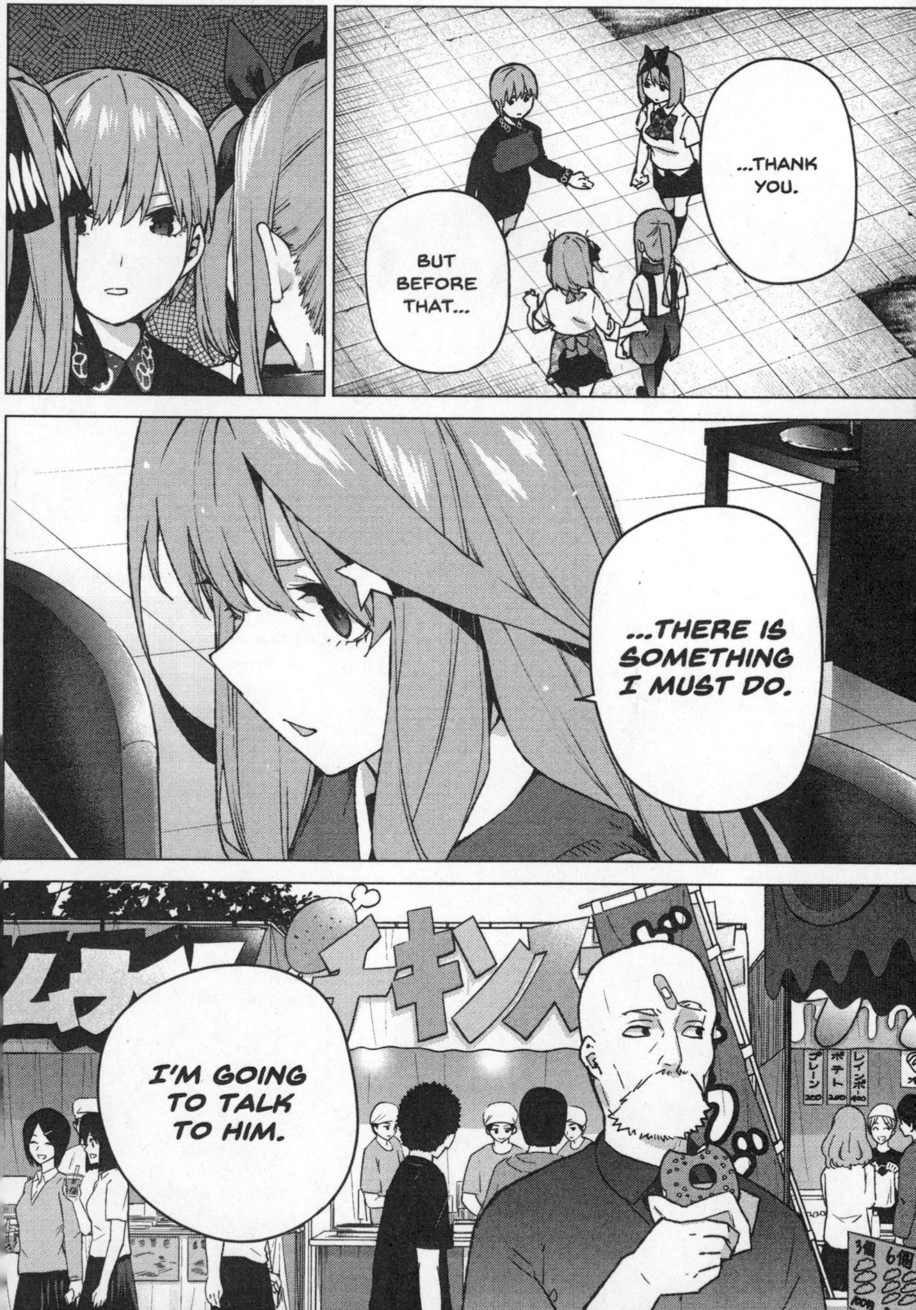
...THANK YOU.
BUT BEFORE THAT...
...THERE IS SOMETHING I MUST DO.
I'M GOING TO TALK TO HIM.

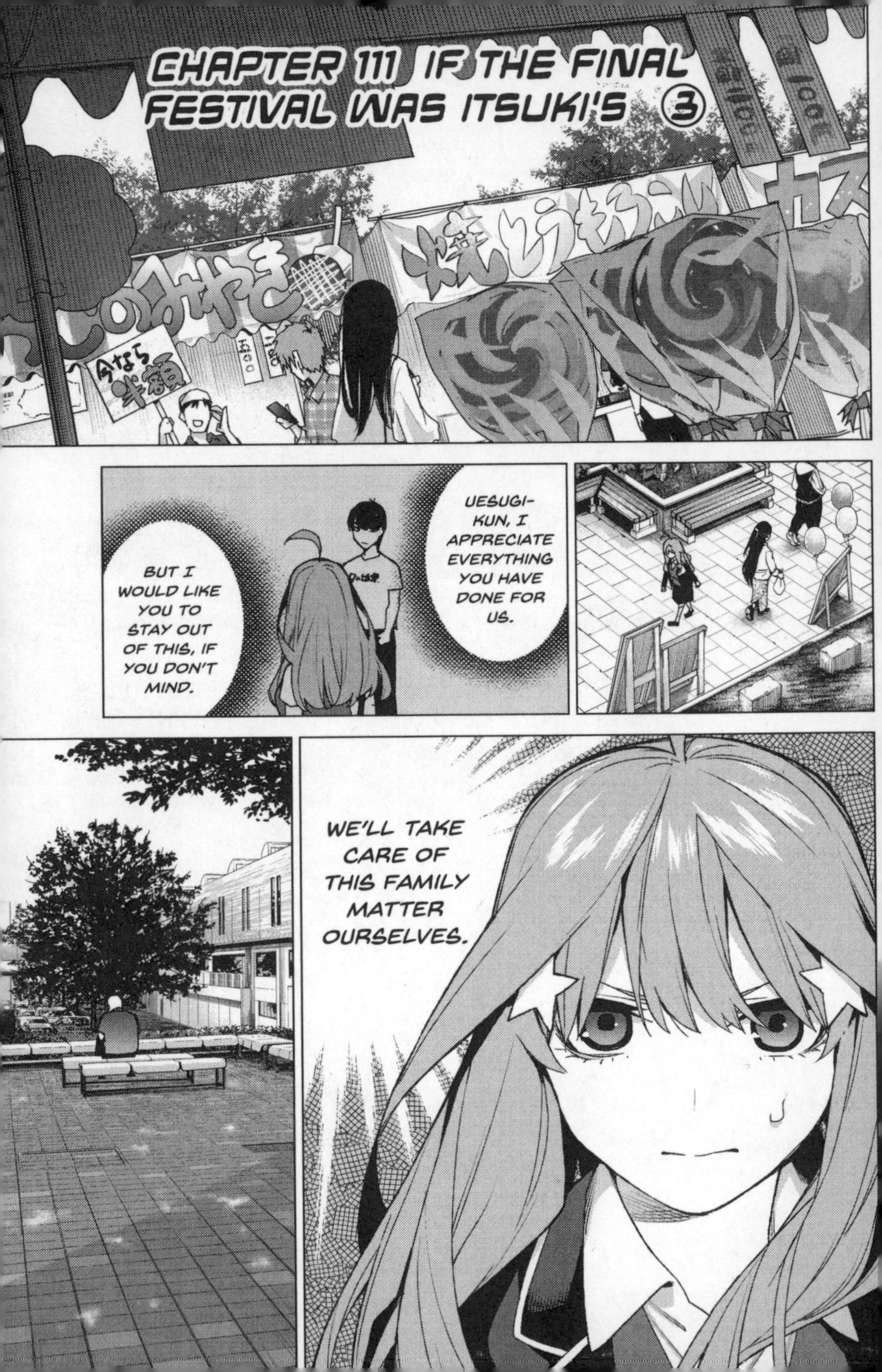
CHAPTER 111 IF THE FINAL FESTIVAL WAS ITSUKI'S ③
今なら 半額
UESUGI-KUN, I APPRECIATE EVERYTHING YOU HAVE DONE FOR US.
BUT I WOULD LIKE YOU TO STAY OUT OF THIS, IF YOU DON'T MIND.
WE'LL TAKE CARE OF THIS FAMILY MATTER OURSELVES.

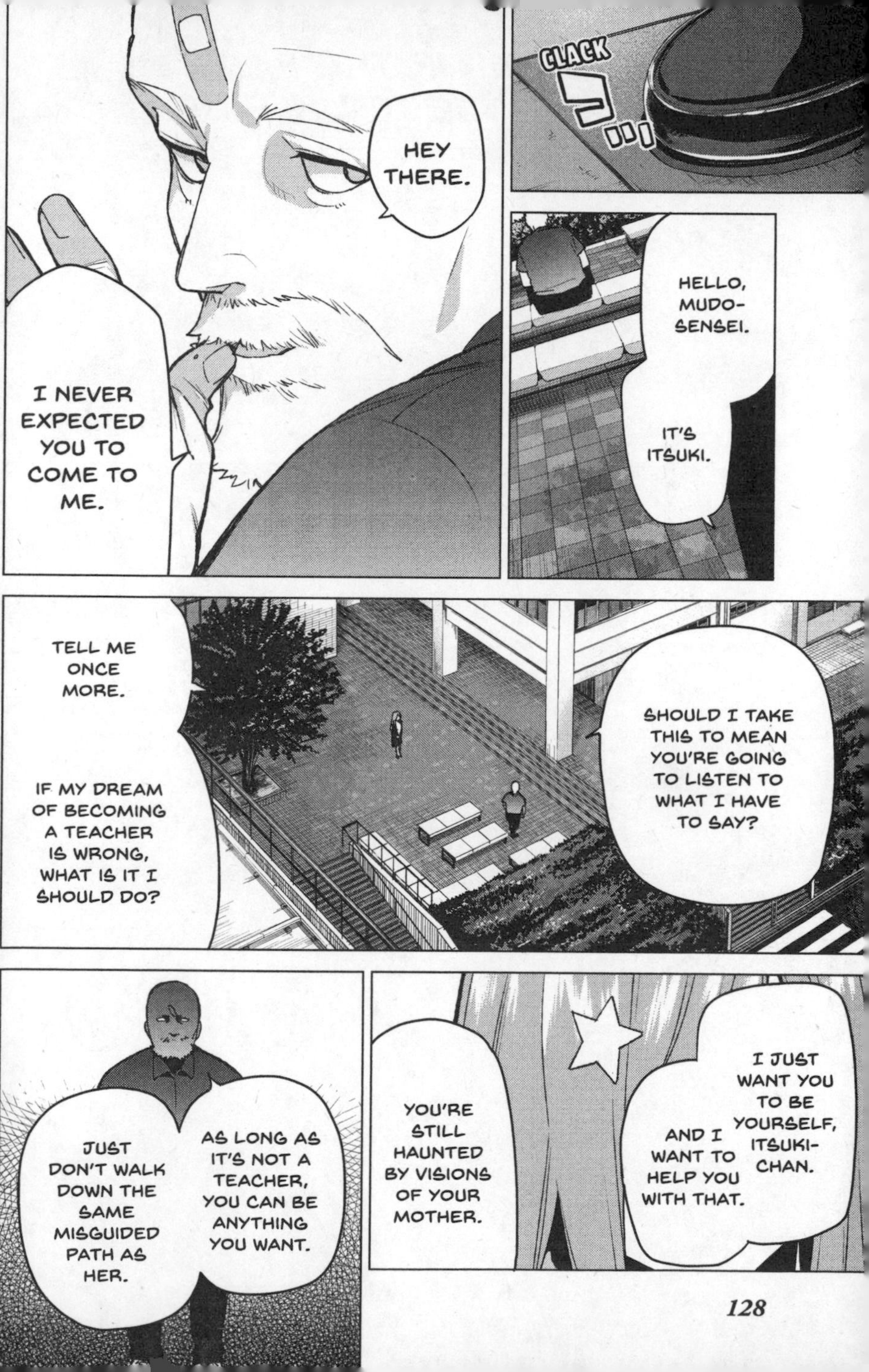
CLACK
HELLO, MUDO-SENSEI.
IT'S ITSUKI.
HEY THERE.
I NEVER EXPECTED YOU TO COME TO ME.
SHOULD I TAKE THIS TO MEAN YOU'RE GOING TO LISTEN TO WHAT I HAVE TO SAY?
TELL ME ONCE MORE.
IF MY DREAM OF BECOMING A TEACHER IS WRONG, WHAT IS IT I SHOULD DO?
I JUST WANT YOU TO BE YOURSELF, ITSUKI-CHAN.
AND I WANT TO HELP YOU WITH THAT.
YOU'RE STILL HAUNTED BY VISIONS OF YOUR MOTHER.
AS LONG AS IT'S NOT A TEACHER, YOU CAN BE ANYTHING YOU WANT.
JUST DON'T WALK DOWN THE SAME MISGUIDED PATH AS HER.

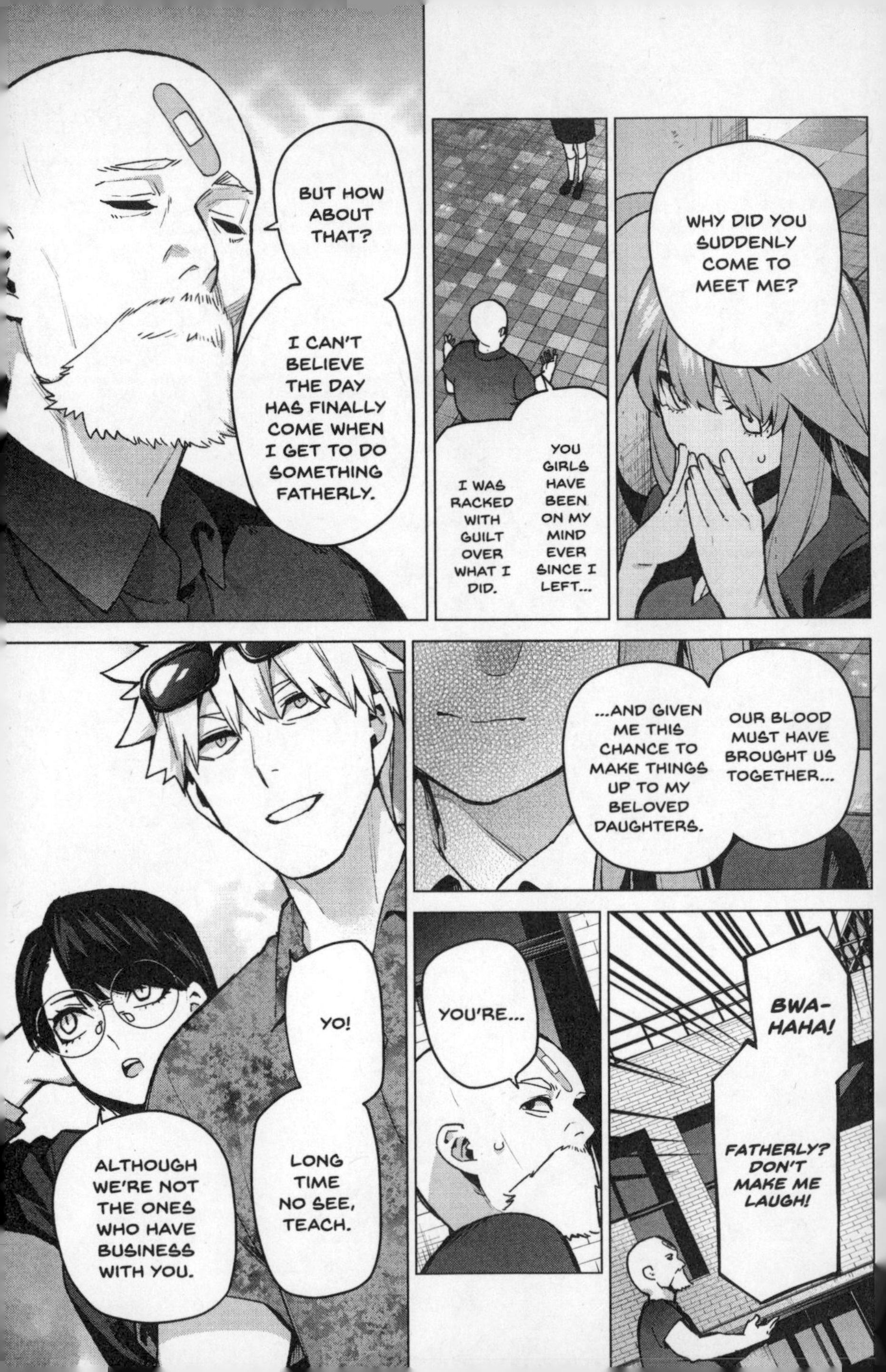
WHY DID YOU SUDDENLY COME TO MEET ME?
YOU GIRLS HAVE BEEN ON MY MIND EVER SINCE I LEFT...
I WAS RACKED WITH GUILT OVER WHAT I DID.
BUT HOW ABOUT THAT?
I CAN'T BELIEVE THE DAY HAS FINALLY COME WHEN I GET TO DO SOMETHING FATHERLY.
OUR BLOOD MUST HAVE BROUGHT US TOGETHER...
...AND GIVEN ME THIS CHANCE TO MAKE THINGS UP TO MY BELOVED DAUGHTERS.
BWA-HAHA!
FATHERLY? DON'T MAKE ME LAUGH!
YOU'RE...
YO!
LONG TIME NO SEE, TEACH.
ALTHOUGH WE'RE NOT THE ONES WHO HAVE BUSINESS WITH YOU.

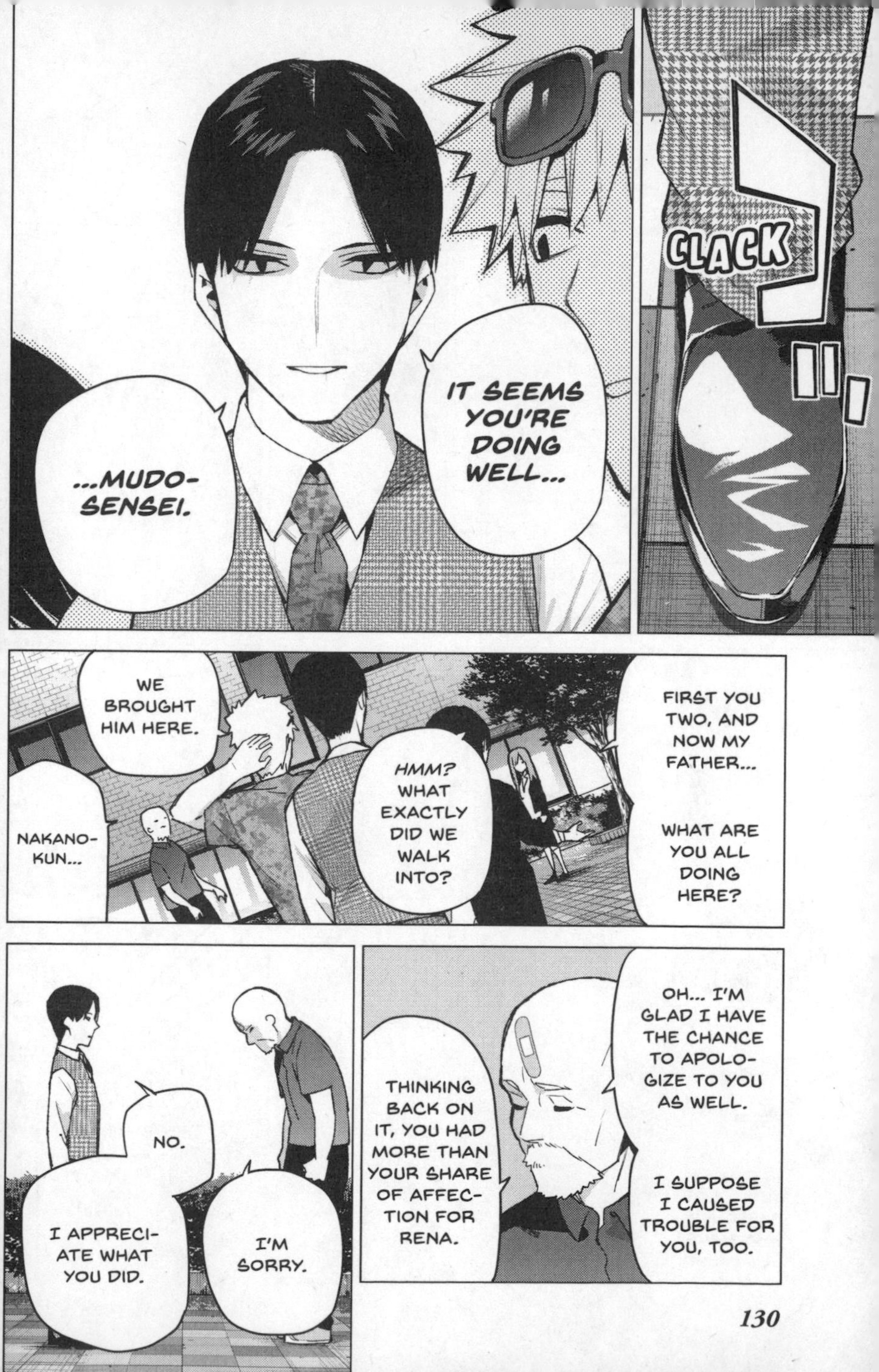
CLACK
IT SEEMS YOU'RE DOING WELL...
...MUDO-SENSEI.
FIRST YOU TWO, AND NOW MY FATHER...
WHAT ARE YOU ALL DOING HERE?
HMM? WHAT EXACTLY DID WE WALK INTO?
WE BROUGHT HIM HERE.
NAKANO-KUN...
OH... I'M GLAD I HAVE THE CHANCE TO APOLOGIZE TO YOU AS WELL.
I SUPPOSE I CAUSED TROUBLE FOR YOU, TOO.
THINKING BACK ON IT, YOU HAD MORE THAN YOUR SHARE OF AFFECTION FOR RENA.
NO.
I'M SORRY.
I APPRECIATE WHAT YOU DID.

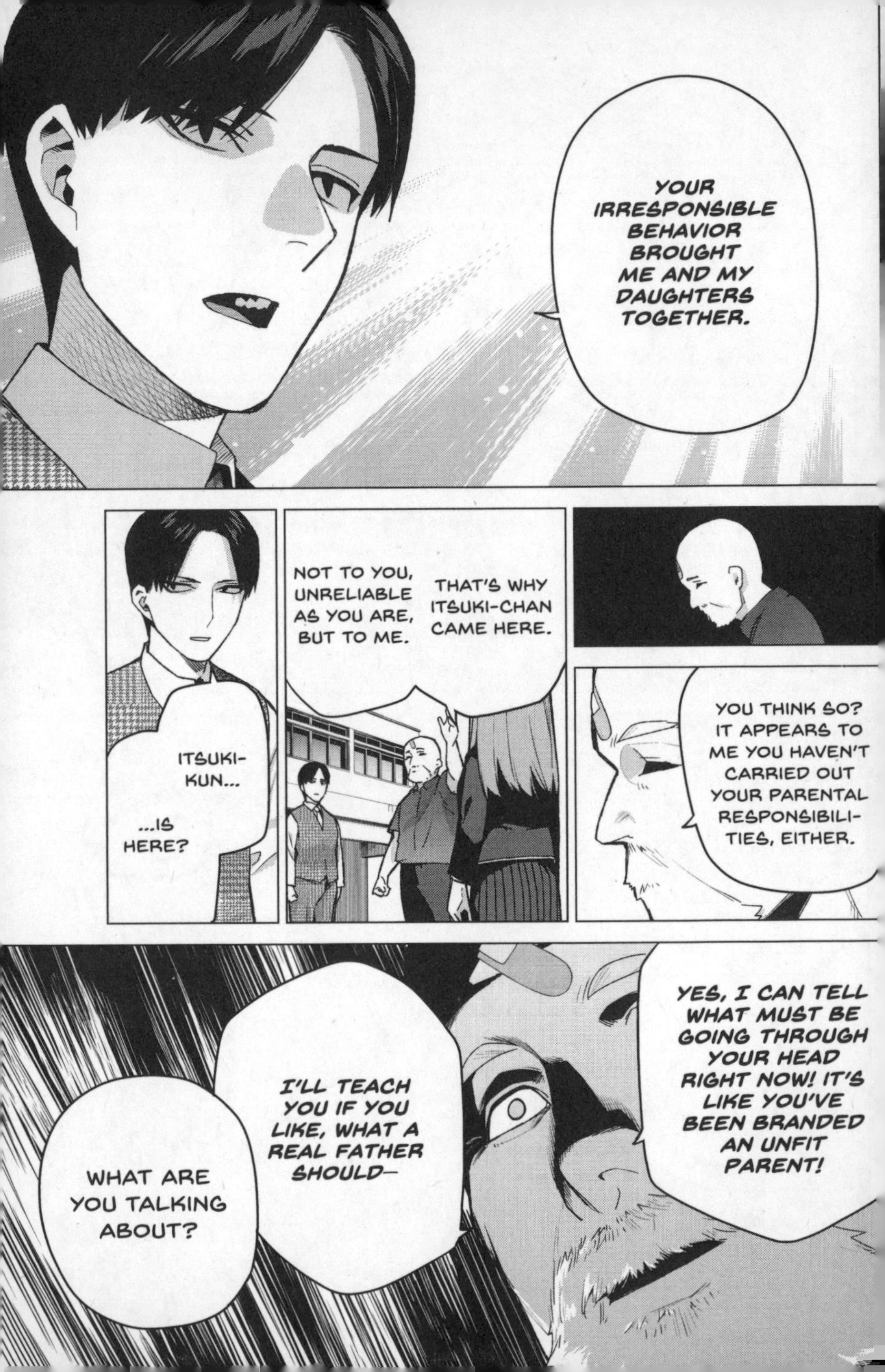
YOUR IRRESPONSIBLE BEHAVIOR BROUGHT ME AND MY DAUGHTERS TOGETHER.
YOU THINK SO? IT APPEARS TO ME YOU HAVEN'T CARRIED OUT YOUR PARENTAL RESPONSIBILI-TIES, EITHER.
THAT'S WHY ITSUKI-CHAN CAME HERE.
NOT TO YOU, UNRELIABLE AS YOU ARE, BUT TO ME.
ITSUKI-KUN...
...IS HERE?
YES, I CAN TELL WHAT MUST BE GOING THROUGH YOUR HEAD RIGHT NOW! IT'S LIKE YOU'VE BEEN BRANDED AN UNFIT PARENT!
I'LL TEACH YOU IF YOU LIKE, WHAT A REAL FATHER SHOULD—
WHAT ARE YOU TALKING ABOUT?

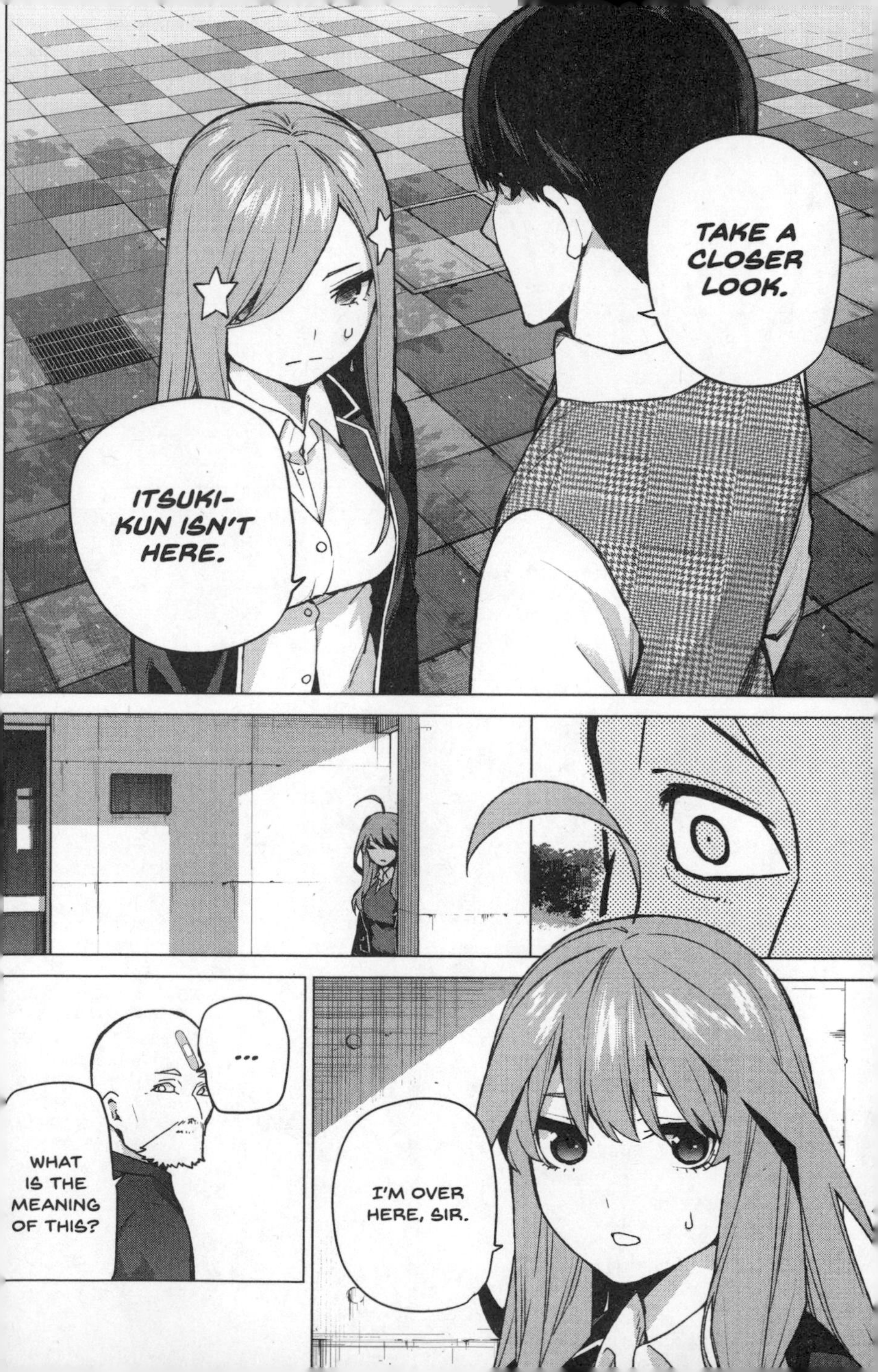
TAKE A CLOSER LOOK.
ITSUKI-KUN ISN'T HERE.
I'M OVER HERE, SIR.
...
WHAT IS THE MEANING OF THIS?

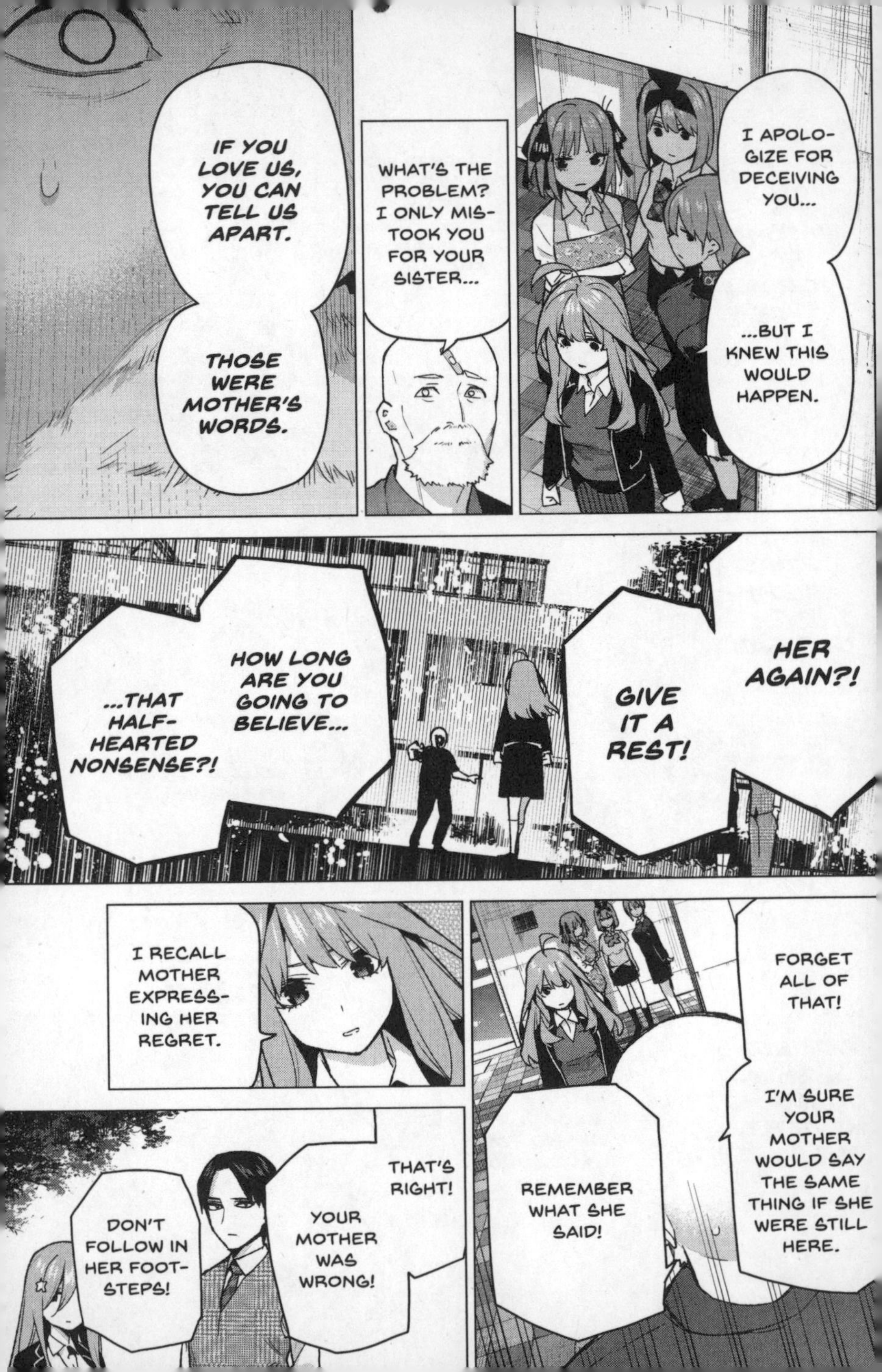
I APOLO-GIZE FOR DECEIVING YOU...
...BUT I KNEW THIS WOULD HAPPEN.
WHAT'S THE PROBLEM? I ONLY MIS-TOOK YOU FOR YOUR SISTER...
IF YOU LOVE US, YOU CAN TELL US APART.
THOSE WERE MOTHER'S WORDS.
HER AGAIN?!
GIVE IT A REST!
HOW LONG ARE YOU GOING TO BELIEVE...
...THAT HALF-HEARTED NONSENSE?!
FORGET ALL OF THAT!
I'M SURE YOUR MOTHER WOULD SAY THE SAME THING IF SHE WERE STILL HERE.
REMEMBER WHAT SHE SAID!
I RECALL MOTHER EXPRESS-ING HER REGRET.
THAT'S RIGHT!
YOUR MOTHER WAS WRONG!
DON'T FOLLOW IN HER FOOT-STEPS!

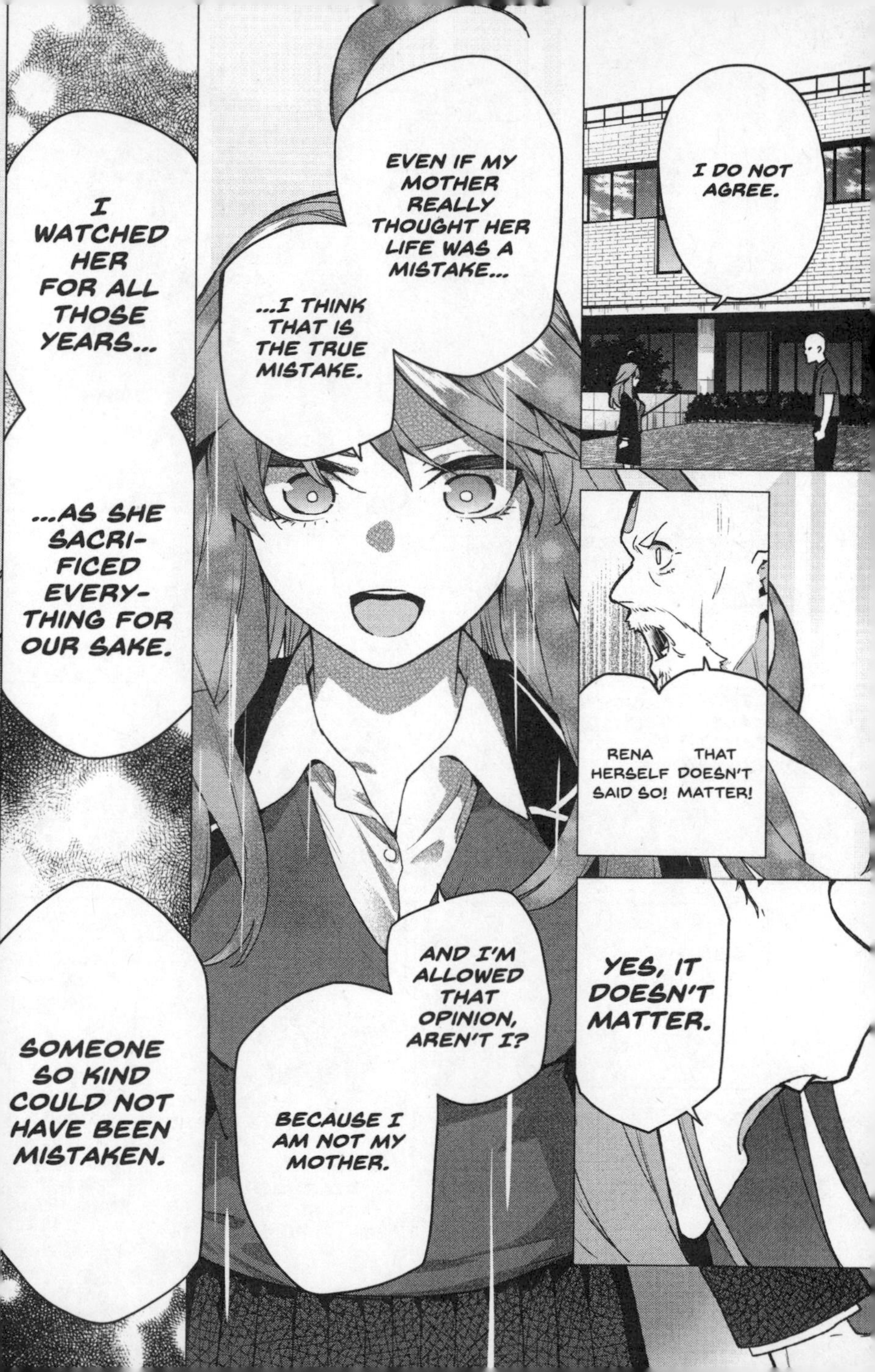
I DO NOT AGREE.
THAT DOESN'T MATTER!
RENA HERSELF SAID SO!
YES, IT DOESN'T MATTER.
EVEN IF MY MOTHER REALLY THOUGHT HER LIFE WAS A MISTAKE...
...I THINK THAT IS THE TRUE MISTAKE.
AND I'M ALLOWED THAT OPINION, AREN'T I?
BECAUSE I AM NOT MY MOTHER.
I WATCHED HER FOR ALL THOSE YEARS...
...AS SHE SACRIFICED EVERYTHING FOR OUR SAKE.
SOMEONE SO KIND COULD NOT HAVE BEEN MISTAKEN.

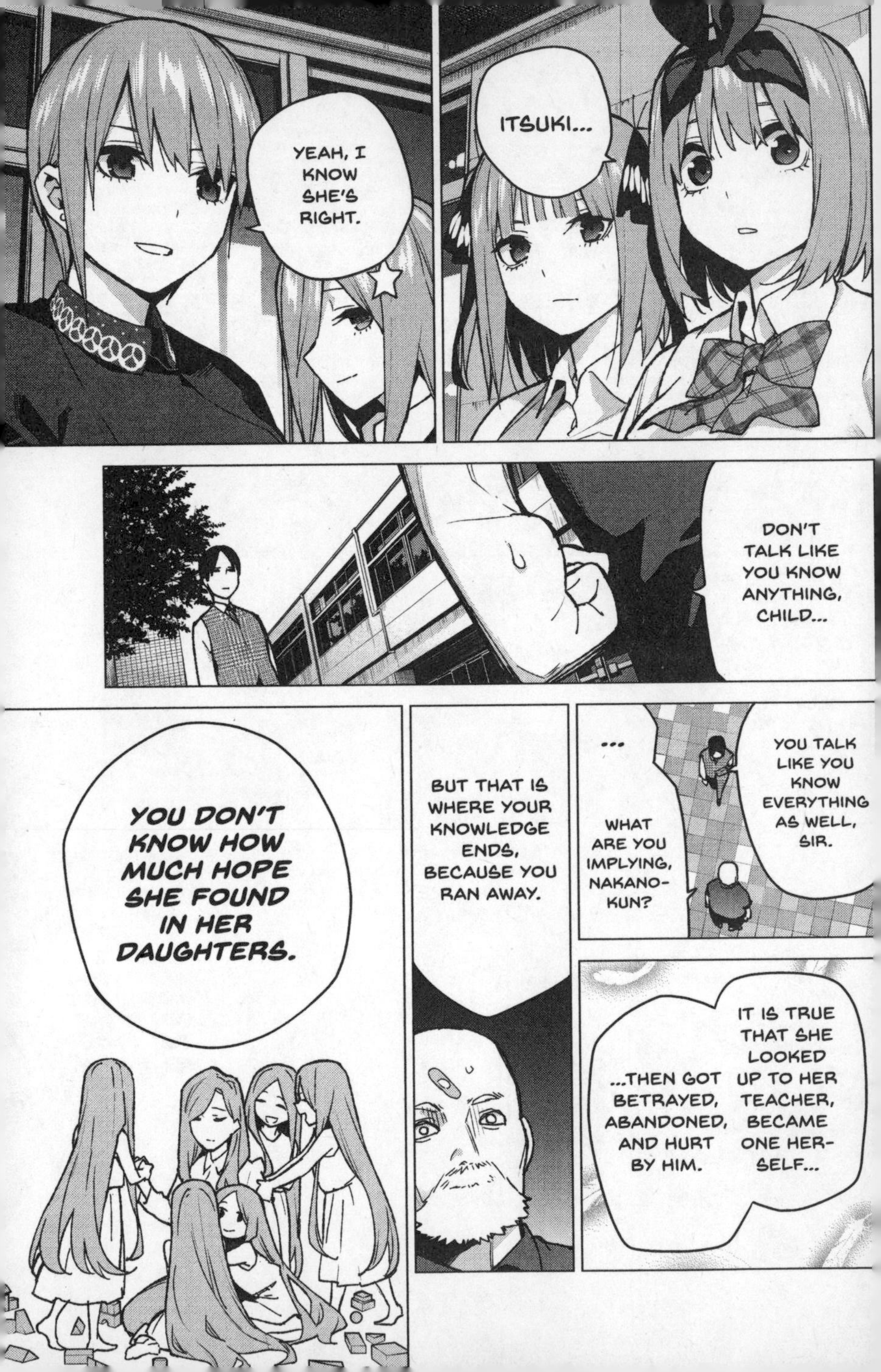
ITSUKI...
YEAH, I KNOW SHE'S RIGHT.
DON'T TALK LIKE YOU KNOW ANYTHING, CHILD...
YOU TALK LIKE YOU KNOW EVERYTHING AS WELL, SIR.
...
WHAT ARE YOU IMPLYING, NAKANO-KUN?
IT IS TRUE THAT SHE LOOKED UP TO HER TEACHER, BECAME ONE HER-SELF...
...THEN GOT BETRAYED, ABANDONED, AND HURT BY HIM.
BUT THAT IS WHERE YOUR KNOWLEDGE ENDS, BECAUSE YOU RAN AWAY.
YOU DON'T KNOW HOW MUCH HOPE SHE FOUND IN HER DAUGHTERS.

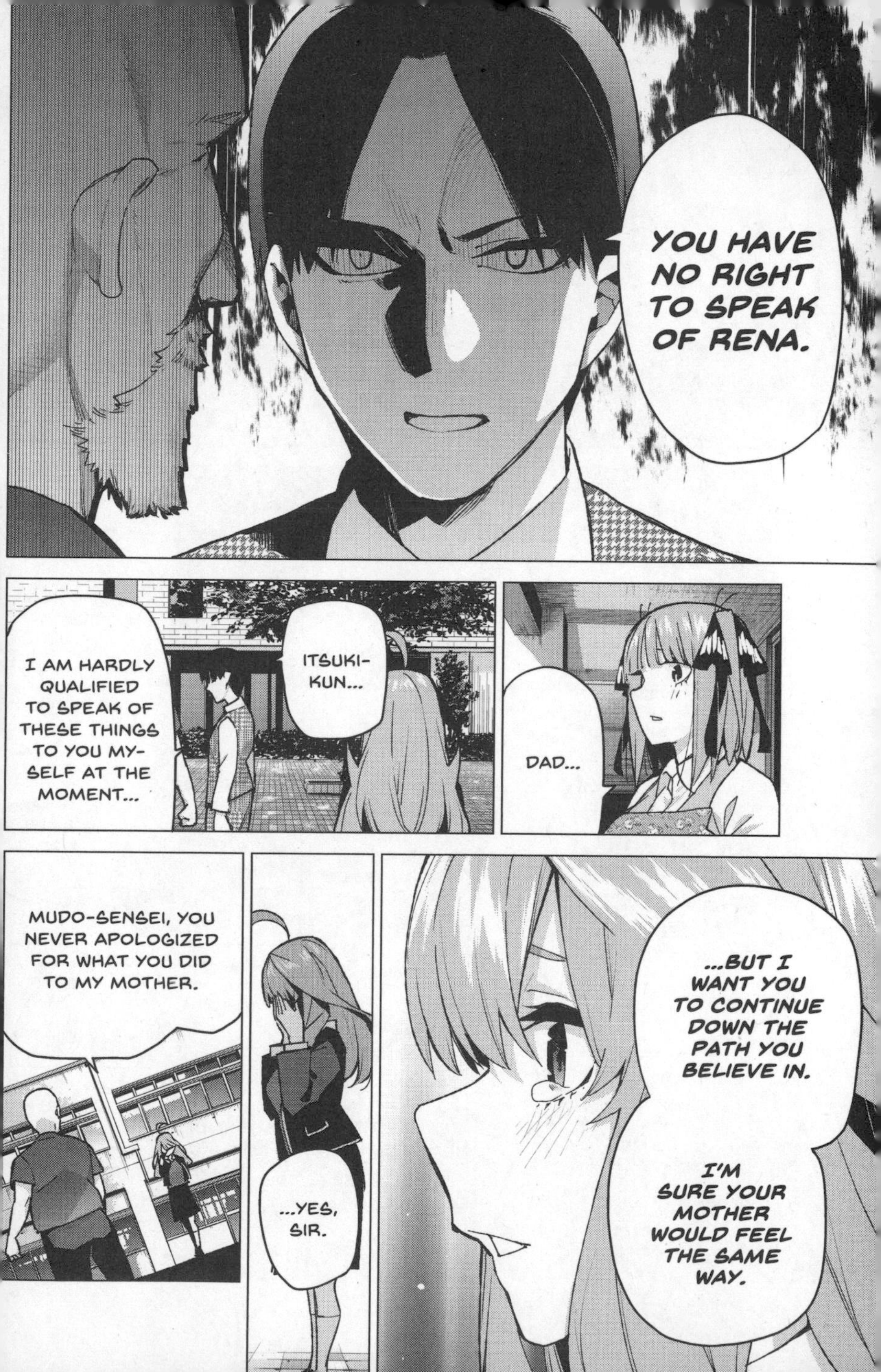
YOU HAVE NO RIGHT TO SPEAK OF RENA.
DAD...
ITSUKI-KUN...
I AM HARDLY QUALIFIED TO SPEAK OF THESE THINGS TO YOU MY-SELF AT THE MOMENT...
...BUT I WANT YOU TO CONTINUE DOWN THE PATH YOU BELIEVE IN.
I'M SURE YOUR MOTHER WOULD FEEL THE SAME WAY.
...YES, SIR.
MUDO-SENSEI, YOU NEVER APOLOGIZED FOR WHAT YOU DID TO MY MOTHER.

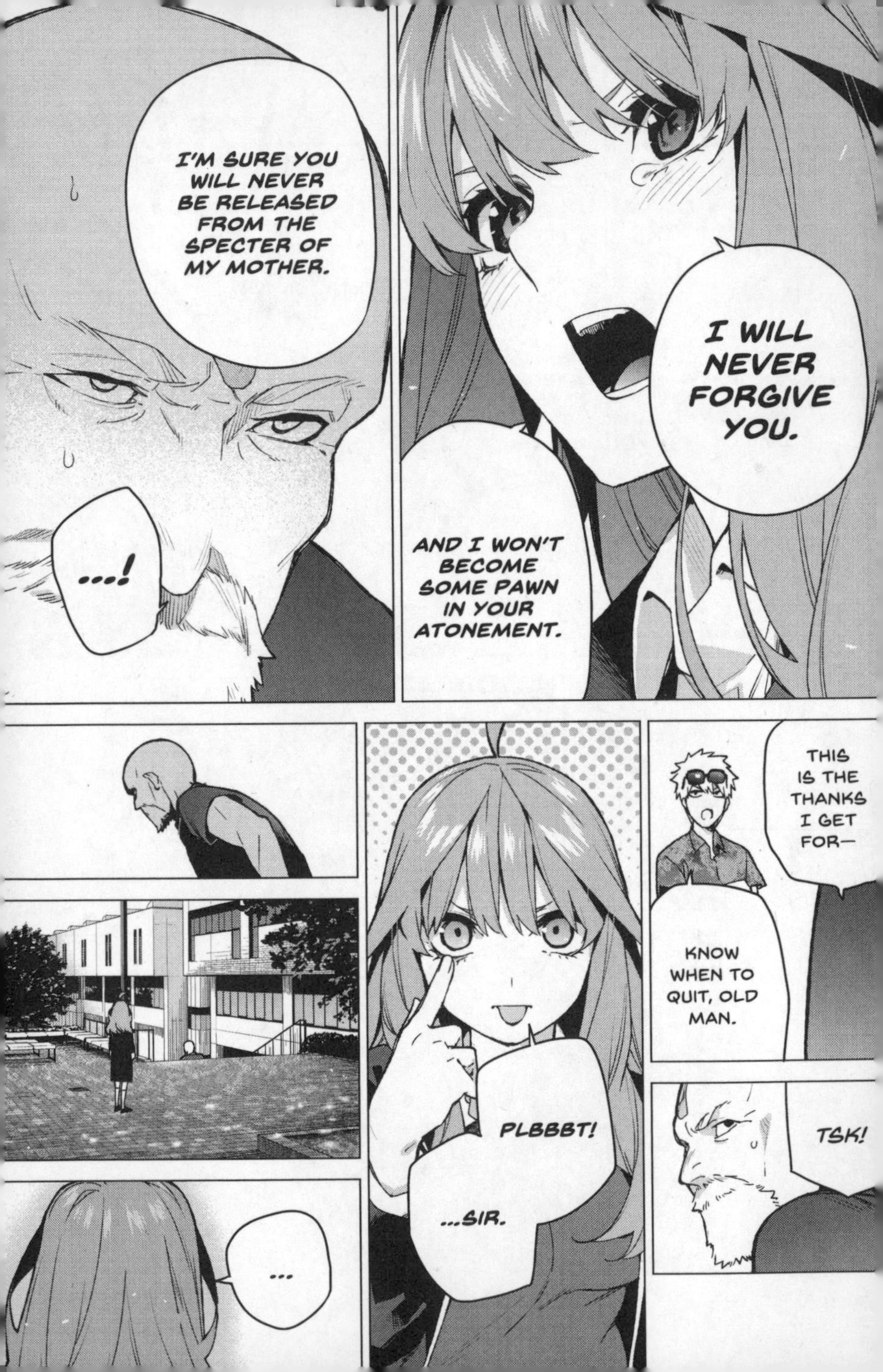
I WILL NEVER FORGIVE YOU.
AND I WON'T BECOME SOME PAWN IN YOUR ATONEMENT.
I'M SURE YOU WILL NEVER BE RELEASED FROM THE SPECTER OF MY MOTHER.
...!
THIS IS THE THANKS I GET FOR—
KNOW WHEN TO QUIT, OLD MAN.
TSK!
PLBBBT!
...SIR.
...

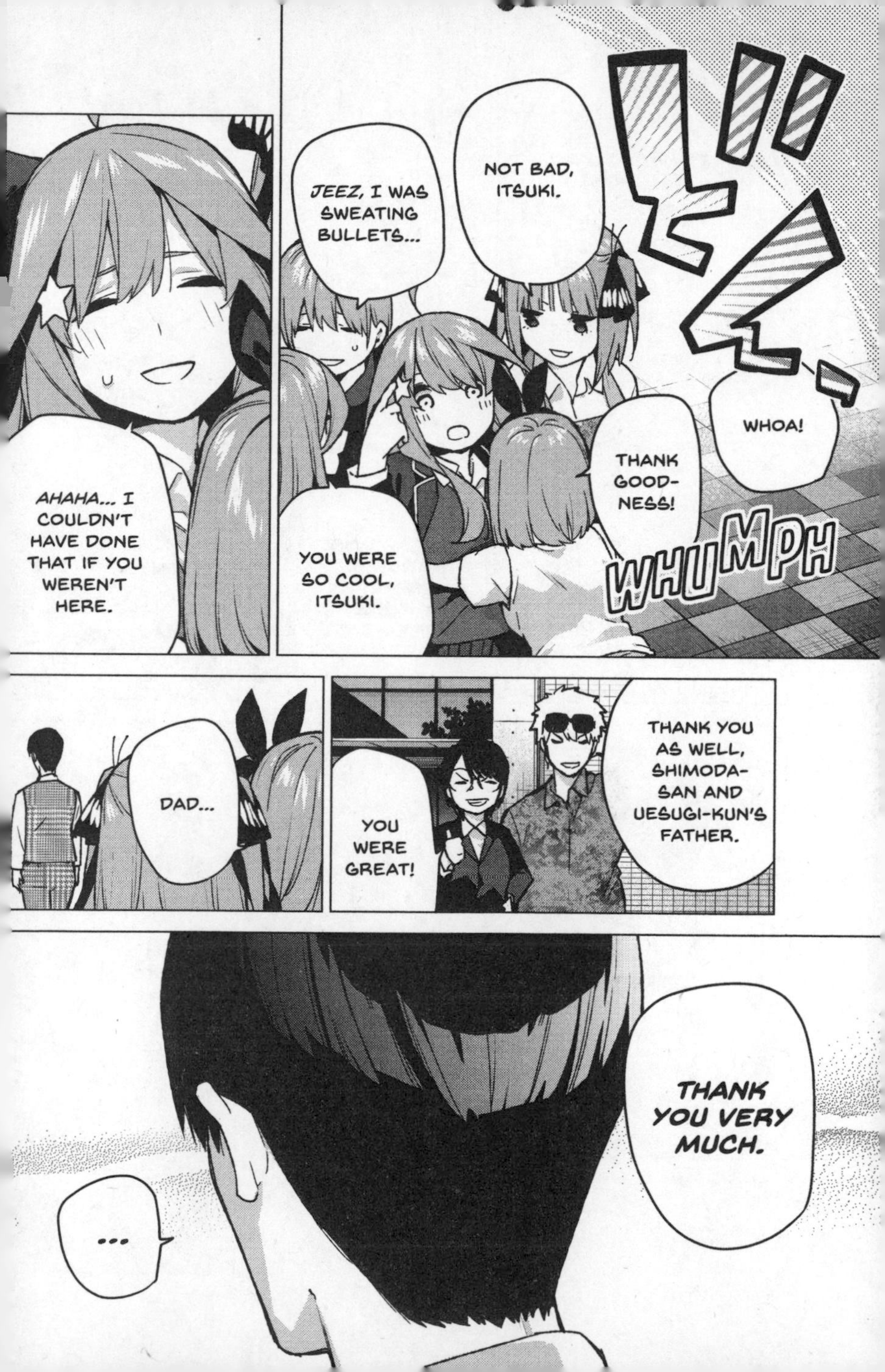
WHOA!
NOT BAD, ITSUKI.
JEEZ, I WAS SWEATING BULLETS...
THANK GOODNESS!
WHUMPH
YOU WERE SO COOL, ITSUKI.
AHAHA... I COULDN'T HAVE DONE THAT IF YOU WEREN'T HERE.
THANK YOU AS WELL, SHIMODA-SAN AND UESUGI-KUN'S FATHER.
YOU WERE GREAT!
DAD...
THANK YOU VERY MUCH.
...

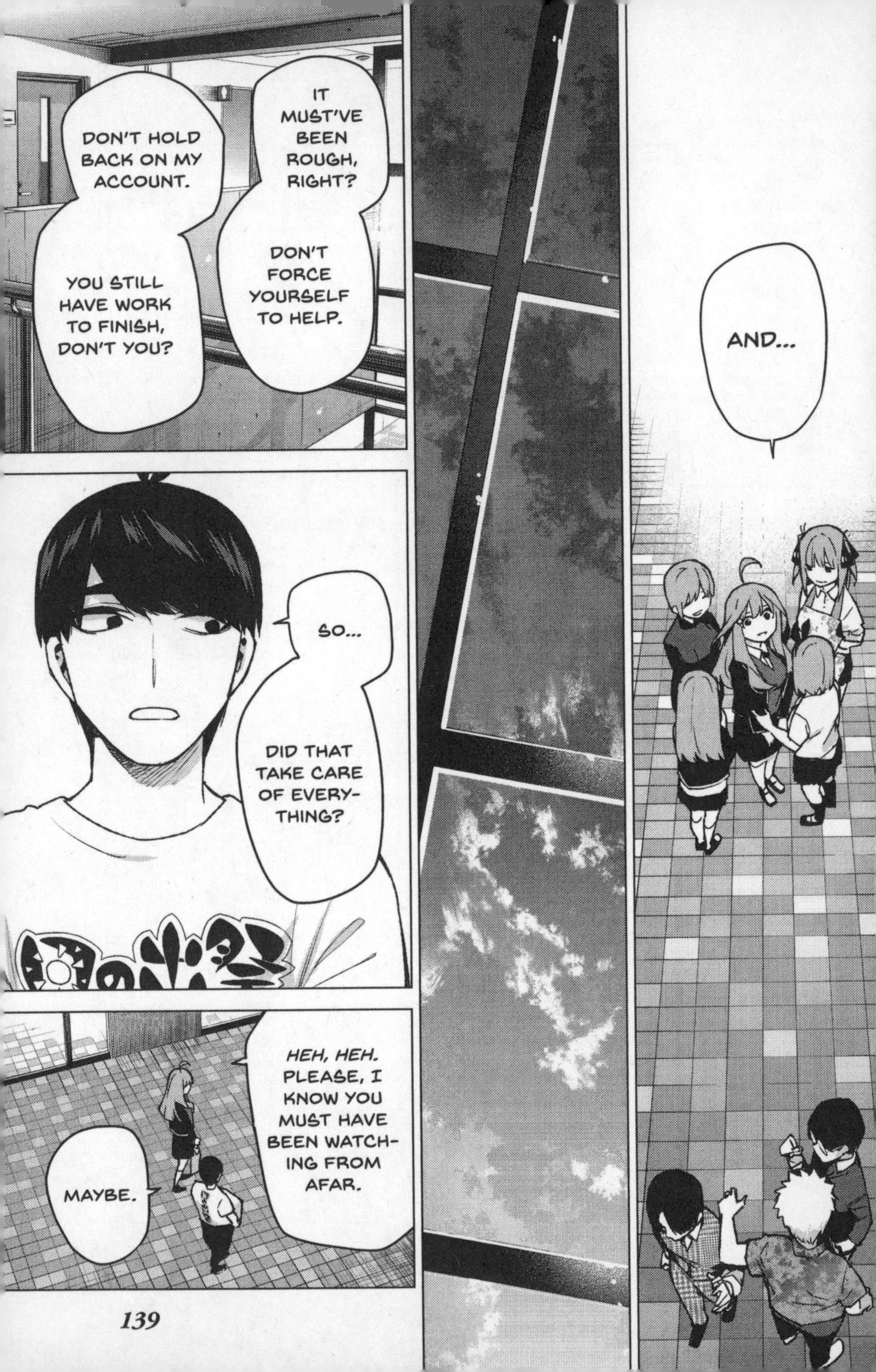
AND...
IT MUST'VE BEEN ROUGH, RIGHT?
DON'T FORCE YOURSELF TO HELP.
DON'T HOLD BACK ON MY ACCOUNT.
YOU STILL HAVE WORK TO FINISH, DON'T YOU?
SO...
DID THAT TAKE CARE OF EVERY-THING?
HEH, HEH. PLEASE, I KNOW YOU MUST HAVE BEEN WATCH-ING FROM AFAR.
MAYBE.

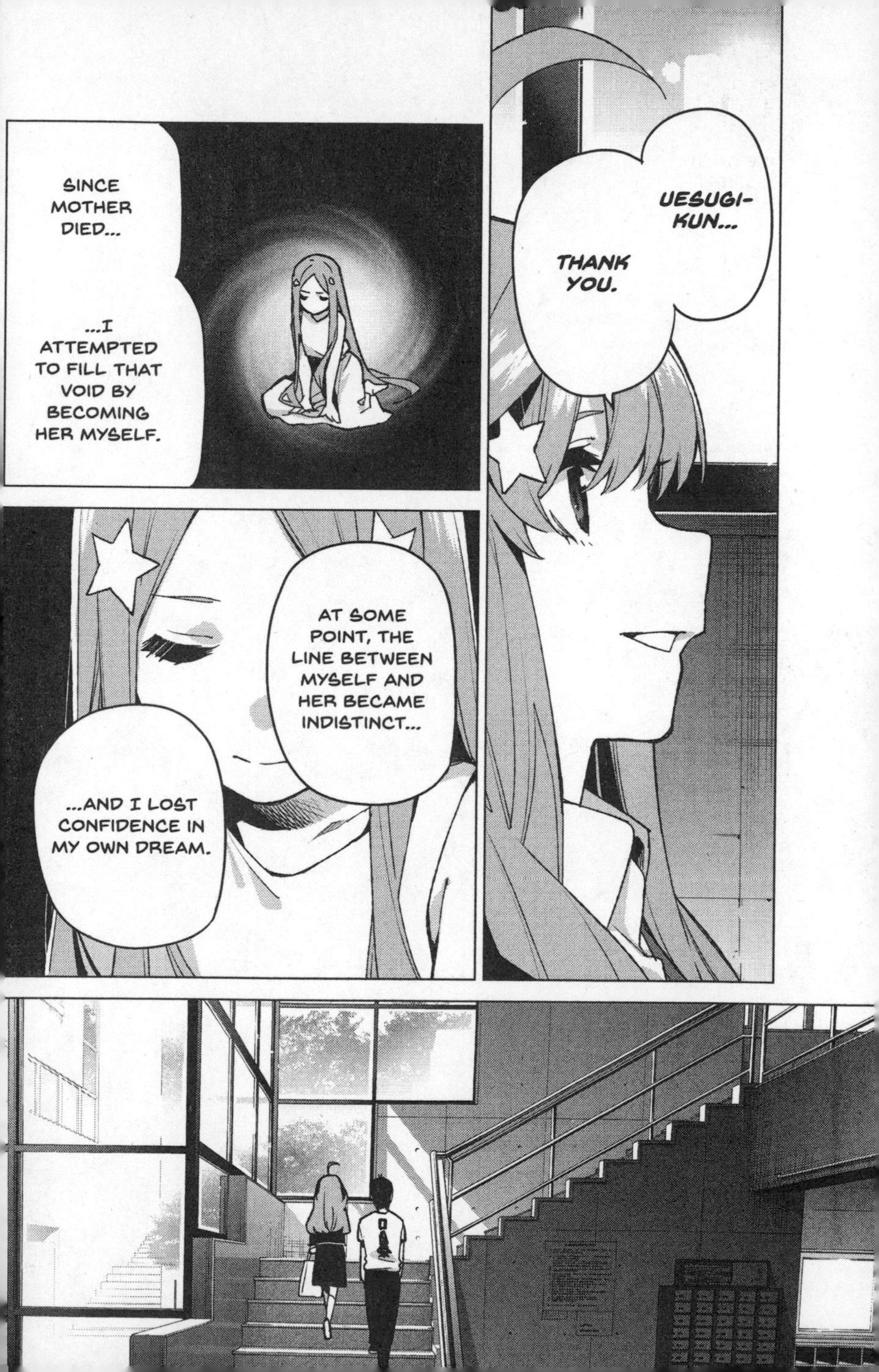
UESUGI-KUN...
THANK YOU.
SINCE MOTHER DIED...
...I ATTEMPTED TO FILL THAT VOID BY BECOMING HER MYSELF.
AT SOME POINT, THE LINE BETWEEN MYSELF AND HER BECAME INDISTINCT...
...AND I LOST CONFIDENCE IN MY OWN DREAM.

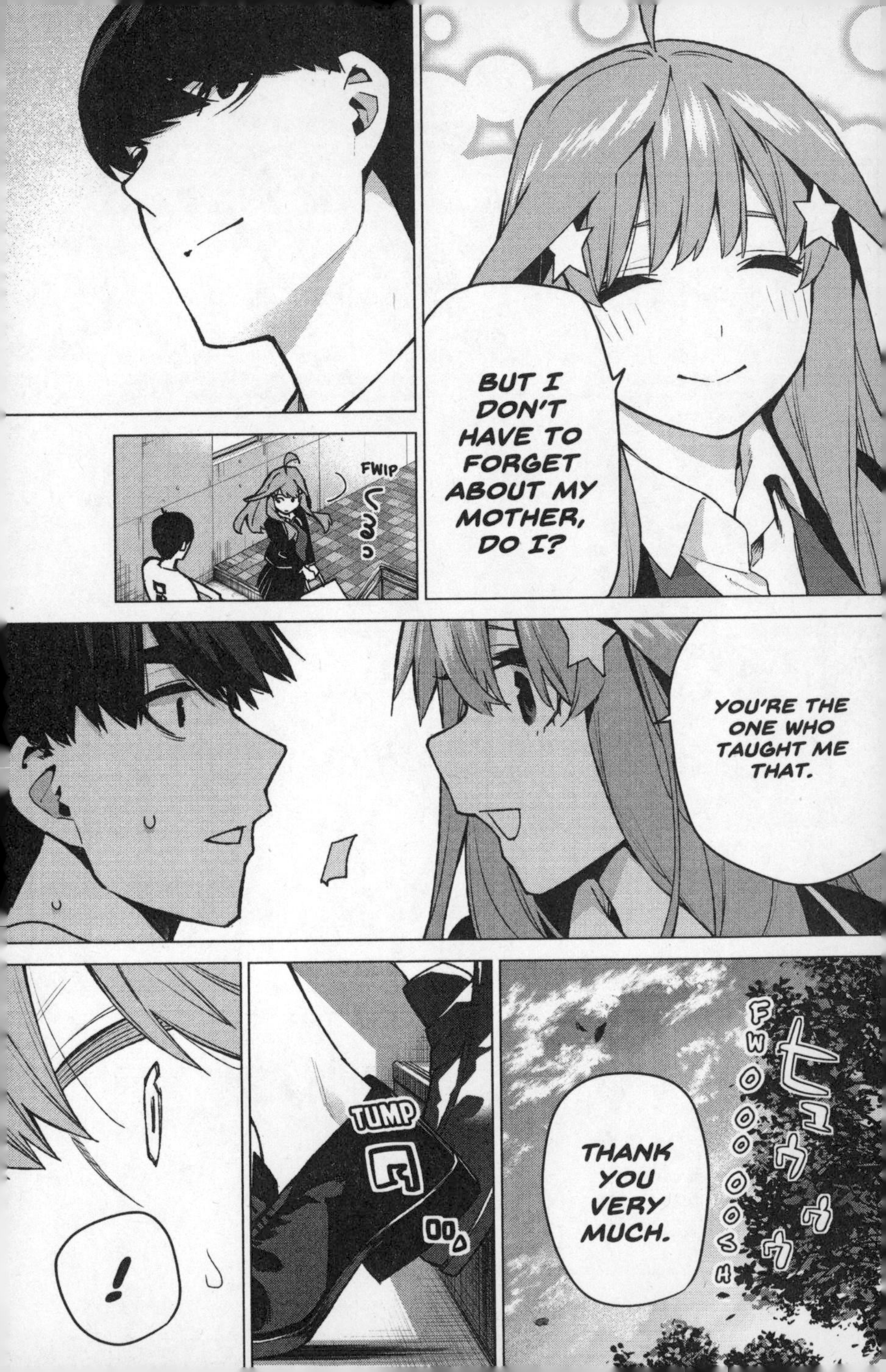
BUT I DON'T HAVE TO FORGET ABOUT MY MOTHER, DO I?
FWIP
YOU'RE THE ONE WHO TAUGHT ME THAT.
FWOOOOOOSH
THANK YOU VERY MUCH.
TUMP
!

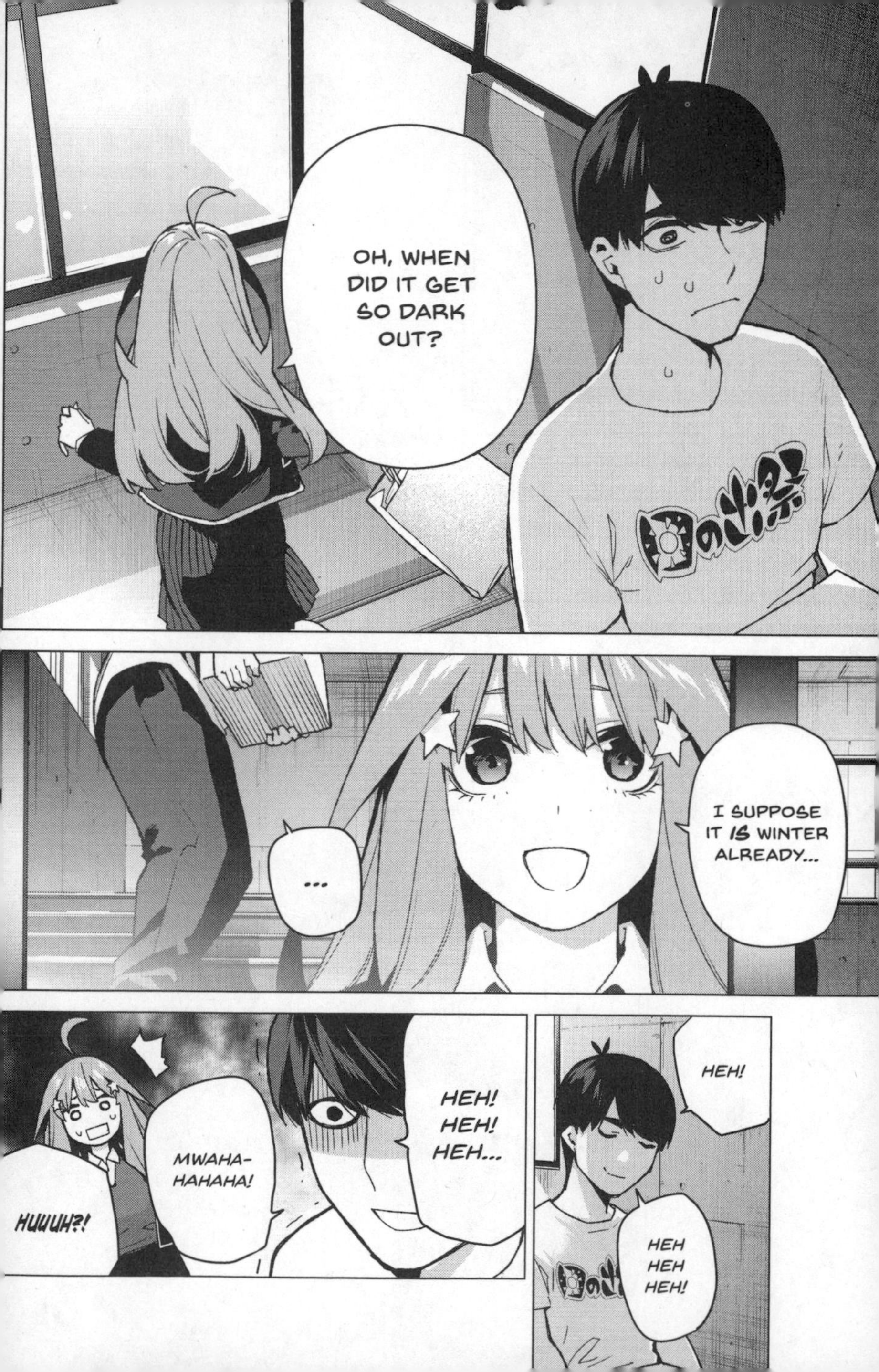
OH, WHEN DID IT GET SO DARK OUT?
I SUPPOSE IT *IS* WINTER ALREADY...
...
HEH!
HEH HEH HEH!
HEH! HEH! HEH...
MWAHA-HAHAHA!
HUUUH?!

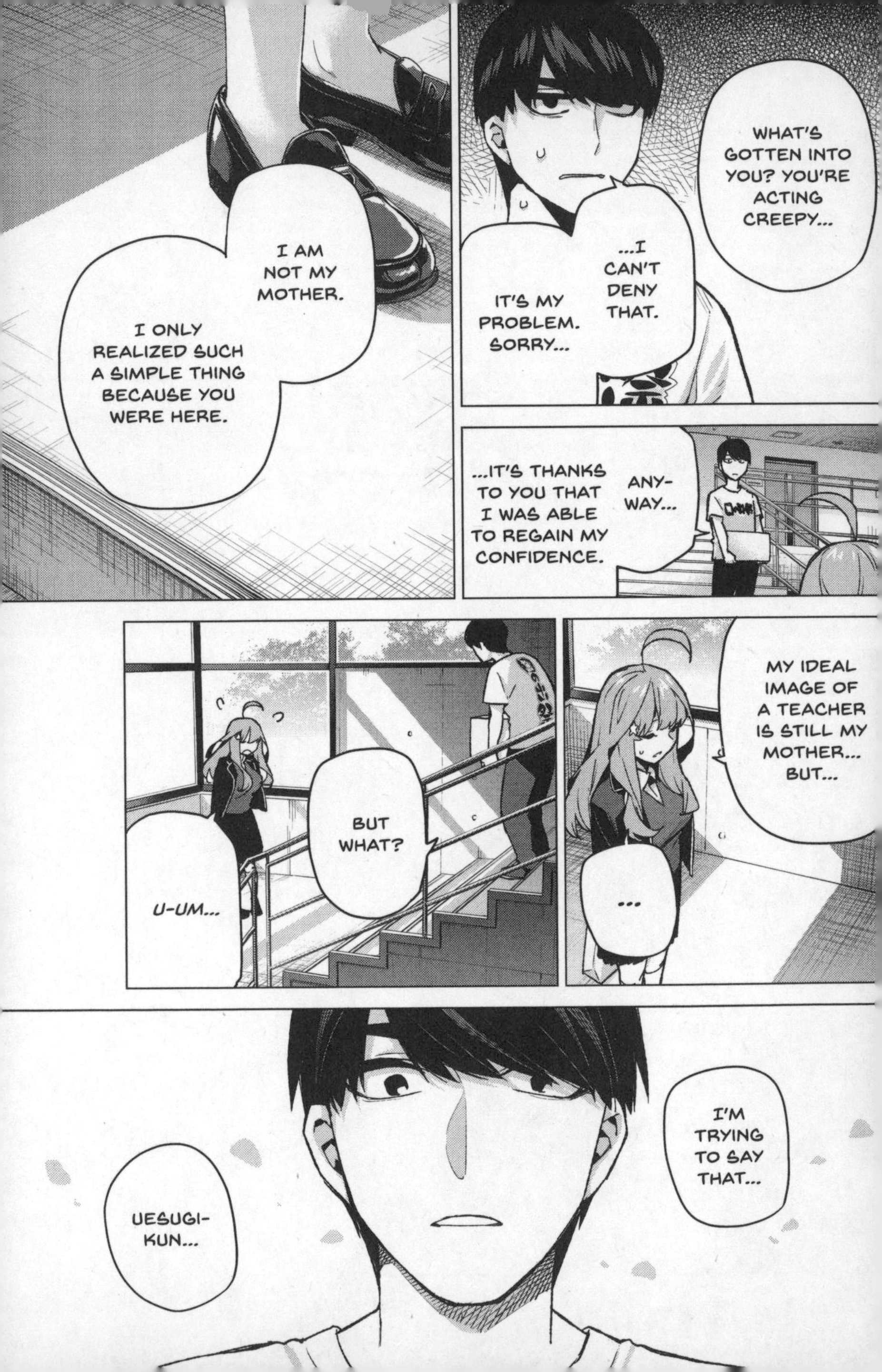
WHAT'S GOTTEN INTO YOU? YOU'RE ACTING CREEPY...
...I CAN'T DENY THAT.
IT'S MY PROBLEM. SORRY...
ANY-WAY...
...IT'S THANKS TO YOU THAT I WAS ABLE TO REGAIN MY CONFIDENCE.
I AM NOT MY MOTHER.
I ONLY REALIZED SUCH A SIMPLE THING BECAUSE YOU WERE HERE.
MY IDEAL IMAGE OF A TEACHER IS STILL MY MOTHER... BUT...
...
BUT WHAT?
U-UM...
I'M TRYING TO SAY THAT...
UESUGI-KUN...

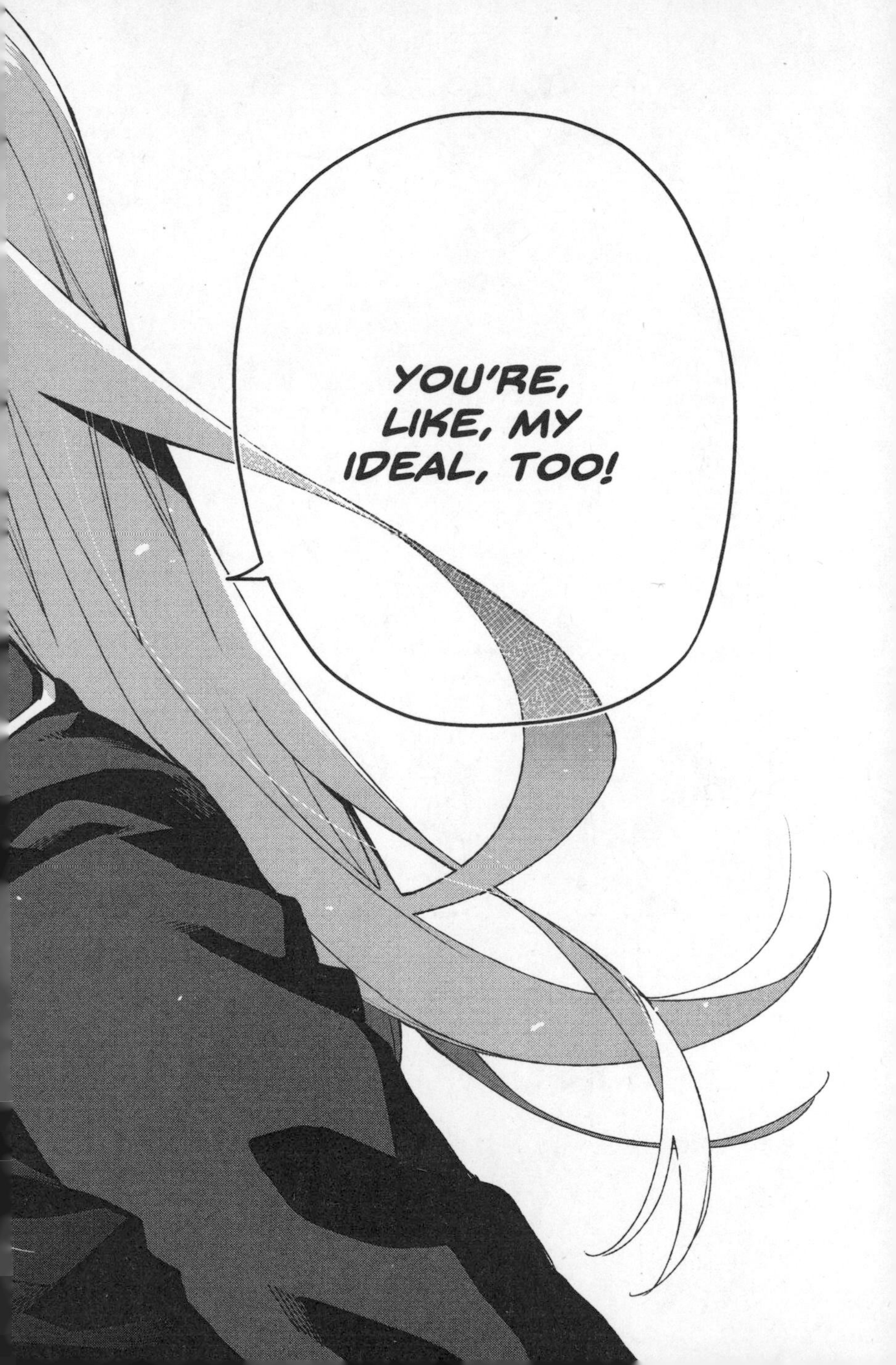
YOU'RE, LIKE, MY IDEAL, TOO!

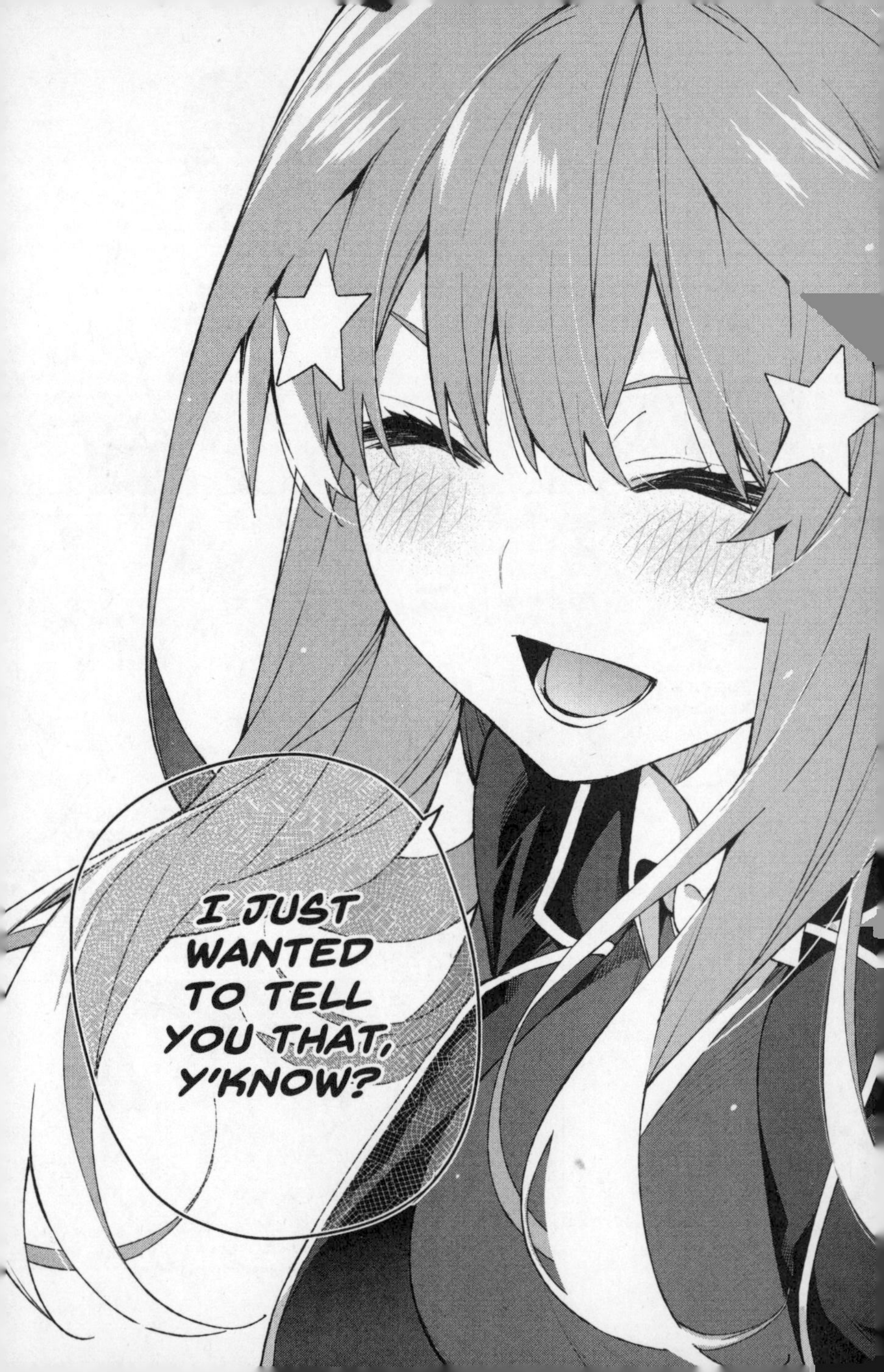
I JUST WANTED TO TELL YOU THAT, Y'KNOW?

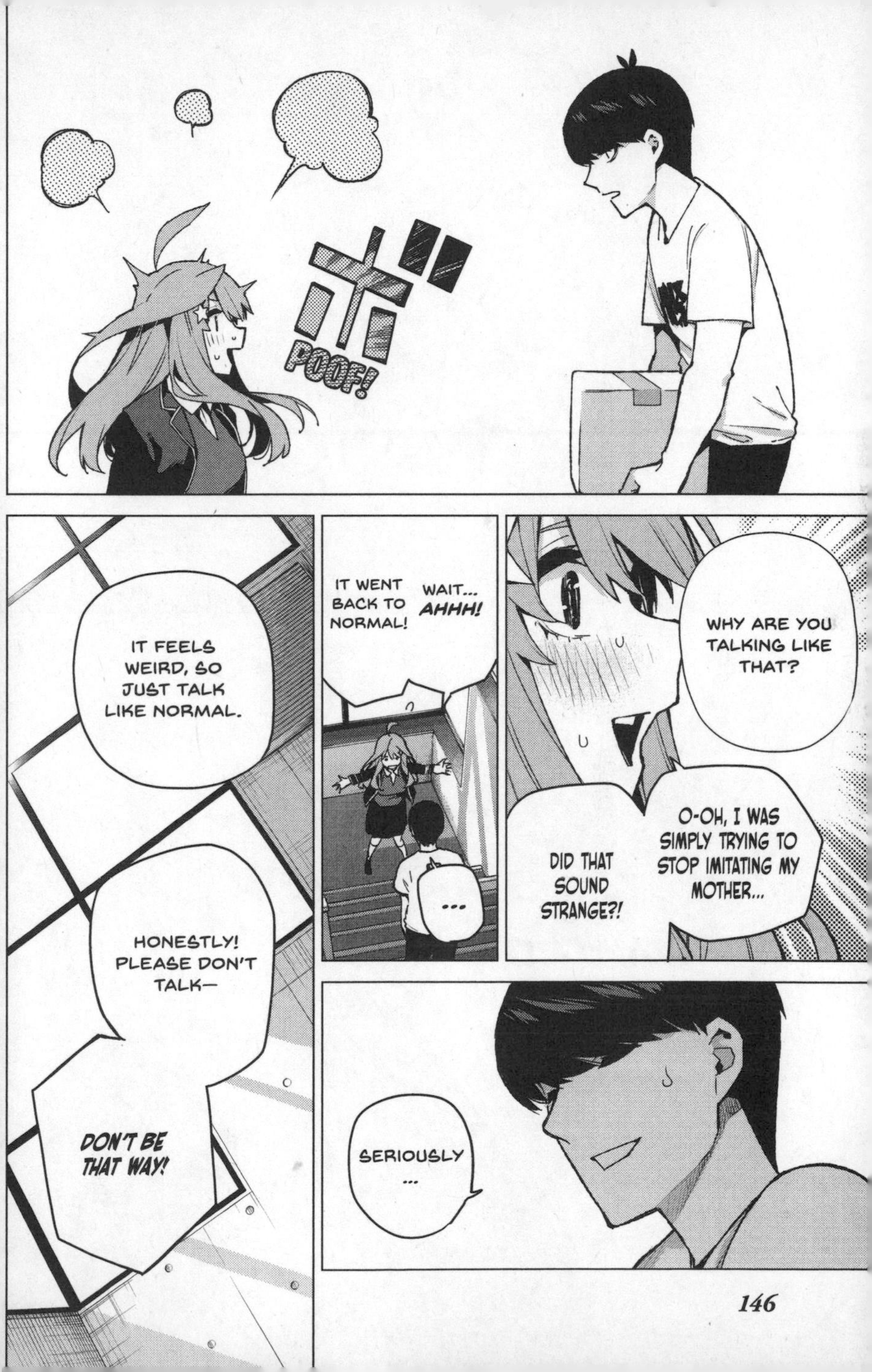
POOF!
WHY ARE YOU TALKING LIKE THAT?
O-OH, I WAS SIMPLY TRYING TO STOP IMITATING MY MOTHER...
DID THAT SOUND STRANGE?!
IT WENT BACK TO NORMAL!
WAIT... AHHH!
...
SERIOUSLY ...
IT FEELS WEIRD, SO JUST TALK LIKE NORMAL.
HONESTLY! PLEASE DON'T TALK—
DON'T BE THAT WAY!

CHAPTER 112
IF THE FINAL FESTIVAL WAS THE QUINTS'

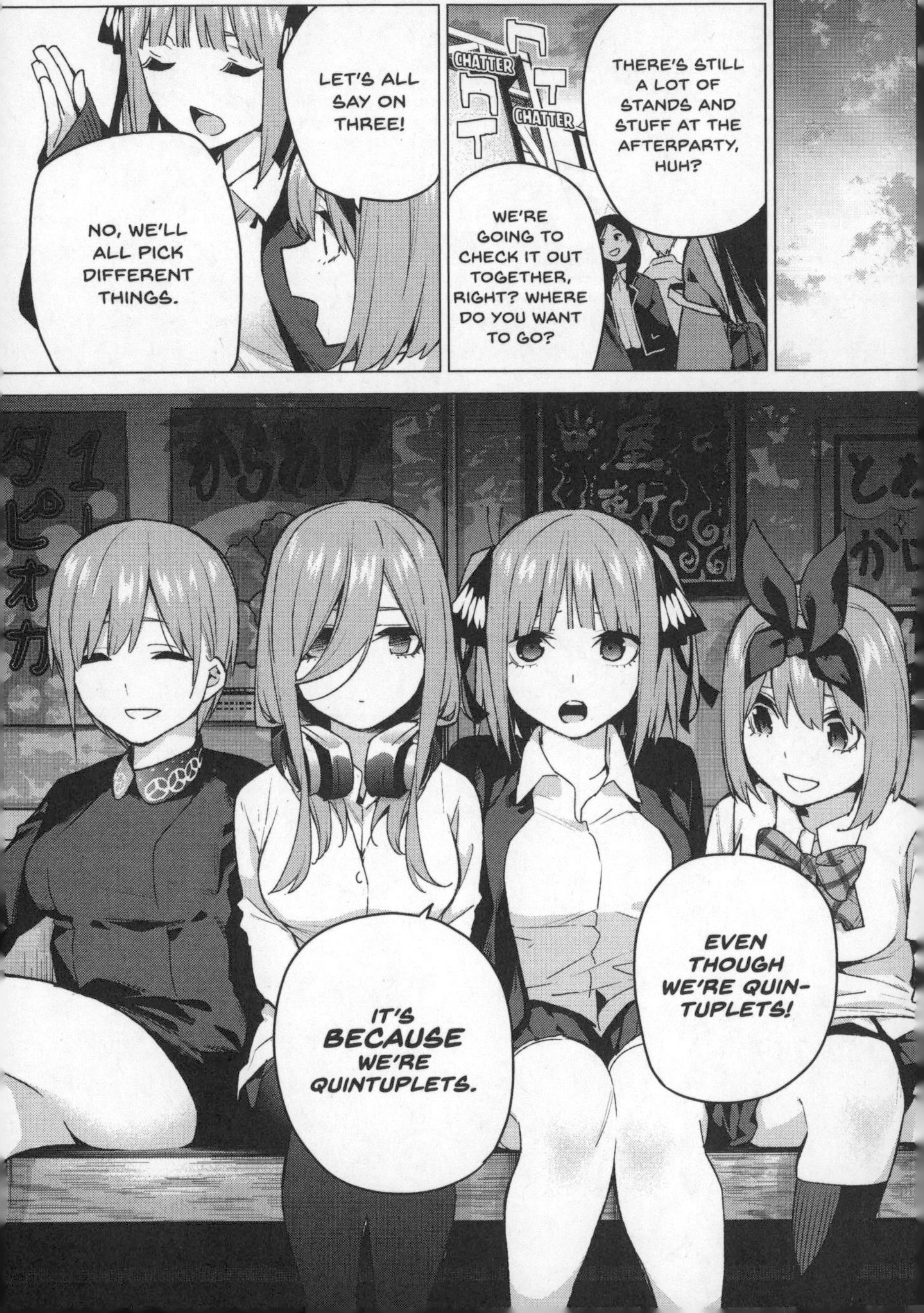
CHATTER
CHATTER
THERE'S STILL A LOT OF STANDS AND STUFF AT THE AFTERPARTY, HUH?
WE'RE GOING TO CHECK IT OUT TOGETHER, RIGHT? WHERE DO YOU WANT TO GO?
LET'S ALL SAY ON THREE!
NO, WE'LL ALL PICK DIFFERENT THINGS.
EVEN THOUGH WE'RE QUIN-TUPLETS!
IT'S BECAUSE WE'RE QUINTUPLETS.

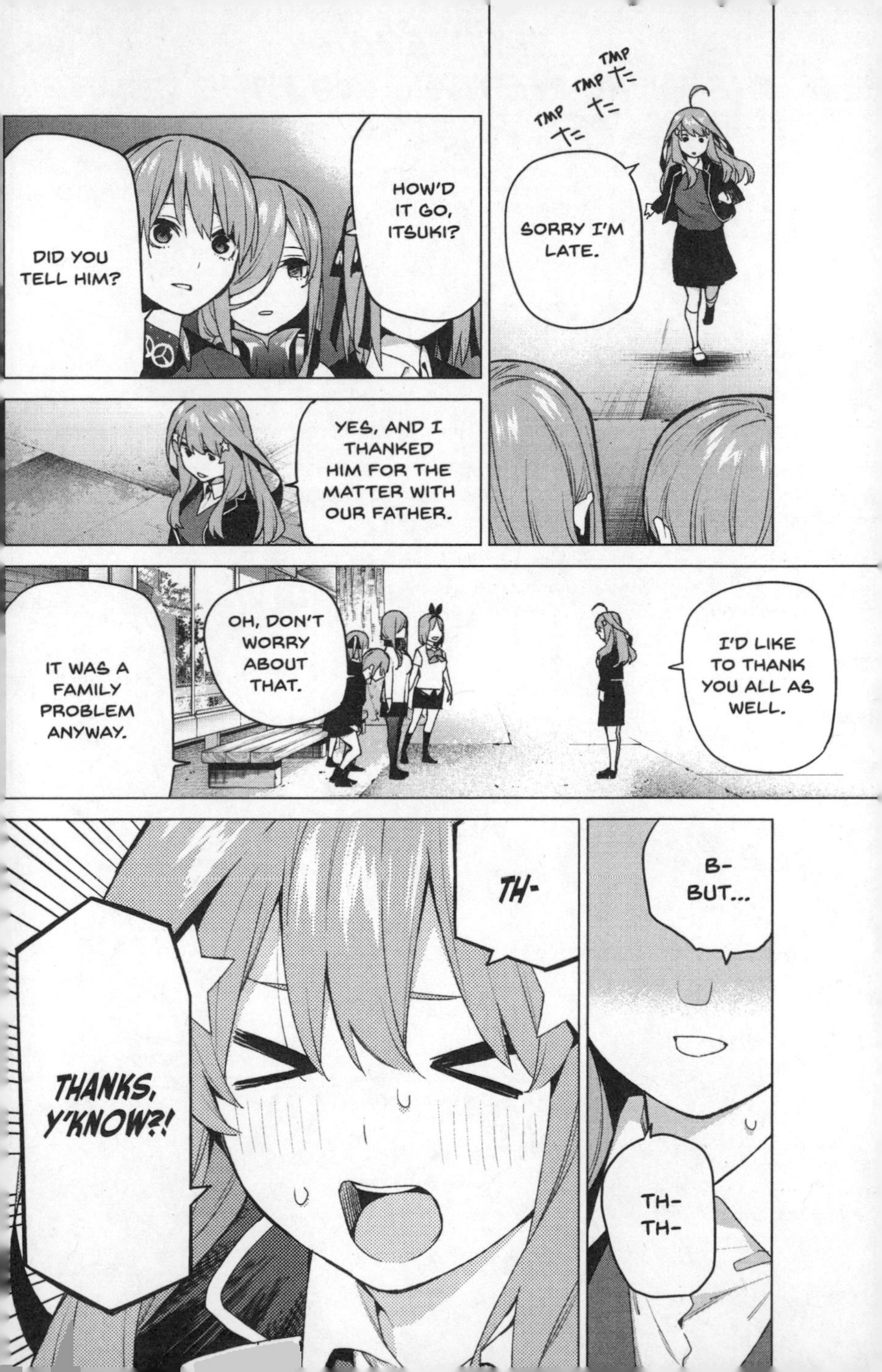
TMP
TMP
TMP
SORRY I'M LATE.
HOW'D IT GO, ITSUKI?
DID YOU TELL HIM?
YES, AND I THANKED HIM FOR THE MATTER WITH OUR FATHER.
I'D LIKE TO THANK YOU ALL AS WELL.
OH, DON'T WORRY ABOUT THAT.
IT WAS A FAMILY PROBLEM ANYWAY.
B- BUT...
TH- TH-
TH-
THANKS, Y'KNOW?!

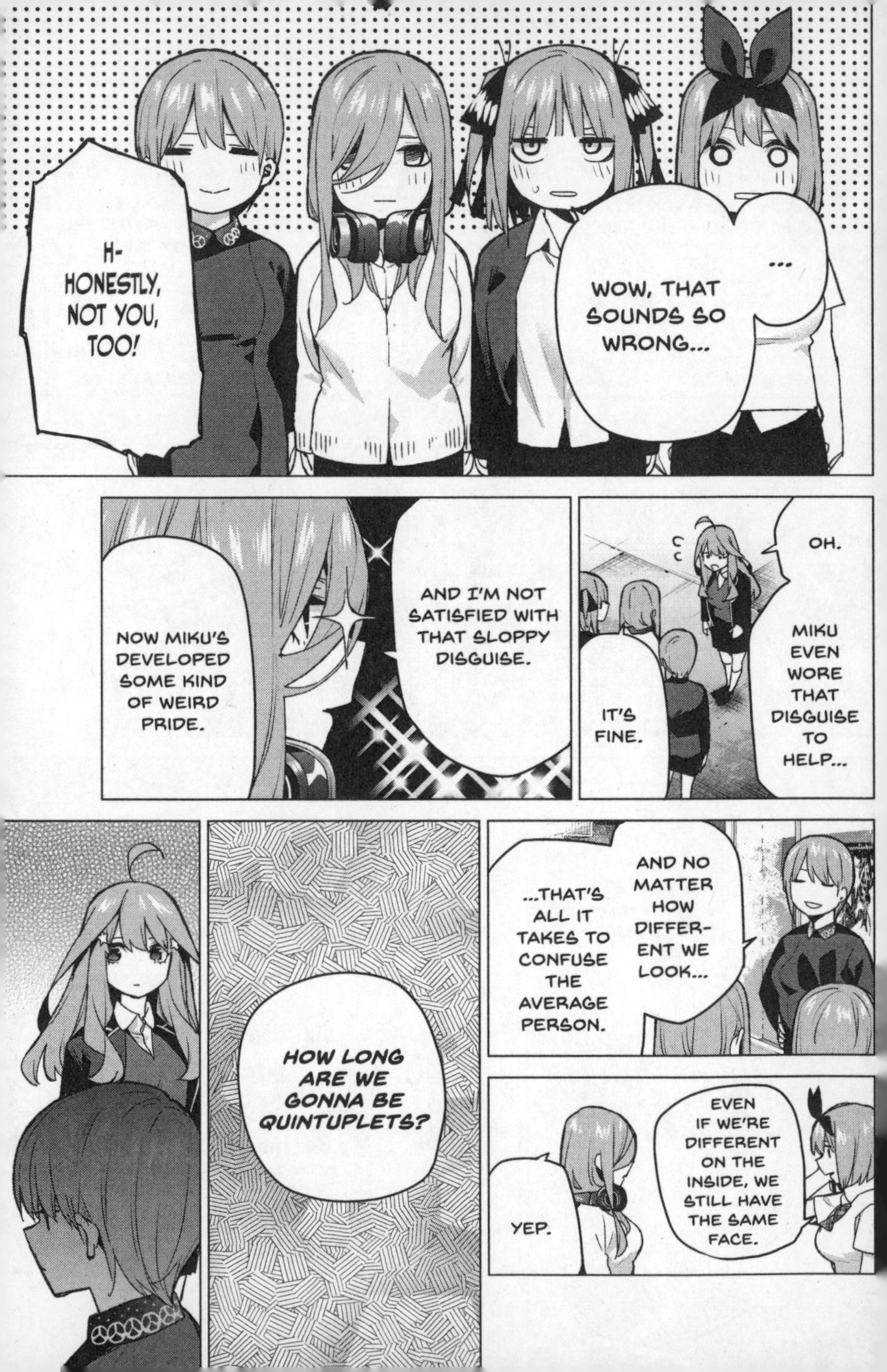
...
WOW, THAT SOUNDS SO WRONG...
H-HONESTLY, NOT YOU, TOO!
OH.
MIKU EVEN WORE THAT DISGUISE TO HELP...
IT'S FINE.
AND I'M NOT SATISFIED WITH THAT SLOPPY DISGUISE.
NOW MIKU'S DEVELOPED SOME KIND OF WEIRD PRIDE.
AND NO MATTER HOW DIFFERENT WE LOOK...
...THAT'S ALL IT TAKES TO CONFUSE THE AVERAGE PERSON.
EVEN IF WE'RE DIFFERENT ON THE INSIDE, WE STILL HAVE THE SAME FACE.
YEP.
HOW LONG ARE WE GONNA BE QUINTUPLETS?

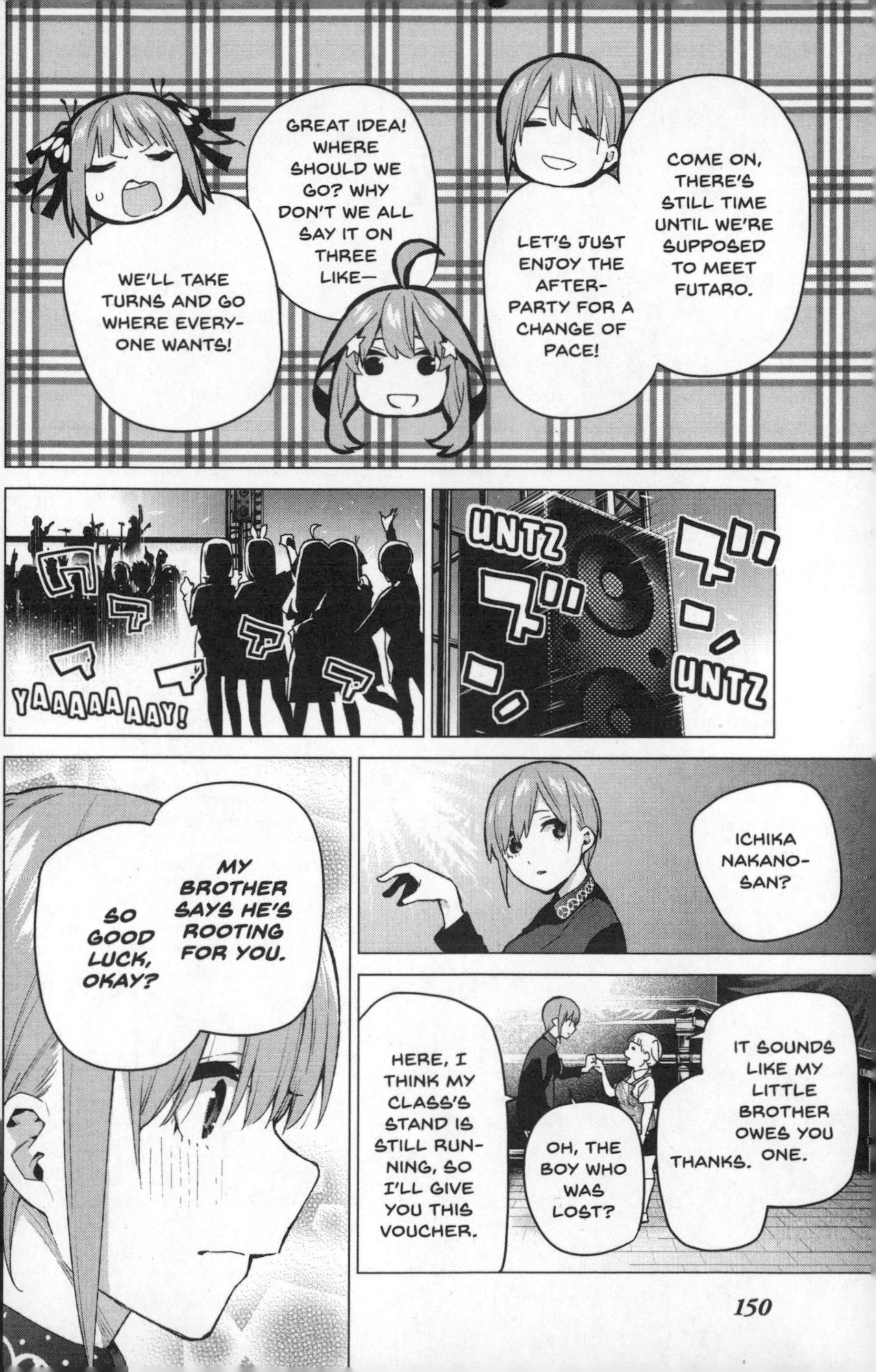
COME ON, THERE'S STILL TIME UNTIL WE'RE SUPPOSED TO MEET FUTARO.
LET'S JUST ENJOY THE AFTER-PARTY FOR A CHANGE OF PACE!
GREAT IDEA! WHERE SHOULD WE GO? WHY DON'T WE ALL SAY IT ON THREE LIKE—
WE'LL TAKE TURNS AND GO WHERE EVERY-ONE WANTS!
UNTZ
UNTZ
YAAAAAAAY!
ICHIKA NAKANO-SAN?
IT SOUNDS LIKE MY LITTLE BROTHER OWES YOU ONE.
THANKS.
OH, THE BOY WHO WAS LOST?
HERE, I THINK MY CLASS'S STAND IS STILL RUN-NING, SO I'LL GIVE YOU THIS VOUCHER.
MY BROTHER SAYS HE'S ROOTING FOR YOU.
SO GOOD LUCK, OKAY?

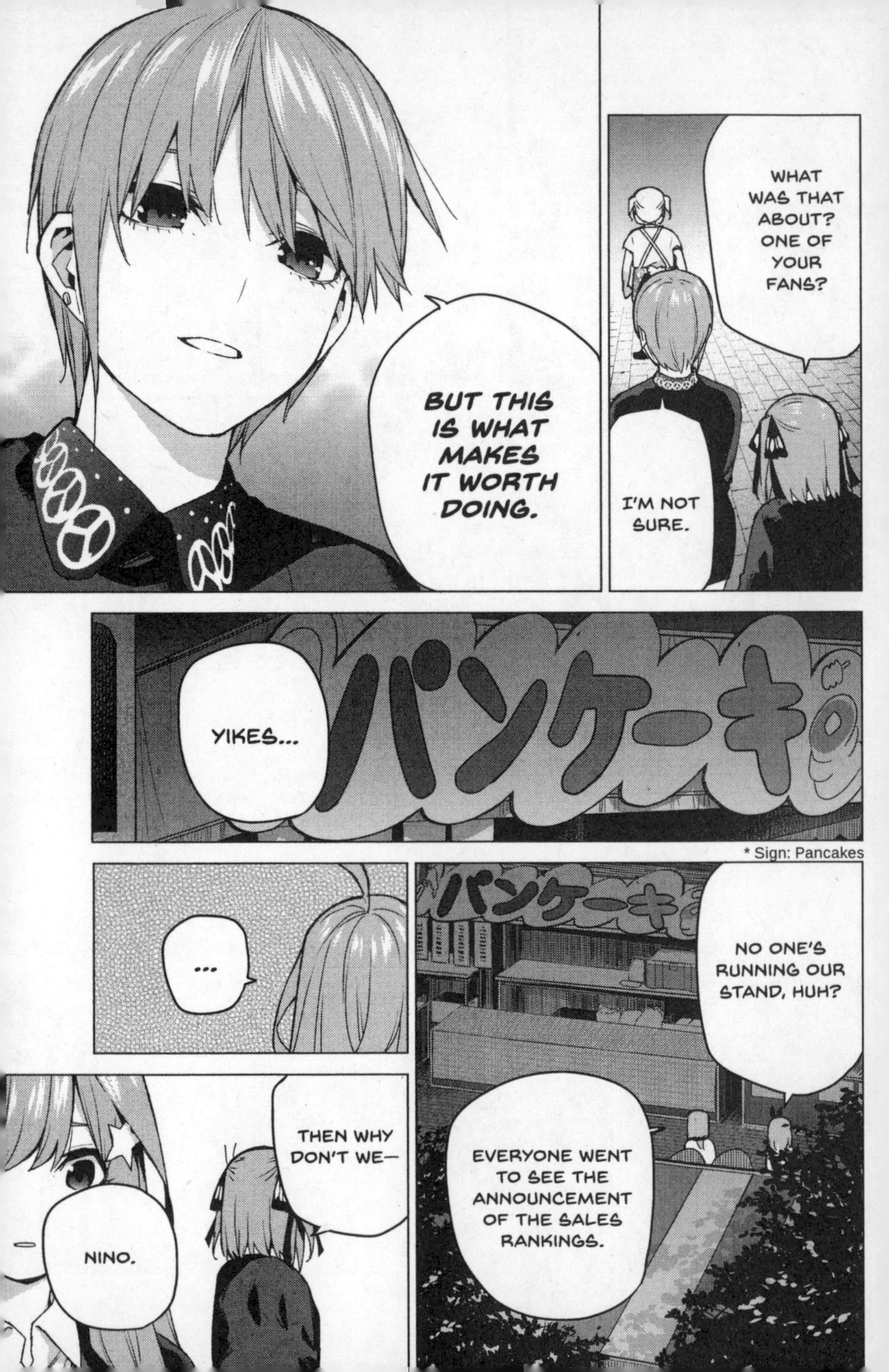
WHAT WAS THAT ABOUT? ONE OF YOUR FANS?
I'M NOT SURE.
BUT THIS IS WHAT MAKES IT WORTH DOING.
パンケーキ
YIKES...
* Sign: Pancakes
パンケーキ
NO ONE'S RUNNING OUR STAND, HUH?
EVERYONE WENT TO SEE THE ANNOUNCEMENT OF THE SALES RANKINGS.
...
THEN WHY DON'T WE—
NINO.

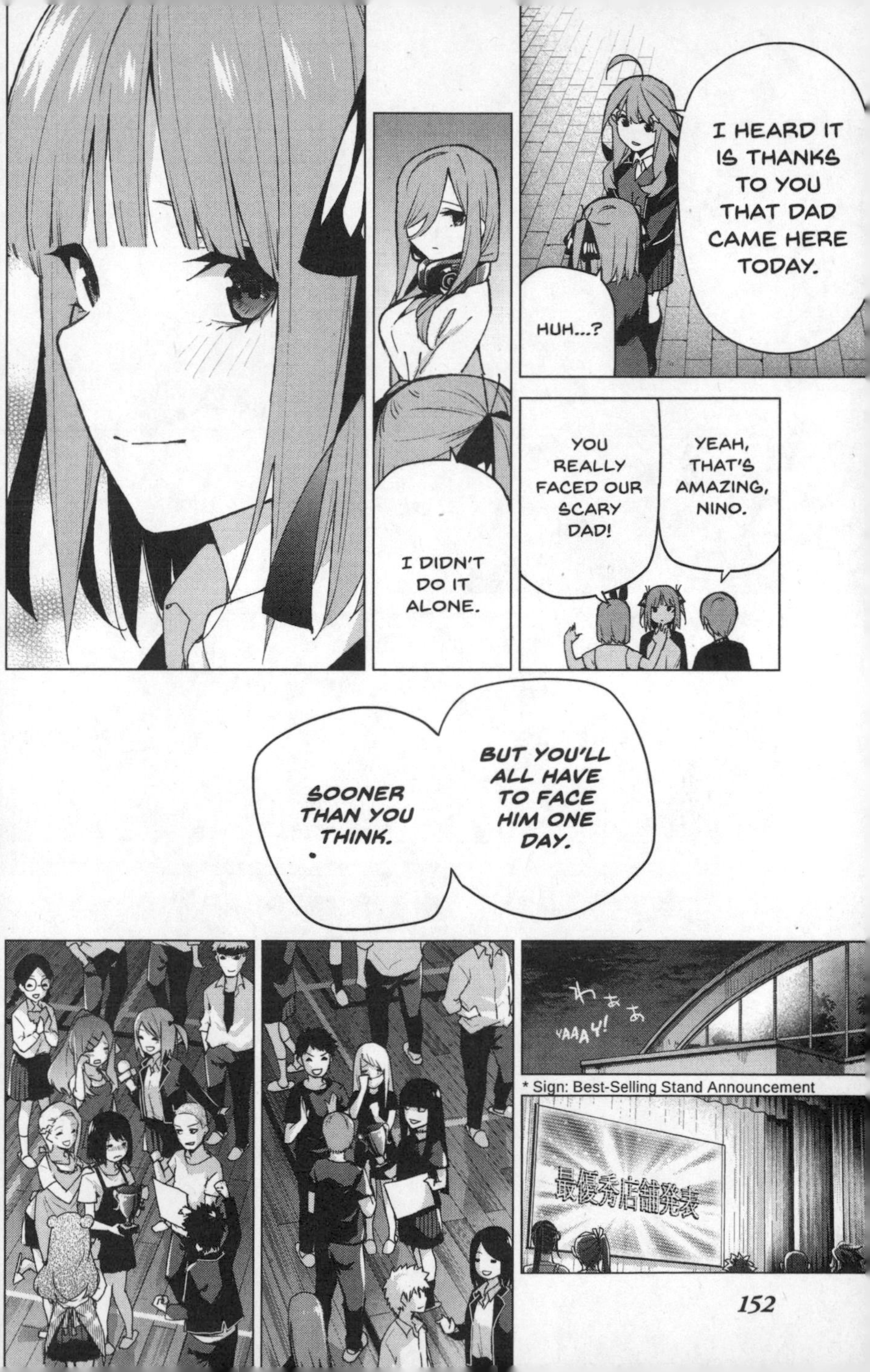
I HEARD IT IS THANKS TO YOU THAT DAD CAME HERE TODAY.
HUH...?
YEAH, THAT'S AMAZING, NINO.
YOU REALLY FACED OUR SCARY DAD!
I DIDN'T DO IT ALONE.
BUT YOU'LL ALL HAVE TO FACE HIM ONE DAY.
SOONER THAN YOU THINK.
わあぁ
YAAAY!
* Sign: Best-Selling Stand Announcement
最優秀店舗発表

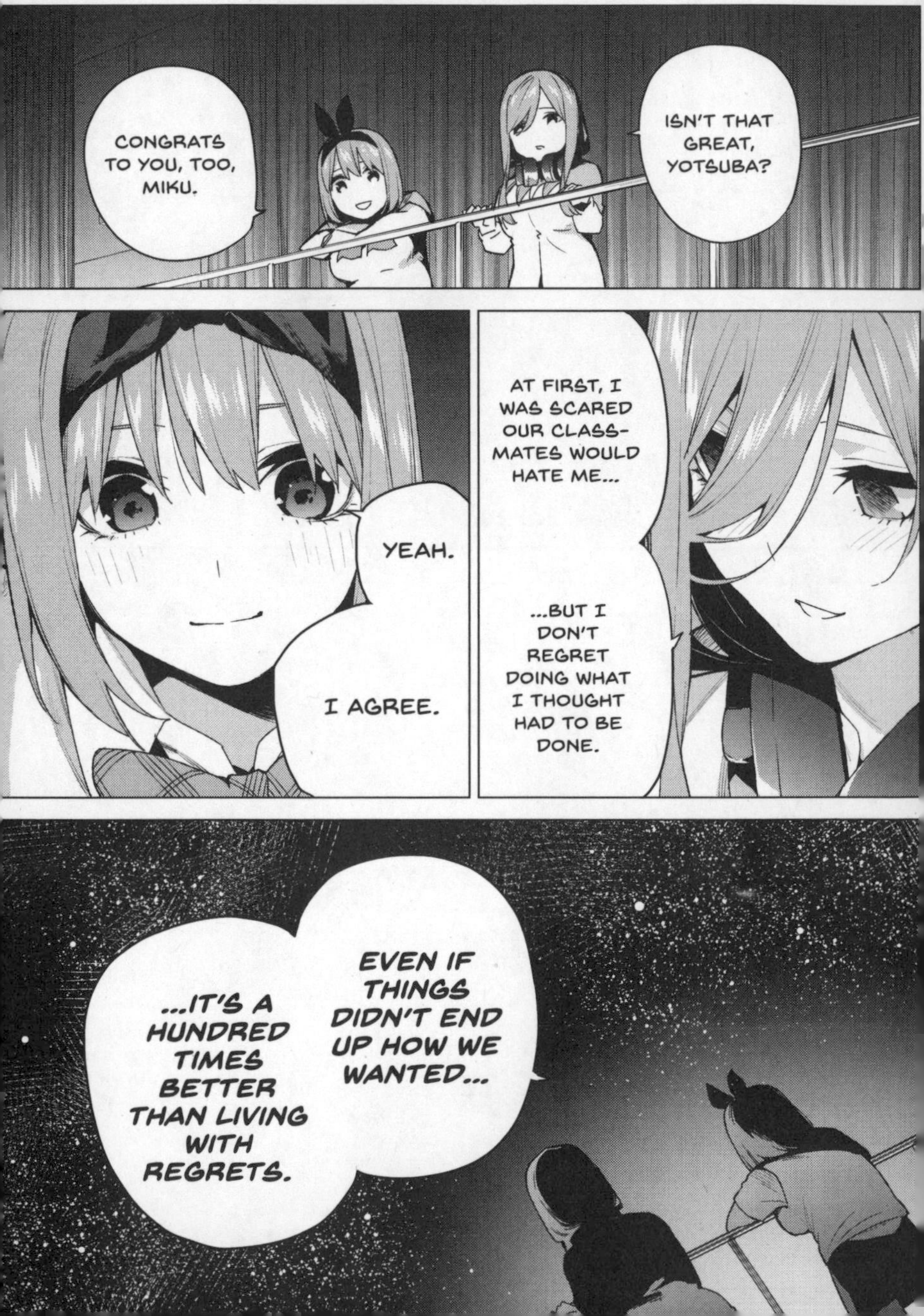
ISN'T THAT GREAT, YOTSUBA?
CONGRATS TO YOU, TOO, MIKU.
AT FIRST, I WAS SCARED OUR CLASSMATES WOULD HATE ME...
...BUT I DON'T REGRET DOING WHAT I THOUGHT HAD TO BE DONE.
YEAH.
I AGREE.
EVEN IF THINGS DIDN'T END UP HOW WE WANTED...
...IT'S A HUNDRED TIMES BETTER THAN LIVING WITH REGRETS.

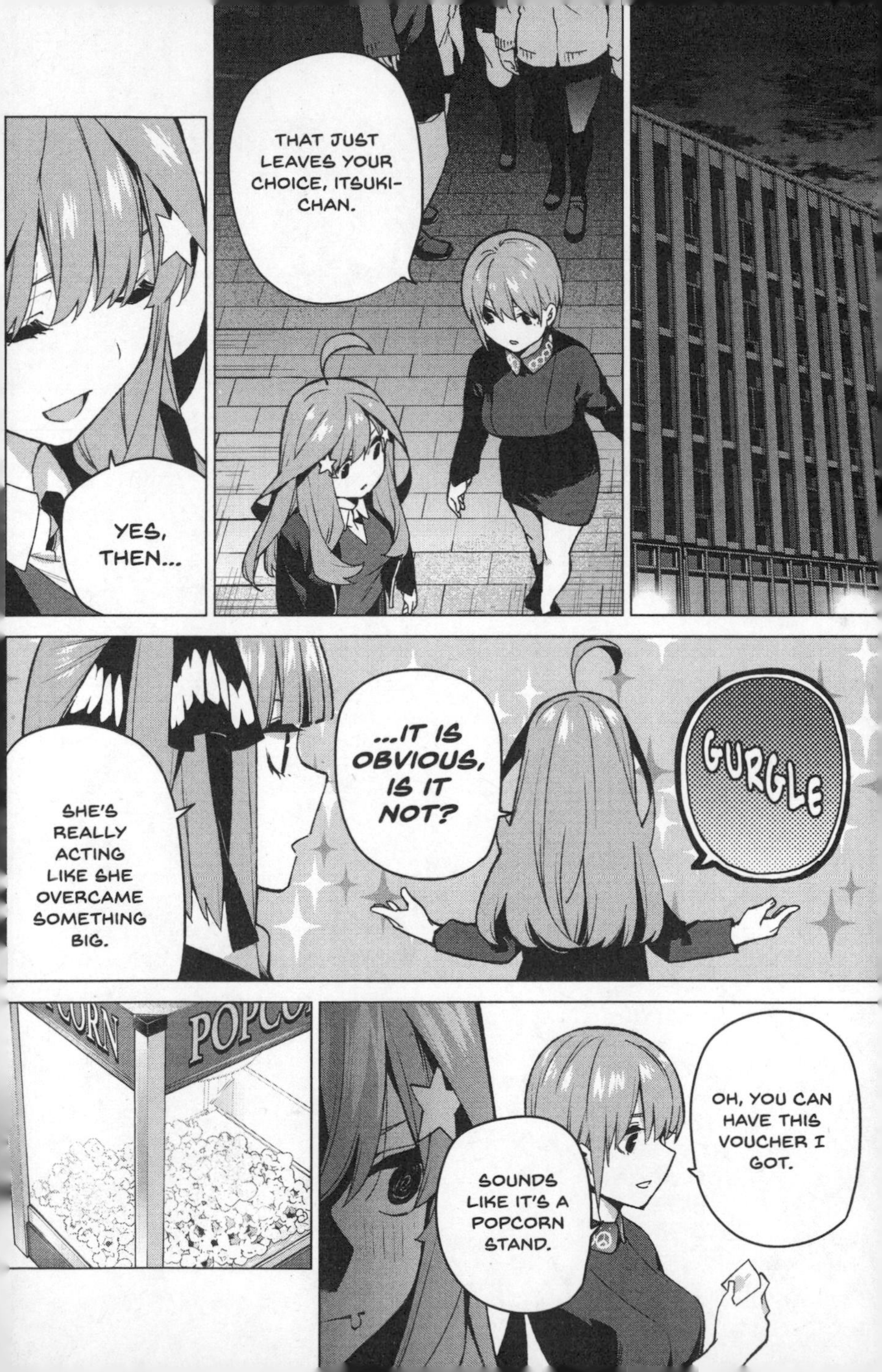
THAT JUST LEAVES YOUR CHOICE, ITSUKI-CHAN.
YES, THEN...
GURGLE
...IT IS OBVIOUS, IS IT NOT?
SHE'S REALLY ACTING LIKE SHE OVERCAME SOMETHING BIG.
OH, YOU CAN HAVE THIS VOUCHER I GOT.
SOUNDS LIKE IT'S A POPCORN STAND.

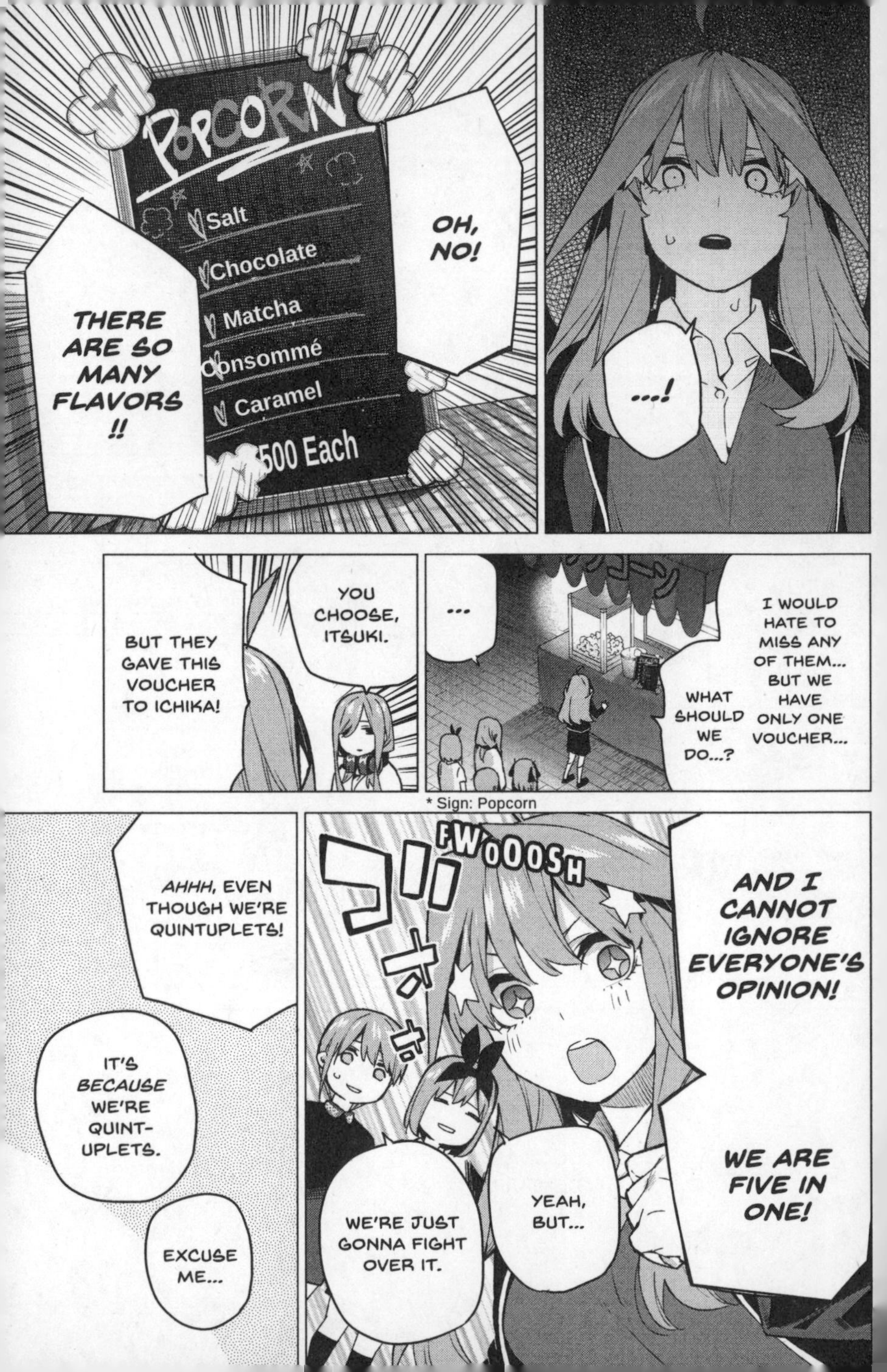
...!
OH, NO!
THERE ARE SO MANY FLAVORS !!
POPCORN
Salt
Chocolate
Matcha
Consommé
Caramel
500 Each
I WOULD HATE TO MISS ANY OF THEM... BUT WE HAVE ONLY ONE VOUCHER...
WHAT SHOULD WE DO...?
...
YOU CHOOSE, ITSUKI.
BUT THEY GAVE THIS VOUCHER TO ICHIKA!
FWOOOSH
AND I CANNOT IGNORE EVERYONE'S OPINION!
WE ARE FIVE IN ONE!
YEAH, BUT...
WE'RE JUST GONNA FIGHT OVER IT.
AHHH, EVEN THOUGH WE'RE QUINTUPLETS!
IT'S BECAUSE WE'RE QUINT-UPLETS.
EXCUSE ME...
* Sign: Popcorn

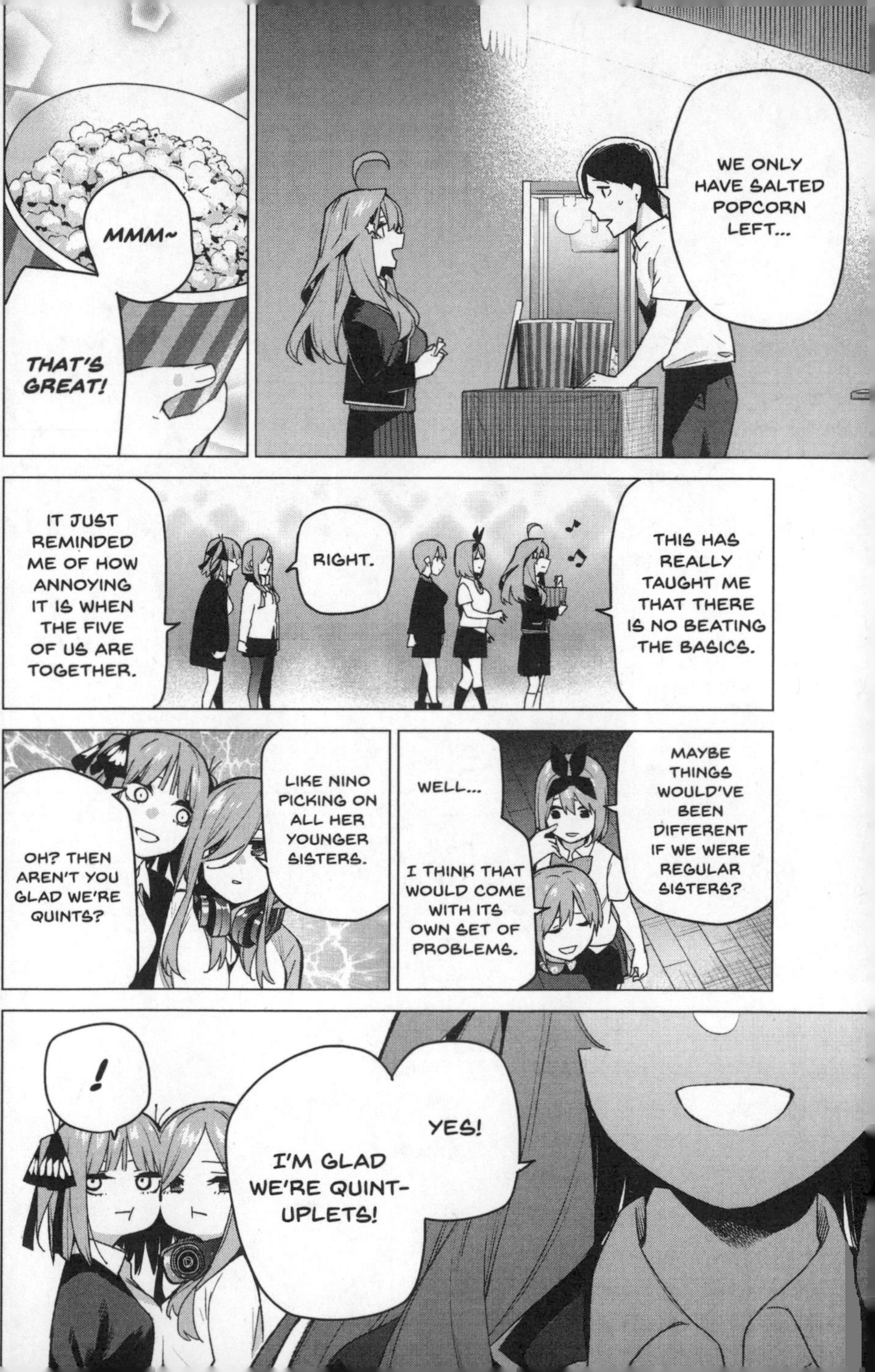
WE ONLY HAVE SALTED POPCORN LEFT...
MMM~
THAT'S GREAT!
THIS HAS REALLY TAUGHT ME THAT THERE IS NO BEATING THE BASICS.
RIGHT.
IT JUST REMINDED ME OF HOW ANNOYING IT IS WHEN THE FIVE OF US ARE TOGETHER.
MAYBE THINGS WOULD'VE BEEN DIFFERENT IF WE WERE REGULAR SISTERS?
WELL...
I THINK THAT WOULD COME WITH ITS OWN SET OF PROBLEMS.
LIKE NINO PICKING ON ALL HER YOUNGER SISTERS.
OH? THEN AREN'T YOU GLAD WE'RE QUINTS?
YES!
I'M GLAD WE'RE QUINT-UPLETS!
!

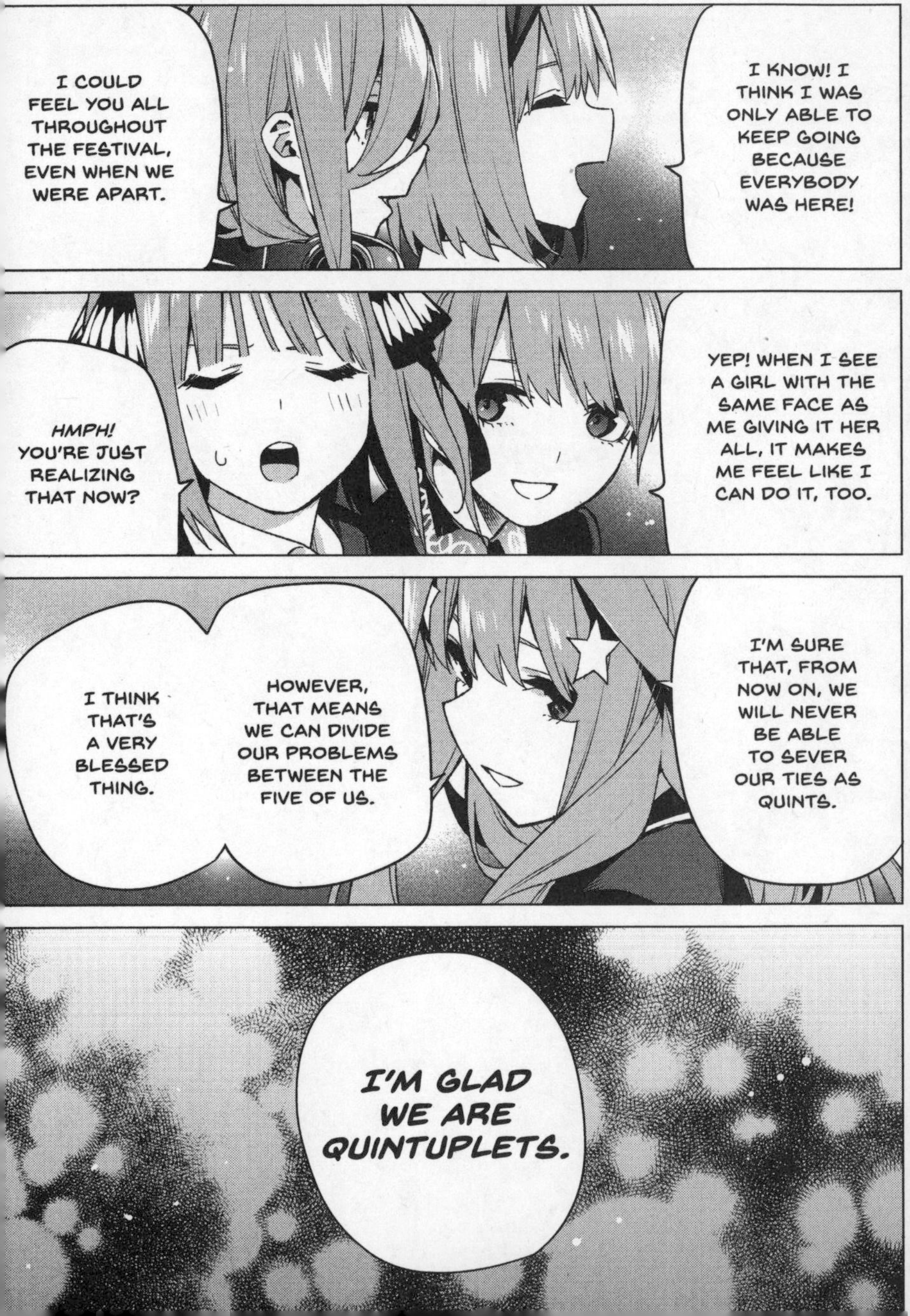
I KNOW! I THINK I WAS ONLY ABLE TO KEEP GOING BECAUSE EVERYBODY WAS HERE!
I COULD FEEL YOU ALL THROUGHOUT THE FESTIVAL, EVEN WHEN WE WERE APART.
YEP! WHEN I SEE A GIRL WITH THE SAME FACE AS ME GIVING IT HER ALL, IT MAKES ME FEEL LIKE I CAN DO IT, TOO.
HMPH! YOU'RE JUST REALIZING THAT NOW?
I'M SURE THAT, FROM NOW ON, WE WILL NEVER BE ABLE TO SEVER OUR TIES AS QUINTS.
HOWEVER, THAT MEANS WE CAN DIVIDE OUR PROBLEMS BETWEEN THE FIVE OF US.
I THINK THAT'S A VERY BLESSED THING.
I'M GLAD WE ARE QUINTUPLETS.

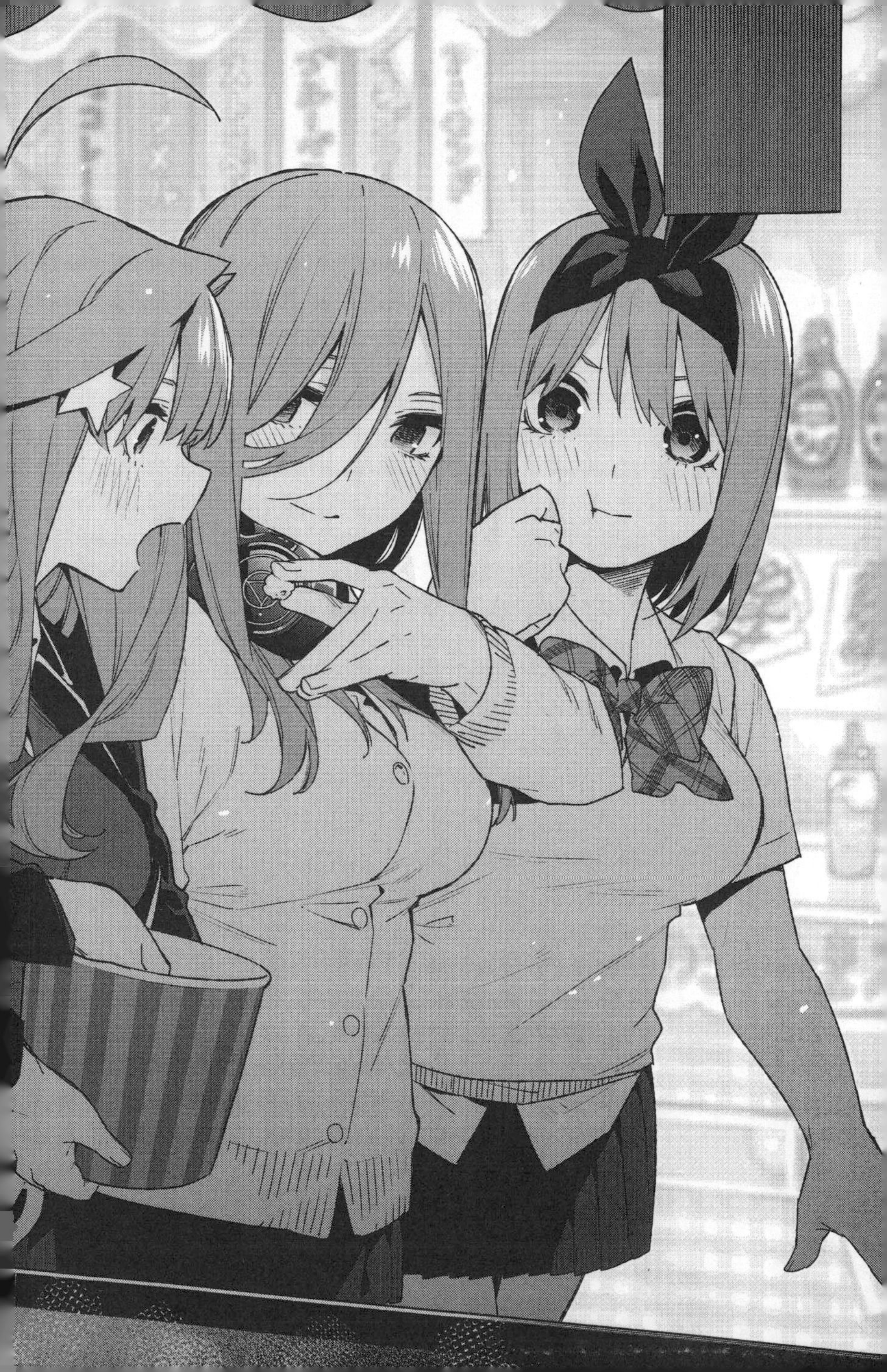

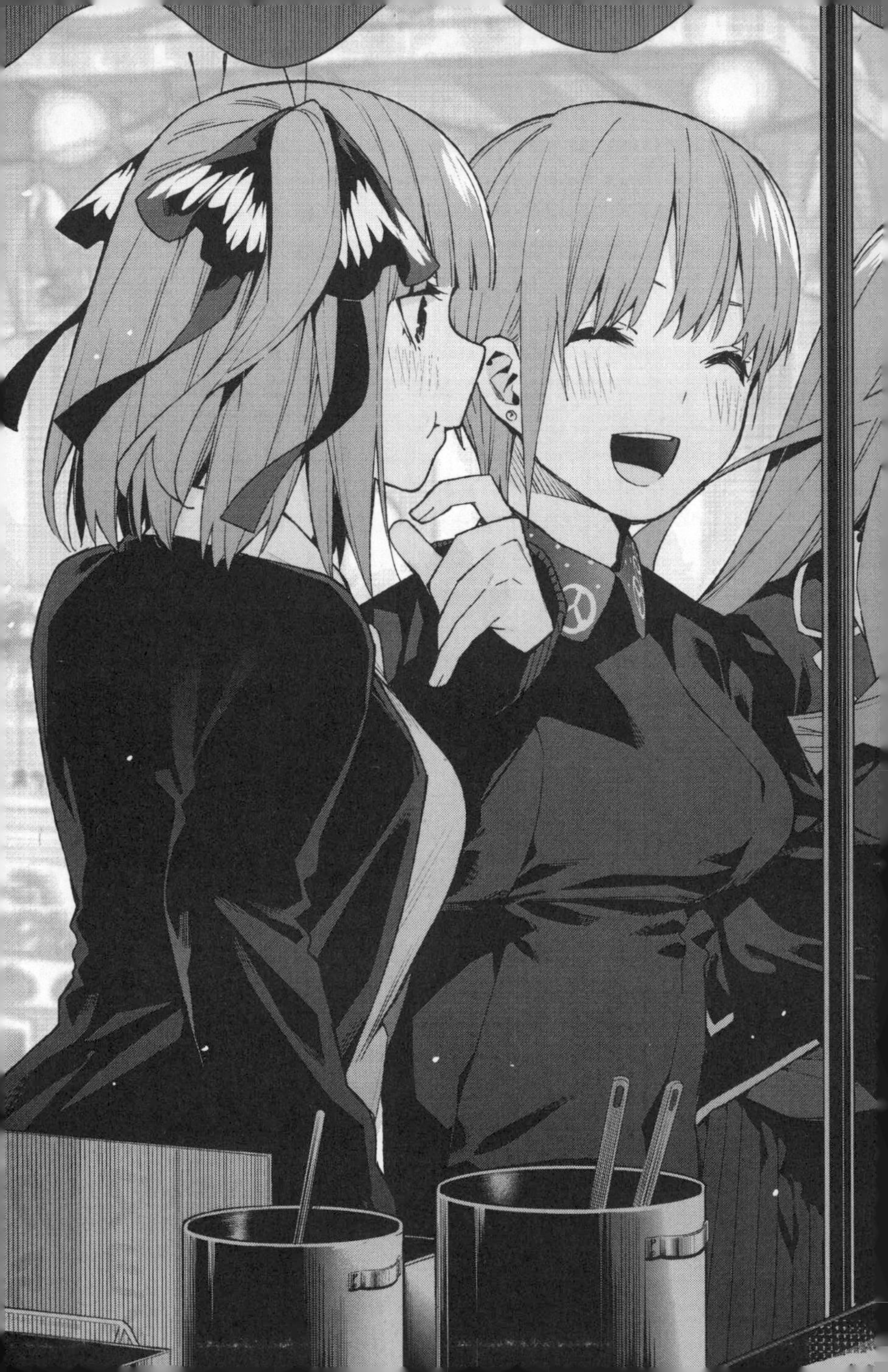

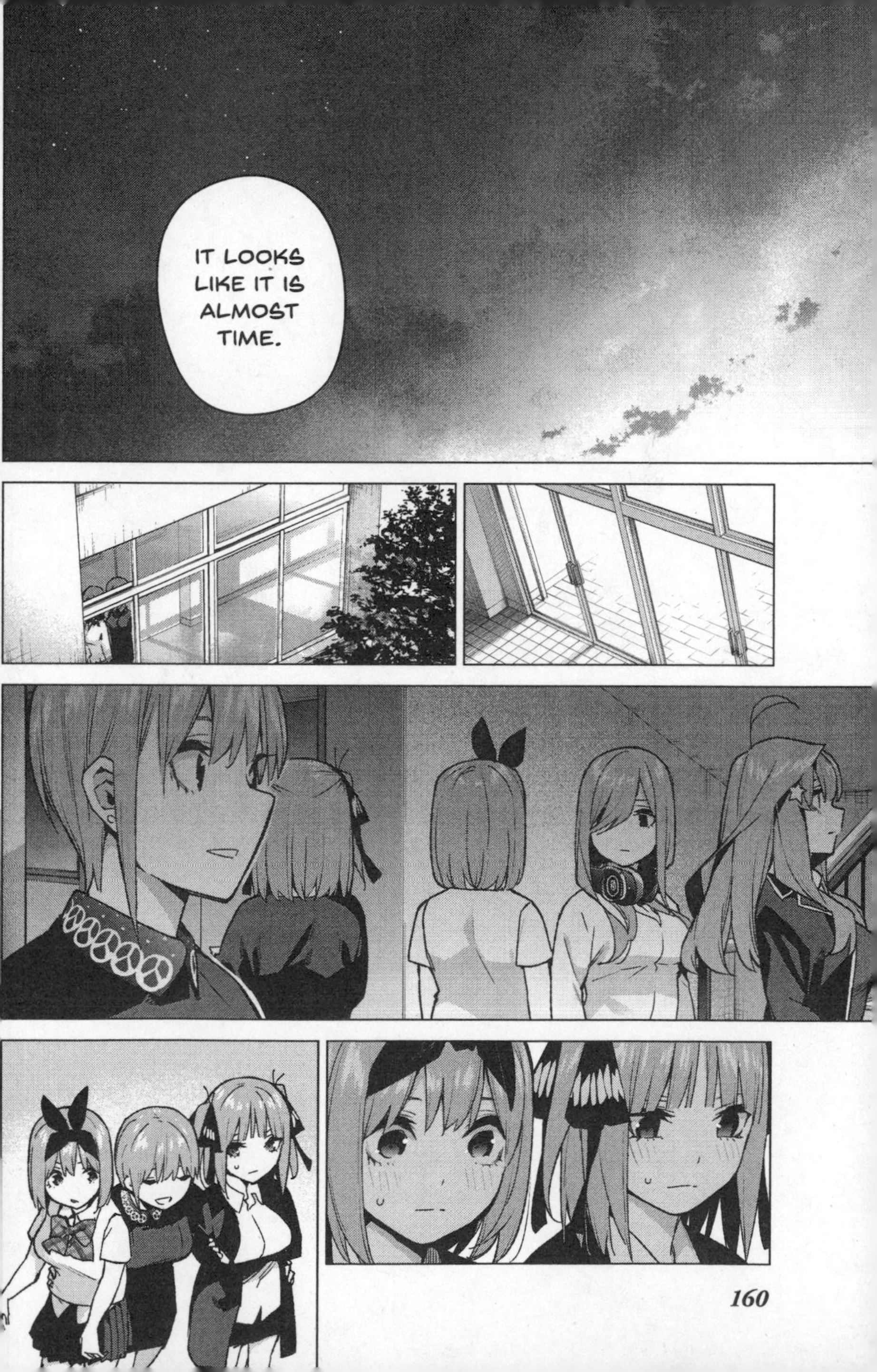
IT LOOKS LIKE IT IS ALMOST TIME.

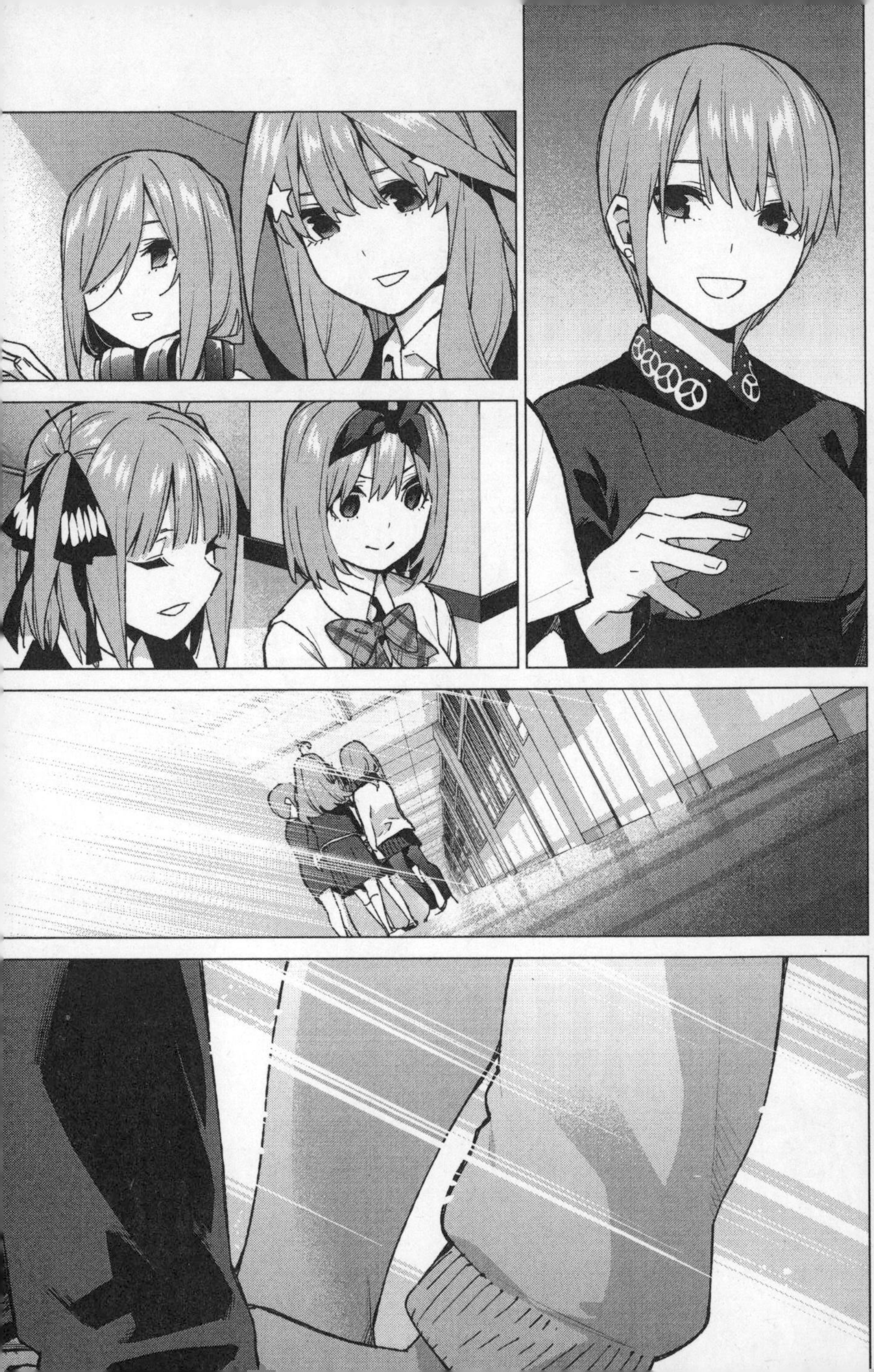

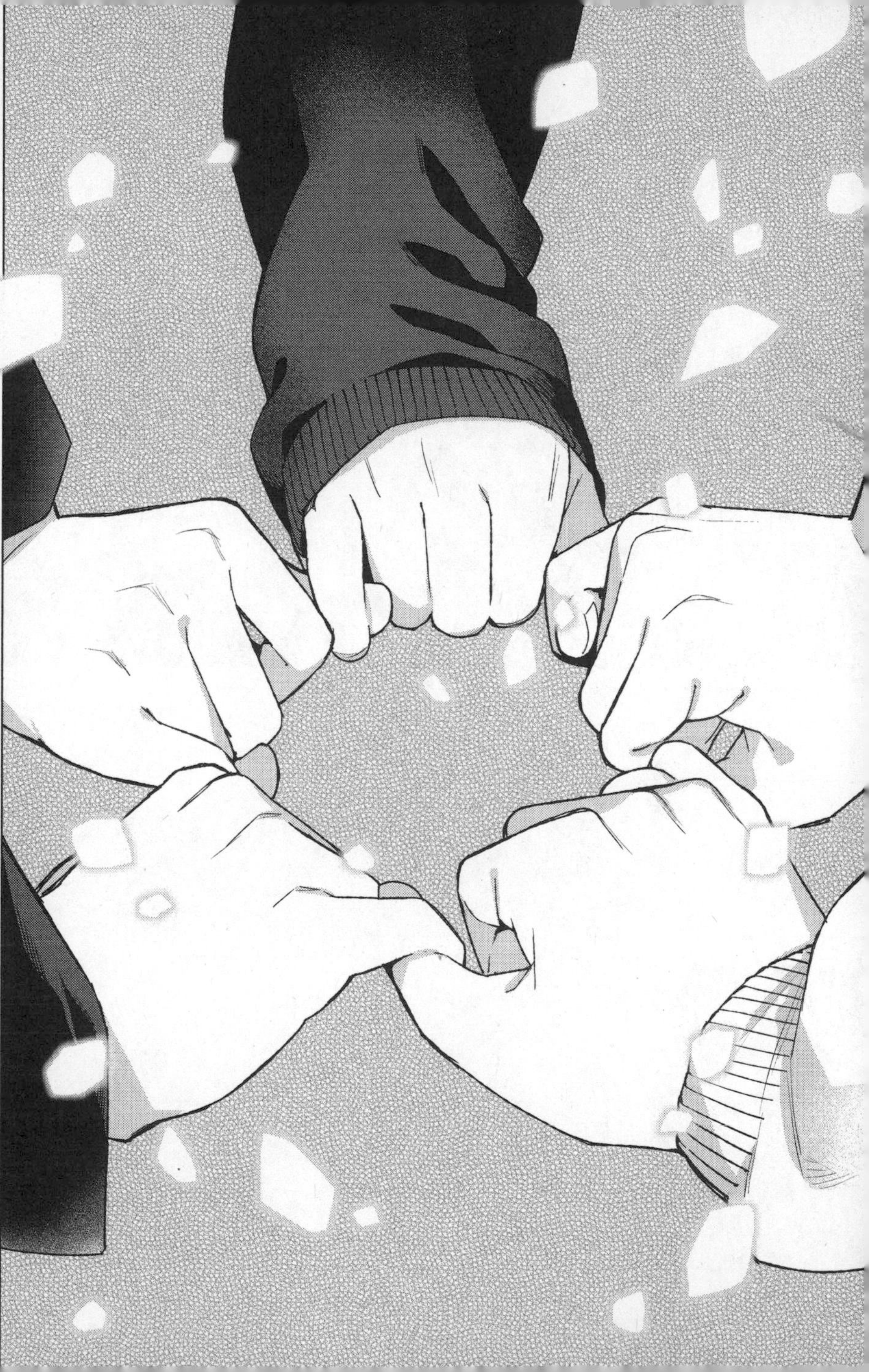

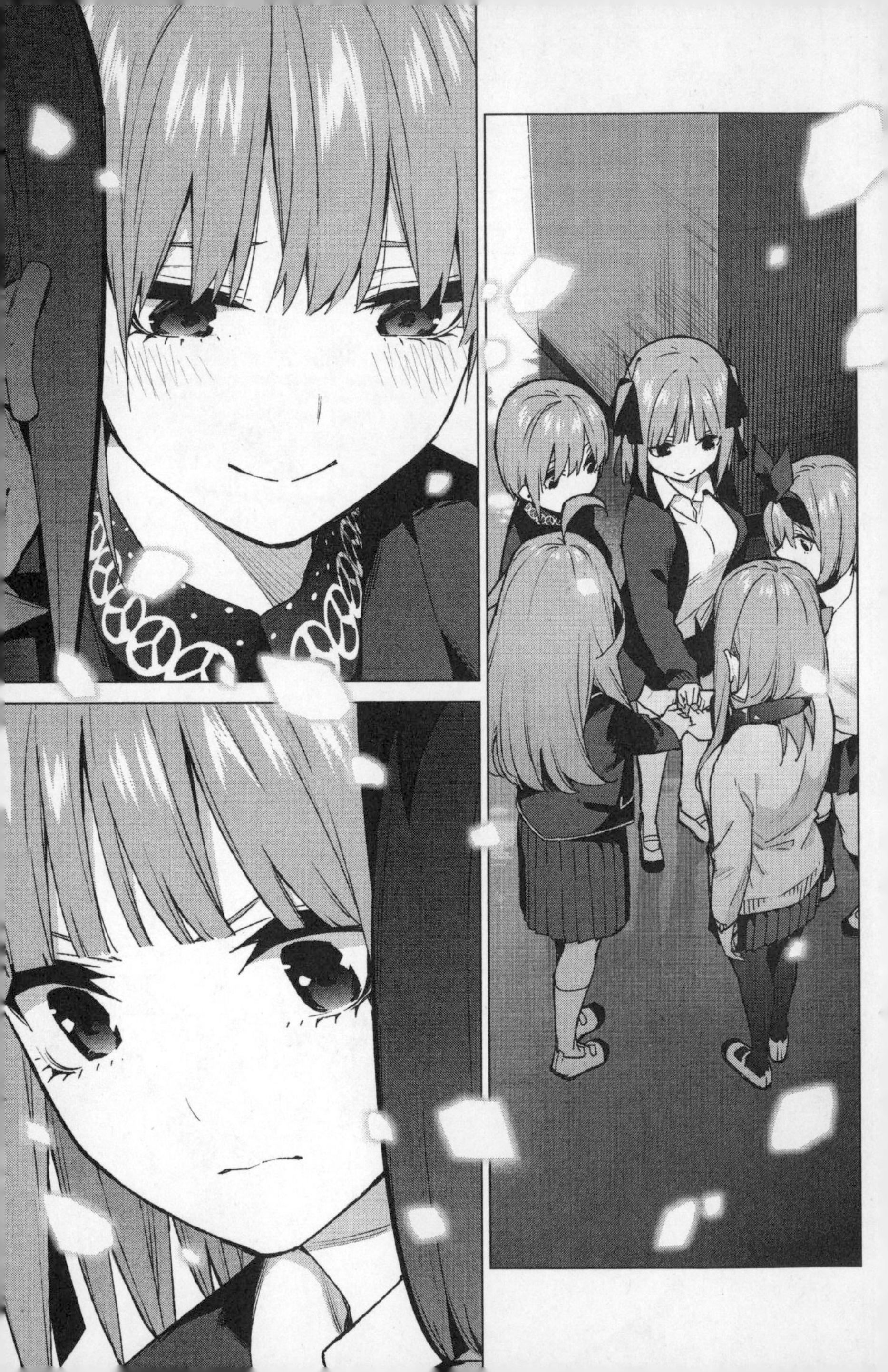

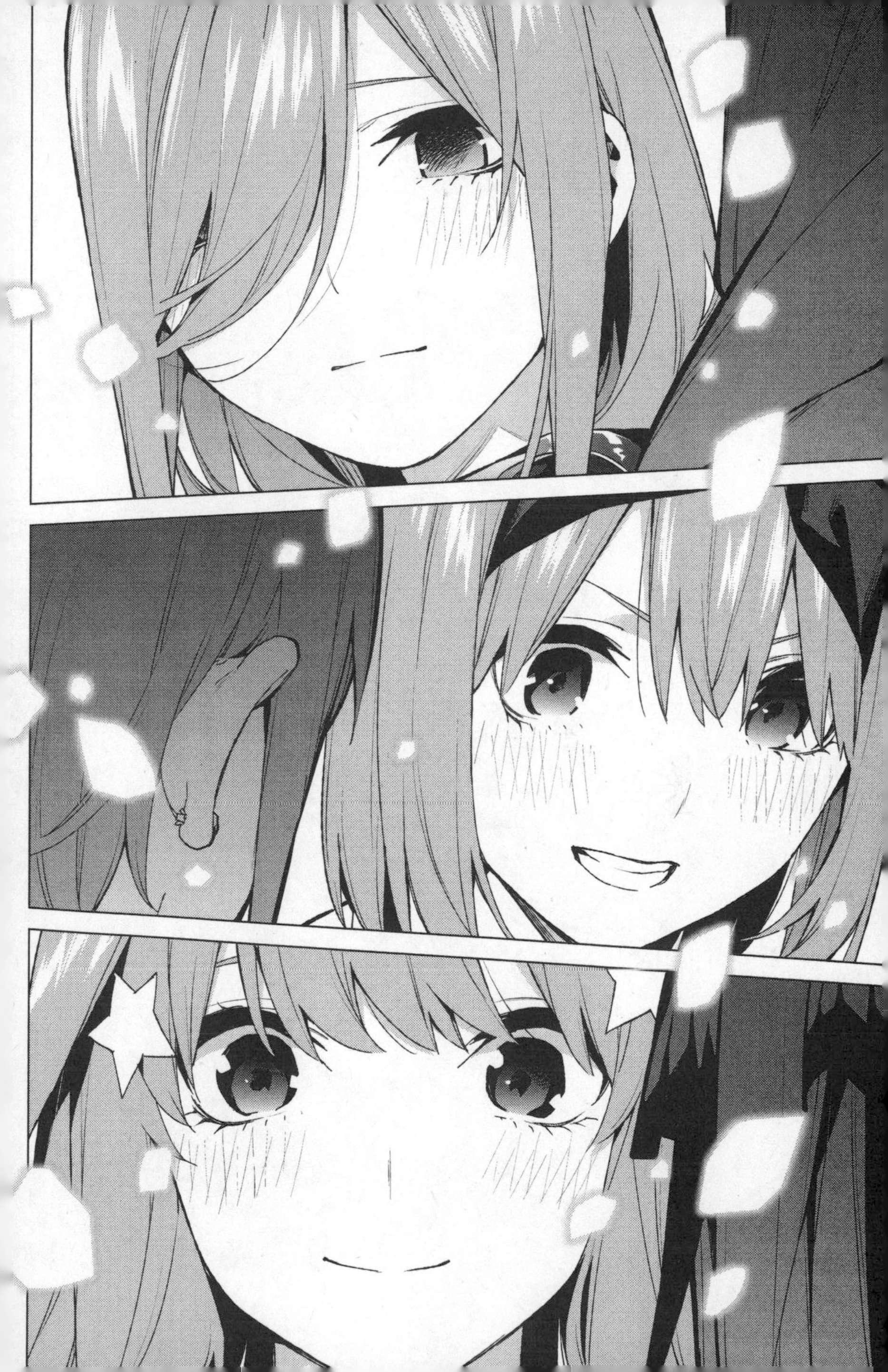

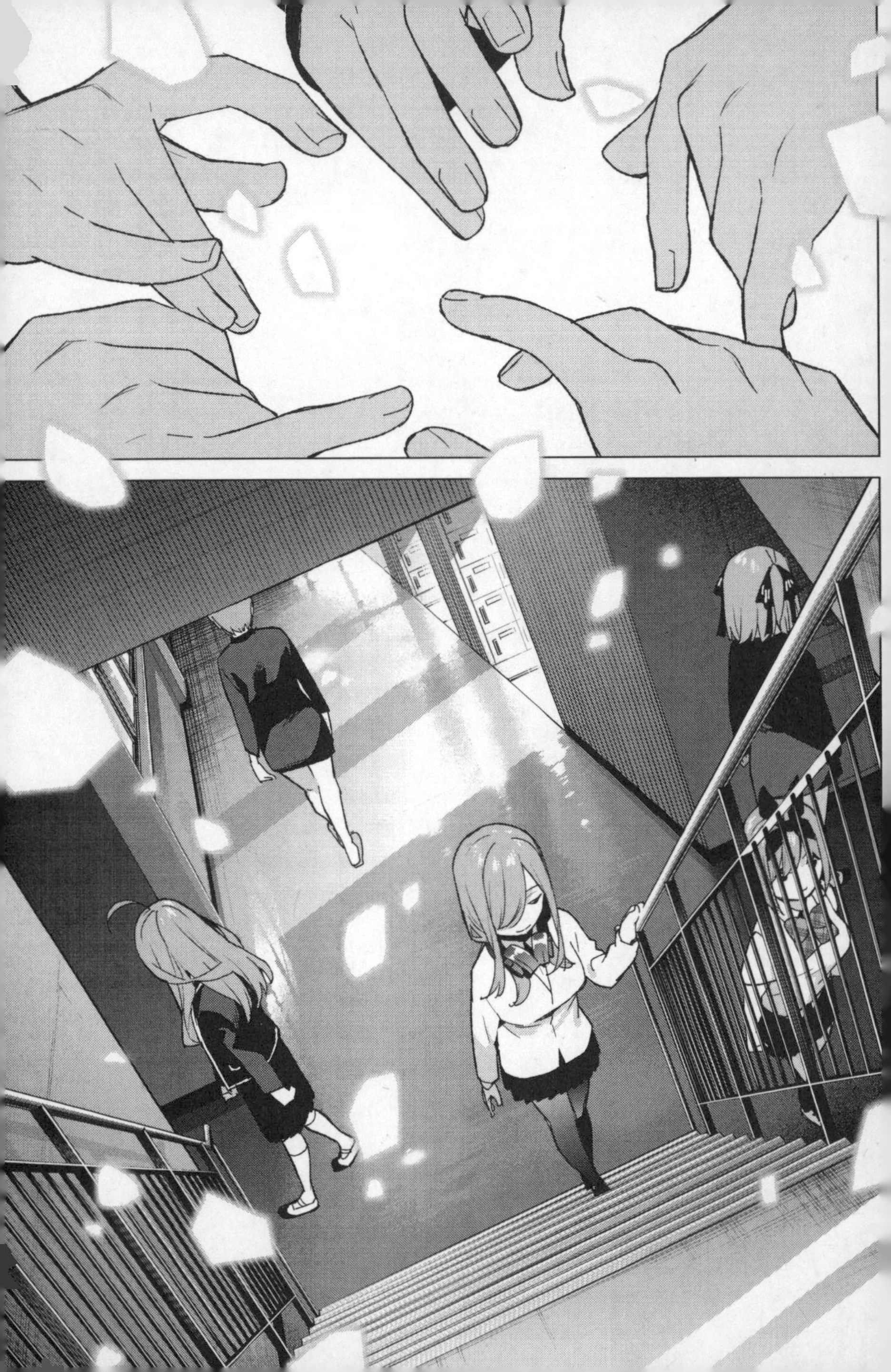

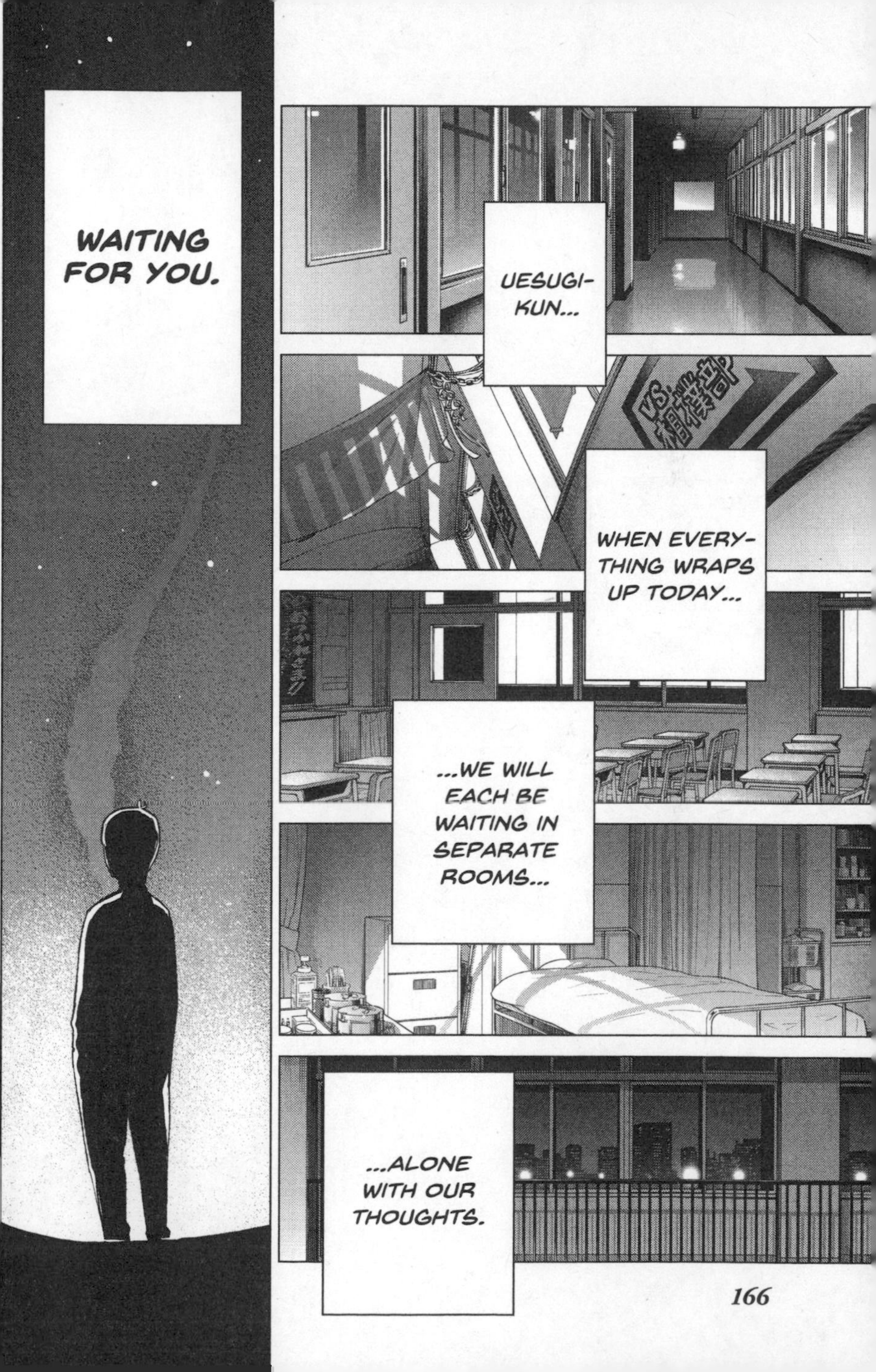
UESUGI-KUN...
WHEN EVERY-THING WRAPS UP TODAY...
...WE WILL EACH BE WAITING IN SEPARATE ROOMS...
...ALONE WITH OUR THOUGHTS.
WAITING FOR YOU.

CHAPTER 113 IF THE FINAL FESTIVAL WAS FUTARO'S ①

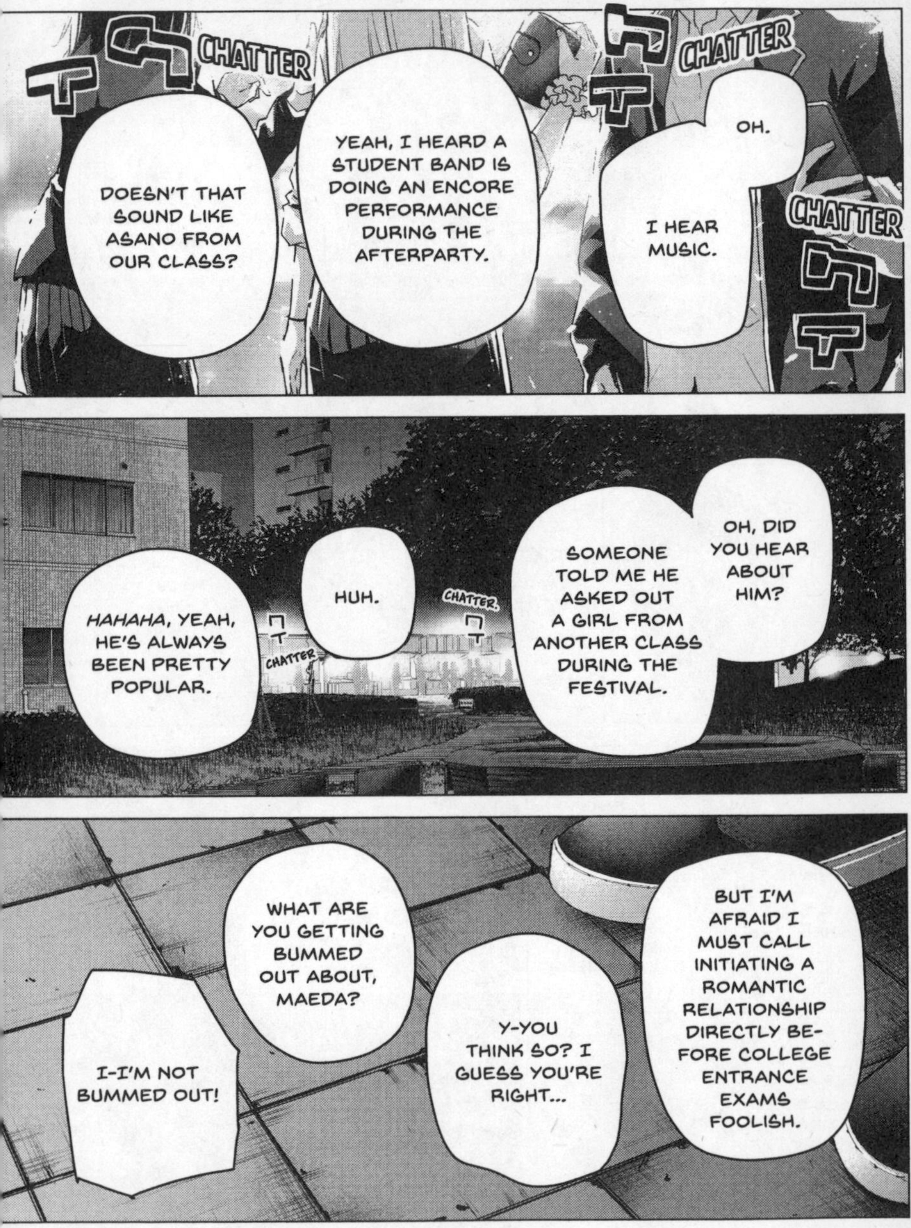
CHATTER
CHATTER
OH.
I HEAR MUSIC.
CHATTER
YEAH, I HEARD A STUDENT BAND IS DOING AN ENCORE PERFORMANCE DURING THE AFTERPARTY.
DOESN'T THAT SOUND LIKE ASANO FROM OUR CLASS?
OH, DID YOU HEAR ABOUT HIM?
SOMEONE TOLD ME HE ASKED OUT A GIRL FROM ANOTHER CLASS DURING THE FESTIVAL.
CHATTER.
HUH.
CHATTER
HAHAHA, YEAH, HE'S ALWAYS BEEN PRETTY POPULAR.
BUT I'M AFRAID I MUST CALL INITIATING A ROMANTIC RELATIONSHIP DIRECTLY BE-FORE COLLEGE ENTRANCE EXAMS FOOLISH.
Y-YOU THINK SO? I GUESS YOU'RE RIGHT...
WHAT ARE YOU GETTING BUMMED OUT ABOUT, MAEDA?
I-I'M NOT BUMMED OUT!

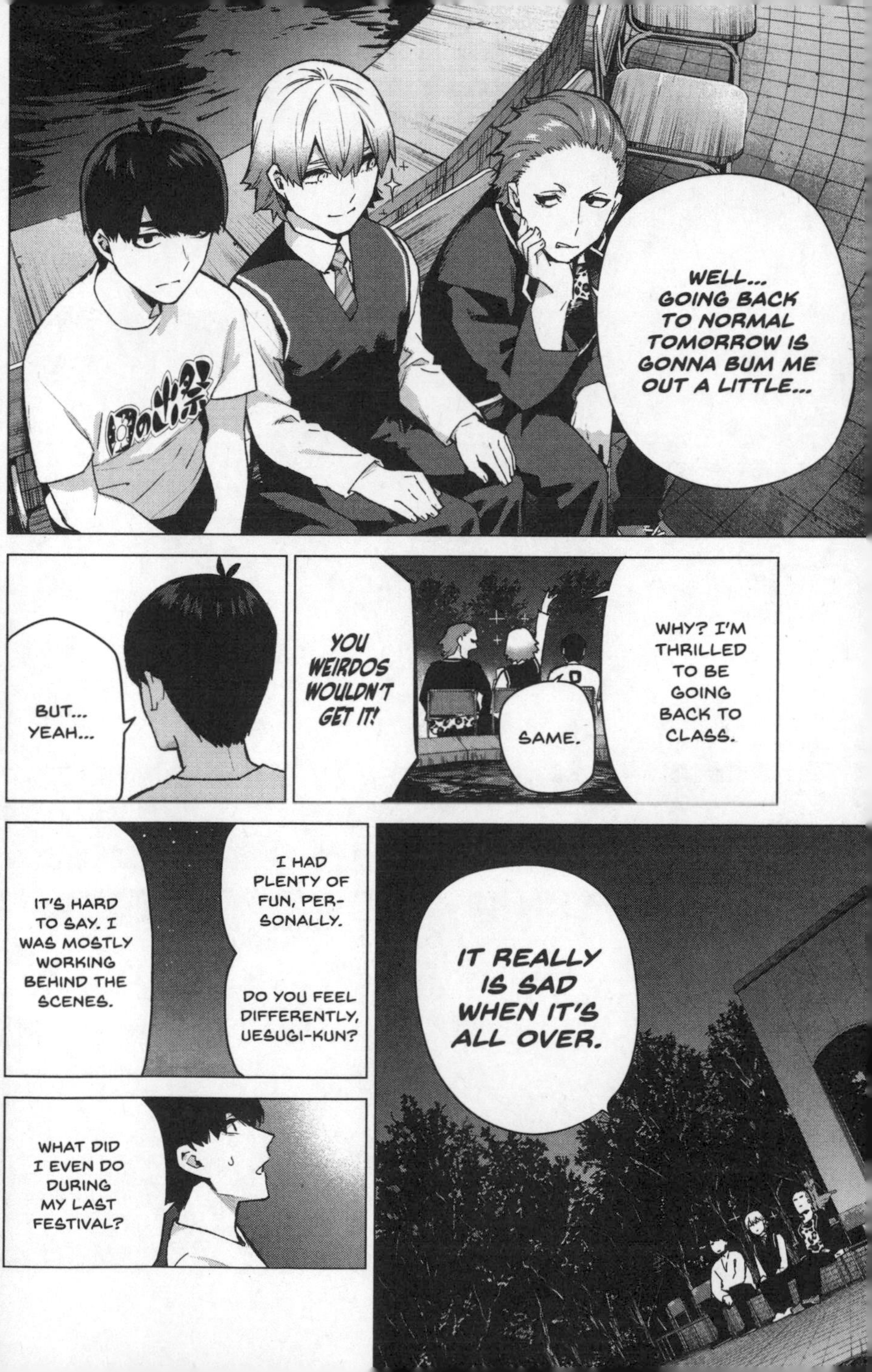
WELL... GOING BACK TO NORMAL TOMORROW IS GONNA BUM ME OUT A LITTLE...
WHY? I'M THRILLED TO BE GOING BACK TO CLASS.
SAME.
YOU WEIRDOS WOULDN'T GET IT!
BUT... YEAH...
IT REALLY IS SAD WHEN IT'S ALL OVER.
I HAD PLENTY OF FUN, PER-SONALLY.
DO YOU FEEL DIFFERENTLY, UESUGI-KUN?
IT'S HARD TO SAY. I WAS MOSTLY WORKING BEHIND THE SCENES.
WHAT DID I EVEN DO DURING MY LAST FESTIVAL?

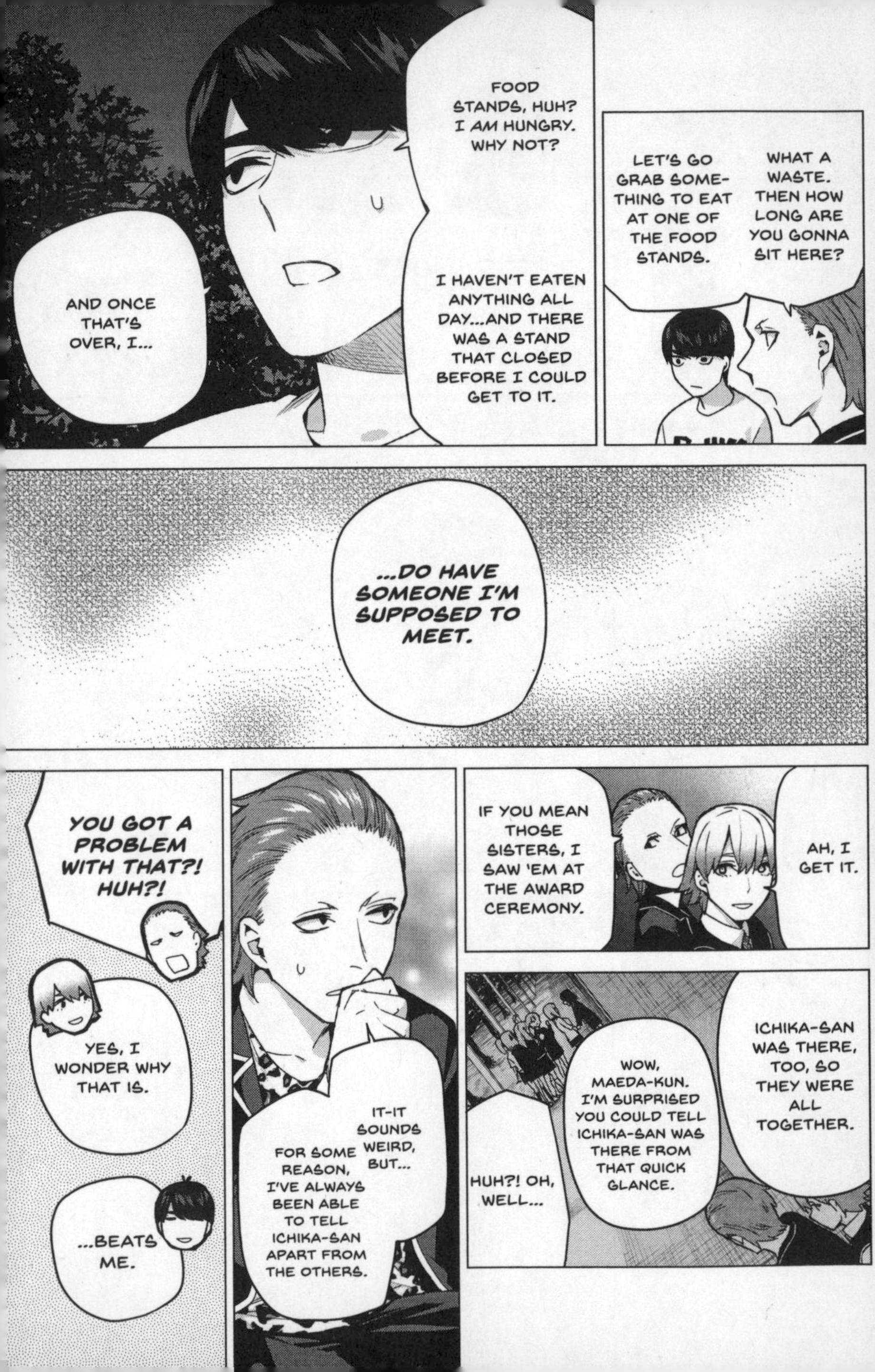
WHAT A WASTE. THEN HOW LONG ARE YOU GONNA SIT HERE?
LET'S GO GRAB SOMETHING TO EAT AT ONE OF THE FOOD STANDS.
FOOD STANDS, HUH? I AM HUNGRY. WHY NOT?
I HAVEN'T EATEN ANYTHING ALL DAY...AND THERE WAS A STAND THAT CLOSED BEFORE I COULD GET TO IT.
AND ONCE THAT'S OVER, I...
...DO HAVE SOMEONE I'M SUPPOSED TO MEET.
AH, I GET IT.
IF YOU MEAN THOSE SISTERS, I SAW 'EM AT THE AWARD CEREMONY.
ICHIKA-SAN WAS THERE, TOO, SO THEY WERE ALL TOGETHER.
WOW, MAEDA-KUN. I'M SURPRISED YOU COULD TELL ICHIKA-SAN WAS THERE FROM THAT QUICK GLANCE.
HUH?! OH, WELL...
IT-IT SOUNDS WEIRD, BUT...
FOR SOME REASON, I'VE ALWAYS BEEN ABLE TO TELL ICHIKA-SAN APART FROM THE OTHERS.
YOU GOT A PROBLEM WITH THAT?! HUH?!
YES, I WONDER WHY THAT IS.
...BEATS ME.

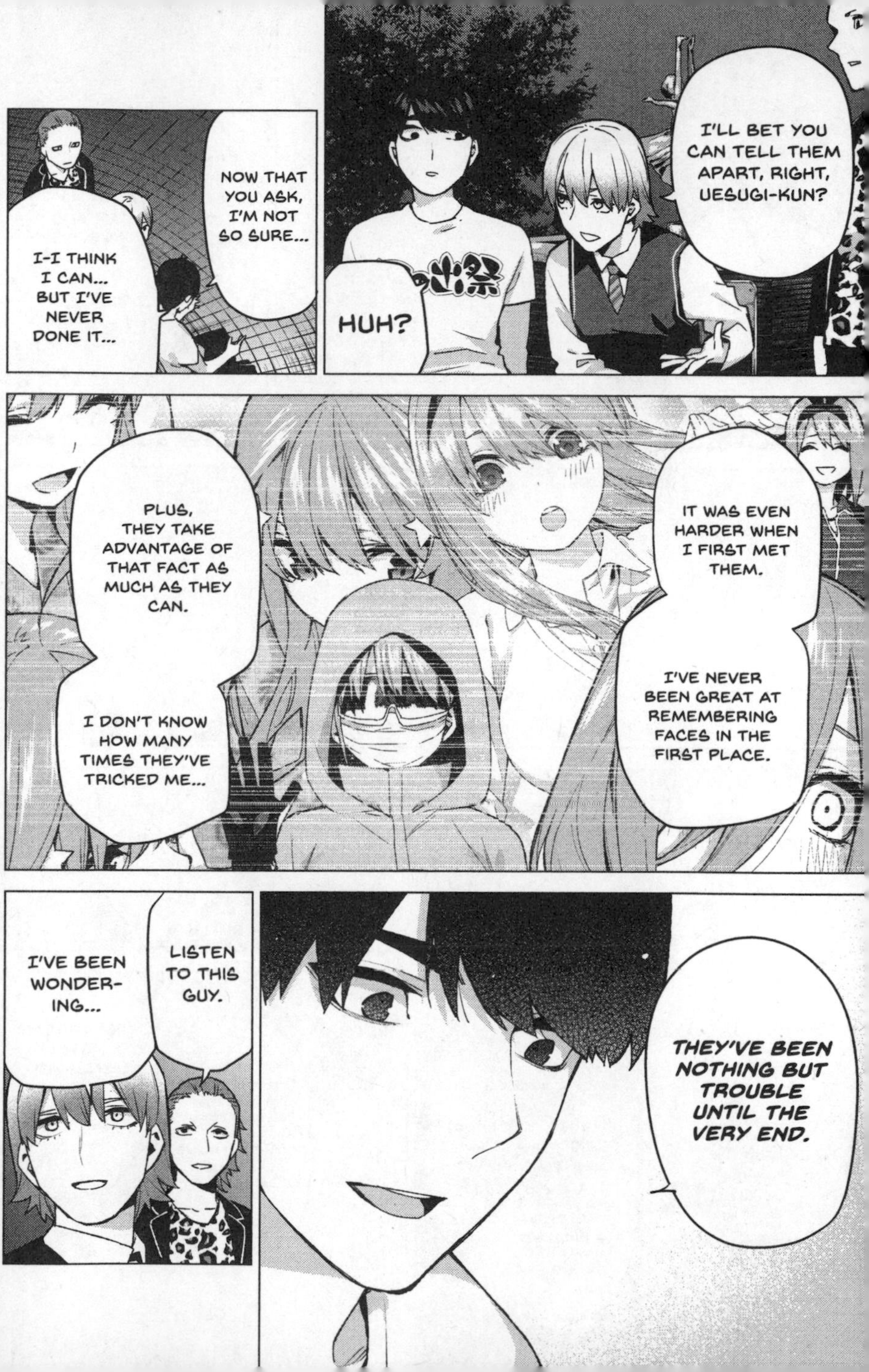
I'LL BET YOU CAN TELL THEM APART, RIGHT, UESUGI-KUN?
HUH?
NOW THAT YOU ASK, I'M NOT SO SURE...
I-I THINK I CAN... BUT I'VE NEVER DONE IT...
IT WAS EVEN HARDER WHEN I FIRST MET THEM.
I'VE NEVER BEEN GREAT AT REMEMBERING FACES IN THE FIRST PLACE.
PLUS, THEY TAKE ADVANTAGE OF THAT FACT AS MUCH AS THEY CAN.
I DON'T KNOW HOW MANY TIMES THEY'VE TRICKED ME...
THEY'VE BEEN NOTHING BUT TROUBLE UNTIL THE VERY END.
LISTEN TO THIS GUY.
I'VE BEEN WONDERING...

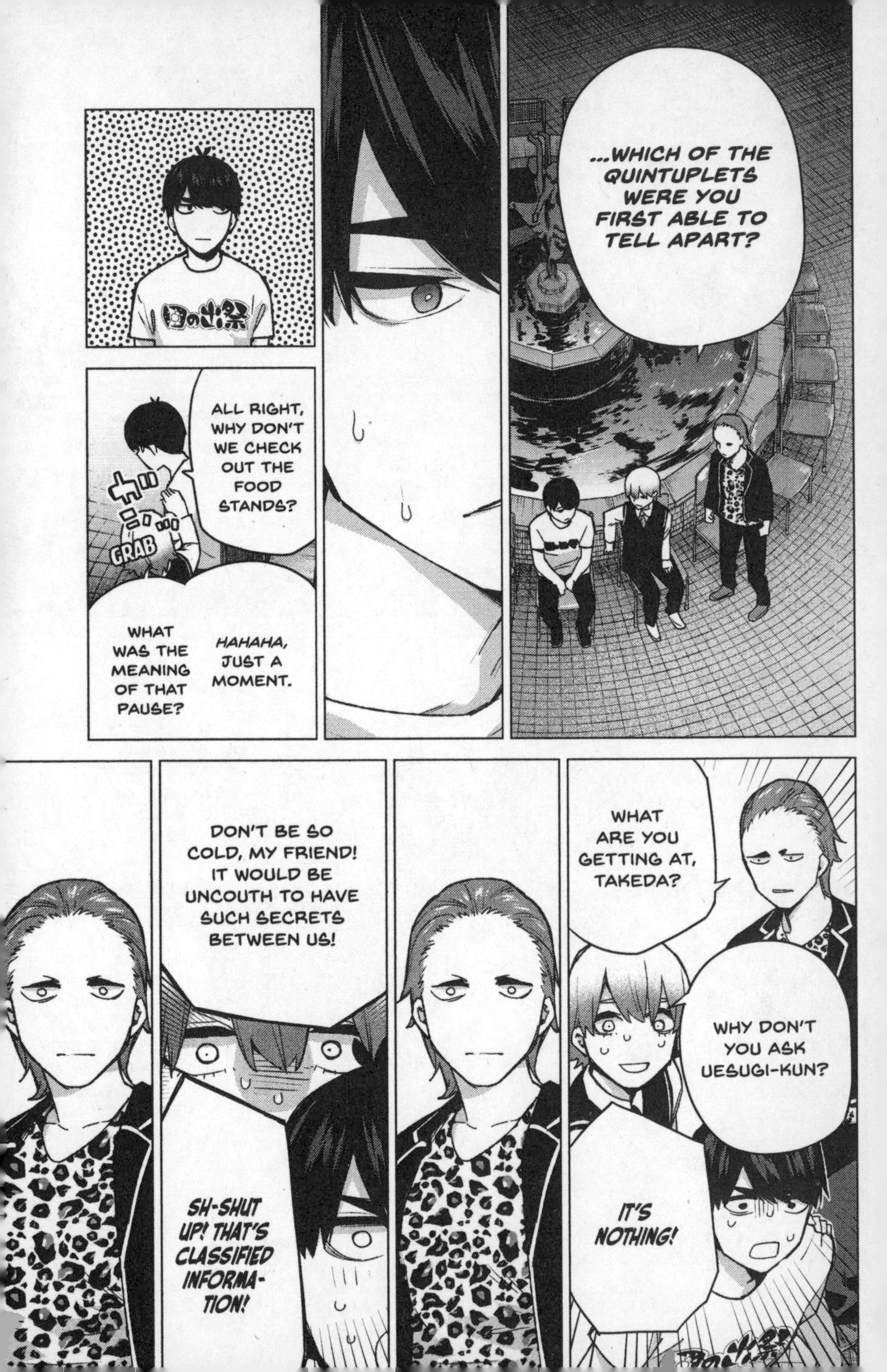
...WHICH OF THE QUINTUPLETS WERE YOU FIRST ABLE TO TELL APART?
ALL RIGHT, WHY DON'T WE CHECK OUT THE FOOD STANDS?
GRAB
HAHAHA, JUST A MOMENT.
WHAT WAS THE MEANING OF THAT PAUSE?
WHAT ARE YOU GETTING AT, TAKEDA?
WHY DON'T YOU ASK UESUGI-KUN?
IT'S NOTHING!
DON'T BE SO COLD, MY FRIEND! IT WOULD BE UNCOUTH TO HAVE SUCH SECRETS BETWEEN US!
SH-SHUT UP! THAT'S CLASSIFIED INFORMATION!

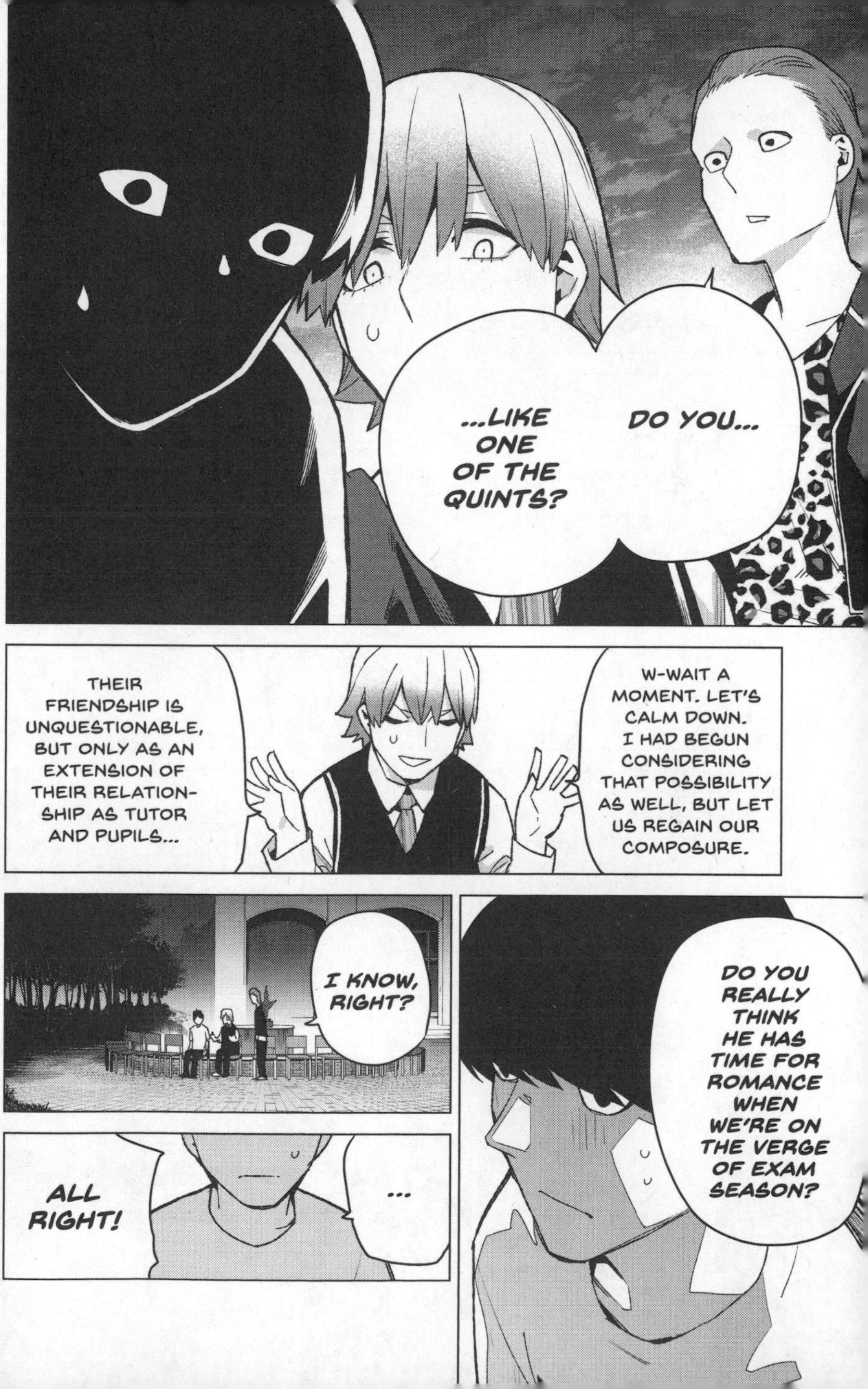
DO YOU...
...LIKE ONE OF THE QUINTS?
W-WAIT A MOMENT. LET'S CALM DOWN. I HAD BEGUN CONSIDERING THAT POSSIBILITY AS WELL, BUT LET US REGAIN OUR COMPOSURE.
THEIR FRIENDSHIP IS UNQUESTIONABLE, BUT ONLY AS AN EXTENSION OF THEIR RELATIONSHIP AS TUTOR AND PUPILS...
DO YOU REALLY THINK HE HAS TIME FOR ROMANCE WHEN WE'RE ON THE VERGE OF EXAM SEASON?
I KNOW, RIGHT?
...
ALL RIGHT!

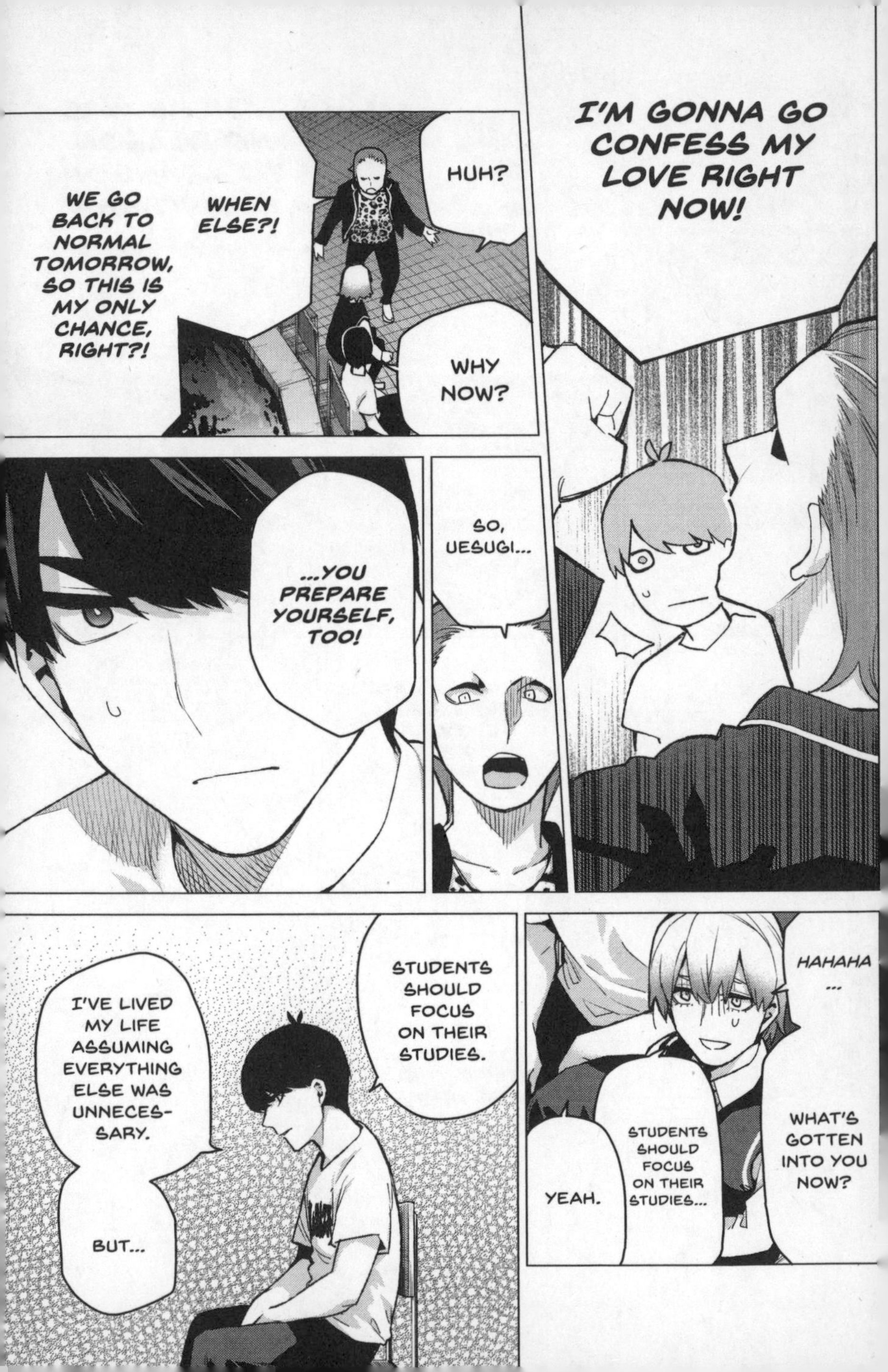
I'M GONNA GO CONFESS MY LOVE RIGHT NOW!
HUH?
WHY NOW?
WHEN ELSE?!
WE GO BACK TO NORMAL TOMORROW, SO THIS IS MY ONLY CHANCE, RIGHT?!
SO, UESUGI...
...YOU PREPARE YOURSELF, TOO!
HAHAHA ...
WHAT'S GOTTEN INTO YOU NOW?
STUDENTS SHOULD FOCUS ON THEIR STUDIES...
YEAH.
STUDENTS SHOULD FOCUS ON THEIR STUDIES.
I'VE LIVED MY LIFE ASSUMING EVERYTHING ELSE WAS UNNECES-SARY.
BUT...

...THERE WAS NO REASON TO ABANDON EVERYTHING ELSE.

ACADEMICS, FRIEND-SHIP...

WORK, ENTER-TAINMENT, ROMANCE...

THEY ALL PUT EVERYTHING THEY HAD INTO EVERY-THING.

THEY'RE THE ONES WHO TAUGHT ME THAT.

BUT I KEPT THEM WAIT-ING UNTIL NOW...

...WHILE I FIGURED IT OUT.

I'M SURE THE OLD ME...

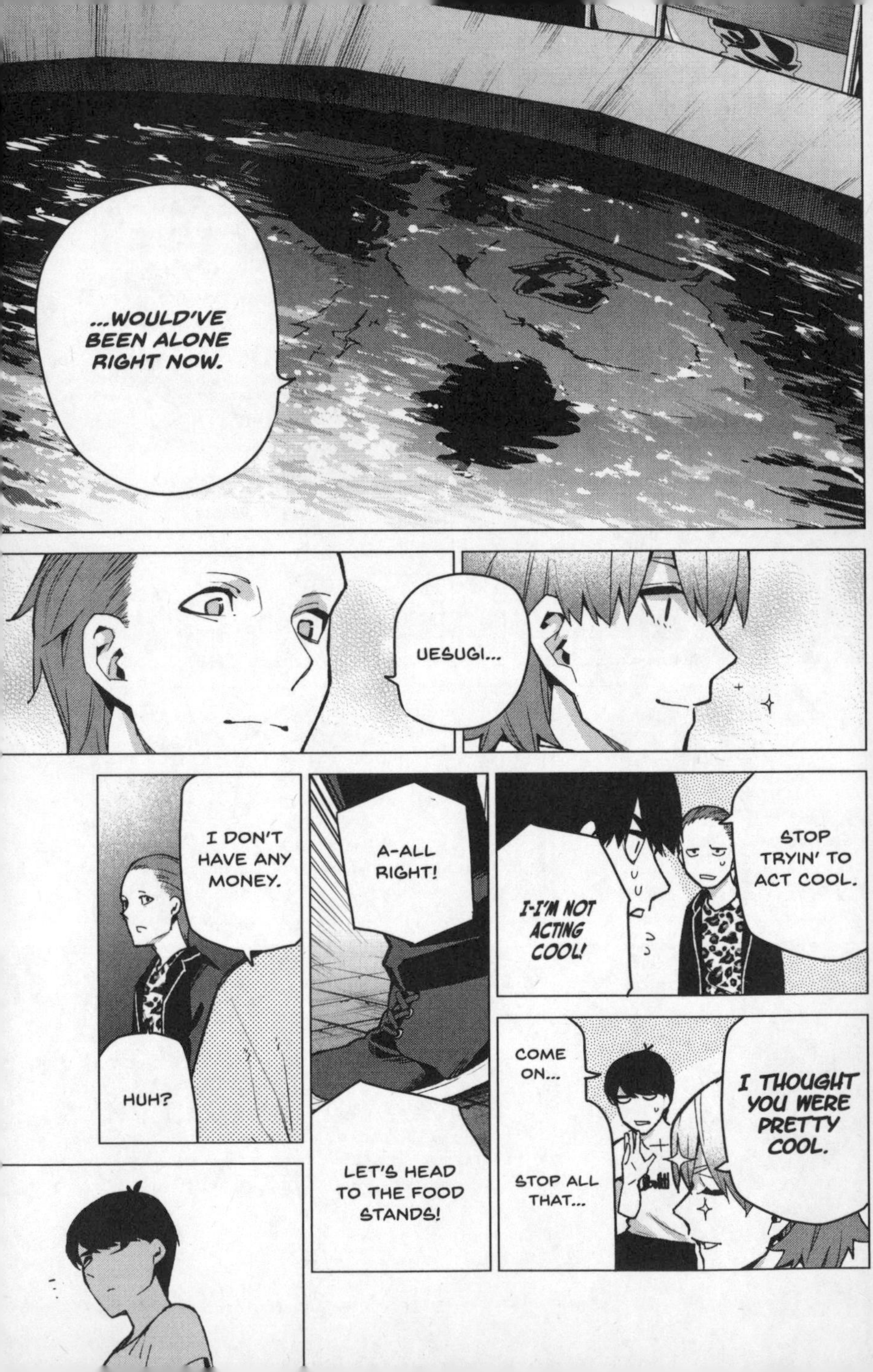
...WOULD'VE BEEN ALONE RIGHT NOW.
UESUGI...
STOP TRYIN' TO ACT COOL.
I-I'M NOT ACTING COOL!
I THOUGHT YOU WERE PRETTY COOL.
COME ON...
STOP ALL THAT...
A-ALL RIGHT!
LET'S HEAD TO THE FOOD STANDS!
I DON'T HAVE ANY MONEY.
HUH?

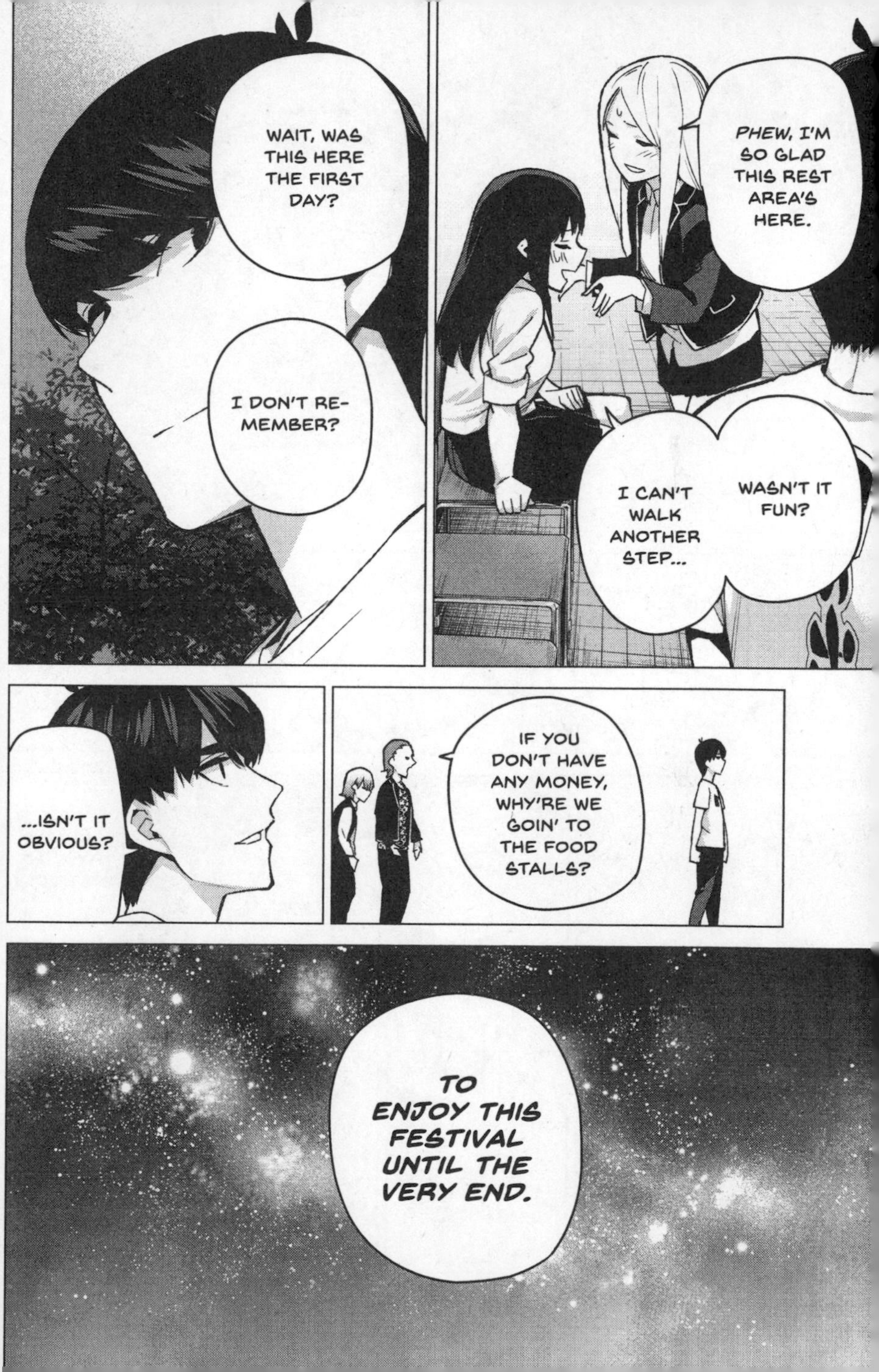
PHEW, I'M SO GLAD THIS REST AREA'S HERE.
WASN'T IT FUN?
I CAN'T WALK ANOTHER STEP...
WAIT, WAS THIS HERE THE FIRST DAY?
I DON'T RE-MEMBER?
IF YOU DON'T HAVE ANY MONEY, WHY'RE WE GOIN' TO THE FOOD STALLS?
...ISN'T IT OBVIOUS?
TO ENJOY THIS FESTIVAL UNTIL THE VERY END.

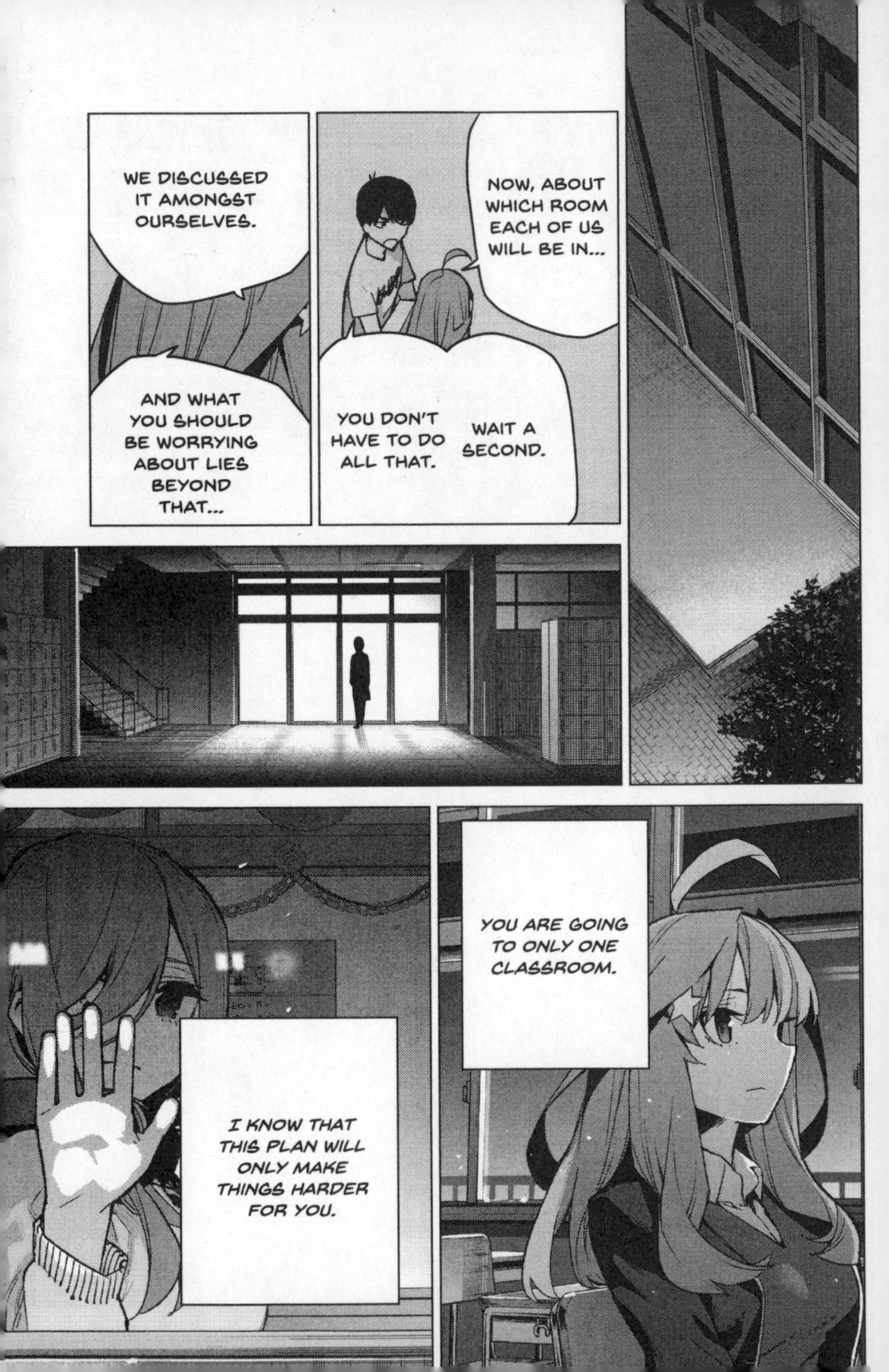
NOW, ABOUT WHICH ROOM EACH OF US WILL BE IN...
WAIT A SECOND.
YOU DON'T HAVE TO DO ALL THAT.
WE DISCUSSED IT AMONGST OURSELVES.
AND WHAT YOU SHOULD BE WORRYING ABOUT LIES BEYOND THAT...
YOU ARE GOING TO ONLY ONE CLASSROOM.
I KNOW THAT THIS PLAN WILL ONLY MAKE THINGS HARDER FOR YOU.

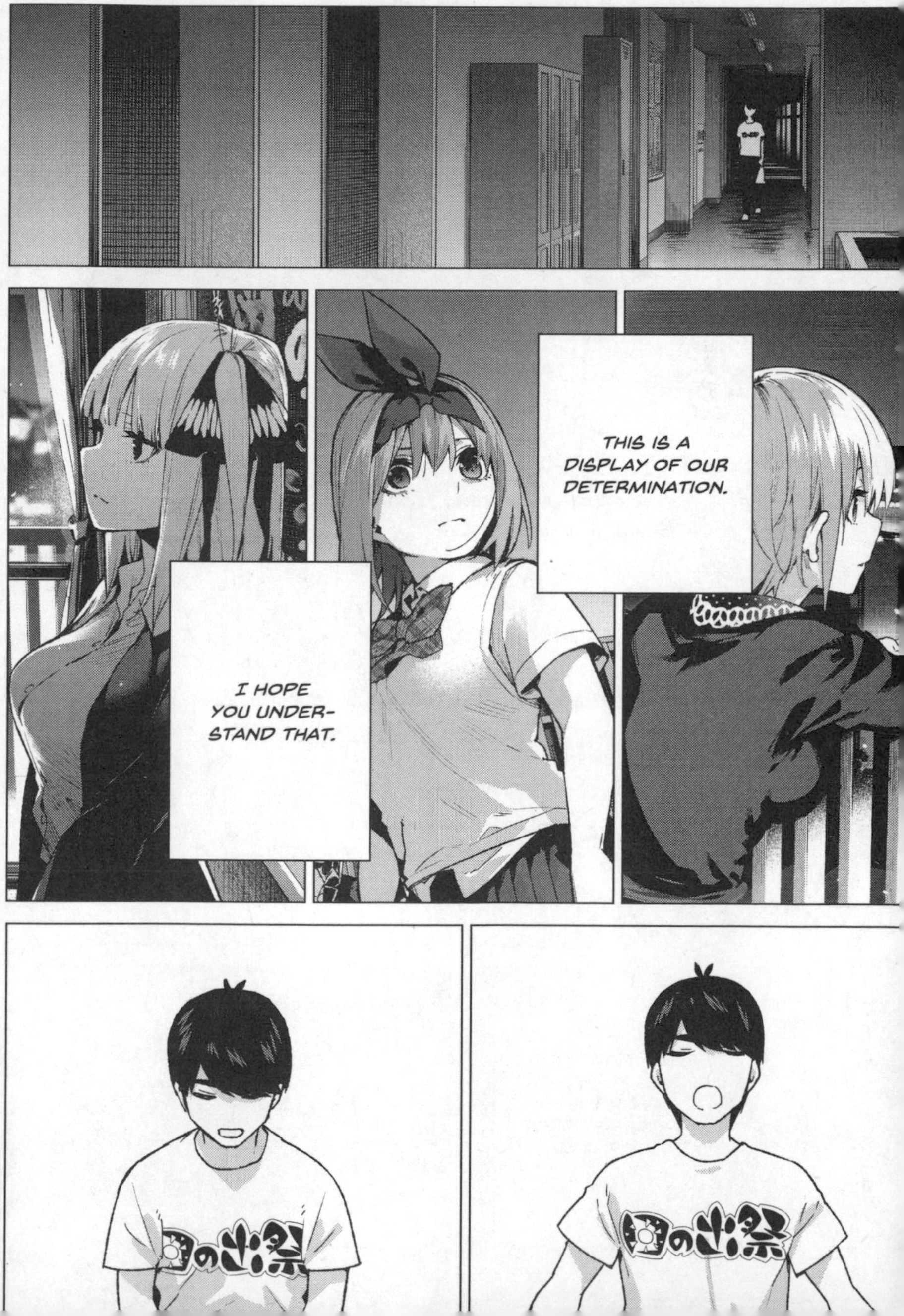
THIS IS A DISPLAY OF OUR DETERMINATION.
I HOPE YOU UNDER-STAND THAT.

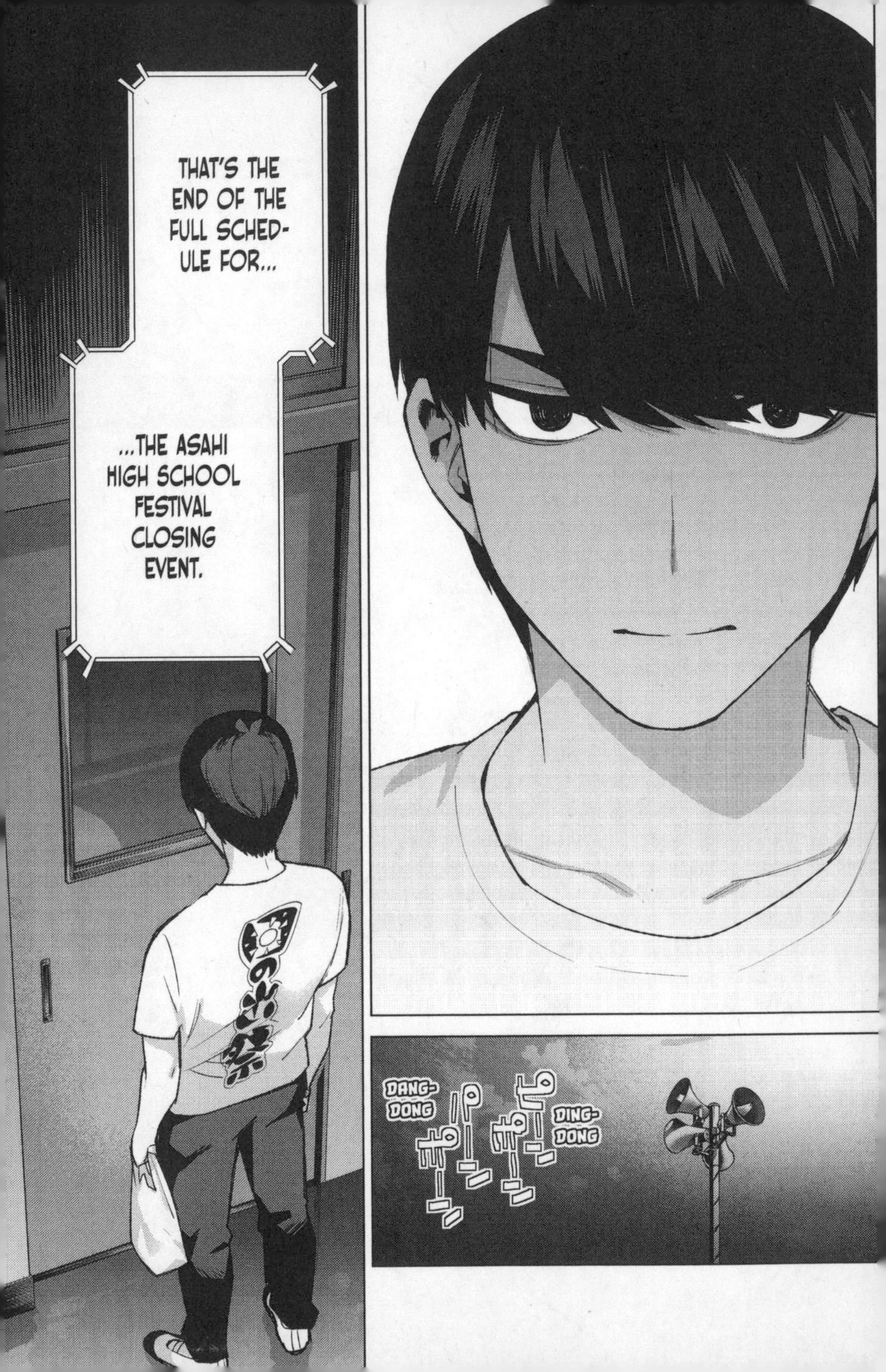
DING-DONG
ピーンポーン
パーンポーン
DANG-DONG
THAT'S THE END OF THE FULL SCHED-ULE FOR...
...THE ASAHI HIGH SCHOOL FESTIVAL CLOSING EVENT.

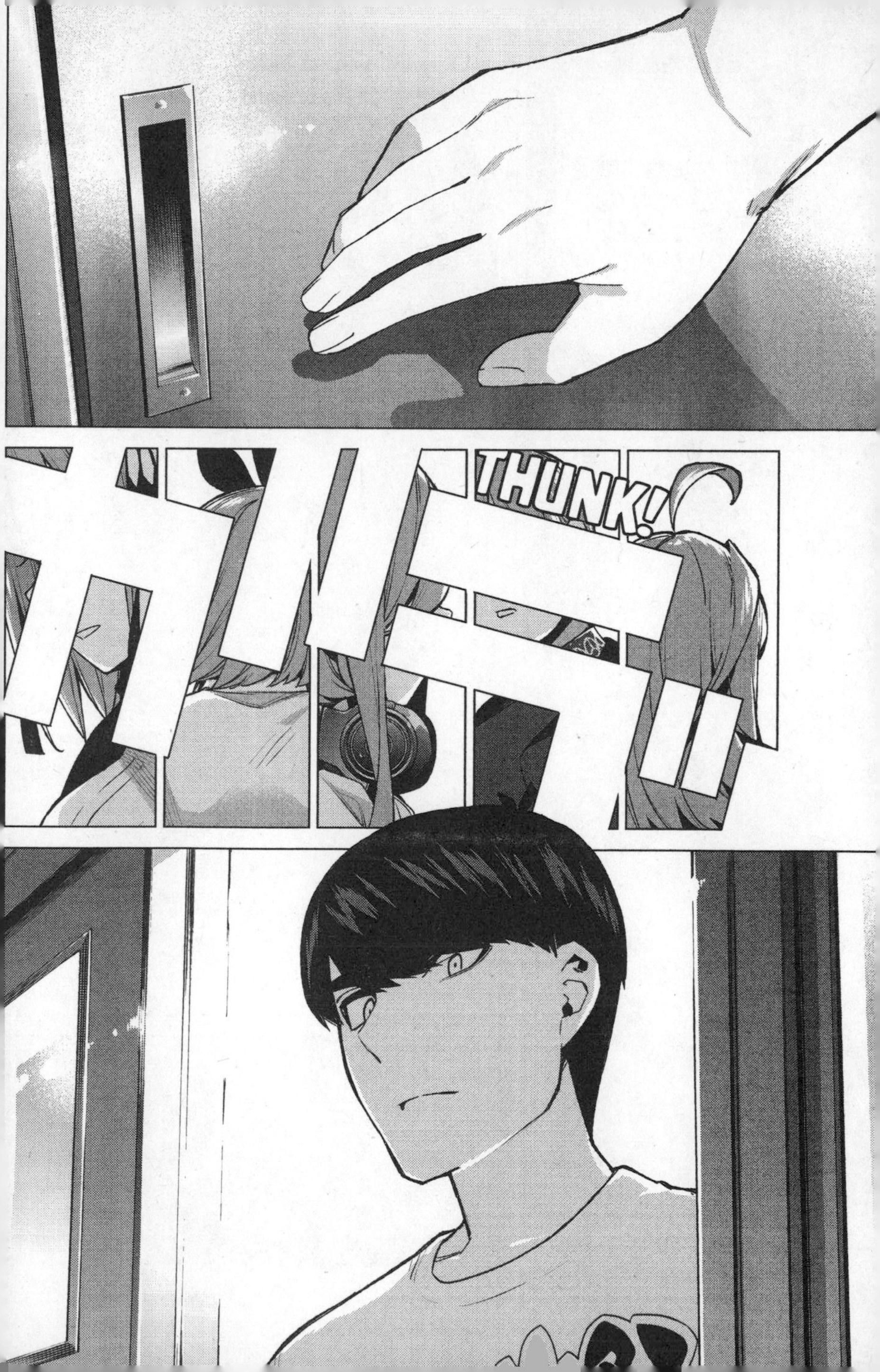
THUNK!

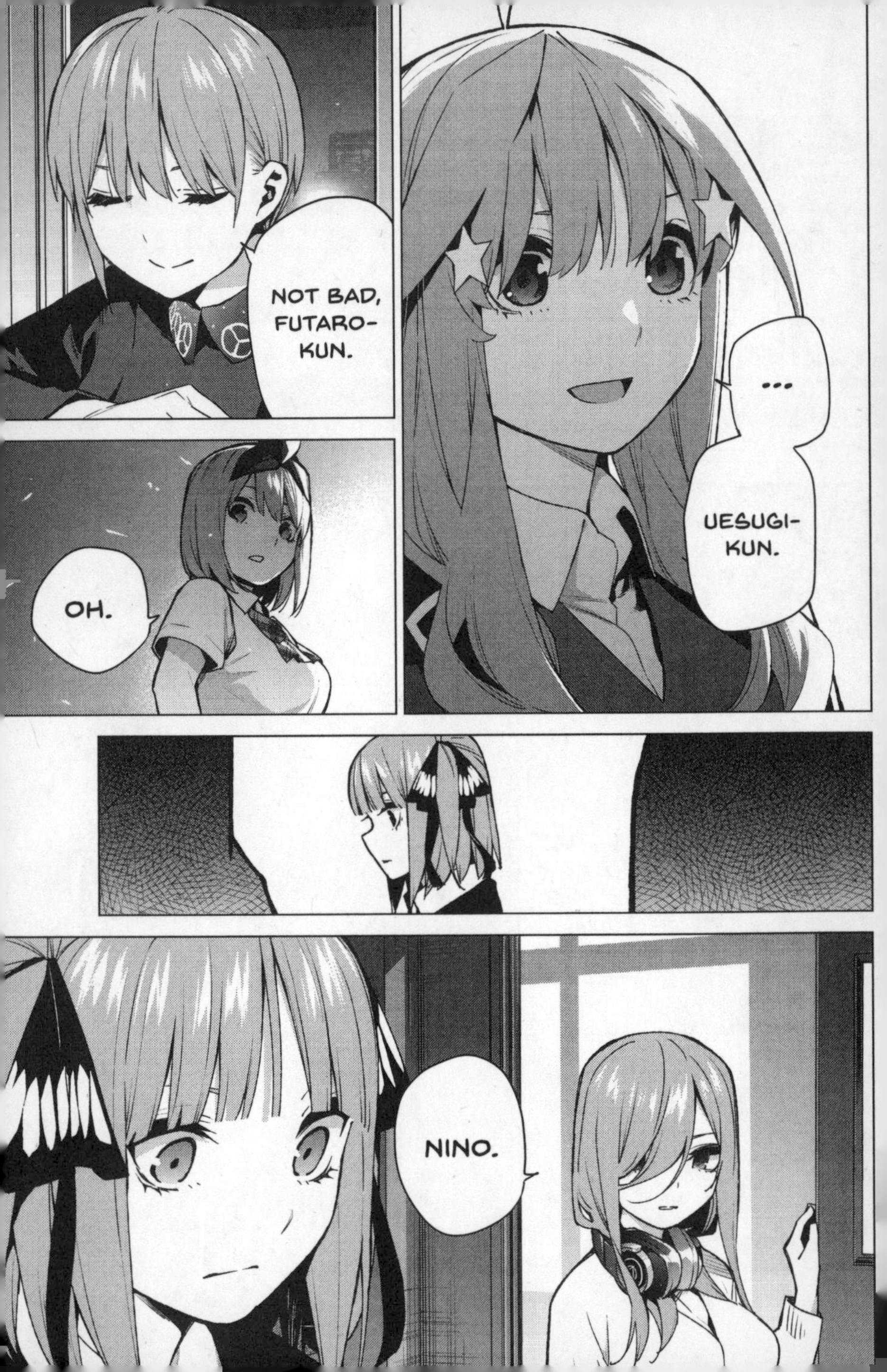
... UESUGI-KUN.
NOT BAD, FUTARO-KUN.
OH.
NINO.

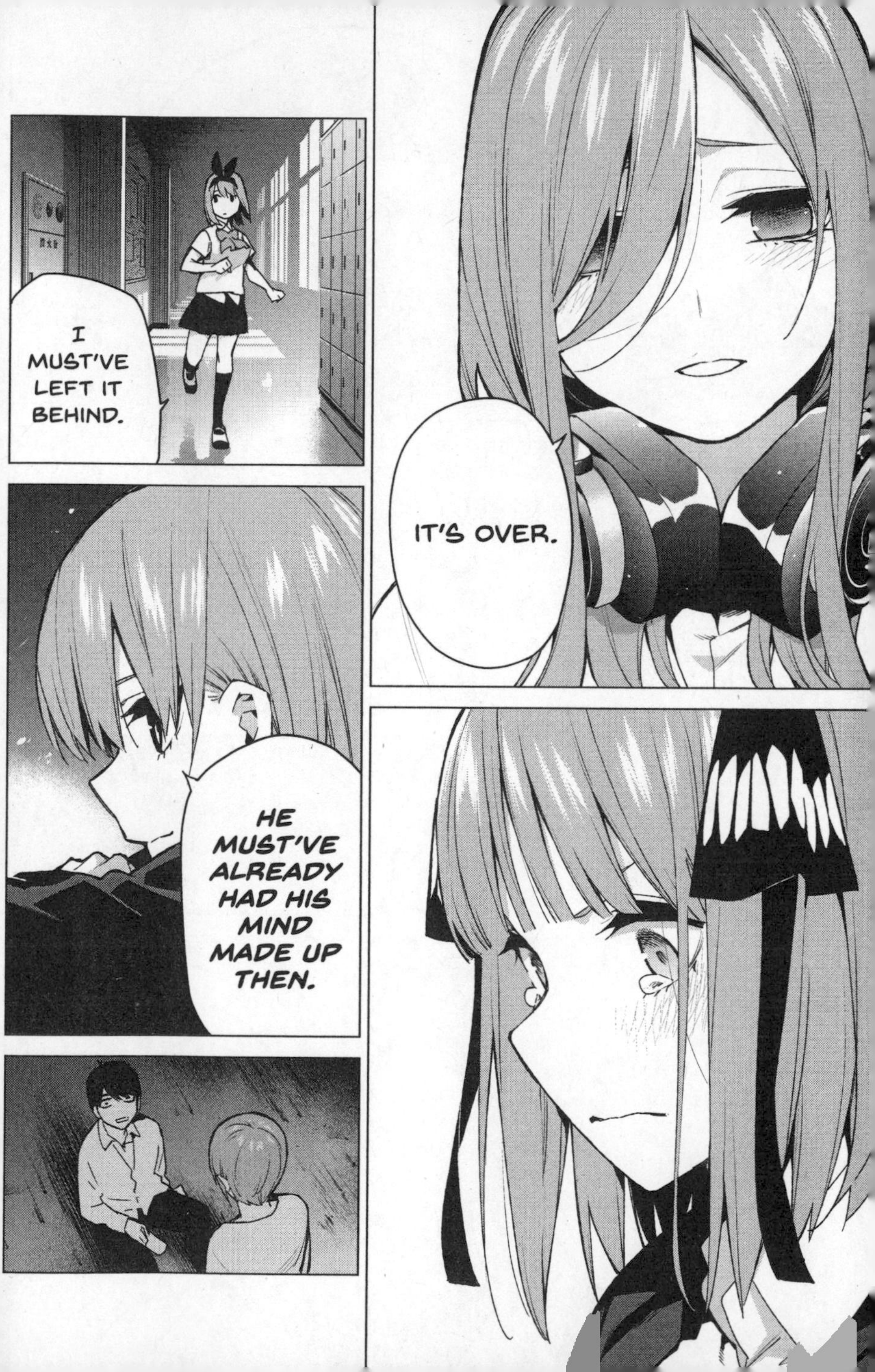
IT'S OVER.
I MUST'VE LEFT IT BEHIND.
HE MUST'VE ALREADY HAD HIS MIND MADE UP THEN.

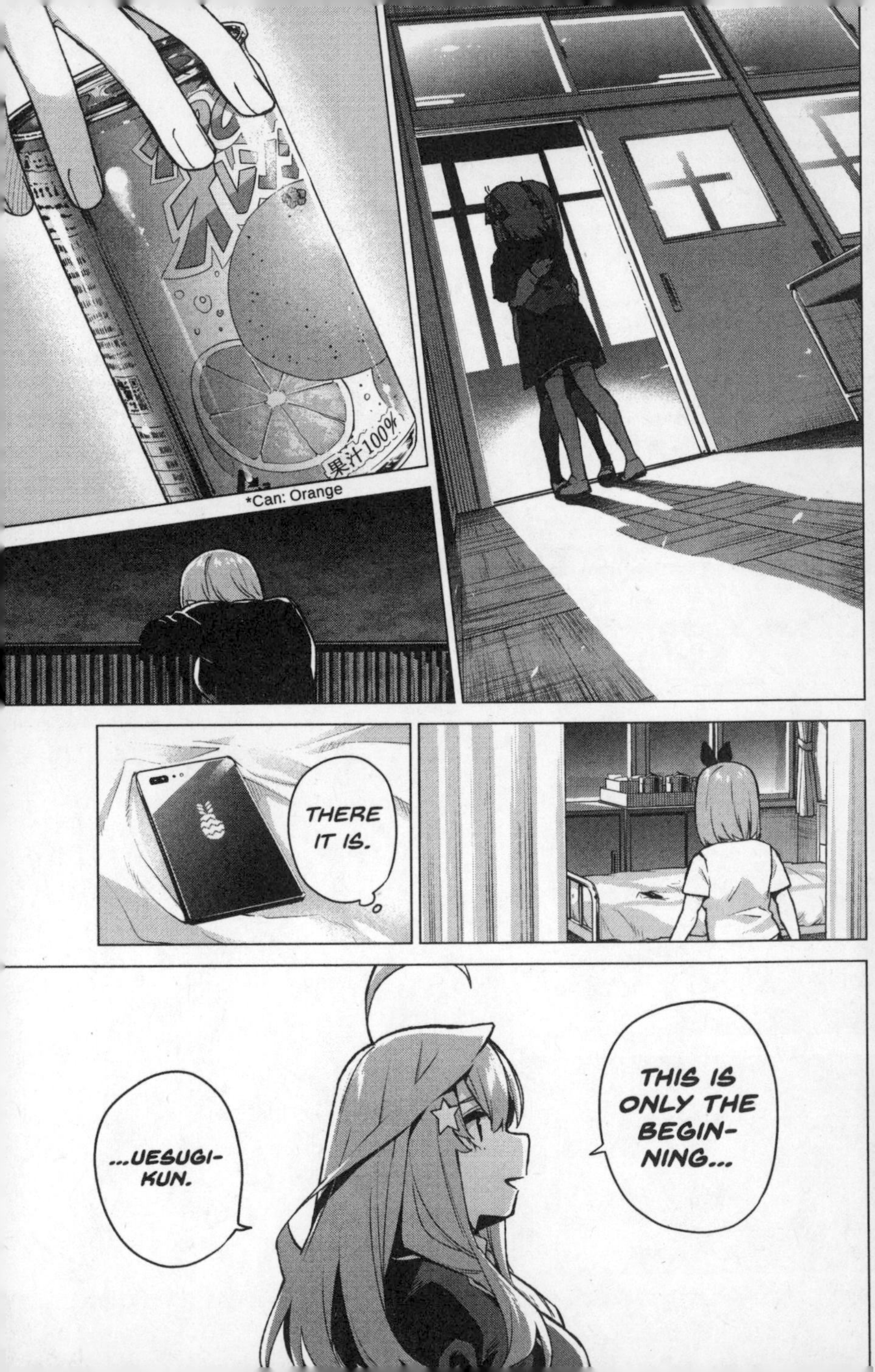
果汁100%
*Can: Orange
THERE IT IS.
THIS IS ONLY THE BEGIN-NING...
...UESUGI-KUN.

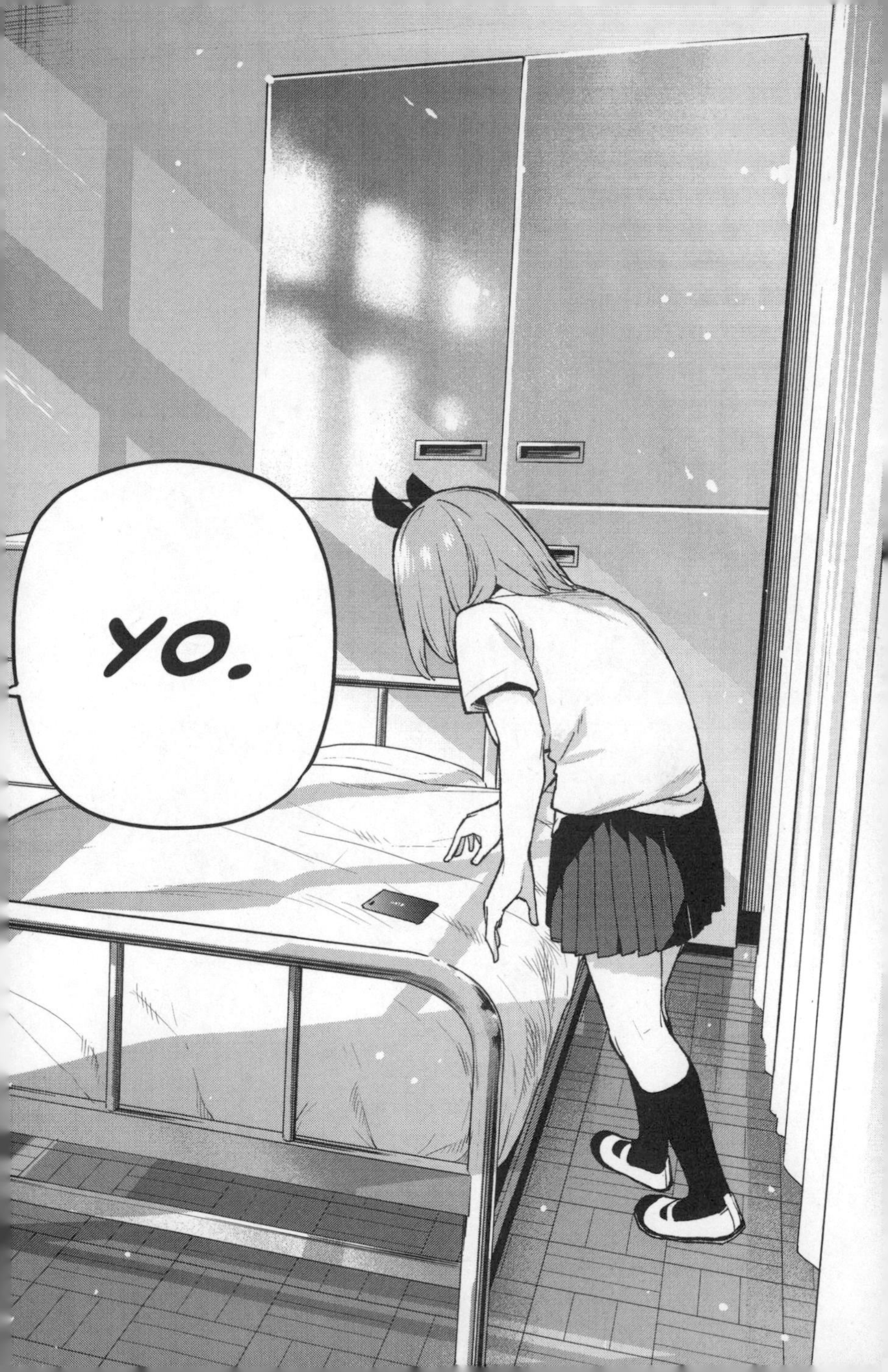
YO.

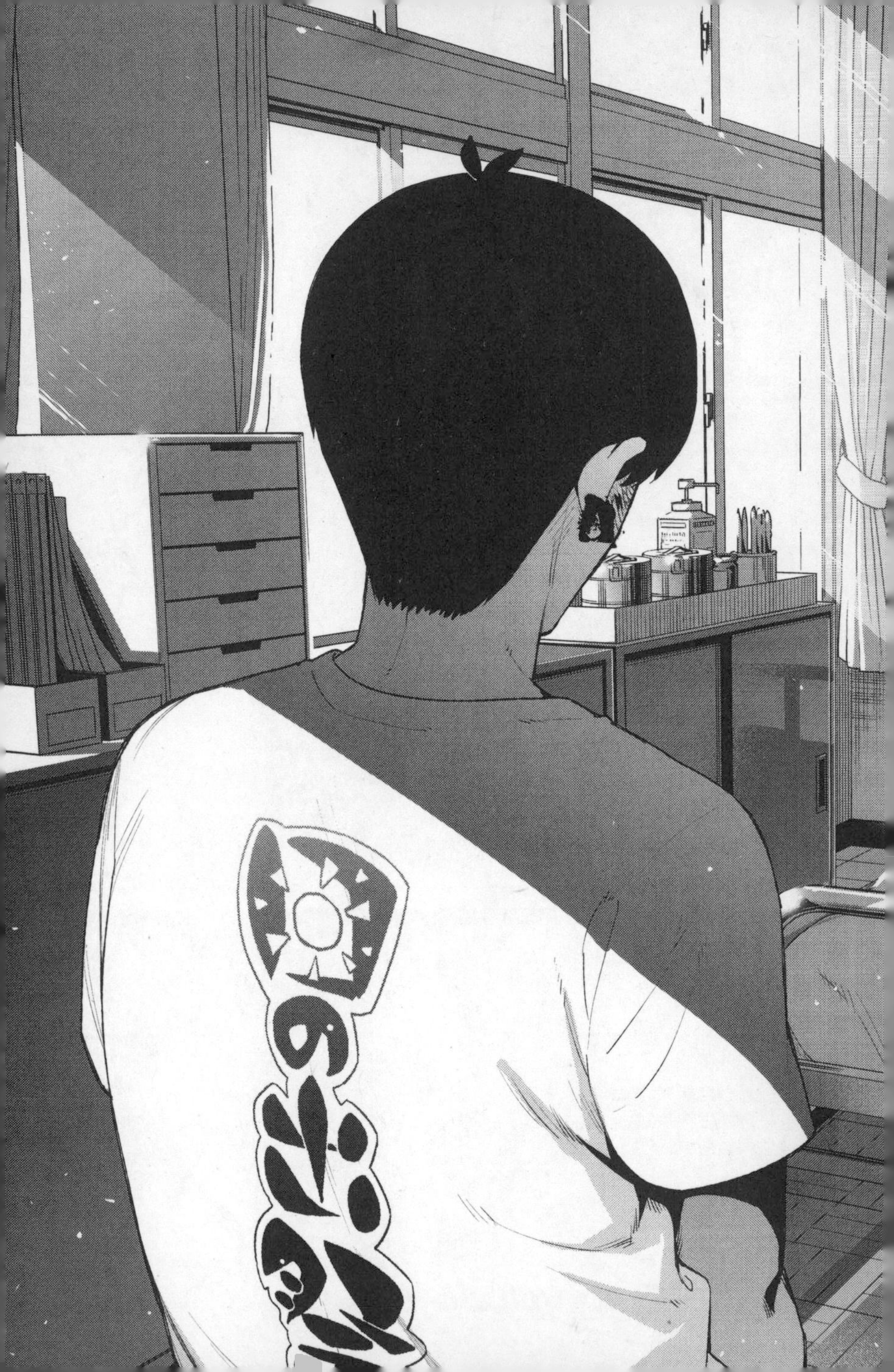

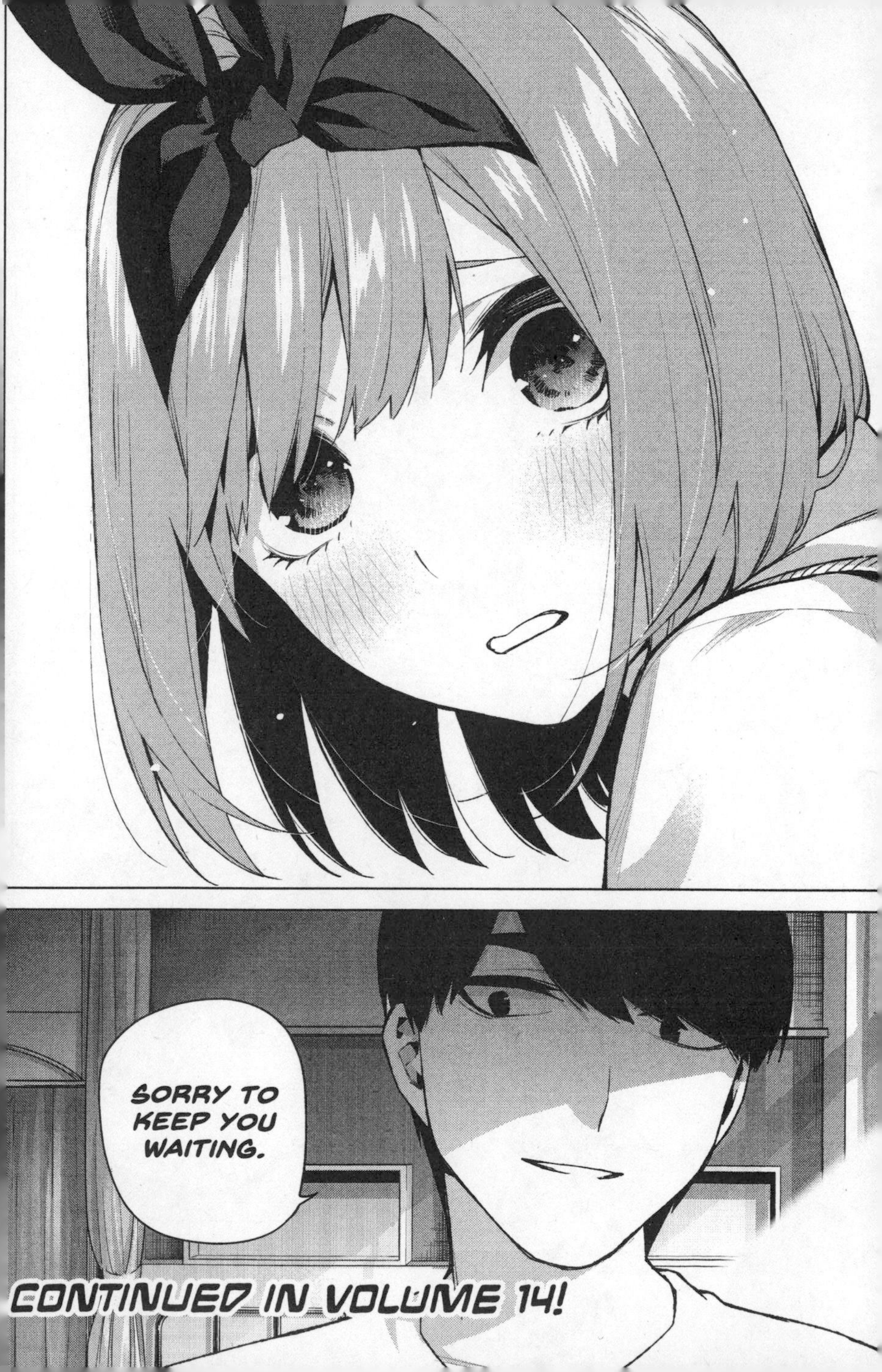
SORRY TO KEEP YOU WAITING.
CONTINUED IN VOLUME 14!

THE QUINTUPLETS CANNOT SHARE DESTINY EQUALLY

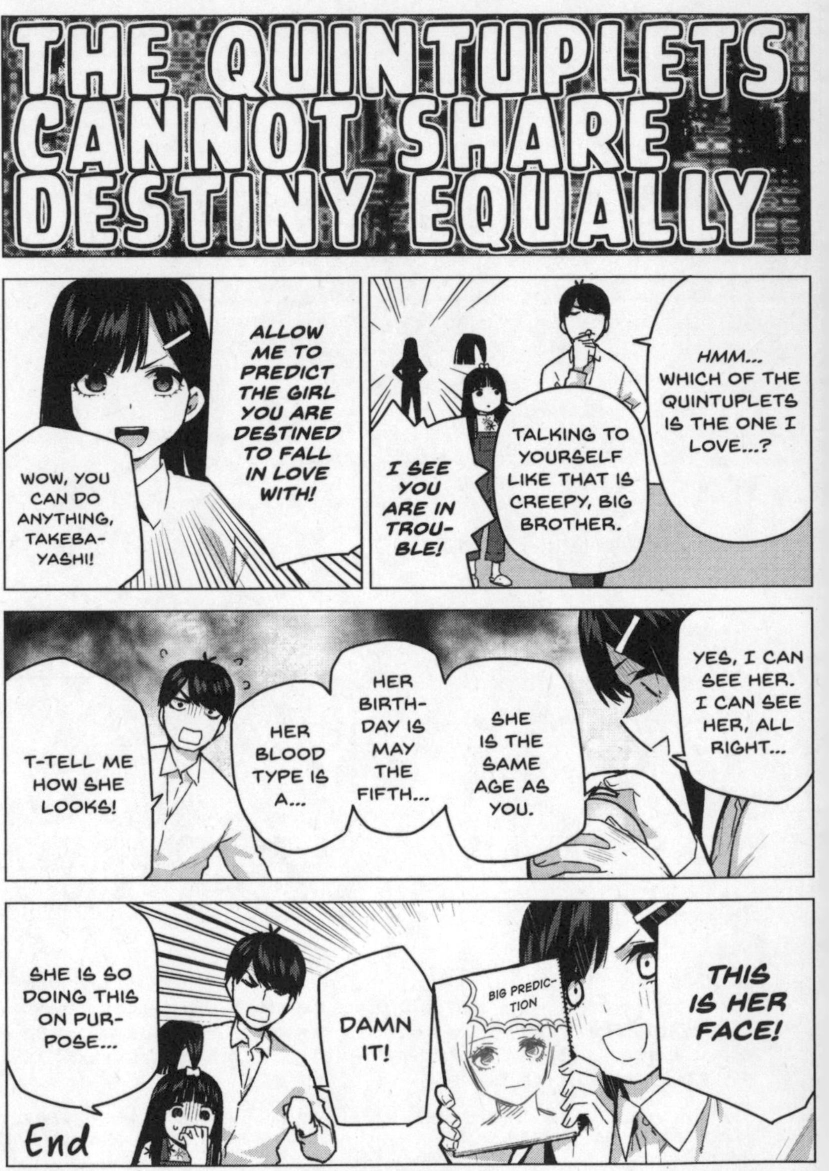
HMM... WHICH OF THE QUINTUPLETS IS THE ONE I LOVE...?
TALKING TO YOURSELF LIKE THAT IS CREEPY, BIG BROTHER.
I SEE YOU ARE IN TROUBLE!
ALLOW ME TO PREDICT THE GIRL YOU ARE DESTINED TO FALL IN LOVE WITH!
WOW, YOU CAN DO ANYTHING, TAKEBAYASHI!
YES, I CAN SEE HER. I CAN SEE HER, ALL RIGHT...
SHE IS THE SAME AGE AS YOU.
HER BIRTHDAY IS MAY THE FIFTH...
HER BLOOD TYPE IS A...
T-TELL ME HOW SHE LOOKS!
THIS IS HER FACE!
BIG PREDICTION
DAMN IT!
SHE IS SO DOING THIS ON PURPOSE...
End

Staff Ueno Hino Cho Naito

PERFECT WORLD

Rie Aruga

A TOUCHING NEW SERIES ABOUT LOVE AND COPING WITH DISABILITY

An office party reunites Tsugumi with her high school crush Itsuki. He's realized his dream of becoming an architect, but along the way, he experienced a spinal injury that put him in a wheelchair. Now Tsugumi's rekindled feelings will butt up against prejudices she never considered — and Itsuki will have to decide if he's ready to let someone into his heart...

"Depicts with great delicacy and courage the difficulties some with disabilities experience getting involved in romantic relationships... Rie Aruga refuses to romanticize, pushing her heroine to face the reality of disability. She invites her readers to the same tasks of empathy, knowledge and recognition."
—Slate.fr

"An important entry [in manga romance]... The emotional core of both plot and characters indicates thoughtfulness... [Aruga's] research is readily apparent in the text and artwork, making this feel like a real story."
—Anime News Network

KC
KODANSHA
COMICS

A SMART, NEW ROMANTIC COMEDY FOR FANS OF *SHORTCAKE CAKE* AND *TERRACE HOUSE*!

A romance manga starring high school girl Meeko, who learns to live on her own in a boarding house whose living room is home to the odd (but handsome) Matsunaga-san. She begins to adjust to her new life away from her parents, but Meeko soon learns that no matter how far away from home she is, she's still a young girl at heart — especially when she finds herself falling for Matsunaga-san.

The adorable new odd-couple cat comedy manga from the creator of the beloved *Chi's Sweet Home*, in full color!

Praise for Chi's Sweet Home

"Nearly impossible to turn away... a true all-ages title that anyone, young or old, cat lover or not, will enjoy. The stories will bring a smile to your face and warm your heart."

—School Library Journal

Sue & Tai-chan

Konami Kanata

Sue is an aging housecat who's looking forward to living out her life in peace... but her plans change when the mischievous black tomcat Tai-chan enters the picture! Hey! Sue never signed up to be a catsitter! *Sue & Tai-chan* is the latest from the reigning meow-narch of cute kitty comics, Konami Kanata.

CUTE ANIMALS AND LIFE LESSONS, PERFECT FOR ASPIRING PET VETS OF ALL AGES!

YUZU THE PET VET

1

BY
MINGO ITO

In collaboration with
NIPPON COLUMBIA CO., LTD.

For an 11-year-old, Yuzu has a lot on her plate. When her mom gets sick and has to be hospitalized, Yuzu goes to live with her uncle who runs the local veterinary clinic. Yuzu's always been scared of animals, but she tries to help out. Through all the tough moments in her life, Yuzu realizes that she can help make things all right with a little help from her animal pals, peers, and kind grown-ups.

Every new patient is a furry friend in the making!

A Kodansha Comics Trade Paperback Original
The Quintessential Quintuplets 13 copyright © 2020 Negi Haruba
English translation copyright © 2021 Negi Haruba

All rights reserved.

Published in the United States by Kodansha Comics, an imprint of
Kodansha USA Publishing, LLC, New York.

Publication rights for this English edition arranged through
Kodansha Ltd., Tokyo.

First published in Japan in 2020 by Kodansha Ltd., Tokyo
as *Gotoubun no hanayome*, volume 13.

ISBN 978-1-64651-062-7

Cover Design: Saya Takagi (RedRooster)

Printed in the United States of America.

www.kodansha.us

9 8 7 6 5 4
Translation: Steven LeCroy
Lettering: Jan Lan Ivan Concepcion
Additional Layout: Belynda Ungurath
Editing: Thalia Sutton, David Yoo
Editorial Assistance: YKS Services LLC/SKY Japan, INC.
Kodansha Comics edition cover design by Phil Balsman

Publisher: Kiichiro Sugawara

Director of publishing services: Ben Applegate
Associate director of operations: Stephen Pakula
Publishing services associate managing editor: Madison Salters
Assistant production manager: Emi Lotto, Angela Zurlo